de Gruyter Studies in Organization 6

Alston: The American Samurai

de Gruyter Studies in Organization

An international series by internationally known authors presenting current fields of research in organization.

Organizing and organizations are substantial pre-requisites for the viability and future developments of society. Their study and comprehension are indispensable to the quality of human life. Therefore, the series aims to:

- offer to the specialist work material in form of the most important and current problems, methods and results;
- give interested readers access to different subject areas;
- provide aids for decisions on contemporary problems and stimulate ideas.

The series will include monographs, collections of contributed papers, and handbooks.

Jon P. Alston

The American Samurai

Blending
American and Japanese
Managerial Practices

Walter de Gruyter · Berlin · New York 1986

Jon P. Alston

Professor of Sociology at the Texas A & M University
College Station, Texas, USA

Library of Congress Cataloging in Publication Data

Alston, Jon P., 1937–
  The American Samurai.
  (De Gruyter Studies in Organization ; no. 6)
  Bibliography: p.
  Includes index.
  1. Industrial management—Japan. 2. Industrial management—United
States. 3. Industrial sociology—Japan. 4. Industrial sociology—United
States. 5. Industrial organization—Japan. 6. Industrial organization
—United States. I. Title. II. Series.
  HD70.J3A45 1985   658'.00952   85–20530
  ISBN 3-11010619-1
  ISBN 0-89925-063-7 (U.S.)

CIP-Kurztitelaufnahme der deutschen Bibliothek

Alston, Jon P.
The American Samurai : blending American and Japanese managerial practi-
ces / Jon P. Alston. – Berlin ; New York : de Gruyter, 1986.
  (De Gruyter studies in organization ; 6)
  ISBN 3-11-010619-1
  NE: GT

Preface

In recent years, considerable attention has been devoted to claims that the American economy is losing ground to Japanese competition. The growing volume of Japanese imports, as well as their diversity and high level of quality, has forced Americans to re-evaluate their traditional managerial and manufacturing practices. The shrinking share of the world's industrial production originating in the United States is cause enough for concern, if not alarm.

It has been argued that obsolete manager-worker relations stifles productivity and quality work performance, and that current managerial policies, once preeminent and respected worldwide, need to be re-evaluated and tailored to better meet a new set of economic competitors, notably Japan and other newly industrializing Asian countries such as South Korea, Taiwan, Hong Kong, and perhaps eventually China.

This book describes and assesses the major features of Japanese managerial and personnel practices as they have evolved during the last decades. Managerial policies seldom transcend the social context from which they evolve. Societies develop assumptions and perspectives from which depend patterns of human relations. A number of chapters in this book discusses the cultural values which underlie corporate behavior and unique Japanese administrative patterns, such as lifetime employment and union-management harmony.

Japanese administrative policies are guided by Japanese social values and cultural traditions. This book offers the reader analyses of how Japanese corporations differ from their American counterparts as well as descriptions of why these differences exist.

Management cannot be separated from culture. Japanese managers rely on traditional values and social customs to achieve high levels of worker productivity in modern industrial sectors. Japanese managerial arrangements reflect, and reinforce, traditional values. It is this melding of modern practices and traditional values that has helped the Japanese achieve international economic preeminence.

Japan's post-war competitive successes are based on a cooperative, group-oriented model of human relations. This traditional Japanese model is based on the assumption that members of a group – whether a work team or a family – should work together on a cooperative basis in order that the group succeed. If the group achieves its goals, this ethos continues, then the members will profit and share in this success. In order to encourage worker harmony, corporate promotions and pay raises are based on seniority rather than individual merit.

Such cooperation demands that the group members submerge their individuality and achieve a consensus motivated toward group success. The group is more important than its individual members, while Japanese culture stresses the primacy of group interests over individual concerns. The individualist who insists on working only for his own advantage is defined as selfish. He is soon punished by the group and kept from enjoying the rewards that accrue from group membership.

Rewards are given to individuals when they contribute to group success. The group, while it demands the complete loyalty of its members, also rewards faithfulness. Japanese workers submerge their competitive urges because it is in their interests to do so. A tangible reward for group loyalty is the Japanese practice of semi-annual bonuses given when corporate profits rise.

By contrast, American culture glorifies competition and individualism. The paradox, though, is that most Americans work for others and with others. The individualist in an endangered species in corporate America. Work practices developed in an earlier economic era when person-centered policies were rational reactions are no longer efficient. The American economy is no longer as expansive as it once was, and it is now made up of larger, more-interdependent work units. Individualism and a competitive ethic no longer fit the modern economic and cultural contexts of the American society. As shown in this book, many American practices which were developed to reward competitiveness are now counter-productive.

Many successful Japanese corporate practices cannot be imported by Americans. Such policies reflect Japanese values too foreign to be borrowed whole and without extensive adaptation. On the other hand, the Japanese have also developed personnel practices which are more universal and thus more easily absorbed into the American society. These industrial policies, such as Quality Control circles and participative leadership styles, can be assimilated into the American corporate structure. This book discusses a nummer of administrative policies Americans can copy from the Japanese.

However, I do not suggest that American managers completely assimilate the Japanese managerial style. Throughout this book, I show that Americans have developed personnel and leadership policies that are as productive and morale-building, or more so, than many Japanese practices. While the focus of the book is on Japanese consensus management and how this was developed from Japanese culture and history, I also describe many American human relations practices which are as good or superior to the Japanese.

The Japanese have much to teach American managers. However, Americans can also learn much from themselves. To meet head on and successfully the "Japanese challenge," Americans need to blend the best of both worlds.

Japanese businessmen have been able to observe Americans and successfully graft to their own traditions the American business and manufacturing practices they felt would be advantageous. Americans too can link East and West into a satisfying synthesis.

I thank here some of the persons to whom I owe a debt of gratitude. T. Stanton Dietrich and Harry E. Moore were model gentlemen and scholars; Norval Glenn gave me encouragement, as have George Lowe, Charlie Peek, Alex McIntosh, Arnold Vedlitz, and Jim Copp. Connie Alexander and Jackie Sandles acted heroically as they typed one draft of this book after another. The Texas A&M University Department of Sociology made available all the resources an author needs. My wife and daughter always supported me.

College Station, USA
Autumn 1985   Jon P. Alston

Contents

Chapter 1
Introduction

1.1 The Plan of This Book

This book describes the administrative styles of modern Japanese and American corporations. Along with an explanation of how and why Japanese managerial styles differ from America's, the first chapters also discuss American corporate practices which are very much like those found in Japan. American and Japanese businesses, in fact, share many managerial concepts and practices: the two corporate worlds are not completely alien. Both IBM and Matsushita, for example, have company songs and slogan. Both have an "open door" policy encouraging employees to openly express their grievances to higher authorities.

Both countries also contain businesses with counter-productive policies that make them less profitable than they could be. Even the Japanese are not all super-heroes. The stress for group harmony in Japanese corporations, for example, results in too much conformity and makes the Japanese less creative. This book presents the negative as well as the positive elements of Japanese management. It's fashionable today to find fault with American managerial practices, and many should be reformed or eliminated completely. But many criticisms can also be leveled at the Japanese.

Contemporary Japanese managers are masters in human relations. They have successfully harnessed individual selfishness and group loyalty so that workers gain – morally, financially, and socially – when their efforts help the group. As this book will show, Japanese corporations are structured so that workers want their work groups and employers to succeed.

Worker loyalty and enthusiasm are achieved because workers who do more than the minimum are rewarded handsomely. Such workers are given fringe benefits, bonuses, and praise. Managers and supervisors are also expected to make their subordinates happy. No one in a Japanese corporation can expect to be in charge of others unless he is adept in social relations.

The education of contemporary American managers is primarily technical. Business courses teach how to draw up a budget, how to evaluate a company's capital/debt ratio, or how to second-guess the solutions of past problems through the analysis of case studies. But most American business administration students do not develop in the classroom the skills they will need the most: how to deal with other persons, whether singly or in groups. This book contains specific information on this critical business skill.

Many Americans still believe that managerial skills cannot be completely taught; that being able to deal effectively with other persons is either an inborn skill or can only be developed over time through experience. This is no longer true. Good managerial practice is more than an art which cannot be taught. Much of the art of managing oneself and others has been reduced to a near-science. Workers – whether senior executives, managers, or machine operators – can now take advantage of what has been discovered about the nature of people and the work activity itself. Managers can educate themselves to learn the human relations skills they need. There is no need to rely on experience by making a series of mistakes over the years. This book offers shortcuts to the education of managers by showing that some managerial practices in Japan are more productive than ours and how to profit from them.

While Americans can profit by learning how the Japanese work together, many Japanese managerial policies cannot be adopted by Americans. Some Japanese ways are too foreign for our culture to absorb easily; their adoption simply demands too much adjustment of American personality and custom. Few Americans, for example, accept the idea that family life should be completely subordinated to work demands. A common Japanese practice, on the other hand, is to spend three or more evenings a week with clients and co-workers, even if this means coming home after nine o'clock. All the while his wife uncomplainingly has kept supper waiting for his arrival.

And Americans will never be convinced that changing employers is a dishonor-able act. Japanese corporate employees expect to work for one employer after being hired right after graduation until retirement. Few Americans feel disloyal if changing employers means higher pay and a promotion, even though lifetime employment is an attractive policy during an economic reces-sion and when unemployment is high. Most Americans are too individualistic ever to become comfortable with the Japanese belief that the group is more important than the individual.

Americans need to know which Japanese customs should be rejected and which ones have value. Though Americans cannot adopt all of the distinctive Japanese work procedures, there are many which can help Americans become more productive as well as happier with their work experiences. Many Japanese work practices encourage a concern with job enrichment. These policies can be valuable to Americans since job enrichment leads to greater job satisfaction and higher work productivity.

The association of morale and productivity has been recognized in America for fifty years. The Japanese are recent converts to this view, but they have become adept in linking productivity with morale. While we have only to look around to see that the Japanese do not have a monopoly on these concerns, Americans can nevertheless profit from the Japanese views of work and the worker.

This book makes practical and concrete suggestions derived from Japanese work practices. These are combined with an analysis of policies sociologists and organizational specialists have found which lead to greater work efficiency. That is why this book's subtitle is *Blending American and Japanese Managerial Practices*. While the Japanese have much to teach us, American managers also have available a native body of knowledge whose practice would greatly increase the efficiency of American management and work in general. Increasing the efficiency and satisfaction of workers even more is a matter of combining the best of these two managerial worlds.

1.2 America's Productivity Gap

It is no secret that the Japanese economy is now more dynamic and expansive than America's. Concrete proof of Japan's commercial success is found in its exports. In 1945, Japan was a shattered, conquered country with its economy almost completely devastated; now Japan's exports challenge America's in a large number of markets, from pianos to television sets, from steel to automobiles, and from transistor radios to computer chips. The list is now almost endless, and increasingly so.

Part of Japan's economic success lies in its managerial philosophies and practices. These derive from Japan's cultural background and postwar experiences. The land of Japan is poor in natural resources such as petroleum and iron ore. This has forced the Japanese to export much of their productive capacity to obtain the foreign financial credits necessary to import raw materials. The Japanese economy is geared toward the import – process – export cycle. This need to export intensified after the Allies defeated Japan and stripped Japan of its colonial empire. The loss of Manchuria, Korea, and other territories forced the Japanese to re-evaluate their relation to other nations.

After 1945, markets could no longer be expanded through military conquests and political intimidation. The Japanese businessman/exporter replaced the samurai/soldier as the national hero. The population understood that "Japan must export or die." There developed a unity among members of the business community, whether a semiskilled worker on Toyota's assembly line or a bank president being asked for a loan to rebuild a bombed-out factory to produce Sony's electronic marvels for export. Each could feel proud that he contributed to the nation's survival as well as to his own profit.

Just as American labor and management worked together to defeat the Axis powers during the Second World War, Japanese workers and managers believe that harmonious work relations and economic development are patriotic duties. And these duties are defined as the responsibility for each worker at all levels to increase his own and his company's productivity. Each worker is asked and expected to develop ways to add to the company's and therefore the nation's production.

What are the consequences of this transformation of the productive worker into a national hero? One has been the national search for ways to increase work efficiency through the development of more productive worker-management policies and strategies. Another has been the active partnership of Japanese governmental, professional, corporate, and labor leaders to develop long and short-range policies promoting economic growth. That is why American manufacturers are faced with "Japan, Inc." as a competitor. The Japanese government, through tax policies, long-range policies, selectively-placed loans, subsidies, and tariffs, has been willing to actively support businessmen seeking to export their goods. The public and private sectors in Japan are partners, though they don't always agree with each other.

Americans, and foreigners in general, forget that the United States economy has a higher overall productivity level than any other country, even Japan. The United States enjoys, or earns, the highest level of real gross domestic product (RGDP) per employed person of any industrialized nation in the world. This RGDP index measures the average output of all employed persons. Using the United States' output as an index of 100, the United States is close to ten percent more productive than its nearest rivals, Canada, France, and Germany. Japan is a poor fourth. This is an overall index, and certain economic sectors in America are less productive than Japan's, especially in steel and in manufacturing.

This American overall productivity superiority is a temporary one. Rather than feeling smug, we should be alarmed with the speed at which Japan is narrowing the productivity gap between herself and America. In 1960, Japan's gross domestic product (RGDP) was a mere 27 as compared to the United States' 100. Now Japan's index is 71. Japan's productivity increase is taking place in leaps and bounds, while ours seems to be standing still.

Let's take productivity changes in the manufacturing sector, since that is so central to a modern nation's economy. The annual manufacturing productivity increase during the period 1960–1981 for the United States was 2.7 percent; for Japan the same annual rate of increase was 9.2 percent. The rate of increase in manufacturing productivity during 1980–81 was 1.5 for the United States and 5.0 for Japan (Bureau of Labor Statistics, Bulletin 2171, 1983:134–5).

The rate of capital formation per employed person measures how much investment for future growth a society is willing to set aside. With the United States as a standard of 100, Japan's capital formation rate during 1974–81 was 114, second only to Canada's (125) among non-communist industrialized countries (Bureau of Labor Statistics, Bulletin 2172, 1983:79). The challenge

Exhibit 1.1: Relative levels in real gross domestic product per employed person, selected and years, 1960–81

Index, United States = 100

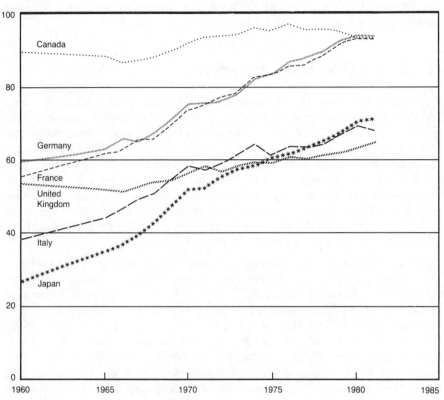

Source: Bureau of Labor Statistics, Bulletin 2172 (1983):23.

for Americans is that our economy must expand faster and become even more efficient than Japan's. We must learn to be more productive. This can be achieved by managing smarter and working cooperatively, as the Japanese plan to do.

During the seventies, U.S. worker output went from 105 to 129, or a twenty-three percentage points improvement. That's not a bad increase, but remember that we compete with other countries for markets. While the U.S. productivity went up a quarter, both Germany's and Japan's output per hour increased almost sixty percent. So did France's. The United States is competing with Great Britain for the slowest rate of increase in labor output (Bolling and Bowles, 1982).

Much of this Japanese success in productivity is based on the distinctive character of its managerial corporate structures. In the same way, America's managerial policies can be blamed for much of our present economic difficulties. This book was written with the hope that Americans can learn from their mistakes, their heritage, and the Japanese way of work.

1.3 Japan's Productivity Advantage

One major advantage the Japanese have is that Japanese workers welcome technological change. Few try to sabotage productivity improvements. This is not so in America. To the average American factory worker, automation can only result in the exchange of people for machines: introduce labor-saving machinery into a plant and someone becomes unemployed. Make one worker more productive and someone else loses his job. Or install a robot which can work twenty-four hours a day on the assembly line and three workers are no longer needed. In contrast to this fear of unemployment, many Japanese corporate workers are lifelong employees. They will not be fired except for criminal behavior, insanity, or the company's bankruptcy.

The Japanese worker with lifelong employment does not fear being replaced by machines. If a worker's duties become automated, he knows he will be retrained for other work. Jamazaki Machinery Works in Japan sells automated machinery and builds automated factories for export to the United States and elsewhere (Bill, 1982:1). The company has also almost completely automated its own blue collar work. But no one has been dismissed after being replaced by tooling machines which work twenty-four hours per day. The two hundred blue collar workers whose duties became automated were retrained and transferred to sales, testing and computer programming. Many of these displaced workers now program the very machines which automated their work.

The Japanese corporate worker enjoys another advantage besides job security. Increased productivity results in higher pay and other benefits. Higher profitablity is translated into higher pay in the form of semi-annual bonuses, often worth four to six months' wages. In Japan, increased profits go to the workers in the form of bonuses and not to the shareholders in the form of higher dividends.

Americans need to re-evaluate their economic and managerial policies if the United States is not to become the economic sick man of the West. This book contributes to this re-evaluation by showing how workers and managers can develop more effective work practices.

1.4 The Goals of This Book

The first part of this book contains discussions of the managerial practices unique to the Japanese. I also pay special attention to the philosophy and social values from which these managerial policies are derived. Every country has its own distinctive ways of viewing how work should be organized and how the worker should be treated, and Japan is no exception. Americans need to analyze these values to discover which ones can be incorporated into American managerial practices.

A basic difference in how the worker is defined in Japan and in America is that Japanese managers expect workers to be so loyal to their corporations that each cares about the company and be willing to increase the company's productivity. And, in fact, Japanese workers are trained to suggest improvements in worker efficiency. By contrast, American managers view workers as being unwilling or unable to improve their work. Workers, management believes, are too inexperienced and ignorant to contribute much else but their obedient labor.

American managers also assume that workers are seldom motivated enough to want to improve their productivity. Japanese managers view their workers as motivated and active agents; American managers define workers as passive and unmotivated. This book takes the stand that American workers can be encouraged to show as much initiative and interest in their work as the Japanese. Only then can the American labor force increase drastically its productivity and compete with the Japanese.

A goal of this book is to describe and explain the Japanese corporate style of management and work in general. And by implication, American readers will be able to compare their own managerial styles with the Japanese.

In spite of recent publicity, not all Japanese managerial practices lead to increased efficiency; conversely, not all of American managerial patterns are inferior to Japan's. American managers do not need to become Japanese to compete successfully with the Japanese, nor with the Germans for that matter. A great many American companies have developed managerial styles and strategies that are the envy of foreigners, including the Japanese. Many American companies are second to none, including IBM, AT&T, McDonalds, Apple Computer, Disney, DuPont, and Xerox. We must not forget our own managerial strengths while envying the Japanese for their successes. After all, Americans are still superior to the Japanese in many fields.

American managers, in partnership with academics, have developed a body of knowledge on managerial practices parts of which are superior to that of any other country. Foreign students still flock to enroll in MBA and other educational programs offered in American universities. Their presence is a measure of how respected American administration science remains. While Japanese corporate programs are the major focus of this book, I do not ignore successful managerial practices developed in America.

American managers have lost touch with many of their most productive strategies. The Americans taught the Japanese how to achieve high quality through quality control. And Americans invented computers, television, computer chips, videotape recorders, semiconductors, and robots. But now the Japanese outproduce and outcompete us in these and many other products. It's time to revitalize the managerial and productive genius which lies latent.

The second goal of this book is to present the most useful elements of contemporary managerial knowledge. The social sciences have made important discoveries in the last decade, discoveries which tell us much about the nature of work and how to make workers more efficient. We don't have to travel to Japan for advice.

Before setting the theme of this book by outlining the basic features of Japanese work practices, there is the need to clear up a number of mistaken stereotypes Americans hold about the Japanese. Too often, we react to Japanese competition with a loss of nerve. It's as if many Americans accept Japanese superiority – the Superman Myth – over American manufacturing capabilities. Examples of this myth are the demands that we close our domestic markets to imports because it's assumed that the Japanese can do things better than we, in terms of price, quality, or product development.

This book exposes this misleading myth, as well as others. The reader of this book will find that many so-called "superior" Japanese work practices originated in America, are already in use today, or can easily be adapted to the American business setting.

1.5 Eight American Myths about the Japanese Worker

To many Americans, the post-1945 commercial successes of "Japan Inc." were made possible by a number of "secret" managerial practices. These Oriental administrative customs and strategies, we are told, are so superior – and therefore more effective – than ours that American corporate managers must rush to learn these rules if American companies are to remain competitive vis a vis Japan's.

Americans have been exposed to a number of stereotypes about the Japanese that are oversimplifications and often contradictory. For example, we have been told again and again that the Japanese are so group-oriented that they are unable to innovate on their own. Without the importation of inventions and fresh ideas from the United States and Europe, Japanese industry, this theme continues, would eventually lag behind in terms of new products and processes. Yet ten percent of all patents awarded by the U.S. patents office are now awarded to Japanese applicants. And in certain fields, such as drugs, electronics, and robotics, the Japanese are now as inventive or more so than Americans.

These myths, like stereotypes in general, contain kernels of truths. Thus they can mislead persons who assume that a partial truth offers the complete picture. This prevents people from realizing that the Japanese have weaknesses as well as strengths. We need to develop a more balanced view of Japanese advantages and disadvantages.

The myths Americans hold about the Japanese can be summarized as the beliefs that the Japanese (1) are total conformists, (2) can copy but not innovate, (3) enjoy unfair economic competitive advantages, (4) enjoy a "free ride" because America bears the costs of Japan's defence, (5) Americans can easily copy any Japanese managerial and manufacturing techniques defined as superior to ours, (6) American cannot copy or adapt Japanese methods because they are too foreign, (7) the Japanese worker is a superman, and (8) there is a historical determinism that Japan is destined to be the next world's leading nation.

The Conformity Myth

Myth: The Japanese are conformists. They obey their leaders and ask no questions. It's like an ant hill. No American could be so passive.

Reality: The typical Japanese worker does respect his leaders, and he wants to be a good team member. But leaders must convince subordinates that their orders are worth obeying. No Japanese executive can be effective in the long run by trying to impose his will on others by administrative fiat. This is why the Japanese spend so much time achieving consensus before a decision is made. Each policy, before it is made official, must be accepted by those who have to carry it out. Americans holding an image of the Japanese being conformists are not aware of the behind-the-scenes compromising and consultation that take place before a decision is made public.

The Japanese seem so conformist to outsiders because the Japanese present a picture of being dependent on the group. This is true in part, but is not the complete picture. A member expects support from the group's members, but helping others is seen as part of an ongoing exchange. When Japanese groups are successful the profit is shared by the members. What may seem to us as group dependency is a member's contribution in return for the expectation of future reward. The policy of lifetime employment, one of the more distinctive characteristics of Japanese management, and discussed in a later chapter, gives the worker a sense of job security while it also places a debt on the worker. A lifelong worker "owes" his company loyalty and dedication.

Lifetime workers are enthusiastically loyal to their employers in part because of their high pay. A worker employed in a large corporation can expect to earn almost twice as much as those working in smaller firms which do not offer complete job security. Within the same company, a young (25–29 years old) permanent employee earns twenty percent more than a non-permanent worker of the same age and his pay will increase regularly through the years of employment.

An important part of a worker's income comes in the form of semi-annual bonuses worth at times as much as six months' pay or more. However, these bonuses are partly based on the financial condition of the company. A part of each bonus is standard, which makes these bonuses a forced-saving or a delayed-payment scheme. But a larger portion of these bonuses varies. Bonuses during a profitless year will be small or nonexistent. And workers, through their unions, accept smaller bonuses when management wants to reinvest the company's profits in order to expand facilities.

The workers know that reduced bonuses involve the premise of higher pay in the future. Smaller bonuses are "loans" the workers make to their companies. It's easier to accept smaller bonuses when you know you will be part of the company for decades. Lower pay will be repaid in the future. In order to maintain a sense of fairness, senior executives accept a larger decrease in their own bonuses than those receiving less.

The flexibility of these bonuses means that labor costs can be reduced even when the work force in constant. Every worker suffers when profits are low even though no one loses his job. In a good year, of course, every worker is "rewarded" for his efforts and loyalty through larger bonuses. Wages follow economic cycles, the company keeps its experienced labor, and workers are secure in that they know their jobs are permanent.

Moreoever, bonuses are visible and frequent reminders that productivity increases result in individual rewards. Workers are more willing to seek out ways to increase their efficiency when they know that their next bonuses will be larger. The Japanese work hard partly because it is profitable to do so. If this were not so, many workers would be less enthusiastic in their work than they are. Even lifetime employed blue collar workers, often pictured as hardworking robots, will threaten to strike if they don't receive what they consider to be a fair share of their company's profits.

The Copy Myth

Myth: The Japanese copy techniques well enough, but they can't originate anything themselves. In the long run, the Japanese economy will stagnate and become less competitive when they run out of other countries' ideas.

Reality: When faced with a successful competitor, the Japanese do become enthusiastic copiers. Realizing that the first step in competition is to outdo the competitor on his own ground, the Japanese are realistic and flexible enough to want to discover a competitor's secrets of success. Then they will copy what seems useful. At this stage the Japanese manufacturers copy more than they create. They are pragmatic in the face of foreign technological superiority. At this stage everyone, even Americans, will take apart a competitor's product through what is known as "reverse engineering."

But once a competitor's product is understood, the Japanese are capable of going beyond the original. The Japanese learned the basic techniques of quality control from Americans, but QC circles and zero-defect policies resulted in Japanese products that were better in quality than American goods. The next twenty years will see whether or not the Japanese are able to innovate as well as copy. Even now, Japanese automotive engine design and robotics are as good or superior to America's.

Copying is merely a short cut to the Japanese. When the Japanese decide that American products are no longer useful models, the emphasis will then shift toward creativity and innovation. It may very well be that in twenty years from now, Japan will be an exporter of knowledge rather than an importer.

Americans do not have a monopoly on originality, and the number of foreign patents being awarded in America is on the increase. Thirty-seven percent of all patents are now awarded to foreigners, mostly to Japanese and Germans, and this proportion has been rising during the last decade. If patents are an indication of creativity, then foreigners are increasing the world's technical knowledge at a faster rate than are Americans. The U.S. patent office issues about ten percent of all patents to Japanese citizens.

The image of the Japanese as successful copiers is correct. But this does not mean they cannot create. Indeed, the Japanese do not merely copy: they also modify to such an extent that few American managerial or production techniques are copied unchanged. The Japanese study what is available and then decide which practices can be successfully adapted by Japanese workers. While the Japanese respect American technology, as well as technology from Germany and elsewhere, ideas, new products, and technology are not automatically accepted.

The Japanese have begun to establish a number of authentic research and development (R&D) programs in contrast to the former practice of limiting research activities to analyses of competitors' products and to minor engineering development. The ministry of International Trade and Industry (MITI) now gives priority to the development of new technologies through basic research. The Japanese feel an urgent need to encourage creativity.

MITI has published a report stating that in the last twenty years, the United States has been responsible for over two-hundred and thirty technological innovations, of which one-fourth were defined as "significant." By contrast, Japan produced only twenty-six innovations, of which only ten percent were "significant." Japan now devotes slightly over two percent of its gross national product to R&D programs, roughly the same percentage as does the United States. Japan's proportion will increase during the 1980's.

To develop an environment which encourages creativity, MITI is developing "technocenters," or small cities devoted to basic research. These will be staffed by resident scientists as well as a rotating number of personnel from Japanese corporations. Successful research developments will diffuse quickly from laboratories to business. MITI plans to emphasize basic research in selected areas, such as robotics, artificial intelligence, and pharmaceuticals. Large corporations with adequate facilities have been encouraged to conduct basic research in electronics and ceramics. Japan is also developing capabilities in military equipment and space technology, including rockets and satellites. In addition, Japanese manufacturers are attempting to integrate modern technology into their products. Thus, Japanese automobile designers are including computer components in their models to develop "talking" cars.

A major edge the Japanese have is that many products are of better quality than American's. Zero-defects is an appealing policy to a consumer who can't repair his TV set or her car. And as the Japanese have increased the quality of their products, they have also decreased costs. American manufacturers tend to assume quality must increase cost.

The myth that Japan enjoys unfair competitive advantages also involves the view that Japanese labor costs are much lower than America's. Wages in Japan are lower. But fringe benefits, including semi-annual bonuses, reduce Japan's advantage. The large corporations provide subsidized housing and vacations, low-cost meals, as well as educational and transportation supports. Most maintain stores where goods and appliances can be bought at a discount. All of this increase labor costs.

The result is that the wage-gap between Japan and America is not as significant as it might seem at first. In fact, some industries in Japan have labor costs as high or higher than their American counterparts.

Lower wages contribute to the fact that Japan can make a car for $ 1,500 less than its American counterpart. But superior automobile technology and quality are not the result of lower wages. Lower wages are not a significant reason for the Japanese "economic miracle." The Japanese have been able to export goods to countries where local wages are lower or about the same as Japan's.

Japanese exporters, like OPEC, change their prices to meet demand. The Japanese would rather sell at cost or at a short-term loss than close down a plant and lay off workers. What is seen as "dumping" to Americans is often an attempt to keep machines busy no matter short-term pofit considerations. The Japanese are hesitant to lose a market. They would rather lower profits to maintain brand visibility and customers' loyalty than temporarily leave the field to competitors. If there is any hope of a future turnaround in a specific market, then a Japanese manufacturer will stubbornly maintain a long-term stance in the face of short-term losses.

Due to their long-term perspective, the Japanese view short-term profits as less important than a gradual increase in their share of a market. They also assume that mass production and design improvement eventually decrease costs even as quality improves. The first task is to develop product recognition and customer loyalty. Profits become more important at a later stage. The Japanese are also willing to desert a market if it becomes too competitive or if they feel no long-term profitability can be obtained.

Japanese industrial associations and government ministries plan ten to twenty-five years in the future. Industrial and government spokesmen take long-range planning and forecasting very seriously. Current losses are measured against profits in the decades ahead. By the same token, current profits are compared to possible future losses.

After capturing the transistor radio market, Japanese manufacturers realized that the market was becoming saturated with cheaper copies from India, South Korea, and Hong Kong. Capital investments were pulled away from radios to newer products even while the former were still profitable. Americans tend to stay in once-profitable markets too long, hoping to continue to eke out profits. Detroit automakers resisted changing production from high-profit large cars to smaller units with lower profits.

In the same vein, the Japanese are willing to eliminate relatively inefficient equipment and facilities even when they are still profitable. The scrap-and-build policy of the Japanese gets rid of marginally profitable equipment or even whole industries (such as ship building) when they become increasingly competitive and less profitable. The scrap-and-build strategy operates in this fashion: a company wishing to expand its facilities by twenty percent will be lent by banking partners (or the government) enough assets to build fifteen percent new facilities and replace five percent of the *least* efficient equipment, even if that equipment were still marginally profitable. Thus the company expands as well as replaces its oldest equipment.

Over the decades, a steel-making company using the scrap-and-build policy both expands and modernizes. Imagine the competitive advantage U.S. Steel would now have if it had adopted a scrap-and-build policy during the last twenty years. Its facilities would now be as modern and efficient as its Japanese competitors.

The age of American equipment is not always at a disadvantage in comparison with Japan's. In some areas, machinery is newer on the average in the United States. The picture is not as grim as is sometimes pictured, though America does not have an across-the-board advantage. In the steel industry, Japanese plants had an average age of seven years in 1983; America's steel plants were a non-competitive eleven years old (*The Japan Economic Journal*, August 14, 1984:3). Japan's equipment in high-tech industries is also younger.

The U.S. and Japan are equal in the age of equipment in the automobile, pulp and paper, and chemical chemistry industries. However, in oil and cement, America's equipment and plants are newer. If manufacturing companies in the U.S. Standard and Poor and in Japan's equivalent list are compared, U.S. firms' plant facilities were a total average of three months younger. High-level investments since 1980 has resulted in a narrower gap in plant age between Japan and America.

However, the age of plants and their facilities is only one aspect, and a minor one, of the differences between Japan and the United States. This book's theme is that the most important advantage Japan has over America is that Japan has developed over the last forty years a better managerial philosophy. The Japanese manage and work smarter. Even with older equipment, Japanese manufactured products will be of better quality and cheaper. These advantages continue when labor costs differentials are held constant.

The blame for any American lack of competitiveness, in this book, is placed on management rather than on workers. America's relative declines in world markets and economic vigor are due to the manner executives, administrators, and supervisors define their work responsibilities.

Not all American companies are in decline; nor are most Japanese companies "better" (however defined) than their American counterparts. There is more than enough American vitality and administrative know-how to challenge Japan. This demands a different way of looking at how people work. The Japanese can teach Americans how to work in more productive ways. As important, the Japanese economic challenge forces Americans to re-evaluate their traditional work patterns. Not all of these are inadequate, though many are. This book shows how Americans can learn from American as well as Japanese practices.

The Myth that the Japanese Lost the War but Won the Peace

Myth: The Japanese economy had to rebuild after the Second World War. That's why their factories and machinery are more modern than ours. Also, we helped rebuild their economy and Japan profited by the Korean and Vietnam conflicts. If the Japanese had a military budget of their own instead of relying on an 'American umbrella' for defense, their economy would not have developed so fast. They've used us for a free ride.

Reality: It is true that most of the Japanese manufacturing capability was destroyed during the war. But the war ended forty years ago. America has had plenty of time to build one, two, or more generations of new factories and manufacturing facilities. A number of American industries, such as steel, have been reluctant to invest heavily in needed capital improvements. Meanwhile the scrap-and-build policy of the Japanese has allowed them to modernize gradually while they expanded facilities.

It is also true that the Japanese burden of national defense is light compared to America's. But other countries, notably West Germany, France, and South Korea, have been able to revitalize their devastated post-war economies and still support a military program. The lack of a large defense budget is a relative advantage, not an absolute one.

The export success of the Japanese has been based on technologies or products which did not exist before 1941. Japanese auto manufacturers decided to export small cars to America late when compared with France, England, and West Germany. Transistor products, pocket calculators, motorcycles, and television sets are postwar items. These products are based on new investments too long removed from the prewar era.

Competitively-priced sandals, clothes, sports equipment, toys, china, and tourist items, as well as simple tools, are continuations of Japanese traditional export practices. These cheap, labor-intensive goods have been exported by Japan for over one-hundred years. But high-quality steel exports, oil tankers, digital watches, and electric musical instruments are modern products. The success of these and other products depends on being internationally competitive. There is no "free ride" for these products.

The major advantage the Japanese have over Americans is not lower labor costs, but that they stress "working smarter and together" not "working cheaper." At the Toshiba electronics firm, ninety-nine percent of the blue collar employees are members of Quality Control circles (see chapter eight). These are organized to increase productivity even though most work tasks are highly automated.

Sixty percent of all industrial robots in the world are found in Japan. Only three percent of all industrial robots made in Japan are exported. The rest are used to increase Japan's productivity and reduce costs. Why Japanese workers have welcomed these robots more than workers in other countries is discussed in a later chapter.

An advantage of the Japanese which I have noted is that they eliminate products when they begin to be less profitable, when markets become saturated, or when goods become increasingly competitive. Declining industries in America, however, are likely to continue their former habits. This is especially true for the leading companies in older industries. Even when declining, these corporations have great political influence. They use this power to limit competition through government aid, protective tariffs, loans, and the like. Too many declining corporations have stakes in America's status quo or in the past. They look to the past rather than plan for the future.

By contrast, Japanese government officials and bankers are ruthless when considering matters of export. Companies are discouraged from exploiting over-saturated markets even though they might continue to be profitable in the short run. If government officials were to decide that the export motorcycle market was becoming saturated, they would "suggest" to officials at the Bank of Japan that loans not be issued for the expansion of plants manufacturing motorcycles. The bank would formulate this policy for its branches and sister banks, and companies would find it difficult to obtain loans for expansion of their motorcycle production capacity.

Those which went ahead anyway would find it difficult to obtain export licenses or future loans. The proposed policy would have been discussed by all concerned before being made official, and all arguments given careful attention. But the result would have been an eventual change in motorcycle production. Those companies hurt by this policy would be given preference for other ventures.

This does not mean that Japanese leaders in and out of government do not make errors of judgment. During the 1981 fiscal year, over eighteen thousand companies in Japan declared bankruptcy (Saso and Kirby, 1982:29). And the Japanese government delayed for years the export of cars to America while West Germany enjoyed a near-monopology on low-cost cars.

The Japanese enjoy one very important psychological advantage over Americans not related to the Japanese enjoying a "free ride." Japanese businessmen and government leaders are export-oriented. They think very earnestly about manufacturing goods which are going to be internationally competitive. American businessmen are more domestically oriented. Exporting their products is often an afterthought.[1] Even industries where a few companies enjoy a near

---

[1] An exception is IBM, which established foreign subsidiaries long before a foreign market for mainframe computers developed.

monopoly rarely think of their international competitive edge until too late. The motorcycle and steel industries, for example, were slow in taking the threat of Japanese competition seriously. Unlike the Japanese, we underestimate what goes on outside our own borders.

The Myth that Americans Can Copy Everything the Japanese Do

Myth: People are the same no matter the culture. If a managerial technique works in one country, it can easily be copied somewhere else. Americans can easily copy the Japanese if it's to our advantage.

Reality: This Americans-can-copy-the-Japanese belief is a very dangerous myth. Few cultural customs can be directly translated from one country to another. Each culture has its own definitions of authority, obedience, individualism, and work norms. These cannot be uncritically taken from one cultural setting and imposed on members of another society. The Japanese are famous for having copied other cultures but each time the borrowing was adapted to the Japanese culture.

The Japanese accepted Buddhism from China in the Sixth Century, but they also adapted the Buddhist way of life to fit Japanese values. Thus the pacifist Chinese Buddhism became altered into the morality of the samurai warrior class. The search for manufacturing quality as copied from Americans in the 1950's became adapted into QC circles. The Japanese are very careful to study how borrowed foreign traits will fit into their culture. Few items are borrowed without being adapted and improved.

Many of the more effective Japanese managerial traits can be found in the American human relations and participative management theories. We need to re-learn forgotten and ignored American managerial knowledge before we borrow from other cultural settings. Some advantages the Japanese enjoy can be adopted to the American scene. Group-level rewards, worker's involvement in work decisions, and profit-sharing bonuses would be welcomed by many Americans. Lifetime employment, the emphasis on group consensus and group rewards, and a strict policy of promotion by seniority would never completely set well with Americans. But they can be modified to fit American values.

Another reason for the Japanese economic success is the strong partnership of business and government. Through tariffs, export loans, tax advantages, and import restrictions, the Japanese businessman sees that his federal government takes an active part in the development of the economy. It has also been rather ruthless in discouraging local economic activities it saw as not as supporting the national interest. We are more likely to allow individual companies as well as industries to commit their own mistakes. On the plus side, this gives companies the chance for creativity Japanese companies may not enjoy.

The Japanese government, though, actively "encouraged" steel and computer industries to modernize facilities in order to compete in international markets. The American government has been willing to allow our steel industrie to diversify into non-steel activities offering higher short-term profits. The American business community would never allow the federal government the power to influence (or interfere with) the private sector to the extent found in Japan.

The Myth that Japanese Business Practices Cannot be Copied

Myth: American culture is too different from Japan's and nothing the Japanese do can be used by Americans. Workers and employers in Japan operate through values which are too foreign for Americans to adapt. Besides, American business methods have been superior to the Japanese until recently. When times return to normal, we will show foreigners how superior Americans are.

Reality: This is another very dangerous myth. The above myth smacks of snobbism and dangerous closed-mindedness. Only the ostrich sticks his head in the sand; he does so at his peril while he looks ridiculous. Americans must admit that they are not perfect, and that others – including the Japanese – can teach us things of value. We must not become so arrogant that we begin to believe that any failure on our part is due to unfair (diabolic?) forces outside our control, such as OPEC, chance, cheap foreign labor, etc. The Japanese have successfully invaded many American markets, and their successes are not due solely to often imagined unfair practices. Perhaps the Japanese can actually manufacture higher quality products more efficiently than we can. The challenge Americans face is to see if, in fact, the Japanese have something to teach us. The fact that the Japanese-managed ventures in the United States are highly productive and produce goods of higher quality should alert the fact that the Japanese way of work is worth studying.

We should study the Japanese and adapt what we see as useful. The key term here is "adapt." Few managerial or manufacturing customs can be directly copied from the Japanese. Fortunately, there is a large number of Americans familiar enough with Japan and with American business to offer suggestions. While Japanese culture contains many elements and concepts that are different from ours, some can clearly be adapted to the American scene.

The Myth of the Japanese Worker as Superman

Myth: The Japanese are dedicated, loyal workers. They are highly skilled, have an instinct for craftmanship and quality work, and are willing to work harder for longer hours. There is no way Americans can compete head-on with the Japanese and win.

Reality: Japanese workers are not supermen, nor are they necessarily more productive than Americans. Over half of the Japanese labor force works in firms employing less than 100 workers. These workers are less efficient than those in large corporations. Their working conditions and job security cannot be compared favorably with those enjoyed by corporate workers. When the economy is depressed, a small firm's workers are laid off and rehired only when needed. Partial reasons for the competitive successes of the large corporations are the lower wages and benefits received by subcontractors rather than high levels of productivity.

There is nothing instinctual about the craftsmanship of Japanese workers. Again, before the 1950's Japanese products were famous worldwide for being cheap, of inferior quality, and generally shoddy. One reason many foreigners discounted the Japanese military before Pearl Harbor was the belief that the Japanese manufacturing capability could never construct a modern, high-quality military machine. Interest in quality in the export manufacturing sector began when Americans convinced the Japanese that economic survival de-pended on increased product quality. At this time American quality experts such as J. M. Juran and William E. Deming went to Japan to lecture Japanese engineers on quality control.

Quality performance exists only when quality production is a major demand of corporate leaders and when workers are rewarded for quality performance. Quality would decline if Japanese managers ignored quality. Any desired work habit can be developed when based on the correct motivational and reward systems. It's a matter of first knowing which goal is wanted and then motiva-ting and rewarding workers for the appropriate work procedure.

This myth of the Japanese as super workers and managers replaced an earlier, equally misleading stereotype: the Japanese of the traditional Japan. This view sees Japan as a nation of rice growers and samurai warriors. This is the Japan of the movies, or what I call the "Madame Butterfly myth." This myth pictures the Japanese as highly aesthetic and emotional, as if they had no interests other than in growing hundred-year old bonsai trees, tea ceremonies, garden viewing, and swordsmanship.

If Japanese males are either simple farmers or arrogant suicide-prone samurai, then it follows that they could never threaten us in modern manufacturing sectors such as steel refining, automobile technology, or electronics. It was this view that encouraged us to underestimate pre-1941 Japanese military technology. This view should have been buried during the Pearl Harbor attack.

But decades after 1945, Americans again underestimate Japan's ability to rebuild and develop a modern, dynamic economy. Now, of course, some have adopted the opposite of the Madame Butterfly myth. But this view of the Japanese as industrial supermen is as simplistic and misleading as its opposite.

The Myth of Japan as Number one

Myth: The 1980's begin the 'Japanese Century.' America is tired and lazy, as are the European nations. The West has had its day and now it's Japan's turn. No one can fight historical trends.

Reality: There is no convincing proof that Japan will become the greatest nation in the world (Kahn, 1971; Brzezinski, 1972). There is no question that Japan will become even more important than it currently is and will remain so for some time, but Japan faces as many potential pitfalls as possibilities for success (Woronoff, 1981 and 1982a). For one thing, Japan is going to be faced with a number of increasingly capable competitors. South Korea is a rising star on the international scene, as are Taiwan, Hong Kong, and perhaps mainland China. Soon Japan will no longer be the only industrial, politically stable nation in the Far East. Even India has successfully competed against Japan in recent years. And the United States still enjoys having the world's strongest economy.

Because of the enthusiasm for long-run planning and forecasting, the Japanese government is encouraging companies to become even more multinational and develop joint ventures with foreign nationals. This policy, it is hoped, will provide added capital for expansion as well as defuse the growing resistance against the flood of Japanese imports. Whether the Japanese will continue to enjoy the benefits of other countries' low tariffs and free trade policies is doubtful, given the political situation in many of Japan's markets.

There are social as well as economic problems on Japan's horizon. Japan's educational system through high school and junior college is recognized throughout the world as excellent. But the quality of university-level education is low, and relatively few Japanese are attracted to graduate work. Japan's universities may not be able to provide the resources that a modern, industrial society needs.

University residency is a near-vacation for many Japanese students. This leads to the question whether or not Japan can produce enough well-trained technicians to keep the economy up-to-date. Can Japan's educational system produce enough computer scientists to compete successfully with the United States?

It's not certain whether Japan's engineers will be numerous enough to meet future technical challenges. Japan now produces more engineers than the United States, but many are ill-trained, and most are hired upon graduation as managers and sales personnel.

Nor will it be easy to increase the number of college students wishing a technical education: there will simply not be enough young persons around to meet future demand. Japan's birth rate is one of the lowest in the world and the population is aging because life expectancy is high. Low birth rates and long life result in more and more older persons in Japan. Twelve percent of the Japanese will be over sixty-five years old in 1995.

Japan's total population is growing at a low rate of 1.1 percent per year, but the labor force is growing at only 0.7 percent. The trends of low birth rates and an increasing aging population mean that the labor force will also age, with relatively fewer younger workers supporting a larger and larger retired group. Even now, many companies are finding it harder and harder to hire enough university graduates. Japan is experiencing a labor shortage of young workers. The increasing competition for younger workers can only increase labor costs as companies are forced to offer higher beginning salaries.

Some of this labor shortage can be met through higher productivity. But the prognosis is that Japan's lack of a large enough youth population could inhibit future economic expansion. A short-run solution to this problem beginning to be considered is the recruitment of older workers. But recruiting skilled older mid-career workers threatens the lifetime employment system discussed in a later chapter and weakens the notion of worker loyalty. Workers are less likely to sacrifice themselves for long-run benefits if mid-career mobility is an option. And the encouragement of more mid-career job changes increases the labor supply only for companies able to offer larger salaries and wages.

Another problem Japan will contend with is the growth in wealth of the Japanese themselves. The Japanese public is presently obsessed with economic development because of the poverty experienced prior to, during, and right after the war. The energy older Japanese workers exhibit is partly due to the determination to avoid their former poverty. A sign of this is that the term describing the post-1945 decade is "the hungry cage." The generation which experienced these years of privation sees hard work as a necessity to avoid past sufferings. A post-1950 generation born and raised in relative prosperity does not feel driven to work as hard.[2] Japan's postwar economic emergence was made possible by those who believed that only hard work could ensure economic security.

---

[2] It is possible, of course, to argue that the same phenomenon is present in the United States. However, differences in attitudes between generations is greater in Japan than in the United States.

The paradox is that this immense effort of those over thirty has been su-
premely successful; the Japanese can now begin to enjoy the fruits of their
labor. Future generations of Japanese workers will not want to work as hard as
past generations and will want to enjoy more leisure. Instead of the problems
of poverty, the Japanese will be faced with the problems of affluence (Woronoff, 1982). Younger workers now want to work less hours in order to be able
to enjoy their prosperity.

A related problem of affluence is the matter of industrial pollution. Until
recently, low-cost productivity and industrialization were considered more
important than the effects of industrial wastes. Factories were allowed near-
complete freedom to discard their wastes in the cheapest manner. This
resulted in the pollution of much of Japan's most beautiful coastlines and
coastal fisheries, the spread of painful and often fatal diseases caused by
contamination of foods – especially mercury-laden fish – dense smog in Tokyo,
and other environmental crises. These have alarmed the population and will
not be allowed in the future. All industries must now decrease their pollution
of the environment, which adds costs to their products. Third world countries
less concerned with environmental quality do not accept such costs and will
enjoy a competitive advantage over Japan, in addition to their lower labor
costs.

Increasing wealth will also make the Japanese less willing to perform unpleasant labor. Wages will increase for labor which until now has been cheaper than
in other countries. As examples of this trend, unpaid overtime was made
illegal in 1955, and Saturdays are no longer accepted by workers as regular
work days without overtime pay. Prosperity will produce in Japan the same
type of labor problems found in Western Europe and in the United States.

People speak of the "English disease" or the "American problem of affluence." But these problems will eventually be found in Japan. There now is in
Japan the complaint that "Japan is rich and the people are poor." Eventually
(though certainly not for several decades), more Japanese will insist that they
be allowed to enjoy being citizens of one of the world's economic leaders.

Some of this excess wealth will be spent on foreign goods, and changing
consumption tastes will force Japan to import more than it does now. Aside
from enjoying McDonald's and Wendy's hamburgers, Kentucky Fried Chick-
en products, and Coca Colas, the Japanese are developing decidedly western
tastes. Most younger Japanese adults are eating more wheat-based than rice-
based products, and Japan must import almost all wheat consumed. Japan will
have to re-consider its relationships with foreign countries as its citizens
consume more and more imported goods, notably wheat, fruit, and meat
products.

Changing consumption preferences as well as political pressures will force an increased openness of the Japanese markets to foreign products. Government subsidies, for example, support rice prices which are three times higher than those paid by American consumers. Americans could easily export rice to Japan to the benefit of American farmers and Japanese consumers.

As the Japanese increasingly become meat-eaters, tariff barriers limiting beef imports from America and Australia and Argentina will have to be lowered.[3] Few consumers enjoy paying as much as twenty dollars a pound for beef when cheaper imported beef is available.

Then too, the fear that foreign countries will place restrictions on Japanese imports will force the Japanese to lower their own trade barriers. These will cause political as well as economic problems which the Japanese will have to fact in the coming decades.

It may be that the Japanese will soon face their greatest challenges yet to their cultural survival. There are many internal as well as external pressures for change. There is no guarantee that Japan's "economic miracle" will continue without pause. The national and international conditions which made Japan's postwar renaissance possible will not continue to exist over the next few decades. The high cost of energy, for example, will make Japan less competitive with oil-rich and coal-rich industrial nations.

1.6 Four Basic Principles of Japanese Management

Four general principles underlie the major difference between Japanese and American managerial behavior. Americans operate from almost the direct opposite point of view of the following Japanese managerial axioms:

1. The worker who is able to perform any work duty is intelligent enough to improve the productivity and quality of that work.
2. Given the chance, workers want to improve the quality of their work.
3. Members of a corporation form a "family."
4. The group is more important than the individual.

These four principles underlie the Japanese way of work. They may seem simplistic, but they form the foundation for the post-1945 expansion of the Japanese economy into the world's markets. No one can understand the Japanese economic miracle of the sixties and seventies without understanding the above principles.

---

[3] Opening Japan's markets to foreign importers would not automatically offer American goods as entry. Other countries are quite able to sell to Japan the same goods Americans have to offer.

The first principle says that *the worker is not stupid*. This means that if the typical factory worker, clerk, or junior manager knows enough to do a specific job, then he also knows enough to improve the work being done. In Japan, the first step taken to improve productivity is to ask the worker how it might be done. Each worker understands his own duties as well or better than any outsider.

Even an experienced engineer is not as familiar with a specific procedure as the person who is actually doing the work. No doubt every reader of this book has sneered at a so-called efficiency expert who has told him how to do his job more efficiently. We all know how to do our work better than an outsider. Imagine a woman who has soldered connections onto a computer chip for six months using a microscope. She can certainly tell an outsider how it feels to make hundreds of solders each day. Since she is doing the work for seven hours or more each day, she is the one best suited to evaluate how she could become more productive. The problem, of course, is how to motivate this worker to want to be more efficient and to volunteer to make suggestions. We assume she knows how. Does she want to?

Any change in a Japanese factory begins by asking those directly involved for their input. That is why experts first ask manual workers for their help in re-designing machines to the users' specifications. A factory floor worker may not have the engineering skills to re-design his tools and machines, but he can tell someone under what conditions his machines overheat. Or he can indicate which hand tools are clumsy and need to be re-designed for faster production.[4] There probably has never been a worker who couldn't have told a superior how the work can be done faster. Whether we want to make such suggestions is another matter. But the principle remains: workers are smarter than they are given credit for.

Japanese managers and supervisors look to subordinates for advice, and it is common for foremen to consult with manual workers. The Japanese assume that a task can be done more efficiently when the worker provides on-the-spot expert suggestions. Workers are consulted whenever work changes are antici-pated.

How can this principle be used systematically in the United States? The Japanese developed two administrative practices which encourage workers to use their initiative. The first is the Quality Control circle policy in which workers make productivity suggestions. The second practice is the policy of encouraging all employees to develop new skills over the years during their work careers. Most younger workers in Japan take evening courses or learn

---

[4] In one suggestion, a Japanese factory worker showed that moving two machines closer together allowed one worker to operate two instead of one machine without added effort.

new skills by observing someone in the plant. No one hired by a corporation expects to stay in he same job classification until retirement. Workers become more valuable to the company over the years as they develop added skills and abilities.

Japanese QC circles, discussed in a later chapter, are made up of eight or more workers and their supervisor. This group meets monthly or more often to study how to increase productivity. QC members are given lessons on productivity problem-solving and quality control. They are taught how to seek out and solve low-productivity situations. Some even visit customers and suppliers to improve the quality of their products and materials.

In some Japanese factories, up to ninety percent of the workers are members of QC circles. These workers not only are asked for suggestions, but they develop the skills needed to find solutions for production problems. How many Americans have been seriously asked to suggest improvements where they work? In comparable companies having suggestion systems, the number of suggestions per worker is thirteen in Japan and less than one in the United States. Both managers and workers in America must change their belief that workers are not fit to take part in quality developments.

A corollary to the first principle is that a worker able to understand what he is doing can also learn other skills. A Japanese worker is expected to take evening courses to upgrade and extend his skills. Both male and female workers enroll in a number of courses aimed at self-improvement, whether job-related or not. According to Rafael Steinberg (1975:58), who lived in Japan for nine years, corporate employees – he mentions Matsushita Electric Industrial Company specifically – take evening courses to improve their occupational and cultural skills. Employees study English, Judo, and flower arranging as well as welding and quality control. Steinberg found that some employees at Matsushita complained when work on Saturday was ended. They were afraid that a five-day work week would result in more overtime and end the possibility of attending evening classes.

The second principle is *workers want to do better work*. Few of us want to do less than possible, although no one wants to be taken advantage (McGregor, 1960:47–8). The Japanese avoid this trap by rewarding workers when they do more than the minimum. Any worker who becomes capable of doing more is immediately given more responsibility or else is transferred to another division. In this way, Japanese companies encourage continuous upgrading of their labor force.

Once workers learn to perform more than one technical job, they are able to relate their work to other departments. These workers can then better evaluate their own responsibilities. They become their own productivity experts.

When a Japanese factory becomes automated, the displaced workers are taught programming or other skills. The robots then do the dirty, repetitive work and humans do the more important, challenging work. Work is made more meaningful for humans when the Japanese robots take over. At the present stage of robotic technology, robots can only perform work that is simple and repetitive in nature. These are the types of duties most workers are glad to discard if they can do so without losing their jobs.

Japanese workers are rewarded when the company's profits increase. Semi-annual bonuses are based on how well the company does. In a depressed period when profits are less, all workers receive less. In fact, during a very bad economic period, the higher-level executives will receive *higher* percentage pay cuts than lower-level workers. The reason for this is that it's assumed workers are so motivated that they are already doing their best. They should not be "punished" as much when profits are low. The senior executives are in charge; leaders must take the blame for any errors in policy.

In America, we punish the lowest-level workers – those with the least seniority and skills – when sales take a downturn. They are the ones who are first laid off and the first to suffer pay cuts. No wonder it is hard to motivate these persons to do their best. Their temporary status makes it hard for them to identify with their employers.

The third general principle of Japanese management is that *workers form a family*. The Japanese accept the premise that employees and employers form cohesive social units. All members of a corporation develop systems of mutual obligations beyond what they are being paid to do. Being part of the corporate "family" entails debts on both management and workers. Pay is only one reward. There is also a sense of belongingness and support that employees receive from their corporations. This sense of belongingness develops when others have done you favors that should be paid back eventually. Being part of a corporate "family" means accepting the notion that "family" means mutual responsibility for everyone's well-being.

One consequence of this belief is the practice of lifelong employment. Many workers in Japan, barring bankruptcy, insanity, or criminal behavior, enjoy complete job security. After all, adults don't "fire" their children and rela-tives. Once you hire someone, you find a place which uses his best talents. The "family" corporation makes adjustments and provides the best environment for every worker. While not all Japanese workers are able to have total job security, the practice is one example of this view of the worker as family.

On the worker's side, the person-corporation relationship is more than a financial one. The worker offers the corporation a loyalty similar to what is owed family or village. Confucius taught that all persons owe parents and civil leaders complete devotion. The Japanese corporation is the modern equivalent to the traditional family.

Japanese white collar workers, called salarymen, are likely to use the same word for home and company. The term, *uchi*, is used interchangably for either (Fields, 1983:69). A reason for this is that a worker's friends tend to be business associates. No one with a middle-management job is likely to have much free time to spend with non-co-workers. Males spend most of their free time with co-workers rather than with their wives. The male-female worlds remain very separate in Japan, and the sexes have little in common with each other. Leisure activities are usually spent with members of the same gender. The sexes have so little in common after marriage that spouses spend most of their free time apart.

"Salarymen" living in large cities do not to make friends with neighbors. These workers are rarely at home long enough to become acquainted with next-door neighbors, whether they live in apartments or single family houses. The ideal Japanese worker is one who comes home near midnight due to business responsibilities.

Another reason why Japanese make bad neighbors is that most of one's friends – except former school mates, childhood friends, and family – are co-workers. The Japanese seldom entertain at home, and business calls are good excuses to meet at bars and restaurants. To corporate workers, *"uchi"* means the company is "family," or at least a home away from home. If in trouble and needing help, a "salaryman" goes to his supervisor or division chief for help before he asks his family.

The worker owes the corporation loyalty to work at peak efficiency and to develop his talents to help the corporation. Given lifelong employment, a worker has the time and work security to be able to learn whatever helps the profitability of the company.

Irwin Ross (1982:41) offers a good example of the opposite attitude of worker loyalty. He quotes a former inspector at Ford describing the attitudes of his fellow workers during the boom years: "When I worked there ... people's attitude was 'take all you can get and screw the company.'" This is opposite from the Japanese ideal. Most efforts of supervisors are focused on avoiding the attitude shown above.

To increase worker loyalty in the automobile industry, writer Irwin Ross recommends the adoption of profit-sharing plans. American Motors Corporation has such a plan. The first layer of profits (10%) is reserved for shareholders; then the workers receive 15% of the remaining pretax profits. Irwin Ross also proposes that manufacturers give complete job security to anyone who has worked for the same employer for ten years or more.

Other Americans besides Irwin Ross are beginning to consider seriously the advantages and disadvantages of lifetime job security, or at least schemes which encourage group loyalties. Labor union officials as well as corporate executives now realize that complete job security can result in advantages to both the workers and the company as a whole. For this reason, a later chapter describes the Japanese lifelong career policy and its advantages and disadvantages.

While many Japanese corporate employees enjoy lifelong job security, the term is more restricted than it might seem at first glance. It is the Japanese custom to retire people when they reach about their fifty-fifth year. Most Japanese workers can expect to live many years beyond fifty-five and must seek work elsewhere. Unfortunately, retirement benefits for most are too low to support a retiree and family in their accustomed standard of living.

This financial pressure forces most Japanese males in their fifties to find new employers, usually at salaries lower than their previous ones. Whether Americans would accept early retirements and lower wages after age fifty-five as one price for "lifelong" employment is questionable. Lifelong employment is a Japanese concept which must be thoroughly analyzed before its utility for Americans can be demonstrated.

The third principle places obligations on management as well as on the worker. The worker on his part owes the company loyalty; the other side of the agreement is that management must "take care" of the workers. As "elder members," corporate officials are expected to be concerned with the welfare of the workers and with each person's special needs. A newly-married male manager will receive a pay raise because, as a married man, his financial responsibilities have now increased. He will also receive extra pay raises after each child is born, though his work has not changed.

A division head may "suggest" that it is time for a male assistant to get married. He would either present the names of eligible girls or be willing to hire a marriage broker at company's expense. If there is mutual interest between the bachelor and a prospective bride, the superior may even hire a detective or investigate himself to see if the girl has "proper" character and family background.

Like any family, the corporation's interest in its employees may become too smothering, and not all Japanese enjoy this much support from their employers. Similarly, many Americans would reject this extreme type of corporate paternalism. Most of us accept guidance during work hours but reject the right of employers to interfere with off-work activities. In Japan, the family orientation developed by corporations makes it difficult to separate work from nonwork. The "family" obligations of the employee are complete and do not stop at the end of the work day.

When talking about the family, Americans think of parents supervising children. Parents take care of children because they are too immature to be independent. This attitude forms the paternalistic model of management. Since children are seen as immature, parents have to tell these dependents how to behave. Only parents know what is good for children. The paternalistic model is authoritarian: the worker should obey the superiors. Seen as a child, the worker is also seen as stupid – or at least as incapable of independence.

The Japanese are not paternalistic in the American manner. The better term to use for the Japanese style of management is "familial" or maybe even "matriarchal." Here, workers are part of a family, but they are adults, not children. There exists inequality in every family; there are uncles, aunts, brothers, the grandfather, as well as others. The grandfather is the leader, and all members contribute what they can to the common good. But being part of a "family" does not mean all are equal. It does mean that all members share a common identity and share a common "love." The Japanese expect all work-related relationships to be warm emotionally and very personal.

Japanese workers expect to be consulted because they feel a responsibility to help the corporate "family." That is why management seeks consensus before issuing orders. Workers are expected to point out, very politely, when management errs. Lower-level workers are lesser members of the community, but they are members nevertheless. Being part of a large family, all members of a company want to be cared for and liked. In ways I discuss later, the Japanese company offers employers love and emotional support as well as paychecks.

The last principle of Japanese management is that *the group is more important than the individual*. No one shoud be so selfish as to think only for himself. This reflects the Confucian ideal that a person always owes a debt of gratitude to parents and leaders. This debt can never be completely redeemed and the group forever has a hold on the individual. This debt continues no matter how long the relationship lasts.

How can someone who has been at the same company for ten years settle the debt he owes? This worker has learned valuable skills and been given work and respect as well as a living. To go to another employer offering a higher salary would be a sign of ingratitude. In the same way, how can a son ever repay the debt he owes his mother? She gave birth to him and took care of him when a child. This debt could never be paid off. The Japanese worker feels a similar debt to the corporate family.

Since the group is more important than the individual, the Japanese have developed a number of techniques to ensure harmony among members of a group. Corporate workers are paid partly on the basis of seniority, not on individual productivity. And promotion is also based upon seniority. These policies decrease the likelihood of individual jealously and competition.

This book discusses in detail these four principles of Japanese work philosophy. Of these, the last is the most difficult for Americans to accept since we are a nation of individualists. After I present how these principles operate in Japanese corporations, I will then suggest a number of ways they can be applied in an American setting.

Chapter 2
The Cooperative Japanese

2.1 The Japanese Insistence on Cooperation

As was shown in the previous chapter, Japanese executives view workers from a different perspective than do American executives. Japanese corporate officials assume that the individual worker is loyal to the company and its goals. The worker, at whatever level, is more than a wage earner. He is an active partner with co-workers and superiors in the search for economic success, whether that goal is quality performance or higher productivity.

The rationale for this worker-management partnership is that production – especially that aimed at export – is believed to benefit not only the worker and the company, but also the nation.[1] The Japanese population has achieved a remarkable consensus described as economic nationalism: economic success is seen as the only way Japan as a society and a culture can survive in the modern world. The major sectors of Japan – government, business, workers, organized labor, the public – all must work together so that the economy becomes and remains a successful international competitor. This consensus is more of an ideal than reality, because various economic sectors in Japan at times conflict with one another. Not all Japanese cooperate wholeheartedly. Even export companies will ignore goverment "advice" if it is not to their advantage. But the ideal of cooperation is a strong one in Japan and influences behavior to a remarkable extent.

National unity developed during the 1950s as the Japanese gradually recovered from the devastation caused by the Second World War. The first four years of the postwar era is still remembered by older Japanese as "the hungry cage." Government officials, managers, workers, and the general public agreed that the peaceful development of the economy was everyone's task.

This attitude resulted in the belief that management and labor must become partners in the development of the economy. When discussing the Japanese economy, the Japanese use the term *"uchiwa,"* which means "all-in-the-family economy" (Johnson, 1982:11). The term suggests that workers are part of a cooperative effort more important than the search for individual rewards. The term also infers that the nation must prosper before individuals are able to do so.

---

[1] The belief that the three divisions of state-firm-worker formed a large family *(kokka)* became official policy during the late 1880s (Fruin, 1983).

Cooperation is seen as a necessity as well as a traditional virtue. That is why workers are expected to actively contribute to ensure the success of their employers. Doing so means that the country and future generations also benefit. To achieve this success, workers must do more than merely follow their work instructions: they must also be motivated enough to want to do more than the minimum. The survival of their society demands this extra effort. There is a sense of crisis among the Japanese that Japan's existence is threatened by outside economic and political forces.

Whether this sense of societal crisis is a strong among younger workers as among those who experienced postwar hardships is another matter. Many of today's Japanese teenagers want to enjoy the benefits of economic prosperity.[2] They are much less willing than their fathers to work overtime and ignore their spouses and children for the demands of employers. But the Japanese superiority in international markets cannot be understood without a knowledge of the importance the Japanese place on economic strength.

2.2 The Japanese Sense of Inferiority

The Japanese feel isolated from other nations. This isolation is partly self-imposed because the Japanese believe themselves outnumbered and over-powered by more industrially-advanced foreigners, and therefore weaker. While the Japanese have historically considered themselves to be equal or better than non-Japanese in terms of culture and spirit, they have also felt their nation to be poor, overcrowded, and threatened by outsiders.

This sense of insecurity was augmented in 1853 when Commodore Perry entered Japan with a modern fleet of warships overwhelmingly outclassing the Japanese naval capability. The Japanese realized that Japan would have to modernize if it were to resist the western powers. Japan did not want to become another Asian colony of a western imperial power such as France, England, or even the United States.

The Japanese today continue to see themselves as forming a small nation whose people live on an overcrowded, resource-poor set of islands. If there is a sense of ruthlessness in the way the Japanese compete in international markets, it is because even today they believe themselves threatened by the superpowers. Their business activities are attempts to adopt whatever measures necessary for cultural survival. That is why it is possible for employers to urge workers to improve their work productivity and quality by appealing to

---

[2] Younger Japanese ask why "the Japanese are poor and the nation is rich?" They want to enjoy the advantage of economic prosperity, especially better housing and more consumer products.

their patriotism. As of now, the cultural hero in Japan is the efficient producer/ worker. The businessman is today's samurai warrior.

I am not trying to paint Japan as a nation of self-denying saints. Instead, the beauty of the situation is that the Japanese have linked private selfishness to the public interest. The same spirit can be found whenever any nation is faced with a national crisis. An example of this was the effort of American women during the 1940's. During this time many women worked as riveters, welders, and in other occupations in war-related industries. They were being paid for their labor, of course, but work had a meaning far greater than just economics: they were also being patriotic. The same for the Japanese today.

Corporate employment in Japan is more than a contracted agreement. The employee accepts the company much as a samurai accepted employment with a feudal lord. This relationship was lifelong and unlimited. A samurai was to follow the *bushido* or warrior's moral code, irrespective of the dangers or personal hardships involved.

The *bushido* code stressed self-sacrifice and total loyalty through self-efface-ment. A samurai was humble (toward superiors, not toward inferiors whom they could kill at will) and considered the lord's *(daimyo)* interests over his own (Masatsugu, 1982). The samurai literature in novels, plays, and movies contains many plots in which one or more samurai sacrifice themselves for lord and clan. A favorite samurai story (the "Revenge of the 47 samurai") in both Japan and the United States is the one in which a group of samurai work and suffer for years to revenge their dead lord. After finally killing the one who had caused the suicide of their *daimyo,* the followers went to his grave and committed suicide. Their loyalty was so complete that they were willing to suffer for their acts of revenge.

Modern executives do not expect their workers to die for their company. But the feeling of personal loyalty is very strong. In fact, many executives do consider themselves to be modern-day samurai. Corporate workers, like the former samurai, are expected to place the company ahead of themselves and their families. New workers spend from three to six months in indoctrination programs. They live together during this period to learn their company's history, goals, and songs. They learn to be loyal employees. They also learn that through their efforts, the company can benefit Japan as well as customers. When they do, then everyone will also benefit. At this point, new employees develop the "spirit" and determination to work for the corporate good.

Some recruits – the term is more correct than "new employee" – may be sent for several weeks to what can only be described as boot camps. There they prepare their own meals and perform their own housework, do strenuous exercises, listen to lectures on business affairs, character formation, and the past and present glories of Japan. More senior workers are sent for a week or more to a Zen temple for a course on meditation and subordination of the self.

The purpose of all of this indoctrination is to instill in workers a sense of total loyalty and sense of duty in employees. On the other hand, the samurai-businessman is expected to be loyal in turn to retainers-subordinates. Japanese management cannot be understood without reference to the fact that the worker-employer relation is in large part a feudal one.

2.3 The Importance of Group Membership

Another distinctive characteristic of the Japanese is their reliance on the group rather than on the individual. *The group is always more important than the individual.* Corporate success is seen as the result of group effort and not through the exceptional activities of individuals. Ideally, there are not production heroes in a large company. There are instead persons whose work groups, teams, or departments have improved their productivity and gone beyond quotas. The company's goals are achieved through group effort. This emphasis of the group is the most important difference between American and Japanese work philosophies.

This "groupism" is reflected in the Japanese definition of the word "individualism." The original term in the Japanese language denotes selfishness, isolation from others, and that the person is concerned with his own advantage as against being willing to work for the welfare of others. To be individualistic means that the person gains by weakening the group, or in spite of the group. On the other hand, everyone gains when each member seeks to make the group more efficient, or when the individual works to help the group as a whole, whether a team or a company.

The example of Soichiro Honda, founder of Honda Motors Co. illustrates the power of group membership in Japanese corporations. In many ways Honda was not a typical Japanese: he built up his company by becoming an entrepreneur instead of a "corporation man," he was not a college graduate) and Honda stressed hiring new employees on the basis of expertise rather than sociability. These are cardinal sins in the view of most corporate Japanese. But he too emphasized the group element. He believed that each worker should be encouraged to work for the good of Honda Motors Co. This belief in the power of group motivation is illustrated by Soichiro Honda's comment that:

There is a limit to what can be thought out by big shots sitting at their desks. Where 100 people think, there are 100 powers; if 1,000 people think, there are 1,000 powers (Schnapp, 1982).

To the Japanese, the group does not threaten the individual. The reverse instead is true: the group supports and helps individual members. The underlying belief is that the person is too weak to defend himself against the world by himself. He needs the protection and support of a group if he is to be successful. For Americans, the group stifles the individual. Most of us believe that the group inhibits individual success rather than the opposite.

Japanese society is an essentially closed society based on membership in interlocking groups. Japanese society is made up of a number of groups each of which demands partial loyalty. By the same token, those outside one's groups are considered as outsiders and strangers. This makes the Japanese ruthless at times when dealing with strangers. To these, you owe little loyalty or concern.

Loyalty to one group often means a rejection of members of the other groups. This allows the Japanese to exhibit an intense competitive spirit. Except for athletics and education, competition in Japan is almost always based on group competition. Work teams will compete to see which one will fulfill a quota first. And there is no reluctance for Japanese companies to compete against foreign ones. It is important to note, though, that this competition is group vs. group.

One theory why the Japanese armed forces seemed disorganized at times during the Second World War is that there existed a large amount of inter-service rivalry. Each service was jealous of its own prerogatives and honor, and each would seek to protect its own interests. The Imperial Navy, for example, would refuse to transport supplies to island-based army troops if the plan endangered too many ships. This is the other side of group loyalty. Non-members are outsiders whose concerns are less important than your own group's. In order to defend themselves, Japanese individuals must join a group, or else form one.

There are two important group ties in a Japanese company. General loyalty lies with the company as a whole and within the immediate division or department. Intensely loyal feelings also exist among age equals fellow univer-sity graduates. University graduates employed in a corporation are hired once a year, and the members of each graduating class go through company training and indoctrination together. Workers remain very close to members of their entrance class, and this weakens the loyalty they owe the company as a whole. Members of the same entrance class are likely to help one another and exchange favors before helping non-members. A junior manager in a Japanese corporation is more likely to do a favor for a fellow entrance-class employee than for someone who's younger or older. He's also more likely to ask this same person for help in getting the information needed to complete a competi-tive bid.

An example of this type of loyalty would be a salesman who wants to pad his expense account a little. This is not a matter to discuss with your immediate superior. But a Japanese would be willing to invite out for a drink a company classmate who's now in the accounting division. The two of you could talk about hypothetical situations such as which types of expenses the company's accountants frown upon and which ones they accept. If nothing, else, your former classmate can be trusted to keep quiet. And he might be willing to give you some inside information. On the other hand, this accountant would feel free to ask you for a favor later on. The point is that the tie established when Japanese employees join the company provides the rationale for trust and cooperation throughout their careers.

At best, this tie encourages employers to help each other and exchange favors. This reduces red tape and increases interdepartmental communication. On the other hand, this entrance class tie encourages workers to become more loyal to some than to others. You can't trust everyone equally. They too may be more loyal to their former classmates than to you.

This emotional tie among members of an entrance class makes seniority a significant element in the workplace. Those who belong to the same company entrance group have also the same age. In a nation where age is strongly respected, seniority is reinforced by age: those who have equal seniority are also age peers. This results in a double bond. Workers who join a company later, of course, are also younger. All of a worker's superiors are older and enjoy influence because of both their higher position and seniority.

Employees of the same age feel more comfortable with one another than with someone younger or older. Age peers by definition have equal seniority in their company and belong to the same entrance group; they have experienced many events in common; and they have learned to trust each other. Any favor to help fellow workers, or to hide errors, will be more likely among age peers. These ties can threaten efficiency if allowed to develop too extremely. If kept with bounds, these ties encourage cooperation and consensus. This serves to decrease interdepartmental conflict and increase communication.

This age/seniority tie is weakened by another demand for group loyalty: the school tie. If anything competes with age as a source of group identity it is a worker's school alumnus status. The school tie is a major one and is influential throughout a person's working career. The Japanese remain loyal to their elementary schools and high schools, as well as their universities. Many of these alumni return to their former grade and high schools for annual events in their honor. High schools with winning baseball teams attract former students who cheer as loudly as current students. This school loyalty is carried over to loyalty to fellow graduates. Friendships made at school or based on a school tie are very important and continue throughout life.

Companies tend to "adopt" one university, college, or high school as a source of recruits. This is not an absolute rule, but most Japanese corporations favor a limited number of educational centers. A company hires most if not all of its accountants from one university, its engineers from another, and so on. Each company recruit will find a large number of fellow alumni within the higher (and older) ranks. He automatically has a group tie with them that he can call on.

Age and position may intimidate a new employee, but at least some of these "elders" are equal to him due to educational background. An allumus tie between older and younger employees already exists. This makes coming to a new company a little less fearful, and it also provides a competing source of group identity against seniority. A worker, in fact, may be caught between conflicting demands. He might be expected to support a project because an older fellow alumnus asks him to do so. But a friend with the same age working in another department may ask him to reject this project and vote against it.

This unfortunate worker may also be expected to act in another way by his immediate superior. To get along with everyone and not appear to be disloyal to one group or another is not always easy in Japan. In the example above, the first tendency of someone pulled by such cross-pressures is to be noncommital and do nothing. The hope is that a consensus will gradually develop until everyone has agreed to one plan or at least compromised. Or maybe the plan will be dropped.

It is easy to see why foreigners doing business in Japan believe that negotiations take a long time to complete. No Japanese dares to make a unilateral decision even if he has the power to do so. Any decision is preceded by a large number of meetings and consultations. In essence, there are few persons in Japanese companies who are completely "in charge." Americans with urgent business to conduct in Japan will find the Japanese unwilling to make quick decisions.

I pointed out that the Japanese society is made up of a series of connected groups and that each person belongs to a number of groups, each of which demands a certain amount of loyalty. This overlapping series of memberships links one member of a group to a member of another group. A member of a university class can expect support from older fellow graduates as well as classmates. He also owes loyalty to his work team mates, his political party, etc., as well as his family.

If we picture group membership as forming a circle, then Japanese society is made up of overlapping circles, each connected to a number of others. A junior executive owes loyalty to his company and age peers, but he also feels close to senior executives who have graduated from his own university. If he seeks a special promotion, he can appeal to an older fellow university alumnus who plays golf with a vice-president. Or he can ask a former professor to recommend him to his immediate superior who also was a student of the same professor or a graduate from the same college.

These interlocking circles of loyalty may seem as if there are too many social responsibilities and demands on loyalty. But that is an American response. A Japanese feels secure because of these multiple group memberships. With multiple loyalties, the individual can count on more persons for help. For every potential call for support there is also the potential of receiving support in turn. An American feels inhibited with such a mass of group demands while a Japanese sees these ties as potential sources of support.

An illustrative example of group support is found in the Japanese practice of giving gifts to someone going on a vacation. Family members' co-workers, and friends will give the vacation goer gifts of money to ensure that the traveler can afford to have a good time.

However, it's assumed that at least a fourth or so of the money given will be returned in the form of tourist momentoes and souvenirs. That is why Japanese tourists appear to foreign observers to be fanatic souvenir buyers. They seem to be almost frantic in duty-free airport shops and elsewhere. There is more to this behavior than a strong Yen currency. The reason is that not buying gifts before returning home would insult friends and relatives. Americans experience the same feeling of anxiety when they try to decide how much to spend on a relative's Christmas gift or whose name to strike off the Christmas card list. To the Japanese, group ties are double-edged: they offer benefits as well as responsibilities.

2.4 The Japanese Concern for Group Harmony

The Japanese hold that conflict, disagreement, and overt competition are harmful if they result in lessened group harmony and consensus. Japanese executives may disagree with one another in terms of certain policies, but these disagreements are not allowed to develop into open conflicts. Those who disagree must discuss their differences privately until a compromise is ached.[3]

The maintenance of a group consensus is more important than allowing conflicting parties the chance to compete directly against each other. The typical American response is that competition allows a winner to emerge. At least open conflict results in a clear-cut winner with a clearly defined policy. But the Japanese feel that intra-group antagonisms weaken rather than strengthen a company. The harmony of the whole (i.e. the work group or the company) is more important than having any one part achieve a clear victory on a specific issue.

---

[3] If two persons can't agree, a common practice is to ask a third party to mediate and settle the difference.

An American group leader typically cares less for group harmony than results. This is one reason why American executives become impatient when subordinates fail to agree with one another and time is "wasted" discussing what to do next. The one in authority is likely to decide to "knock heads" together and order everyone to do what they've been told to do. Group harmony and morale can come later, but first there's a job to do.

The Japanese manager, by contrast, believes that team morale and harmony come first. Once achieved, they will automatically result in better work performance. The Japanese are willing to spend – and do so – as much time as needed to achieve a group consensus. Leaders prepare carefully to make sure group harmony develops over a proposed plan. The project can begin only when all involved are satisfied and in agreement.

The Japanese are inhibited by the fact that their society is group-oriented; all Japanese are taught to want to live up to group expectations. Their cultural ideal is based on persons helping the group through individual sacrifices. A Japanese worker may not always want to subordinate himself to his work group, or a wife may at times chafe against her subordinate position vis-a-vis her husband or mother-in-law. But both have been taught to comply with the traditional value that individual feelings are less important than maintaining group harmony. As important is the fact that the group rewards the individual. The Japanese worker receives a bonus when the company does well; he receives praise and prestige when he performs for the group's advantage. A loyal wife is supported by her own family and friends.

The Japanese do not work hard for its own sake: few persons, even in Japan, are that altruistic. Japanese workers are motivated by the way they are rewarded to be group-oriented and motivated workers.

Much of this motivation can be developed and encouraged by American managers. The task is to develop reward systems which encourage people to work together instead of competing. A bonus system which rewards every member in the most productive work team follows Japanese logic; rewarding only the top three salesmen with bonuses is American. It's common sense to assume that, in the first instance, workers will be motivated to work together and help each other out. In the second example, our hypothetical American salesmen are forced to compete against one another. In this case, helping someone out means you're helping a rival. Salesmen in Japan are not given individual bonuses. They receive bonuses when the sales group as a whole does well. The Japanese worker is more cooperative than his American counterpart partly because it's to his advantage to do so.

Japanese culture, through the influence of Buddhism and Confucianism, stresses the value of cooperation over competition. The individual should cooperate with groups, and all groups should cooperate with one another. This traditional belief is still an influencial ideal today.

There is no classical Japanese word for the western term "competition." The word was first discovered by Yukichi Fukuzama, who was translating an English text on economics (Ballon, 1980:119). Fukuzama translated the word into *"kyoso"* (*kyo* = race; *so* = fight) and was criticized for introducing such an un-Japanese concept. Even today the term is not a respectable one in Japan.

"Competition" to the Japanese assumes group-to-group competition. Except for carefully defined individual contests such as in athletics, competition in Japan nearly always takes place on the inter-group level. Whenever a Japanese strives to better himself, he does so through the group for the group (De Mente, 1981:60).

The concept "competition" in Japanese has the added connotation of a crisis being present. A person or group "competes" because it's a matter of group survival or group prestige. Otherwise it is more natural for the Japanese to compromise and cooperate harmoniously.

This makes the Japanese aggressive competitors when they do compete. There must first be a sense of emergency, of a crisis, of a threat to the group. Then all energies and talents are mobilized to combat this threat. However, this mobilization of resources takes place within the group. Individual advantage and rivalries must be set aside. This results in a solid front and in often ruthless behavior. If a danger exists then it must be conquered as quickly as possible.

That is one reason why Americans are competing against "Japan, Inc." instead of individual corporations such as Mitsubishi or Yamaha. Japanese businessmen, as modern samurai, see themselves as the defenders of modern Japan against western threats. It is also why Japanese businesses, government, financial circles, labor unions, and workers themselves develop and follow the same policies.

2.5 The Concept of *Wa*

One extremely important concept gives great insight into Japanese thinking. The Japanese term for group harmony and consensus is *wa*. *Wa* refers to a balance or limitation of individual needs and desires in favor of the good of the group. It is the search for or the existence of mutual cooperation so that each member works for the success of the group. A close American equivalent to *wa* is the term "group morale." Better yet is the U.S. Marines' motto, "Gung-Ho!," which is translated as "work together" and "be enthusiastic." Notice the phrase is Oriental in origin.

The search for *wa* or group harmony does not mean that Japanese executives never personally favor one policy over another, or that employees always agree on how a company goal should be achieved. Instead, *wa* encourages members of a group to emphasize what they have in common and to search for ways to eliminate any remaining differences. They must try to convince each other that one favorite policy or another is the best. The process of agreement involves compromise, promises of future agreement in exchange for present acquiescence, and the like. These backroom techniques are common in American businesses as well as in politics and diplomacy, but they are even more common in Japan.

A state of group harmony cannot be forced on conflicting parties. Members must be allowed to debate, try to convince each other, and eventually compromise until all persons agree on a solution. The emphasis is on reaching an agreement that all can accept. As discussed below, the Japanese have developed a number of bureaucratic mechanisms to develop *wa* in corporations. Many differences between Japanese and American corporate practices can be traced to the Japanese interest in maintaining a feeling of *wa*. This search for consensus is partly responsible for the enthusiastic and loyal feelings Japanese workers have toward their companies.

The concept gives every Japanese worker the responsibility to improve production. Each worker is expected to look for ways to improve his efficiency because in that way *wa* is maintained. On the other hand, in this concern for group harmony, superiors explain to their personnel why a specific policy exists and continuously ask for suggestions for improvements. Future policies are discussed by all workers at all levels; this ensures that a policy won't be introduced until a consensus is reached. Afterwards, no one resists when an agreed-upon policy is made official.

Maintaining *wa* can only be done through a strong belief in what Americans call team spirit. Members must identify with the group and be loyal to its goals. Hopefully, the members of a work group will develop goals that are the same as the larger company's. When that is the case, the group will be a high morale one with a high productivity record. The enthusiasm of the members will support the company. If not, the group will be made up of complainers who will not only refuse to work as hard as possible, but will also exhibit high absenteeism, high error rate in production, and so on. Groups develop their own morale level and work standards. Japanese supervisors have the responsibility to ensure that the groups they oversee have *was* that support the company's goals.

Japanese managers spend much of their work days and evenings making sure that each worker develops a team spirit supporting the company. This is the major responsibility of those responsible for others. *Wa* must be focused toward the company or else the manager fails in his duty. No Japanese, no matter his technical knowledge, will ever be given supervisory responsibility over others if he cannot develop and maintain a group spirit loyal to the company's goals. In this context, production goals are secondary. It's assumed that group morale *(wa)* results in high production and quality performance. The opposite is usually true in America. American managers are taught (and expected) to stress production and profit first. Only then does morale become the focus of managerial behavior.

When asked what the goals of corporations are, Japanese managers will always first answer that a company's primary goal is to take care of the workers *(wa)* and next to help the Japanese nation survive international competition by increasing exports. Then they will say that the company exists to serve customers. Only afterwards, if at all, will there be mention of stockholder profits and the company's credit balance. If these same Japanese managers were asked how these goals can be achieved, the unanimous response will be "team spirit and company loyalty."

Team spirit has both advantages and disadvantages. Team spirit encourages members to be faithful and enthusiastic workers. They will want to work hard to ensure group success. Team spirit encourages high productivity and quality performance.

Team spirit is also beneficial when close supervision is not possible or becomes too expensive: the ideal is that members will want to work on their own initiative. The result is that supervision costs decrease with the development of team spirit. And the workers themselves will want to maintain quality performance. This is a reason why the Japanese are now among the world's leaders in manufacturing productivity and quality. These have been achieved through the achievement of workers' high morale.

There are also disadvantages to having too strong a team spirit. Loyalty to one group may mean rejection of others and in a lack of coordination with non-members. Members may hoard supplies for themselves instead of sharing with others or may keep valuable information to themselves. After all, team spirit is based on the belief that others are outsiders: loyalty stops with the immediate group. Too much team spirit gives rise to a competitive spirit which challenges overall cooperation.

Japanese managers encourage inter-group competition, and a group will be rewarded over others for higher attendance, above-quota production, neatest/ cleanest work area, giving the largest number of efficiency-improving suggestions, and so on. Managers also try to develop company-wide enthusiasms which are stronger than any lesser loyalty. Such a balance is hard to achieve. This is done by company-wide rewards and bonuses, frequent team rotation, and the like. The Japanese are aware that a delicate balance exists among a person's multiple group memberships and loyalties. But company loyalty is more important than any others, even those based on a worker's family ties.

Because of this concern for group harmony, the individual Japanese is rewarded when he thinks of others before himself. Instead of acting "selfishly," he is encouraged to advance the fortunes of his immediate work group, his department or division, his company, his nation, and his family. He also must maintain harmonious, unselfish relations with members of his company's entrance class, fellow alumni, company, team, and so on. This may seem repressive to an American who sees himself as more of an individual, and it is. But these groups in turn support their members, and the Japanese in question can expect support and aid from each of these ties. *Wa* forces a Japanese to give up his individuality; it also protects and rewards him.

This pressure toward group support has made Japanese workers highly productive. The following examples of the positive influences of the *wa* spirit in the next sections illustrate its power and significance.

This search for *wa* takes many interesting twists in Japan. In 1966, Soichiro Honda became convinced that, in the future, popular automobile engines would be air-cooled. And, in fact, the first mass-produced air-cooled Honda, the N-360 Minicar, became a top seller. President Honda ordered all research on water-cooled engines ended and asked the Honda engineers to develop only engines which were air-cooled.

A number of engineers in Honda's Research and Development Center disagreed with this emphasis on air-cooled engine research. Naturally, they obeyed the boss and developed a number of research programs on air-cooled engines. But they also continued to work on water-cooled engine technology. These engineers made a hideaway in a secluded and unused upper room where they could work on their own schemes. They would sneak away to their own project, even though Soichiro Honda would come to the bottom of the stairs and shout, "Your guys upstairs, come down!" Though he was the founder and president of Honda Motors, he did not want to be so dictatorial that he would force workers to ignore their own pet projects (Sakita, 1982:158). Doing so would threaten the company's *wa*! Even when disobedient, he trusted them to want to do good for the company. He never formally forbade their working on water-cooled designs, though he did show his displeasure.

Finally, the stubborn engineers asked Takeo Fujisawa, Honda Motor's then co-leader with Soichiro Honda, to talk to Honda. Fujisawa's specialty was finance and seldom interfered with the company's technical projects. These were Soichiro Honda's expertise and interests. But after talking with the engineers, Fujisawa decided he had to intervene for the good of the company's *wa*. Honda was convinced by Fujisawa that air-cooled engine research had to be abandoned. The next day, Honda told the R&D engineers to work on their cherished water-cooled engines. Honda realized that *wa* demanded that he follow the majority and that as a minority of one, he might very well be mistaken.

Honda was still personally convinced his engineers were wrong, and according to one report, "Honda never smiled when anyone talked about water-cooling" (Sakita, 1982:160). He admitted his error by testing the first water-cooled prototype himself when completed and admitted that the design was superior. *Wa* demands that superiors trust their assistants when they insist on making unorthodox contributions. In this instance, they were right. Honda's policy of encouraging worker initiative proved correct.

Sharp Corporation, a Japanese electronics corporation, follows a cooperative philosophy similar to Honda Motors. Like all Japanese companies, Sharp has a formal company creed, mottoes, and an official philosophy. Its business philosophy, reported in *Nation's Business* (January, 1984), is:

We do not seek merely to expand our business volume but, by using our unique technology, we intend to contribute to the upgrading of the culture and welfare of all people around the world. By encouraging the development of our employees' potential and by improving their living standards and welfare, we intent to parallel the growth of our corporation with the well-being of our employees.

The last sentence is a typical Japanese corporate statement and is found in most corporate creeds. The company exists to advance the well-being of the employees and to provide a service to customers. If the managers, workers, and customers all work together in harmony, then the company will be a success, financially and otherwise. While such statements as the one above are more ideals to work toward than ones already achieved, they provide insights into Japanese motivation. Japanese corporate leaders see themselves as driving forces for the good of workers as well as for themselves or stockholders.

2.6 *Wa* and the Worker

The search for *wa* is continuous in Japanese corporations. There are few occasions when *wa* is not encouraged. Japanese companies sponsor weekend retreats *(gasshuku)* for employees at all levels. Many countryside inns and resorts cater only to members of large organizations who come in groups.

These weekend retreats are supposedly organized for professional and educational purposes, and most of the costs are met by the corporations involved (Schreiber, 1983). But in fact, weekend *gasshuku* are also seen as company-sponsored leisure events. They offer breaks from work routine as well as encourage a feeling of *wa* among participants. At times a supervisor may feel the workers need a rest and "suggest" that a *gasshuku* take place.

The weekend is structured, given the Japanese preference for organization, around a detailed schedule of events. The typical weekend begin with a wake-up call, group calisthenics or walks, and breakfast; then come several work sessions on productivity, efficiency improvements, and the like, and a light lunch. There might then be lectures by specialists on quality control techniques and afternoon sessions on specific work problems faced by the workers. Then comes light exercise, usually through team sports. A short rest takes place before a group supper. This banquet would generally have as a guest speaker a senior executive of the company. His speech would include praises of both the company and the workers and formal thanks to those present for their loyalty and hard work.

After speeches, testimonies and toasts, the evening would be devoted to a party with games, group skits, songs, and heavy drinking. A top-ranking executive or the banquet's keynote speaker will visit for a while and join in the fun. His presence makes the weekend "official" and indicates the personal interest executives take in subordinates. He will make a short speech, offer and receive a few toasts, and leave. Now the fun can really begin!

The weekend's work and play activities encourage a feeling of togetherness among workers; the office's *wa* emerges as workers develop friendship ties with each other. The whole weekend reminds the participants that their company cares for them. The company is interested in their leisure activities as well as their work.

It is hard for a non-Japanese to realize how important such company-sponsored activities as the *gasshuku* weekend retreats are to the workers. Many Japanese corporate employees work long hours; nor do they like to take long vacations away from their jobs.[4] But company-sponsored retreats "force" them to enjoy leisure without guilt.

More important, though, is the fact that these weekends improve morale and company loyalty. Imagine a group of workers from the same office soaking together in a hot bath and then drinking and singing through the evening. They relax together, can work out any hostility they might feel toward co-workers, and feel even more thankful to be working for "their" company. Obviously, the group's *wa* as well as company loyalty is increased.

Japanese supervisors can "reward" workers by inviting them out on the town because, at least for older Japanese, most males spend little time at home. The home is a territory belonging to wives, and most husbands spend very little time there. Those who live and work in the Tokyo metropolitan area will

---

[4] Japanese workers do not take all of the vacation time they are legally and officially entitled. White collar workers, especially, will spend the first and last days of their vacations at the office to show how dedicated and loyal they are to their work.

commute as much as two hours to and from work. Men often leave before anyone else is awake and return after dark. Japanese apartments are small and crowded, even those rented by the more affluent. Husbands have little to do at home in the evening except watch TV and drink beer.

Tokyo night life caters to businessmen and expense accounts. Most bars have hostesses who flatter and flirt with male customers. It's very easy for a group of co-workers to spend a few hours at a bar together before separating to go to their respective railroad or subway stations. Tokyo at night is a man's city.

Managers have expense accounts for entertaining clients or co-workers, or both and entertaining business contacts is normal and expected. The result is that "having fun" for most Japanese males takes place among colleagues or within a business setting.

A supervisor's hosting workers to a few drinks or a salesman taking potential customers out on the town for an evening describe very normal business behavior. A *wa* relationship is developed outside of working hours as much as during the work day.

The presence of *wa* in a group can exist only when there is mutual respect. The Japanese are very proud, and deference to rank is a major part of good etiquette. Although a supervisor may spend an evening drinking with his staff, he expects deference from the workers during working hours.

Wa is not based on equality. Few Japanese want to eliminate social differences due to rank and prestige. Cooperation at work does not demand complete democracy. A good leader in Japan does not assume himself to be equal to others. The only times there is leader-subordinate equality is during drinking sessions, when alcohol operates as a safety valve.

Instead, a "good" leader in Japan is one who helps his assistants and who respects their talents. That's why a good leader asks subordinates for advice. And he listens very carefully to what they have to say since by doing so he shows respect. A good leader also shows a personal interest in the lives of his workers. He does favors for them, offers advice on personal matters, and tries to develop mutual debts between himself and his followers.

All of this is done, ideally, because the leader views workers as worthy persons without whose help he could not be a good manager. I say "ideally" because not all Japanese treat their subordinates that way. They may at times be dictatorial, authoritarian, and treat workers as inferiors. But the ideal has pressures of its own, and Japanese leaders feel this pressure even if they would rather not give in to it.

This ideal is that leaders treat workers as if they were valued parts of the company. Even those who hold low company rank are worthy of respect and dignity. They are "decent" individuals whose feelings are important. These persons also have talents – no matter how small – that must be given respect.

Managers who view workers as "decent people" will not only treat them more considerably, but will also expect more from them. Japanese executives seldom give anything without expecting something in exchange since. Japanese culture demands that debts be discharged. Supervisors who respect their workers also assume that their contributions to the company should be greater.

The Japanese value on cooperation can be seen in many ways at Yokoyama Electric Manufacturing Co., a world's leader in the manufacturing of certain electric components. Although small (322 employees and five plants), it is the leading manufacturer of certain speaker components.

Workers attend research meetings, during which employees lecture other employees. Each worker is expected to be an expert on some aspect of the company's work. President Morio Yokoyama meets with all workers at the main plant once a month to explain policy and operations changes. The managers of each factory and heads of each section also hold morning meetings. Workers are expected to offer suggestions on how to improve productivity.

2.7 Learning by Observing

Workers in Japan are culturally predisposed to help each other. Traditional crafts and occupations were learned by observation and doing *(Minarai)*. *"Minarai"* means watching skilled workers and copying their techniques. In America this would be called an apprenticeship, though the *minarai* process is more than that.

In classic Japan, the new worker helped a skilled worker and observed. The skilled craftsman, on his part, was expected to work slowly at times and allow himself to be copied by the younger worker. Contemporary workers are not different. Workers are not supposed to keep their craft a secret. In a group, workers are expected to be willing to learn from one another in the *minarai* tradition.

The experienced worker and the trainee form close ties as they develop a web of mutual exchanges: the pupil owes a debt to the other for being taught a trade. The teacher receives honor and respect as an exchange for his teaching. It is easy for workers to accept the *minarai* procedure: workers teach each other. This personal relationship brings workers together and enhances a feeling of group loyalty.

Minarai fits the Japanese personality. Many Japanese corporate leaders distrust formal education. They believe that people learn what they really need to know while at work and through personal guidance. That is why the Japanese stress on-the-job training. Formal education provides basic skills and tests for innate aptitude, but that is never enough. After graduation, workers are expected to learn as they work.

An American example of *minarai* learn-by-doing-and-observation is found in McDonald's. McDonald's is in many ways a very Japanese company in terms of its administrative style. McDonald's founder Ray Kroc, was anti-education. He felt that formal education was less important than "spirit" and "enthusiasm," both highly respected qualities in Japan. That is why McDonald's gives preference for franchises to employees who have been with the company for ten years or more. Their practical experience makes their success more likely, according to Kroc. To today's Japanese and Ray Kroc when alive, determination and a willingness to work hard are more important than classroom knowledge. Ray Kroc's business philosophy was (Kroc, 1977:168):

What does it take to get a McDonald's franchise? A total commitment of personal time and energy is the most important thing. A person doesn't need to be super smart or have more than a high school education, but he or she must be willing to work hard and concentrate exclusively on the challenge of operating that store.

The potential franchisee works part-time at a McDonald's before investing any money. Later, he will spend 500 hours working full-time in a McDonald's restaurant and be sent to Hamburger University for orientation and management classes.

Ray Kroc's dislike of formal education[5] does not allow licensees to operate their McDonald's outlets in any fashion they wished. They must learn standardized operation in complete detail before receiving a Bachelors degree in Hamburgerology. They learn all this (including making cold drinks and fries, store control, and employee training) through learning-by-doing *(minarai)*.

Hamburger University accepts as students only those who have already learned their trade through *minarai*. Each trainee is teamed with a manager or trainer and learns personally each facet of a McDonald's outlet operation (King and King, 1983). The Japanese would approve of this philosophy, and they place it in practice as much as possible.

Ray Kroc's (1977:189) favorite inspirational is so Japanese that it could be posted on the walls of any Japanese factory or head office:

Press on: Nothing in the world can take the place of persistence. Talent will not; nothing is more common than unsuccessful men with talent. Genius will not; unrewarded genius is almost a proverb. Education will not; the world is full of educated derelicts. Persistence and determination alone are omnipotent.

---

[5] Although Ray Kroc supported many community projects and charities and expected franchisees to do the same, he did not support higher education.

2.8 Children Companies

The Japanese prefer to personalize every business transaction. They feel more comfortable when they deal with people they know and trust. All business transactions should contain a personal element. One manifestation of this cultural pattern is that manufacturers establish close and long-lasting relationships with suppliers, so that the relationship is almost that of a partnership. The relation is non-contractual and informal, but the smaller concerns become well-established satellites of the larger corporations. These satellite dependents are called "children companies," and they are looked on as a part of the corporate family. The concern for *wa* extends to these suppliers. They are in essence adopted into the corporate family.

Major corporations will each have over one-hundred satellite companies attached to them, each specializing in a different sector of production (Ouchi, 1981:18).[6] These satellites are often headed by former executives of the central corporation. When senior managers retire they will often establish or join a smaller company whose function is to meet their former corporation's specific needs. The central corporation and its supporting banks will offer whatever financial resources are necessary for the establishment of these new enterprises if investments are not available elsewhere.

American suppliers to large corporations are hesitant to be so closely tied to one supply source since this would make them overly dependent on one company. Japanese executives, though, see this arrangement as merely an extension of the company's "family" and not as a threat to their independence, which in any case is less important than a company's permanent well-being. If a "child company" fulfills all requirements and provides special service, it develops debts owed to it by the parent company. The child company has a moral hold on the larger corporation not easily broken.

These suppliers are familiar with the parent company, know its special needs, and feel loyal to its success. They are also less likely to seek other markets. If a better customer is available, the supplier will merely ask for a comparable reward. A more profitable contract with an "outsider" might also be rejected if it were to be a short-term relationship. Japanese suppliers prefer a reliable, longterm relationship rather than a one-time affair. Remember also that a good supplier has a monopoly over its product. The parent company may not be able to easily secure a part elsewhere and obtain regular shipments. Mutual dependency encourages a *wa* relationship between parent-child companies.

---

[6] The Japanese automobile industry has developed the subcontrast system to the highest degree. Automotive firms subcontract seventy percent of the parts-cost content of their autos. Many of these suppliers are "children companies."

There are many advantages for both parties to this satellite arrangement. The parent company can trust its supplier and depend on its loyalty. Being part of the larger corporate identity, the supplier can be counted not to raise prices when supplies are scarce. The supplier can also rush orders, increase quality, or increase production when necessary. The fact that this company is a small one means it can shift schedules relatively quickly, change standards, and even deliver parts several times a day.

A long-range relationship of this type helps in planning expansion. By including the suppliers during the early stages, a company is better able to avoid unanticipated problems. It's one thing to plan a twenty percent expansion; it's another to make this expansion problem-free. A long-term supplier is more sympathetic and more aware of potential problems than a stranger.

It is easier to achieve high quality and zero-defect policies when subcontractors are permanent suppliers. There can be an exchange of personnel to discuss problems as they arise. These "children companies" can be trusted with manufacturing and production secrets. And parent companies can "suggest" to the subcontractors that a certain type of machine or process is preferred. Since there is the assurance of a captive market, the suppliers know that a contract is long-term; any investment made will be repaid over time.

McDonald's is an American example of the advantages of loyal satellite suppliers. It is a policy of McDonald's to stay with the same suppliers and give them long-term markets. McDonald's profits depend on rigid standardization and the company wants every hamburger to taste the same no matter where sold. Its success is based in part on the customer's trust that each McDonald's item tastes as expected. Every patty weighs 1.6 ounces, and each bun conforms to rigid specifications. This is not only makes McDonald's hamburgers the same wherever sold, but they can be produced more cheaply. McDonald's is the food industry's direct descendant of Henry Ford's assembly line technology.

The problem is how to make sure each local outlet uses the same materials in the same way. The solution is that each outlet uses exactly the same procedures and machines to cook french fries or hamburgers. The training of workers is specific. Each standardized procedure must be duplicated by all trainees.

Uniformity of materials is achieved through the use of long-term suppliers who conform to standards established by McDonald's. Keeping the same suppliers ensures uniformity of standards. It also encourages supplier loyalty to McDonald's. It is to their interest to maintain the specifications demanded by McDonald's since they are guaranteed long-term contracts if they do so. Suppliers grow with McDonald's and many suppliers began when McDonald's was just starting. McDonald's has made millionaires of suppliers as well as of franchisees.

The Japanese satellite company has another reason for maintaining a close relationship with its parent corporation. Parent companies practice a policy of temporary personnel transfers *(shukko)* to satellite companies. These transfers can last two, three, or less years. At times specialists will be sent to a "child company" to help develop quality control measures or to install new machines. These transferees maintain their official ties with their original employers, and the company continues their pay. They are "loaned" to solve certain problems. These transferees keep their seniority in the original company. Someone may be sent to a "child company" to teach the supplier a cheaper way to make a certain part, or to show packers how to more efficiently box parts to be sent to the "parent company."

A second type of transfer is more permanent and takes place when the transferee approaches retirement age. He is sent on a permanent basis to work for the "child company." This person can then join the company on a permanent basis after reaching mandatory retirement age in the first company. Since he is older, he will be promoted to a senior position in the "child company" (Ballon, 1980:122).

These types of transfers have a number of advantages. The temporary transferee gains training and experience valuable to the parent company. He learns about supply problems and quality control. He is also able to solve specific problems. Smaller companies may not be able to hire highly educated technicians or engineers. Nor may they be able to apply the findings of new research. The transferee offers the child company temporary expertise not usually available to it. Suppliers also receive information on how to cut costs and increase quality. The problems solved will be those related to the problems of the "parent company," but many solutions will help over-all productivity.

These transfeers also strengthen the "parent-child" relationship. The parent company has an employee whose loyalty is ensured working in the other company. The one who has been transferred and returned has established personal ties with the subcontractor. The dependency partnership now becomes a personal relationship.

Permanent transfers offer other advantages. Retired personnel who return to work receive lower salaries than pre-retirement workers, so the "child company" is able to hire an experienced, well-trained worker at a relatively low cost. More important is that this worker, by virtue of his seniority, knows the senior executives of the "parent company" very well. The chances are that they have known each other since they first joined the company. He can ask for favors and special treatment because they are on a close, personal footing.

This transferee knows his former company and can suggest shortcuts and ways to cut red tape through his personal contacts. Then too, this person has probably dealt with the supplier for years. He knows the relationship from both sides. He becomes a bridge linking the two companies.

An American equivalent to the above type of transfer would be a military general stationed at the Pentagon who resigns his commission and goes to work for a company which manufactures military supplies. The former general knows the military side of the industrial-military connection well. He can offer valuable advice to his new company on contracts, recent Pentagon strategy, and the like. As important, this general (ret.) knows the Pentagon personnel well. His friendships make entry into the Pentagon more likely.

Another obvious example of the value of such transfer in the U.S. and elsewhere is found when government officials retire (voluntarily or not) and become employed by the industries they were regulating. Or when a former U.S. Senator becomes a lobbyist for an organization wishing special representation. The advantages of such situations are obvious.

The central company can also use *shukko* transfers as ways to ease out employees who are not qualified enough to be promoted into the highest levels. Not promotable, they may nevertheless be quite capable in new settings. At the very least, the transferee has personal ties with the central company. This makes him valuable to the supplier even if he's considered to be administratively or technically substandard. There are times when a *shukko* transfer is forced on a "child company." If so, the accepting of this transfer means that the "parent company" owes a debt to the other party.

2.9 The Just-In-Time-System

The satellite arrangement does more than provide a dependable source of supplies. It also allows for the Japanese Just-in-Time system. The JIT system keeps inventories as low as possible: parts are brought into the plant to where they are assembled only when they are needed. Inventory is almost nonexistent because parts are delivered to the assembly line instead of being stored nearby (Monden, 1981). Toyota, for example, has over 200 suppliers. Matsushita has over 500. Many of these, of course, are "child companies."

A standard strategy used to increase productivity in any plant is to decrease the waiting time for supplies. Workers and machines have less idle periods if parts are always available. Less time is wasted because supplies are available when they are needed. The American response to the problem of idle time is typically to increase the company's inventory. The Japanese policy is to have small batches of supplies delivered as often as is necessary, even if this means several times a day.[7] The JIT system can also be called "stockless production," though it includes more than that.

Lower inventories save. Charles G. Burck, a member of the board of editors of *Fortune* magazine, estimates that U.S. auto manufacturers carry $775 worth of inventories for each car while the Japanese carry $150 (Burck, 1982:36). This allows Japanese companies to pay less interest for the cost of idle material. As important, JIT reduces the amount of needed floor space. There is less need to store material on-site if there are no large quantities on hand. Automobile factories need one-third less floor space in Japan than in the United States (Hayes, 1981).

Richard J. Schonberger (1982:121) presents a graphic example of the savings involved in the JIT system. Schonberger recounts the experience of Bill Harahan, director of manufacturing planning at Ford Motor Co. Two companies, American and Japanese, had prepared bids for the same product, an automotive power train. The Japanese plans called for 41 machines; the American plans called for 39 machines of the same type. The Japanese company offered the lower bid.

The Japanese won the contract because their proposed plant was to be 300,000 square feet in size for a total investment cost of $100 million. The American company lost the bid because its plant was to be 900,000 square feet in size at an investment cost of $300 million (Schonberger, 1982:121). Think of the savings the Japanese made on interest alone!

The major difference in the two plants – holding about the same number of machines – was in the space needed for inventory: the Japanese plant needed no space for inventory. Parts were to be delivered when needed for assembly; then each sub-assembly would immediately be passed to the next worker for the next assembly, and so on. No parts sat waiting, and no batches of partially-assembled pieces lay idled in stores until needed at a distant work station.

The small batch JIT system is an ingrained policy in Japanese manufacturing strategy. At Kawasaki, workers are allowed to be idle rather than having them make parts not immediately needed (Schonberger, 1982:152). Idle periods, if they appear often enough, are matters of rescheduling work and supply shipments and can be ended soon enough.

The JIT system is one Japanese productivity strategy which has been successfully adopted in the United States. Ormark Industries, based in Portland, Oregon, has conducted an extensive reorganization based on the JIT system (called Zero Inventory Production Systems – ZIPS – at Ormark.) In a log-

---

[7] I highly recommend Richard J. Schonberger's *Japanese Manufacturing Techniques* (1982) as the most detailed analysis of the JIT system and how it can be adopted in the United States.

processing plant, Ormark was able to reduce inventories 45 percent by reducing batch size and relocating machines. Two machines were placed side-by-side so that parts now traveled 18 inches instead of 2000 feet before the next assembly. Before, parts waited as much as sixty days before being fed to the second machine. In addition, each piece is now checked for quality one at a time instead of being inspected after sixty had been processed (Waters, 1984:87). In another Ormark plant, large-size drill inventory was cut 97 percent and the time it took to go from order to finished product went down from three weeks to three days.

At Ormark, small is beautiful! Under Ormark ZIPs' small-batch system, loss due to defects is kept to a minimum since almost every machined piece is inspected instead of waiting until a large batch has been processed. In the past, the defects in a large batch might not be noticed for weeks, until the next step in the process had begun. By then it would be too late to correct the mistake. Valuable time as well as material was being wasted.

The small-batch system allows for more job rotation and worker flexibility than is usual in the United States. The system could not work unless workers (and labor unions) accepted the idea of flexibility. The system can be success-ful only if workers are willing to learn a number of different operations. Small batches demands a flexibility where workers shift from one small batch to another as needed. At times, a worker follows his work from station to station. He might complete a batch of sixty units, then take them to the next station where he performs himself the next process, and so on.

An idle worker can repair or clean equipment and work station. He can also observe another worker to learn new assembly skills and help in the work. This preparation for the next small batch is important, since each batch must be completed on schedule, or else the whole process grinds to a halt. Once begun, the sequence must be completed uninterruptedly, even if this means overtime or shorter rest periods. On the other hand, since batches are small, each worker knows that the sequence will be a relatively short one. There is less time to become bored and make mistakes. The shift ends soon.

There are other savings in the JIT system. Other than savings in capital investments, physical maintenance and heating costs are also reduced when plants are smaller. Fewer personnel are needed. Lower inventories demand less paperwork and less people who take care of storage. Inventory systems are kept simpler and therefore are less costly to maintain and supervise. And there is less need for the forklifts and other equipment needed to move objects to and from storage.

JIT offers the Japanese another advantage which is not directly applicable in the United States. By their very nature, satellite suppliers are smaller than their manufacturers, and smaller firms in Japan offer lower salaries and wage benefits than large ones. The pay scale in firms with 500–999 employees is eighty-one percent of the wages in firms with over a thousand employees (Taira, 1970:175). The cost of parts is as a result lower if bought from a smaller supplier than if produced internally.

Small suppliers could not provide large batches of parts without increasing their inventory costs or their size. It is simpler to produce small lots continuously and deliver them once a day or more. Continuous delivery of small lots also use smaller delivery trucks and smaller moving equipment in general. This lowers capital investment costs.

Japanese products are competitive in international markets because of more than their relatively low prices. More important than price is quality, and the JIT system is one source of Japan's competiveness. The JIT system offers one of the best ways for American manufacturers to increase the quality of their products. Just-in-time is based upon the use of small lots of parts, and small batches are a major key in achieving higher quality.

Imagine an American assembly line. It is typically run as fast as possible for as long as possible. An assembly worker on this line is forced to work constantly. If he stops he creates backup problems all along the line. There are no problems if all goes well, but this is seldom the case.

Suppose this worker is faced with a faulty sub-assembly or a part which doesn't meet specifications. He has two choices. He can install the faulty part if he can. This may pass inspection and the problem eventually becomes the customer's. The assembler can also throw away the faulty part and select another. After all, American manufacturers have on hand an oversupply of parts "just-in-case." There is a larger than needed inventory of parts nearby. So far so good. Excess parts are always available to replace the ones that are rejected.

The problem is that a few faulty parts in one assembly point is statistically irrelevant. This causes the faults to be ignored until later, if ever. Meanwhile, quality is low, inventory is high, and the parts rejection rate is also high. And large batches of parts take longer to discover if they contain faulty or substandard parts.

The JIT system catches substandard supplies very quickly, at least after each shift, though usually sooner. When a small batch is completed, the supervisor can ask workers during the pause before the next job if any problem emerged. There will be time to correct any fault before the process begins again. Also, these shift pauses allow workers to clean their machines and get them ready. Machines in Japan last longer than their counterparts in America because Japanese workers are encouraged and have the time to take care of their machines.

The JIT system, with its small-batch process' has another, more emotional, advantage. Smaller work sequences give Japanese workers more chance to socialize with one another. These breaks allow workers to talk together, whether for social or work purposes. This encourages the team's *wa*. Japanese supervisors use these breaks to talk to workers informally, and even to lead them in gymnastic exercises. These breaks also allow higher-level executives to visit workers and become more visible. There are morale as well as economic advantages to the JIT system.

The major advantage of the JIT system, if one facet needs to be pointed out over the others, is quality performance. JIT makes it possible to maintain high manufacturing quality: faults are caught earlier and below-standard assemblies can be more easily spotted.

Large-batch production forces lower levels of quality. With the mass production of large-batch systems, it is easier and cheaper (in the short run) to ignore a small number of rejects and faulty assemblies. Even if the finished product is substandard, it is cheaper to replace it if the customer later complains than to tighten quality control procedures. The JIT system allows for higher quality manufacturing as well as makes possible a policy of zero-defect production.

A warning to American managers wishing to introduce the JIT system to their companies. The system demands that the final assembler be able to rely on a larger number of loyal suppliers. Some Japanese manufacturers receive shipments every two hours or so. The suppliers must be willing to work closely with the central company; this usually means that suppliers must be located nearby. This is easily achieved in a country like Japan, where most manufacturing facilities are located in a limited geographic area. Toyota Motors has solved this problem by establishing Toyota City, an area which concentrates most suppliers into one area. Toyota City contains 250 parts suppliers within easy reach. Communication as well as transportation does not involve great distance. It is easy for Toyota engineers to visit a nearby supplier to discuss the quality of a specific small batch of parts.

2.10 The Advantages of Worker-Management Consensus

Achieving consensus before a policy is made official causes higher-level unilateral decisions to be small in number. In essence, few orders are given unless there is an agreement that these orders will be accepted and obeyed. This agreement cuts down on the need for paperwork. Memos, notes, and the like are less common in Japan than in America. Communication in a Japanese corporation is more likely to be verbal and face-to-face than written, though the oral process takes more time.

There is less need for close supervision in a Japanese work setting. If all persons involved agree after discussion that something must be done, then no supervision is needed to make certain that anyone avoids performing the work in question. Being part of the decision-making process leading up to a consensus, a Japanese line worker must accept the responsibility for his production. He has in essence been co-opted into becoming a member of management. The factory worker has made an exchange: he receives fewer unilateral commands, but he must be self-motivated. He gives himself his own orders by remaining alert to what the group wants accomplished.

The situation is different in an American factory. Authority is highly structured and an assembly line worker is given detailed instructions on what he must do. He would not normally be encouraged to use his initiative. Instead, this factory hand is told that he has to obey the foreman and mind his business if he wants to keep his job. The advantage, if one can call it that, of this situation is that he has no worries beyond his own immediate work instructions. Any unusual situation is handled by saying, "It's not my business. I was told to do only my job."

But the Japanese worker enjoys no such limitations on his responsibilities. His job instructions are much vaguer than they would be in the United States and he is expected to do whatever needs to be done without being told. He is his own foreman. That is why Japanese factories are so much cleaner and safer than America's. Each worker is expected to clean up his work area and the surrounding space. A machine operator will clean up grease and oil spots around his work station rather than wait for the janitorial staff to do so. He will also repair his machine if it becomes overheated or inoperative.

The search for consensus and group harmony *(wa)* in Japan has resulted in a number of curious production and management practices. Some of these can be exported to non-Japanese situations. The N.S.K. (Nippon Seiko K) company established a ball bearing factory in England. Using a primarily British labor force, the N.S.K. management nevertheless introduced a number of consensus-encouraging policies. One of these is that shifts overlap by ten minutes.[8] This gives each incoming worker the chance to talk to his predecessor about any problems encountered during the previous shift. They can together try to solve any snags or see that someone else is called in to do so.

In this way, no one can blame production problems on the previous shift (Deacon, 1983:277) or on inadequate communication. In addition, overlap-

---

[8] Many Japanese factories overlap shifts slightly. The members of the incoming shift line up in two rows outside the work area. As the workers from the outgoing shift file out, they are given a series of "Banzai!" to thank them for working for the company.

ping shifts allows for a member of the previous shift to help the successor get started. At the very least, this practice encourages worker cooperation.

N.S.K. in England encourages worker loyalty and enthusiasm in another way, among others. Each worker receives a small check on his or her birthday as a reminder that management cares. Most American companies officially recognize a worker's age only when it's time for retirement.

Honda Motors Company has instituted a program which reflects this Japanese view that workers are expected to contribute to the company's *wa*. The problem is that being willing to help the company is not enough; workers must also have the skills to be capable of making contributions. As a result, Honda administrators developed their "expert system."

This program assumes that workers want to be involved in the company's decision-making process and that *wa* demands that they become involved. This program reflects Soichiro Honda's belief that workers should be encouraged to continuously upgrade their skills. It is based on his view that formal education is not as valuable as "hands on" experience.

The "expert system" involves a long-range commitment on the part of the company to train workers until they can be certified as "experts." This is done in two ways. The typical Honda blue collar employee takes a series of courses over the years to upgrade his technical skills. In addition to attending lectures and lab courses, he is shifted from one job to another. This gives him practical experience in a variety of work settings (Schnapp, 1982).

Workers are also expected to keep personal journals of their work experiences, courses taken, and special programs attended, as well as unique contributions they have made to the company. This includes suggestions which have cut production costs and improved quality plus any awards won by the worker. This journal gives them a resume of their personal development as well as a record of what they have done for Honda Motors.

The "expert-system" derives from Soichiro Honda's view that all workers must develop their talents. This program makes long-term workers more valuable to the company and allows many to be promoted over the years. At the same time, workers experience a wide range of work duties. They can contribute more when proposals are discussed and when they have the skills to take part in the decision-making process itself.

Another advantage to Honda's "expert program" is that a more technically-skilled labor force demands less specialization and fewer rules. The workers increasingly know how to perform a greater and greater number of duties. This, in turn, reduces boredom. Morale and quality performance suffer when work is repetitive, specialized and boring. Boredom is supposed to be unknown at Honda Motors. Below (Schnapp, 1982)is how Soichiro Honda sees what the ideal factory is like:

The workshop should be a place where everybody finds a joy in working and earns his living. An organization that enforces monotonous labor and deprives the workers of the right to think may work well for a while but is bound to get decayed in the long-run. I noticed at auto factories in the U.S. that the working environment was bad. Decent people don't want to work at such places, and as a result the quality of labor at those workshops is poor.

2.11 *Wa* and Labor Unions

The value placed on the importance of the company's *wa* is found even during labor-management confrontations. Three-fourths of the workers in Japanese manufacturing firms with over five hundred employees are unionized. Membership consists of manual and clerical workers and non-supervisory junior managers (Sasaki, 1981:50). But union membership does not split a worker's loyalty between the labor union and the company/management as it does in America and elsewhere. Doing so would inhibit the search for an achievement of *wa*.

Union members remain loyal to their employers and corporations because each union is organized along corporate membership. Each union is limited to one company instead of being based on occupation or industry. There are no national unions in Japan for welders, secretaries, auto workers, or steel workers. There are a number of nationally-based unions for teachers, railway workers, and students. But these are exceptions to the rule of enterprise unionization. Most (90%) Japanese Labor unions are enterprise organized (Sakurabayaski and Ballon, 1963).

Enterprise (company-wide) union membership is open to all permanent workers except those in supervisory levels. The membership includes all blue-collar and white-collar workers and all staff workers. Newly-hired university graduates, although future managers, are also expected to be union members. Given the Japanese predisposition to join groups, all do so. While not obligatory, union membership is expected of all who are eligible.

Japanese labor-management conflicts are remarkedly few, though they do occur. During 1980 in Japan, 1.5 million hours of work were lost through strikes, as compared to 39 million in the United States. Since the population of the United States is roughly twice as large as Japan's, it is easy to see that the Japanese enjoy greater union-management harmony, even though a larger proportion of the Japanese labor force is unionized. When the different sizes of the two countries' industrial work force is controlled, the United States industrial sector loses ten times more hours through strikes (Richmond and Kahan, 1983: 69–70).

Such union-management harmony was achieved only after the Second World War. Before, labor unions were barely tolerated and most union activity illegal. Around the turn of the century, there were instances of labor-management violence as disruptive as any in the United States at that time. The labor peace the Japanese enjoy today is primarily a post-war phenomenon.

An example of this radical change from labor conflict to harmony was experienced by the Kikkoman company. During 1927–28, the company experienced a 218-day strike, the longest in prewar Japan (Fruin, 1983:6). Over 3,500 workers took part, and one-half of the workers were fired, though eventually two-thirds of these were re-hired after the strike's settlement (Fruin, 1983:206).

It was after this strike that Kikkoman executives began a campaign stressing that workers as well as managers formed a corporate family. Before, the notion of the company as a family was restricted to the owners. After 1928, Kikkoman became very much family-oriented toward its workers. But this happened only after a violent strike and very damaging publicity. While not typical, Kikkoman's experiences suggest that Japanese corporate familism is not completely a traditional pattern.

The development of enterprise unions parallels the policy of lifetime employment, which is discussed in a later chapter. The basic feature of lifetime employment is labor immobility. That is, the worker is expected to stay with one firm throughout his working career. To encourage this labor stability, retirement benefits are linked to years of service while pay levels are determined through seniority.

The development of modern industry in Nineteenth Century Japan was made possible through the importation of modern technology from the West. Firms would buy foreign machines and technology (patents, plans, etc.) and hire foreign experts. Workers would be taught the modern skills needed to operate and maintain these foreign machines. If that were not possible, then Japanese students and observers were sent to Europe and the United States.[9] Foreign workers, called "living machines," were imported during the Nineteenth Century at very high wages with the single aim to teach the Japanese the needed technical knowledge. They were expected to return to Europe or the United States when their tasks were done. The Japanese had no intention of becoming dependent on foreigners. This trait of wanting to comprehensively understand what the West has to offer still exists.

---

[9] Even today, the term "research" in Japan has connotations of studying what the West has already discovered. "Doing research" often means going through western journals and technical reports.

The Japanese do not want to become dependent on foreign knowledge. No western idea or practice is accepted until the Japanese understand it well and can use it by themselves. By contrast, Nineteenth Century Chinese were willing to import western machines and then import foreigners to maintain and repair these machines. The Japanese have always rejected this approach. That is why they would rather buy plans and patents than the machines themselves. A national labor force which cannot build the machines it uses probably cannot operate efficiently or repair them adequately.

Schools at that time could not teach these modern skills since foreign technology was available only in firms wealthy enough to afford it. This encouraged the policy of in-plant training which is still followed today. The corporate recruit was trained to operate the modern machinery available at his place of employment. The worker learned the requirements of one employer, and job skills were developed at the plant itself. Each enterprise developed a work force trained to its specification on equipment nowhere else available. This made the trained worker valuable to primarily only the trainer/employer.

Lifetime employment (discussed in greater detail in a later chapter) was developed at this time to encourage a worker to stay where he was trained. This ensured that the company's investment spent on training a worker would not be lost. The company could feel secure that workers trained at company's expense would remain to repay these investment costs.

From a Japanese point of view, it is understandable that workers trained in an enterprise should stay with one employer. The company provided the worker with skills and employed him when he was less valuable to the firm. Now that he had certain skills, it would be disloyal on his part to work elsewhere. His training becomes a lifelong debt.

On the other hand, a trained worker is a more valuable worker, so the employer should reward him with increased rewards, such as job security and higher pay. Not to do so would be considered selfish and ungrateful behavior. The company would want to keep this worker after he had become an asset instead of a liability. The permanent worker is more valued in Japan and better rewarded than a temporary one. The first repays the investment spent on his training.

In the short run, trained workers are valuable only when their skills can be used. This limits the employment of a worker to the company which provided the training in the first place. Until modern technology became widely available, workers with non-traditional skills had a limited value except where they were first employed and trained. So lifetime employment was a policy which also benefited the worker: he was guaranteed work where his skills were in the greatest demand and where the rewards were highest. Lifetime employment was advantageous to both employer and employee.

Enterprise unionization developed because skilled workers in the modern economic sectors were lifetime workers. Being trained by and in the company, workers identified more with their employers than with their trades.[10] Unions followed suit, and plant-wide unions developed. At first, a punch press operator did not identify with other punch press operators throughout the Japanese nation. Instead, the person was an employee of a specific company and who happened to be a punch press operator. Labor unions had no choice but to accept this company identification and develop into enterprise unions.

The modern unionized worker is not forced to divide loyalties between union and employer. Instead, the Japanese believe that what are essentially local unions should be concerned only with local grievances and matters.[11] Unions and their firms become in essence partners, and they should work together to maintain the company's *wa*.

When compared to workers in America or England, Japanese workers do not see themselves as united nationally in terms of their skills or industry. A worker considers himself an employee of the company first. Only afterwards would he define himself as an accountant or a welder. If asked what he does for a living, a worker first says, "I work for Honda." If pressed he might say he's an engineer or a lathe operator.

In the same way, union membership does not reduce a Japanese worker's loyalty to his firm. Both memberships ideally complement one another. Corporate executives do not hesitate to ask union officials to look for ways to improve worker productivity. After all, they share a common identity.

An enterprise union can be part of a national organization of labor unions, but membership in the union itself is open only to employees of one company. A consequence of this localism is that workers are unwilling to demand pay raises when company profits are too low. Doing so would threaten the economic well-being of the company and thereby also threaten its *wa*. By the same token, workers do not remain passive when considering next year's pay. When profits are high, union members expect a corresponding pay increase and will threaten to strike if they do not feel they are being treated fairly by management. *Wa* means having a sense of fairness on the part of both sides,

---

[10] This feeling of company loyalty was reinforced by the fact that workers were encouraged to be generalists rather than specialists. A worker taught to operate a foreign machine helped to install it and was expected to clean and repair it, perhaps even to help duplicate it. He would later advise management on whether or not such machines were needed.

[11] Labor unions in other countries operate in very different ways. In such different countries as France and India, local labor unions chapters will arbitrarily declare a strike to express a grievance against the local or national government. Local work issues in such cases are irrelevant. Such strikes are completely beyond the control of corporate management.

management as well as labor. The union is not the company's enemy but a partner. The partnership, however, is not one-sided.

Having all of a company's workers as members of the same labor union avoids a number of potential problems. There are few union-management conflicts about job demarcations in Japan. A worker who repairs his milling machine or helps out a friend does not worry about whether these activities should be done only by members of one specific union or another. Nor is management faced with negotiating with different labor unions at different times. Workers of one union are not faced with the problem of refusing to cross a picket line because another union is striking.

This preference for labor-management harmony is an ideal which is never completely achieved. There do exist conflicts between workers and managers, although usually threats to strike or offers of low bonuses are enough to force management and labor to sit down together and negotiate. Leaders on both sides feel embarrassment if someone were being unreasonable. In a culture such as Japan's, conflicting parties have failed if harmony does not exist.

There is labor conflict in Japan, but enterprise unions avoid open confrontations. When they cannot, workers can obtain redress to their grievances by forcing management to do so. While union conflicts exist primarily as threats, they can be effective. Managers too are expected to maintain *wa*.

2.12 Union-Management Relations

It is obvious to any American that enterprise unions cannot be as militant as those based on occupation or industry. Unions want to cooperate with management, since the union's existence and prosperity are dependent on a single employer's success. The welfare of the union is linked to the company's.[12]

Some union members will eventually be part of middle management since all non-supervisory white collars become members. Any militancy on their part will hurt their chances for better job positions, promotion, and pay raises. Union militancy on the part of a future executive would be defined as disloyal and "aggressive behavior." Also, since good mid-career re-employment is almost nonexistent in Japan, older manual, blue collar workers consequently dare not be labeled as troublemakers and agitators.

---

[12] Nationally-organized unions in Japan are much more militant than interprise unions. Student and teacher unions are led by Marxists-oriented members and are much more politically active and ideological.

Management-labor relations are smooth because workers who are too militant become the target of wounded solicitude from management. Management representatives – usually from the personnel division – will spend hours trying to persuade union officials that their militancy is misplaced. This type of pressure toward conformity is effective in Japan.

Union officials, on their part, will not hesitate to lecture managers on their duty. This is done circumspectively, of course, because corporate officials hold high rank and are older; these two features necessarily offer managers prestige. But union officials nevertheless expect that managers on their part will support group harmony.

Management and labor representatives negotiate often with each other because Japanese employment contracts seldom contain many specific clauses that bind the parties. Employee-employer agreements are vague and abstract. Traditional contracts contained such phrases as "Should a disagreement arise, both parties will consult each other in good faith." Many contracts today have similar clauses. Workers' contracts define general policy rather than specific conditions and signers assume that disputes will be settled through negotiation (Hanami, 1979:53). If parties cannot trust each other to deal fairly, then an agreement can't be reached and a contract shouldn't be drawn. Each worker, in essence, enjoys a personal relation with the employer.

While enterprise unions may not seem openly militant, they are influential. Instead, most labor-management issues are solved before they develop into open conflict. Unions are represented on corporate committees dealing with labor issues. And unionized corporations (those that are also larger – the two factors go together) offer larger fringe benefits and higher wages than smaller companies. The search for labor-management consensus (*roshikyocho-rosen* = labor harmonizing path) has brought both company and workers many benefits (Saso and Kirby, 1982:25–28).

One such benefit is shorter working hours. During 1978, small (5–29 employees) manufacturing firms averaged slightly over 2200 working hours per worker per year. The corresponding figure for large (1000+ employees) manufacturing firms was 2050 hours per worker. Larger firms, which are unionized, have shorter work years in part because they offer more paid holidays and more lenient sickness benefits.

The number of hours worked for all Japanese manufacturing firms was an average 2150 hours worked per worker. This compares unfavorably with 1740 hours in German manufacturing firms. Corresponding figures for the United States and France are 1950 and 1800, respectively (Saso and Kirby, 1982:24). Obviously, Japanese unions have not completely gained all of the types of benefits found in other industrialized countries, but in the Japanese context, they have done quite well for their members.

The Japanese work long hours in general. The unions probably couldn't shorten the work week much more unless the government officially instituted shorter working hours for workers in all economic sectors. This hope is not realistic in the near future. In 1979, the average industrial work week was 44 hours, of which 3½ hours were overtime. The corresponding work week for the Japanese manufacturing sector was just under 46 hours, with four of those hours overtime (Saso and Kirby, 1982:159). Other economic sectors have longer hours, especially small family owned and managed retail outlets.

The strength of the Japanese economy lies partly in the fact that labor unions are not openly militant. They are co-partners with management working for the good of the company and the nation. Being seen as co-partners by all parties, Japanese unions are part of the search for *wa*. Union members do have a sense of justice and while they would not demand too much, neither would they accept too little. When there is a perceived imbalance, unions can become militant. Most of the time, though, they are supportive of management (Buss, 1982).

Japanese labor unions conduct union-management negotiations called Spring Offensives *(Shunto)*. These are annual demands for higher wages and fringe benefits. To show their determination and power, workers will threaten to strike, though strikes generally don't occur. When they do happen, these strikes at times will take place after the work day and during the weekend. Such timing avoids a direct confrontation and will be less likely to completely embarrass management. A strike means that group harmony has been disrupted, and management is partly at fault when *wa* has not been achieved. A strike which begins one hour before the end of Friday's work day and continues until Monday morning has a more symbolic intent than the aim of actually stopping production for a long period. The fact that there are pickets in front of a factory during Saturday and Sunday is embarrassment enough for management.

Nor does this union's show of force necessarily decrease production. During a Spring Offensive, workers will often work harder to maintain or increase production levels. Workers thereby show management their loyalty to the company while at the same time expressing grievances. During 1975, there were 8,860 strikes, 5,475 of which lasted one-half day or less (Hanami, 1979:149). Imagine a nation where two-thirds of all strikes last less than one-half a working day each!

Short strikes are the pattern in Japan, though they're not unique to Japan. For the year 1975, the average length of strikes was three days in Japan. This compares to a four day's strike average in the United States, seven for the United Kingdom and two days for Germany (Hanami, 1979:148). Official strikes are distasteful to workers because they represent overt conflict and bring disagreements into the public awareness. They are visible signs of the failure of worker-management *wa*.

There are other strategies available to workers. Slowdowns are common when workers have a grievance. Manufacturing schedules in Japanese factories are very tight, and intentional slowdowns cause havoc with a factory's schedules with suppliers as well as retailers. Floor workers can stage a slowdown and gradually decrease the speed of their work, which is usually faster than in America, and hence relatively easy to do. A slowdown is an indirect act of disagreement and is easier for a Japanese worker to commit.

Slowdowns are a major fear of management. Suddenly, quotas are no longer being met, supply deliveries have to be cancelled, and production figures drop. All of this is very embarrassing. Foremen may find it hard to pinpoint the blame on an individual – which is good reason for a group slow-down and it's hard to loudly order workers to work faster. Even when they last only a short time, slowdowns are effective and indirect signs that the workers have a grievance.

Labor unions have a number of ways to disrupt schedules without calling for a general strike or a general slow-down. Organized labor would rather threaten than actually carry out acts of disobedience, and it is possible for unions to support a strike without actually seeming to do so. If a grievance has not been met, union officials can ask one person to strike by himself. A key worker declares that his grievances have gone unnoticed and he stops work in such a way that other areas in the factory are effected by the stoppage. In this way, a vital part is left untended and in a way that production throughout the plant is disturbed. This is called a one-person or "nominated" strike (Hanami, 1979:165).

Wages are not paid to striking workers in Japan and labor unions don't have the resources to offer strike benefits to many members. It is easy, however, for a union to support a one-person strike. But how does management react when one worker stops a whole assembly line by his actions? Other workers cannot be penalized, the striking worker has the support of the union, and again management is embarrassed. Unhappy workers have a number of strategies available aside from a complete closure of a factory.

The power of Japanese unions to peacefully embarrass management cannot be overestimated. Another strategy labor unions have in their arsenal is the "ribbon struggle." Workers who feel they have not been treated fairly can wear armbands and headbands at work. These ribbons have various slogans printed such as "fulfill demands." These bands publicize workers' unhappiness and embarrass management. Workers wear them to advertise their feelings without disrupting production schedules (Gould, 1984:130).

All large corporations have dress codes, and wearing an unofficial armband or button is an act of defiance as well as individuality. An armband showing a union's slogan is defined as union activity as well as disobedience. The workers, on their part, say that wearing armbands does not distract them from their work. There have been many court cases dealing with whether or not these ribbons are a legitimate right of labor. The wearing of these ribbons is a visible sign that *wa* is threatened even though production continues.

Satoshi Kamata is a freelance journalist and an investigative reporter in a country where criticism is frowned upon. His work *Japan in the Passing Lane* (1982) is based on his experiences as a factory worker during the early 1970's. As a low-skilled, temporary worker at Toyota, he found that Toyota's enterprise union valued harmony more than fighting arbitrarily changed work rules, dangerous working conditions, company spying, and unpaid overtime. Kamata also asked future managers how they had enjoyed their obligatory tour as floor workers on the assembly line. They indicated that this period had been a very unpleasant one. Japanese factories are not the happy places often pictured. Instead, workers are pushed to work as hard as possible. But they are rewarded financially and psychologically for doing so.

One day, Kamata's foreman announced that there would be two extra days of overtime during the next two months. This meant not taking vacations during holidays as well as not receiving overtime pay (Kamata, 1982:136). Kamata did not expect the union representatives to complain about this increased workload. The general foreman is often the shop floor's union representative as well, and most union officials are either foremen or chief clerks (Kamata, 1982:183).

While management-worker harmony is an ideal, it is not always achieved. Surprisingly, this ideal is something that all parties work toward. Without this emphasis on *wa*, the Japanese society would have probably destroyed itself on the way to modernization. The years 1890–1945 did witness tremendous dislocations in the Japanese society. Japanese culture survived a colonial venture, a world war, and international competition with more technologically advanced nations. The culture obviously has great strengths, one of which is its stress on cooperation and harmony. The following chapters show how this emphasis on *wa* has helped to make Japan a major industrial society.

Chapter 3
The Competitive Americans

3.1 Competition in America

"Become Japanese!" This is the password used by many who hope to revitalize the American economy. There is much we can profitably learn from the Japanese. There are also many Japanese practices which, if adopted, would not benefit us. Few Americans, for example, would be happy with the notion that co-workers should spend several or more evenings per week together. Nor would we feel comfortable with the Japanese version of paternalism: we are too individualistic to let our employers dictate how we should live our private lives. How many junior executives in America would appreciate being told it's time to marry?

The miracle of Japan is not its emerging economic dominance – though that's important. Japan was a non-industrial, feudal society just a little more than one hundred years ago. Now it's an industrial giant. The miracle is that Japan became the first Asian country to modernize while still keeping much of its traditional culture. Japan, in short, was able to absorb western technology without becoming culturally demoralized and losing its Japanese identity.

America needs to experience a second industrial revolution to hopefully revitalize the economy. This best can be achieved by copying certain features of the "Japanese miracle," notably its emphasis on cooperation and worker-management consensus. We must be able to borrow from the Japanese whatever is promising without discarding the core of American identity. But doing so depends on understanding ourselves better. We mustn't reject the sources of our strengths as well as our weaknesses. We cannot copy the Japanese or take advantage of our strengths until we know ourselves better. This necessitates having a clearer image of what Americans and American work practices are like.

This chapter focuses on the American personality traits which influence work behavior. No one doubts that the Japanese are hard-working and energetic, and this description also fits American workers. But one major difference between Americans and Japanese is that while both are highly competitive they compete differently. If only one word can be used to describe the differences between Americans and Japanese, this word is "competition." Though the same term can be used to describe businessmen from both nations, each uses the term in different ways. These differences are causing enormous misunderstandings and confusion.

Americans and Japanese compete differently because Americans encourage competition among members of a group while the Japanese encourage competition among groups. American managers believe that business relations involve individual competition among equals as well as unequals. We assume that it's good for members of a work group to compete against each other when rewards, such as promotion, are limited. To be successful in American business you have to do more than good work. You also have to show that you're competitively better than everyone else. We organize reward systems so that workers have to compete to receive rewards.

Americans see competitive situations as zero-sum contests: if one person wins, the others necessarily lose. This is the winner-take-all notion of competition: someone's victory is another's loss. This belief is found in all sectors of our society, from sports to academia to business. In other situations, in order to insure that a clear winner emerges, we set up a quota system: no matter how good five persons are, each one must be ranked from one to five and only the "best" get promoted.

It's a fact of life that we can't reward everyone who deserves it. Someone has to suffer because there are usually not enough prizes to go around. Americans use competition as the major way to distribute scarce goods. The Japanese prefer to use other ways to hand out prizes. For example, the Japanese would rather reward the person who helps the group the most. The one who is most helpful and contributes the most to the group's *wa* is rewarded. American reward systems tend to reward the one who has helped himself the most, and only indirectly the group.

Also, the Japanese, whenever possible, reward the group rather than the most successful member. A car salesman in Japan works so that his sales group and company sells the most cars. At the end of the season, each member of the highest-selling sales group will be rewarded. Unlike American reward systems, the best salesman will not get the highest bonus. Bonuses are given to group members equally and not on an individual basis.

Nor do the Japanese like to establish quotas. They would rather reward everyone who reaches a goal instead of rewarding only the top five or ten. It is more American to say, "the top five salesmen will receive free vacations in Hawaii." A Japanese motivational scheme would more likely state that, "Anyone who sells a three hundred million yen's worth of insurance will win a free vacation in Hawaii." The goal set in the Japanese contest may result in only five winners, but at least everyone has an equal chance to win. No one is competing against anyone. Winning or losing is not dependent on someone else's success or failure.

When necessary, the Japanese can insist on very competitive situations on the individual level. A Japanese university will accept the fifty highest test scores if there are only fifty places for new students out of two-hundred applicants. Japanese executives know full well that only one can become president of the company. But this type of competition is acceptable only when there are no other alternatives. The Japanese avoid face-to-face winner-takes-all competitions unless inescapable.

Americans see competition as one of the most productive ways of distributing rewards. We admire competition so much that we develop competitive contests even when they are not necessary. Instead of permanently hiring one person, for example, a common practice of large companies is to hire two or more on a temporary basis. Then each is told that only one will be retained permanently. These recruits are forced to compete against one another because only one will be kept after the trial period. At the end of the year other recruits are hired, told that they are on trial for a year, and the competitive cycle continues.

One way to avoid this pattern – and it is a common one in the United States – is to hire only the number of workers you plan to keep permanently. They can always be dismissed if they don't work out, but at least they are hired with the understanding that if they are good enough to be hired in the first place they are good enough to keep. To stretch a point, the American system of competition would suggest that a woman should be allowed to marry two men at the same time with the unterstanding that after a year she would divorce one. That way the co-husbands would be very attentive and hard-working for a year! To the Japanese, this logic is distasteful and ridiculous in a business as well as a marriage setting.

Two Types of Competition

I will discuss the negative features of competition after giving three examples of hiring on a competitive basis. The examples of competitive hiring are university professors, first-job accountants in large accounting firms, and beginning lawyers. Universities offer senior professors near-complete job security as part of their reward for appropriate behavior. Once tenured, professors can be dismissed only for immoral and insane behavior (the definitions for these acts are flexible and vague), or when departments are disbanded due to lack of student interest in their courses. Pay raises tend to be automatic and based primarily on seniority, so that an academic career is a secure one once tenure is achieved.

A common university practice is to hire more lower-level professors than can be given tenure. These receive low wages, teach the larger undergraduate classes, and stay busy with committee memberships. They are also expected to do research and publish the results. At the end of a probation period, usually five years or so, the senior faculty offers tenure to a few and the rest are asked to leave. Then a new batch of new Ph. D.'s are hired and the cycle continues.

There are two types of competition in the above situation. First of all, a junior professor competes against others in the field. This I call *impersonal competition*. Two professors from different universities could both be trying to win the same publishing prize. The same type of impersonal competition exists when two milers in different stadiums take part in separate events and both want to break the world's record set earlier by a third.

In this competition, the person essentially competes against himself rather than others, though the aim is still to be the best. Impersonal competition is usually the most effective form of competition from a human relations perspective. It encourages people to work together and help each other because someone's gain is not another's loss. Co-workers can also take pride in each others' successes. Even a player on the bench can feel pride when team mates score a touchdown.

Another example of impersonal competition is when everyone who achieves a goal receives a reward. Each of ten workers can hope to develop cost-savings procedures to save the company at least $100,000 a year. Suppose the company offers a bonus of $10,000 to anyone who does so, irrespective of whether one or ten find a way. This is a different competitive system than one which rewards the one who makes the *best* cost-reducing suggestions. This one allows for one winner and nine losers. The chances are that such a quota system will encourage some workers to give up if they feel they have less chances for success than someone else.

The second type of competition is *personal competition:* individuals compete directly against one another for a prize only one can win. They are competing more against each other than against a standard. Two boxers facing each other in the ring, and three junior accountants each hoping for the same partnership are both instances of personal competition.

At the university, an example of personal competition is a teacher's policy in which students are told that only the top ten out of one hundred will be given A's. The standard is not that the A students need to know ninety percent of the material at test time, but that they must know more than ninety other students. This may demand knowing ninety-five or sixty percent of the material, depending on how well the others do. This example of personal competition stresses doing better than others rather than learning a certain amount of class material.

This type of competition is common in the United States. Unfortunately, it can also become counter-productive. Those involved in personal competition compete against each other. The goal becomes one of bettering the opponent rather than better performance.

The same destructive type of competitive situation is found among junior accountants, as described by Mark Stevens. Stevens is a member of the faculty of the Lubin School of Business as well as an author who has written on how to run small businesses and a history of Bloomingdale's. The book more pertinent here, however, is Stevens' study of the largest accounting firms in America, called the Big Eight.

These multinational firms dominate corporate accounting, and their clients account for over ninety percent of all of the employment in the United States. Stevens (1981:177) reports that the Big Eight hire about 16,000 persons each year, most of them new college graduates. The companies' strategy is to hire a large number of first-job recruits, then expect them to work hard and compete with one another for ten years or so until a few are made partners. They work up to sixteen hours a day because everyone knows that only a few will be kept on. It is no wonder that up to a quarter of new Big Eight staffers quit within the first year, or that most leave within three (Stevens, 1981:188–90).

The Big Eight firms expect that employees straight out of college will compete against one another for promotion and eventual partnership. To succeed, staffers must learn to handle competition as well as auditing. They know that no matter how good their work, only a few will receive better-than-average pay raises and eventual promotions. The system was developed with a very high drop-out rate based on personal competition in mind.

Personal competition is also common at the high-prestige top law firms in America. Prestigious law firms hire new graduates from law schools and evaluate them eight to ten years later. It is then that the decision is made whether an associate becomes a firm's partner or not. Generally, thirteen percent or so of associates become partners (Rosen, 1983). This figure, of course, varies with the economic fortunes at the time of decision. Excellent associates are dismissed because business is currently slow. Their talents and decade of experience are lost to the company. When business picks up again, the company can always expand the labor force with raw recruits, but the experienced workers have already been dropped.

There are also personal costs. Associate lawyers experience a decade of job insecurity as well as being in competition with associates. The Japanese would be horrified at such a competitive situation! They would not want to hire someone they did not think would be able eventually to become a full partner.

Unequal Rewards and Relative Deprivation

There are other competition-based reward systems; these rewards are unequally distributed to competitors and given to only a few. Some are rewarded and others not; this produces a jealous feeling of relative deprivation even though those not rewarded are not punished in an absolute sense. The ones not given prizes are naturally those who have lost the competition. They lose nothing while another is rewarded. This type of reward system causes stress and low morale because every time someone is rewarded, those who are not become by definition losers. Give a raise of $100 to one and each co-worker feels $100 poorer although no one is actually paid less.

This type of personal competition is more negative than positive because more people are punished than rewarded. In addition, this type of competition creates envy. The Japanese try to set up competitive situations where there are as many winners as possible. Americans encourage situations which produce the largest number of losers.

This is one reason why American companies keep salaries as secret as possible. Salaries are rewards which are unequally distributed and employees doing the same work are often paid unequally. If everyone knew what others earned in most American companies, morale would decline. The reason for this secrecy is that recruiters usually tell prospective employees that their salaries will be based on their worth. They are also told that they will receive raises equal to their performance. Money becomes the symbol for a worker's worth and how each is evaluated by employers. This is natural, since salaries and wages are the major rewards most Americans expect from their work.

Newly-hired recruits are not completely paid solely on current performance. Corporations also give higher bonuses and salaries based on potential and promise. An all-A college graduate is offered a larger starting salary than a B-student. The first graduate is paid more because she shows more promise based on past performance. It may not be "fair," but it's assumed that a better student will know more and be a more useful employee than a less successful student. One recruit has been evaluated as potentially better even before the first day of work!

A similar case of separating people is when a graduate from an Ivy League university is given a higher starting salary than someone with a diploma from a lesser-known midwest college. Someone who is seen as potentially more valuable will be offered more pay than another defined as average, if only because she may be in a better competitive position to demand a higher salary. The result is that two junior staffers may be doing the same work equally well at first, but the pay is different.

This is a harmful practice, though it would be hard to eliminate beginning salary differences in the United States completely. The Japanese make salaries among ranks as equal as possible and public: each worker knows what peers are earning and why. The same is true in the United States military and in most universities. Employees there don't suffer from secrecy about what others earn, though they may be bitter over some other type of perceived unfairness.

They know exactly the worth their organizations place on them. Beginning employees all start with the same incomes. Everyone knows what army privates make. When two army recruits both peel potatoes or set up a tent, each knows they are both receiving the same salary. This is not the case in most corporations.

How internally competitive are American companies? Very, especially among new workers. Some companies develop personal competitive strategies bordering on ruthlessness. At Shell Oil Company, department managers get together once a year to rank their personnel, and each junior employee is given a score from one to five with five meaning that he is about to be fired. Competition is heightened through a quota system of ranks. Out of 200 being evaluated the policy will be set that only six or so will be given the highest rank, even if this eliminates a number of equally or almost equally qualified applicants.

One problem with this system is that when a number of highly capable persons with equal work records are ranked, the evaluation eventually becomes based on work-irrelevant characteristics such as personality, dress, or looks. Another problem is that we have to assume these ranks mean something worthwhile. Most tests can't rank very accurately people who are similar. A small difference in rank scores doesn't really mean very much. Close scores, given the state of the art, probably reflect tests-induced differences and personal biases rather than real aptitude levels. At the end, differences in rank are the result of such subjective evaluations as personality, sponsorship, or being test-wise. Whether they mean anything in relation to future or present job performance is debatable. These evaluations, the Japanese feel, should be avoided.

Officially, Shell employees are not supposed to know their ranks. They will probably be told informally what their general standings are by friends or sponsors, as you would expect, but rankings are kept as secret as possible. No one is supposed to know even though most have a pretty good idea what their standings are. Since these scores are officially secret, no one knows exactly his or others' standings, and it's hard to openly complain or discuss them with others. This increases insecurity and uncertainty. Junior-level managers who have been working at Shell for three years or less spend considerable energy trying to guess each others' ranks.

Shell junior managers are also evaluated in terms of how promotable they seem. Based on performance and sponsorship, a new worker can be tagged as belonging to the "fast track." These are what Shell supervisors call the "Early Identifiables" because they are the ones who are pushed for early promotion within a year or so after joining Shell. The EI is rotated from job to job as often as every six months. This provides varied job experiences as well as gives management the chance to see how well the EI operates in different settings.

The EI also becomes highly visible and enviously tagged. Former friends become jealous and guarded in their conversation. Who wants to complain about company policy or a supervisor to someone who might soon be part of management?

The EI is gradually given more responsibility and more resources to control. Then he becomes ready for a series of early promotions. No one is supposed to know for sure who is an EI or not. Naturally, everyone tries to find out whether a job transfer means that someone is an EI or a failure.

This competitive system is so ambiguous that every rotation is accompanied by gossip and dismay. Those who don't get promoted begin to dislike their work since these jobs become badges that promotion has been denied. Who can blame them, since staying too long in one job means that you are not in the fast track? The work itself long ago became meaningless except as a stepping-stone to promotion. The position seems like a dead-end to someone who has been passed-over. Who can take an interest in work which proves he is not promotable?

W. Somerset Maugham, that keen observer of mankind, was correct when he noted that "failure makes people bitter and cruel." American systems of promotion and rewards stress failure rather than encourage success. The Japanese search for more positive systems of rewards. They are not as individualistic as those found in the United States, and they promote coopera-tion and company loyalty rather than person-to-person competition.

There is also the jealousy factor. After being passed-over, it's only human nature to begin to hate a successful competitor as well as yourself and your work. You become angry at anyone recognized as an EI when you are not. It's normal to blame others or the system when we don't get what we want. Competition increases the likelihood of sour grapes. Only a saint would not think "Why can't I get rotated as often as Victoria? If it wasn't for her I would be in line for promotion. She's either very lucky or she's using blackmail." Poor Victoria. Her very success makes enemies of her friends. Victoria becomes alienated from her age peers and she begins to learn the social costs of competition.

Why do Americans encourage competitive inequality? For some, competition, especially personal competition, is seen as necessary because there are fewer higher positions and rewards than there are candidates. Someone has to lose the race for promotion: there are simply fewer positions at the top than there are at the bottom. For others, corporate perks used as rewards become meaningless when everyone receives them. Part of the satisfaction of having a corner office with a large window is that there are only a few corner offices available. Who would value using the executive washroom if too many had keys? Who wants to eat with everyone else? Food eaten at an exclusive executive dining room tastes better than that at the common cafeteria. Competition brings out the snob in us.

Competition is also seen as the best way to motivate workers to do their best. Americans imagine that unequal rewards result in harder-working employees. Take two or three new staffers; tell them only one will be kept on after the end of the year. They are on trial and the best competitor will be rewarded. Then we suppose that this threat encourages the three to work as hard as they can. The supervisor gains an added bonus: the company hopefully has gotten the best efforts out of three workers during the trial period. Two have been proven inferior, so they can be dismissed, passed-over for promotion, or punished in some other way while others take their places.

This type of competition results in an environment which encourages conflict. Younger Americans compete in Little League teams; Boy Scouts compete to see who will earn the most badges or help the largest number of old ladies across the street; Girl Scouts compete to sell the most cookies. When older we compete for grades and peer prestige and later for career promotion and marriage partners. Unfortunately, all of these competitions force attention on winning and not on the activities themselves. We go through life collecting prizes (or not) and ignore the fact that the prizes may not be worth much in themselves. It's like racing through a museum to see more works of art than anyone else without seeing one painting long enough to enjoy, much less appreciate, it.

Most Americans believe that competition should be encouraged in business because the advantages outweigh the costs. This attitude shocks the Japanese. Americans are seldom ashamed of competition and its partner, inequality. Have I been too critical? As my defense I quote the developer and godfather of McDonald's. McDonald's is now a world-wide institution, popular even in Japan, and was made into a success through the vision of one person.

The man who made the McDonald hamburger a household word in many languages is Ray Kroc. During a 1972 interview, Ray Kroc explained how he saw the world of business (Boas and Chain, 1976:20):

This [the food industry] is a rat eat rat, dog eat dog. I'll kill 'em, and I'm going to kill 'em before they kill me. You're talking about the American way of survival of the fittest.

After discussing the disadvantages of competition, we can begin to consider why the Japanese do not accept a level of competition assumed to be so necessary in America. After all, the Japanese have been able to develop cooperative schemes which are more successful than most American competitive policies. Ask any executive in America's steel, motorcycle, and electronic industries! The Japanese see Americans as encouraging competitive environments which are more destructive than constructive. The problem is whether or not Americans can adopt Japanese strengths without their weaknesses while still keeping our own (and many) positive managerial practices.

Disadvantages of Competition

Competition forces co-workers to compete against each other. But the consequences of competition are not always the ones expected. One such consequence is that the work being done becomes less important than beating competitors. Competing now becomes an end in itself instead of a strategy to get more out of employees. The work becomes less important than competing successfully. You look for shortcuts by beating competitors rather than by doing better work.

This is the major disadvantage of competition in the eyes of the Japanese. To the Japanese, cooperation is more productive than competition. It's a question of achieving a balance between competition and cooperation. Americans see (wrongly) competition as the more useful strategy; the Japanese see cooperation as a better strategy.

There are many ways to compete against others without doing better work, and personal competition can easily become counter-productive. The negative character of personal competition is found when salespersons are rewarded when they sell more than others. Suppose there are two types of products. One product is low-cost, easily sold, and has a low profit margin. The other is more expensive, harder to place, yet enjoys a higher profit margin.

If a salesperson is rewarded according to volume, the tendency would be to ignore the high-volume object and push the other. He is rewarded by the number of products he sells and he will sell whatever is to his own greatest advantage. This salesperson might encourage newer colleagues to sell the higher-cost items. He would also try to monopolize selected "best" customers. Probably no reward system can be complex enough to encourage sales personnel to spend equal effort on both high and low volume products.

Peter M. Blau (1955) gives another example of the damaging effects of competition. A well-respected sociologist, Dr. Blau observed an office of social workers over a period of time. Their task was to find work for the unemployed. He found that workers would keep easily-filled positions secret until one of "their" clients came forward. Telling other social workers that an opening existed means that someone else might get the credit for ending a case. No one got any credit for helping co-workers. Social workers would therefore keep secret the best job openings until they could close the cases themselves. Since they were being evaluated in terms of how many clients they found jobs for, it was rational for them to keep an easily-filled job opening hidden until one of their own clients appeared.

Competition was harmful in another way. Senior workers foisted hard-to-employ applicants onto their junior employees. No one wants to be saddled with a case that's hard to close. Competition forced these social workers to keep information from one another and to seek out "easy" cases. If rewards in this office had been less individualistic and competitive, then more clients would have found jobs faster.

3.2 The Prisoner's Dilemma

Research in the social sciences has shown in a number of ways how destructive competition among members of groups can be. Many work situations in the United States encourage self-interest over cooperation while the opposite is found in Japan. Japanese workers are rewarded more often when they cooperate with others and when they work through the group. Out-performing colleagues and rivals is defined as "individualistic" (selfish) behavior. By contrast, those Japanese who help others while at the same time helping themselves are cultural heroes and respected.

A danger with competition – and a problem avoided by the Japanese – is that once begun it's hard to limit. Competition encourages distrust which leads to more intense competition which increases more rivalry and so on. Rivalries snowball and become more intense and more destructive. The end result is more and more distrust which leads in turn to more rivalry and more what was called earlier destructive competition. This is the *Revenge Principle*. Being hurt by someone demands that you avenge yourself by hurting the other person in turn. The other person must react in the same way for self defense if for no other reason. Even if you call for a truce and offer to "forgive" past action, the other can't agree because he wants to commit one more act of revenge. Then you have to get even. Eventually, both parties suffer much more than if each had forgiven the other earlier.

Once this competition-rivalry-revenge cycle develops, competitors lose sight of the real goals as they focus on how to harm each other irrespective of the costs. An example of this downward spiral is two families which have been feuding for generations. The original cause of the feud has long been forgotten. All that the members of each family can see is the last insult which must be avenged, and so on.

The problem associated with the competition-distrust-revenge cycle is that it becomes rational to return blow for blow and motivates participants to continue the cycle. After all, it's common sense to strike back after some one has struck you. Based on past experience, it's normal to distrust someone who has been untrustworthy in the past. At the very least, striking back may stop the other person from continuing the conflict. It's also hard to not try for revenge. Turning the other cheek may be good ethics but it's hard on the one getting hit. The world is full of bullies who do not hesitate to strike again if the victim ignores the previous blow.

The problem of accelerating hostility and distrust is easily understood in what is known as the Prisoner's Dilemma game, which has been studied by many social scientists (Axelrod, 1982). The name of this game comes from the story in which two criminal accomplices have been arrested by the police and kept in different cells. The police give each the choice to confess to a crime and implicate the other. If one confesses, he receives a light sentence and the other a heavy sentence. If both confess, each receives a sentence medium in severity. If no one confesses (if they cooperate with each other), each is charged with a minor offense with the possibility of being acquitted or receiving the lightest possible sentence.

The problem – or the Prisoner's Dilemma – is whether one prisoner can trust the partner enough to not confess and implicate the other. If both cooperate, both receive the lightest possible sentence; if one confesses he receives a light punishment and the other receives the greatest amount of punishment. The two unfortunates are tempted under the rules of the situation to break trust to receive the lightest sentence. It is a matter of self defense not to trust the other and receive the highest pay off (Rapoport and Chammah, 1965).

In experiments based on the logic of the Prisoner's Dilemma game, there are two players who must make a series of decisions based on the "simple" choice of whether to cooperate or not. To make the game more serious for the participants, each choice results in a reward, say one dollar for each point won. The purpose of the Prisoner's Dilemma game is to make the most number of choices resulting in the largest number of points won. It's a poker game. A choice is made in secret, and then the results are shown to the two participants and a score awarded. For the next turn, the choices are again made in secret and then compared and scored. The goal from the researcher's point of view is to see if the two players end up by cooperating or competing. If they cooperate, they each "earn" more points than if each had refused to co-operate.

Note in Figure 3/1 that the player who gets the other to cooperate while he does not receives the largest number of points in a relative as well as in an absolute sense. These instances – cells II and III – are called "sucker options": someone is tricked into losing because of misplaced trust.

Commonly, participants get greedy. They try to trick the opponents into cooperating when they themselves have no intention of doing so. Successful manipulators receive large scores, at least in the short run. The other party eventually learns from this treachery. After losing, the next choice is either to trust the other again (and maybe become a sucker again) or else to play if safe

Exhibit 3/1: The Prisoner's Dilemma

		Player B's	
		Choices	
		Cooperation	Non-Cooperation
Player A's Choices	Cooperation	Cell I A gets 5 points B get 5 points	Cell II A gets 0 points B gets 10 points
	Non-Cooperation	Cell III A gets 10 points B gets 0 points	Cell IV A gets 2 points B gets 2 points

Source: Adapted from Axelrod (1982).

and not cooperate. The second move gives you either two (cell IV) or ten points (the sucker cells II and III).

When the Prisoner's Dilemma game takes place, either trust is established and all moves fall in the cell I combination, or distrust develops and all choices eventually fall in the cell IV combination.

During the first few moves, one player usually tries to sucker the other into a 10-0 cell. The other player may "forgive" and cooperate a few more times to see if the choices eventually fall in the cell I combination. But for that to happen, the player doing so has to turn the other cheek and hope an unfavorable 0-10 combination doesn't happen again. Eventually, though, most players end up using a strategy resulting in cell IV combinations until the end of the game. The players both leave with some cash, but neither makes as much had both cooperated. In Figure 3/1, each player could have won fifty points if both had cooperated during a game of ten turns. If no one had cooperated, each would go home with twenty points.

The world is full of such situations, and the Prisoner's Dilemma is more than a game. Judicial courts often encourage a defendant to plea bargain for a lesser sentence instead of taking a chance of being acquitted. The defendant has to trust that everyone – lawyers and judge – will accept the plea. In the same way, when a bully attacks you, do you forgo revenge and try to make friends? Do you "forgive" the previous blow? Or is the best strategy to ignore the possible benefits of friendship (cooperation) and slug the bully? International relations often involve situations where diplomats and government leaders must choose between revenge and forgiveness, or trust vs mistrust.

Robert Axelrod (1982) has conducted conferences for game theorists and computer programmers to test which strategy of cooperation-non-cooperation and their combinations would be the winning one in terms of points won. One ingenuous program used the strategy of selecting the cooperation alternative whenever the other player did so except every tenth or so times. Then the choice was to not cooperate and "sucker" the opponent to see if the other "forgave" the non-cooperation choice during the next turn.

Robert Axelrod found that the most successful strategy was one called TIT FOR TAT, in which a player repeated an opponent's previous choice. When the opponent cooperated, the second player did the same for the next turn. Non-cooperation was "punished" in the next move if the first player "suckered" the other in the previous turn by non-cooperation. If the opponent continued to choose non-cooperation, our player did the same and both won two points each per trial. If the opponent got wise and cooperated, the other player did the same and both won five points each. They both won more with this strategy.

Japanese managerial strategy encourages every one to adopt the cell I strategy. Over the long run, everyone wins the most when everyone cooperates. A short-time perspective might encourage the strategy found in cells II and III. The reward is high for a short while if you can take advantage of the other player, but the distrust being developed makes cell IV the most likely strategy over time. No one wants to be suckered again and again.

The Japanese business philosophy is that long-term cooperation is more beneficial than short-term high profits followed by perpetual distrust and competition. I discussed in chapter two Japan's "child companies." The relationship between the "parent" and "child" companies is an example of the fourth cell of the Prisoner's Dilemma logic. Whenever possible, the Japanese prefer the profits of long-term cooperation to temporary short-term (larger) profits based on non-cooperation.

The genius of the Japanese work style is based on the realization that long-term profits based on mutual cooperation are greater than short-term profits that result in distrust and non-cooperation. Americans, as we have seen in this chapter, are prone to encourage relations and reward systems which resemble cells II and III in the Prisoner's Dilemma. Americans need to develop ways of working which reflects strategies encouraging mutual trust and cooperations, or cell I. We are too easily tempted to "sucker" others to gain a short-term advantage. This strategy develops into less gain for everyone involved over time.

So-called lower animals avoid the Prisoner's Dilemma trap by establishing trust, even when beginning the process involves some risk. Paul Watzlawik and his co-authors (1967) offer the example of how porpoises establish trust with humans through certain rituals. Some porpoises will establish contact with human strangers by taking a human's hand in their mouths and squeezing gently. Porpoises have sharp teeth and can easily bite a human's hand through.

Allowing a hand to be placed in a porpoise's mouth is a sign of trust. The porpoise then reciprocates by placing its underbelly against the human's hand or foot. By doing so, the porpoise shows its willingness to expose its most vulnerable part of its body to the human. Obviously, these procedures cannot be carried through unless each being trusts the other at the outset. No one wants to place a foot in a shark's mouth! The problem is for potential enemies to begin a series of gestures which indicate both good intentions and trust.

3.3 Overt vs Covert Competition

Overt competition is competition acknowledged and supported by the company or other outside party. It is the officially-supported method through which an employer distributes unequal rewards. A sales department can offer a special bonus to the salesman who gets the most orders. Or a foreman can be evaluated in terms of the absentee rate of his line workers. In this type of competition, the foreman whose workers have the best attendance records receives a cash bonus. All of the members of the winning group could also each receive a special prize. The prize doesn't always have to be cash. In this case, the winning foreman wins a cash bonus, and the workers might be allowed to leave work two hours ahead of time on two successive Fridays. It might be worth more to the company to achieve perfect attendance and let some go home early than to have higher absentee averages.

Unfortunately, competition is not always kept within ethical or officially sanctioned limits. This was the case with Dr. Blau's social workers. One problem with competition is that it's hard to keep it within acceptable boundaries. Competition can take extreme forms when the prize is large enough. A few years ago, the Boy Scouts of America national association was faced with an embarrasing situation. A number of scouting recruiters had falsified enrollments as well as the existence of a number of troops. These recruiters wanted to show increases in their enrollments and had yielded to the temptation to cheat a little in order to improve their performance records.

A similar situation existed when an investigation found that U.S. Army recruiters had falsified test scores so that a larger number of volunteers would be accepted. The recruiters were rewarded by how many recruits each signed on instead of being rewarded for the quality of their recruits. Human nature being what it is, competition will often bring out the worst in us.

The Japanese, on the other hand, fear overt personal competition. Their response to this fear is to offer rewards for cooperation. Rewards in a Japanese company are organized at the group-level. Few employees compete directly and personally against one another. Instead, they compete as members of a group against other groups. Better yet, Japanese workers are encouraged to compete against themselves. There are prizes when group members surpass their earlier averages.

When the Japanese are forced to compete, they prefer to do so on an impersonal basis. Workers are encouraged to become more productive so that their company will be more profitable than their competitors. The group – in this case the company as a whole – now becomes the winner or the loser.

This type of competition is impossible unless workers identify with the company and feel loyalty to its goals. Japanese administrators spend much effort and time developing this personal company loyalty. Most Japanese corporations encourage their workers to wear company symbols and standard-ized clothes fashions, such as jackets and caps with the company's logo. Workers receive pep talks and lectures at the start of each shift.

As important, all workers receive bi-annual bonuses as part of their pay. These bonuses vary according to the profitability of the company during the previous six months. This allows workers to receive a direct benefit whenever their company prospers. Productivity bonuses and other types of rewards are given to a group rather than to an individual. In Japan, work groups compete against each other but not individual against individual.

Covert Competition

Even in America, there are limits to what competitors can do to each other. Doing in the other fellow too openly is bad form and frowned upon, at least officially. As a consequence, competition goes underground. It becomes furtive and sometimes hard to see, but the damage is still real. There are always ways to compete unfairly against others without seeming to do so. Unfortunately, covert competition is counter-productive from an employer's point-of-view because workers now try to weaken opponents and their work. The purpose here is harming the other person rather than doing a better job yourself. The goal is not working better but making others look worse. That is what much office politics is about. There are as many forms of covert competition as there are unhappy workers.

One attempt to reduce covert competition has been to reward each worker according to his or her own production while having at the same time no quota or limitation on winners. This is a classic method of motivation used in the United States and less so in Japan. Establish a work group of eight workers and pay them with a piece rate. Each is competing against the others for higher pay but not against one another. No one is harmed by someone's success because pay is based on a person's productivity. Some make more money while others earn less based on individual production. But no one receives less because another earns more. On an objective level, the system is rational and should cause no problems.

But the situation is not as simple as it might seem. Assume Daniel McIntosh is the rate-buster of this group. The setting is a row of machines where each worker operates a machine independently of the others. The slower workers are going to become jealous. For one thing, McIntosh is placing them in a bad light by being a faster worker. He's made them into losers. There is no way to avoid being compared unfavorably. Also, McIntosh's higher pay makes the others feel inadequate. They will not congratulate him for his good fortune. They will instead blame him for their growing insecurities. Why shouldn't the foreman fire the slower ones and hire new workers who might do better?

The slower workers will feel that Daniel McIntosh is encouraging sweat-shop labor. He doesn't seem to know that there are limits to how hard someone should work. This may not seem rational, but piece work causes more tension and lower morale after its introduction even though some workers can earn more money.

There is another negative result to this type of competition, one discussed earlier in another context. Workers who are less successful become envious. Even when higher pay to one does not mean a real loss of pay, the others feel that they are losing some benefit. Slower workers may intellectually believe more productive workers should earn more. But this sense of justice disappears in real life situations. Even if someone next to you is working harder, it's hard not to feel envious of another's higher rewards. Such competitive settings give rise to very strong feelings of envy.

The slower workers gang up on the faster ones to protect their pride, if nothing else. They tease McIntosh when he begins to pass their daily production levels. If he ignores them, they will refuse to talk to him or share coffee breaks. The next step is to hide his tools, and even sabotage his machine. Why not put sand in McIntosh's driller? Daniel McIntosh has three choices. He can complain to the foreman, but what can a foreman do against teasing and social isolation? This merely makes McIntosh look foolish. He can admit defeat and quit his job, lose his seniority, and go through the efforts to find new work somewhere else. He can also conform and decrease his production. This is the most likely decision. Conformity and lower productivity have been found to be the common reaction when a rate-buster faces covert competition. Much of this covert competition is almost impossible to prove, much less stop, because it takes so many forms. One type of covert competition is passive in nature. Passive competition is avoiding doing something which places a competitor at a disadvantage. Passive competition can take the form of someone who "forgets" to pass on information which might be useful to someone else. Suppose "fast tract" Jim Wilson has left the office to take a potential client out to lunch. The client becomes interested in Jim's presentation and the lunch hour becomes two as he asks for more information.

Jim Wilson gets a phone call at his office from his supervisor before he returns. What can co-worker Paul Edwards say to the supervisor about Jim's absence? Paul can say that, "Jim is still out to lunch and sometimes gets back pretty late. It's hard to know when he might get back." If the supervisor seems angry, Paul can leave a message on Jim's desk mentioning only that the supervisor called. Why mention he was mad and put Jim on guard, or that it's important to return the call as soon as possible? Now the supervisor has the impression that Jim takes long lunches while Paul is hard at work at his desk. This type of office politics can ruin Jim's career by destroying his image.

Women workers are especially threatened by the techniques of passive competition on the part of men. Men who reject women as co-workers can easily and safely (to themselves) refuse to pass on valued information. This happens because much information is exchanged in informal settings such as a bar, the golf links, or during a coffee break. There are times when you want to discuss serious matters informally. Not letting a woman co-worker become part of the office's unofficial information-sharing network can hurt her career.

Marcille Gray Williams, in her book *The New Executive Woman* (1977), points out that a typical strategy used in office politics is the withholding of information. One passive competition technique is to sit on a circulating memo until the deadline for action is passed. Williams recommends that women (and men) make sure that they are part of powerful groups by making alliances and becoming accepted by their members.[1] Women who hope for successful careers need to become members of various leisure groups from work. This means joining in after-work cocktails and coffee breaks until you are accepted. Otherwise you will miss valuable information.

There are other examples of passive competition. Floor workers might not "understand" a foreman's instructions and say they misunderstood their directions. The supervisor gets blamed for not being a good communicator and one of the workers may eventually take his place. Passive competition obviously can take many forms. Just not warning a colleague that the supervisor is in a bad mood can result in someone making a regrettable diplomatic error. This type of non-help threatens a worker's chances of promotion.

---

[1] Many of the stumbling blocks colleagues can use to harm another's career are discussed in Betty Lehan Harragan's books *Games Mother Taught You* (1977) and *Knowing the Score* (1983). Most of these traps are examples of covert competition.

3.4 Competition Encourages Conformity

Competition also results in cautiousness and conformity. Most workers will decide that the best policy is to be cautious if rewards are given only to one. Those who dare and fail are punished; in this environment, it is better to "not-lose" than to take a chance and "not-win." It's naive to assume that competition, especially personal competition, always results in more productive behavior from all parties. The result may be more distructive than productive.

Take the situation where two employees compete for the next higher position. One decides to be energetic, daring, and innovative. She decides she will be rewarded when superiors notice her dynamism and activism. The other worker decides to keep a low profile. He follows established procedures and exhibits an image of dull reliability. He follows orders, obeys the rules, and takes few chances.

What are the possible outcomes of this contest? If the first worker dares too much and fails, the promotion goes to the other by default. The latter, if he has done little that is exceptional, at least has done nothing wrong. He is rewarded through another's failure. Many middle level managers in this situation would adopt the safe, secure way of slow but probably gradual promotion. Remember that someone may fail through no fault of his own. Experiments will fail under even the best conditions just because they are experiments. By their very nature, experiments involve the element of uncertainty and possible failure. When in direct competition with others, a favorite policy of many workers is, "nothing ventured, nothing failed."

Too much competition is harmful to the organization as a whole. The employers who encourages competition will not necessarily get the most productive effort from employees. Even superior workers can be harmed by too much personal competition. It's not just the weak who get cut off from the herd in competitive situations. Because they gain when a "water-walker" (a promotable trainee) stumbles, colleagues are likely to be less than enthusiastic to help such a person. Personal competition forces everyone to look out for his own interests even when this harms the organization. It is unfortunate that competition pits one employee against another, but the system teaches you that everyone is out for himself. Competition encourages co-workers to view one another as opponents instead of partners and helpers.

The safest strategy in a personal competition environment is to be like everyone else. The result will be that most workers will adopt a camouflage of collective anonymity. The Japanese saying "the raised nail gets hammered" recognizes the fact that workers standing out from the crowd make the most enemies and become targets for envy. Competition has the potential of making workers into enemies or into anonymous, cautious members of a crowd. Either alternative inhibits productivity not to mention creativity and innovation.

Competition Brings out the Worst as Well as the Best

If the reader thinks I am being too harsh, let me quote what others say about conformity in corporations. Rosabeth Moss Kanter has published widely in the field of sociology and is a partner in a consulting firm dealing with organizational problems in corporations. She studied a large firm, which she called Indsco, for several years. Here (Kanter, 1979:192) is how she describes the tendency for those competing for promotion to choose the safe path:

Getting everything right is the response of those who lack other ways to impress those about them or to secure their position; and in turn they demand this kind of ritualistic conformity from subordinates, like school teachers more concerned about neatness of a paper than its ideas. Secretarial supervisors at Indsco tended to be known for these traits: a concern with proper form rather than a good outcome. Or, as someone else said, "You don't give freedom or experiment with procedure when you're a first-liner. You try to cover your ass and not make a mistake they can catch you on."

The fear of making a mistake results in many forms of inefficiency even in a highly successful company. William Rodgers published an unofficial and at times critical biography of IBM and its founder, Thomas J. Watson. Though Tom Watson was a maverick as well as an organizational innovator, he expected IBM employees to conform to a large number of rules not directly related to corporate performance, such as those dealing with dress. He also expected results. He rewarded and supported those who promoted IBM's progress, but he was a tyrant to those who were not consistently successful.

Tom Watson's treatment of employees at the bottom half of the corporate ladder was very paternalistic. Watson was very Japanese in his concern for lower-level personnel. But he used punishment as well as reward to encourage good behavior for higher-level executives. They were paid well, but they also paid a price: business mistakes as well as non-conforming behavior could ruin a career (Rodgers, 1969:290):

In general, IBM policy dictated that a man wasn't wanted in power circles if he made a mistake. ... Blame for a mistake meant demotion, sometimes a reduced salary, and oblivion from former associates. His name went up on the bulletin board under promotions and transfers. An executive in charge of manufacturing at half a dozen plants might find himself *promoted* to a management job involving one plant.

It's obvious that the corporate world is not always a rational one. Reward systems based on personal competition may seem at first glance as if they would encourage better performance. But the opposite is often true. The Japanese strongly feel that personal, in-group competition is too potentially destructive to be used extensively.

John Z. De Lorean relates a number of experiences while working for General Motors which show how personal competition can turn a team into backbiting enemies. De Lorean's fortune declined after he left GM, his company went bankrupt and he was arrested for alleged attempted drug trafficking. But his GM observations contain valuable lessons.

He found that GM's senior executives competed against one another and were so suspicious of each other that they seldom could work together. Competition for promotion and prestige resulted in administrative near-paralysis at the central headquarters. De Lorean was in a unique position to observe that GM's senior executives were more concerned with fighting each other than in worrying about what was best for GM.

De Lorean was a General Motors executive when he resigned in 1973. He was then earning six hundred thousand dollars yearly and was considered to be next in line for GM's presidency. His biography, written by J. Patrick Wright, provides a good picture of the competitive conflict taking place in large corporations. Wright (1980:47) quotes John De Lorean describing the effects of competition for attention and notice at GM:

Lower executives, eager to please the boss and rise up the corporate ladder, worked hard to learn what he wanted to know or how he thought on a particular subject. They then either fed the boss exactly what he wanted to know, or they modified their own proposals to suit his preferences.

Emphasis on competition has a final drawback: competition creates losers as well as winners. Competition shows who is inferior as well as who is better. If the winners are superior, then the others are by default inferior. They are losers. The winners look down on the others and this creates an emotional distance between the two groups. Competition makes persons so unequal that they will find it hard if not impossible to work together. Smugness on one side and envy on the other cause friction, not cooperation.

This sense of superiority carries over to persons holding different ranks in a company's hierarchy. By definition, the boss must be better than the department head, and the senior secretary must be superior to a newly-hired secretary third-grade. And so on. If those with lower ranks were smart enough, capable, etc., then they would be in higher positions in the first place. Competition creates inequality; inequality in turn creates a sense of snobbism and disdain of others. The others feel envy and jealousy. Is it any wonder that so many Americans hate their jobs?

Nowhere are the results of competition and inequality so clear as in the Scientific Management school of managerial thought. The American emphasis on competition in its extreme form is found in Scientific Management. The popularity and influence of this school of thought makes it necessary to discuss it in some detail. This managerial philosophy is so opposite to the Japanese managerial model that it highlights how American managers can improve their manners as well as their productivity. Some of the major reasons why many Japanese workers are more productive than American workers can be traced to the influence of the Scientific Management philosophy.

3.5 Scientific Management in America

The competitive, individualistic orientation in American business is a central element of the Scientific Management school, dominant during the first half of the twentieth century. Its influence is still great, and no one managerial philosophy is so opposite to what the Japanese believe.

Developed by Frederick W. Taylor, Scientific Management's goal was to make American workers more productive while they received higher pay. It focused on manual workers, especially in manufacturing, but its influence can be found in all parts of the labor force: from schools to the military, from managers to secretaries, and from factories to offices.

Production is improved in Scientific Management by making the individual a better worker through teaching him how to work faster. This was done by making the work simpler and more specialized, so that it could be performed faster. Scientific Management is based on the assumption that work simplicity and efficiency go together. It was a very rational approach: study the work to be done; break it down to its simplest units; and teach the operator to follow these now-simplified procedures. This type of philosophy works well when a task is repetitive and relatively easy to perform, as is typically found on the assembly line.

The Worker as Stupid

Taylorism, as Scientific Management is also called, accepted the view that workers were basically stupid. That is why work had to be broken down. Workers could not be productive unless management made work duties easier to perform. Workers were also seen as so ineffective that they needed detailed instructions. Any initiative on the part of the worker was viewed as a dangerous threat to efficiency so that workers had to be strickly supervised. The worker was so unintelligent that any variation from established procedures would necessarily be inefficient. Management's claim to leadership was based on the belief that workers performing lower-level work were by definition incapable of doing anything else. Anyone holding this view is tempted to see anyone in a lower position as inferior. One purpose of this book is to show the long-term inefficiency of this belief.

A quote from Taylor shows this rejection of the worth of lower-level workers. The setting is Bethlehem Steel, where Taylor had been asked to apply the principles of Scientific Management. He began with the pig handlers, the least-skilled workers. They were paid $1.15 a day to carry iron ignots (pigs) from the yard of the foundry to a nearby railroad car. Molten iron was poured from the furnaces into molds were they cooled and solidified into pigs. When set, these pigs were placed outside to cool. The pig handlers carried the pigs into railroad cars to be transported to finishing mills. A pig was manually carried across the yard and each weighed ninety-two pounds. Below is how Taylor felt about these pig handlers (Taylor, 1911; Part Two: 59):

Now one of the very first requirements for a man who is fit to handle pig iron as a regular occupation is that he more nearly resemble the ox than any other type. The man who is mentally alert and intelligent is for this very reason entirely unsuited for what would for him, be the grinding monotony of work of this character. Therefore the workman who is best suited to handling pig iron is unable to understand the real science of doing this class of work. He is so stupid that the word "percentage" has no meaning for him, and he must consequently be trained by a man more intelligent than himself in the habit of working in accordance with the laws of this science before he can be successful.

Japanese managers rejected this view of the worker. Scientific Management was never popular in Japan. The belief that lower-level workers are totally inferior is seldom found in Japan today. Only temporary day-laborers and resident foreigners (especially those of Korean descent) are treated so disdainfully.

A contemporary Japanese manager faced with the problem of how to increase the performance of pig handlers would approach it differently than did Taylor. The Japanese supervisor would first ask the workers themselves to make suggestions. He would also take them out for drinks and meals. If necessary he would ask them to take a course on material handling offered by the company. Since pig handling is a manual operation the course would teach the men how to carry loads more efficiently. The pig handlers might also be asked to test various ways of lifting to see which they preferred. The Japanese practice would be to include the workers into the decision-making process. Scientific Management leaves them out completely.

Taylor's work with the pig iron handlers involved teaching them how to carry, when to rest, how to lift. The men were eventually able to transport two and a half times more ignots a day from plant to railroad car than before. Management then did what seemed rational to them and common at this time: they fired half of the pig handlers. The result was increased performance with half the labor. The practice of increasing productivity and then firing excess personnel was another reason why Scientific Management was hated by the workers.

As a final note on Taylor's pig handlers, they were given a sixty percent pay increase after being taught to be two and a half-times more productive. A Japanese supervisor would promise that no employee would lose his job when production increased. Those who were no longer needed would be retrained and given work in another part of the plant. The workers would also profit more from their increased productivity in the form of group bonuses.

A third reason why workers disliked and fought Scientific Management was that its view of the worker was insulting and, if taken to its logical extreme, inhumane. Scientific Management assumed that workers were nothing but stupid, organic machines. Workers were little else than low-IQ robots.

The logic of the Scientific Management approach demands that managers treat workers as if they were machines. This is why time-and-motion studies became popular in American industry from the 1900's to the 1950's. Timing how fast a person should do a task reduces him to a machine analog. All that is important is the worker's movements. There is no room, in this model, for considering his humanity or his intellect. Feelings, emotions, and morale become irrelevant. Along with this attitude, Scientific Management took the approach that workers were so inferior and stupid that they were, in fact, oxen. It is obvious that this view degrades workers.

Scientific Management provides a framework for making manual workers more productive and this part of this school of thought was beneficial. For manual operations, Scientific Management did make workers much more effective. In fact, productivity could be increased and fatigue decreased. This was a plus for the workers who earned more money if they kept their jobs. This approach to how work should be done was based on a very limited and inhumane view of the worker. Scientific Management gave management a rationale for making work simpler through specialization. After all, if workers were really simple persons, work could be made more productive only if tasks were made simpler and easier to perform. Having little presumed ability, workers could also not be expected to have the intelligence to contribute useful ideas for work improvement or perform complicated operations.

Foremen and managers felt superior because workers were defined as inferior beings. All that workers needed were clear and detailed orders telling them how to work and what to do. This is an authoritarian outlook in which nothing is expected from subordinates except obedience. The Japanese have found, by contrast, that very few tasks are so simple that workers can't improve their productivity if motivated to do so.

The supervisor, under Scientific Management, believed that anyone willing to work at a repetitive, specialized task such as on an assembly line was no doubt too stupid to become personally involved in the work. Such a person lacked the intelligence and sensitivity that separated him from the non-manual workers. In fact, it was believed and acted on that the superior and his workers were in a direct confrontation from which only one side would remain victorious. Either the foreman would force high productivity from his charges or they would cheat the company by loafing and reducing their work pace. Close supervision was necessary and the workers should not be involved in making decisions about the work performed. American workers and the superiors form a combative duet where one party expected to win over the other. Their goals are contradictory rather than complementary. This is competition taken to an extreme!

While Scientific Management is over eighty years old, the attitudes which separate manual workers from others persist today. Roscoe Dye spent twenty-one years as maintenance line worker in American automobile plants. Hired by the Japanese venture company the New United Motor Manufacturing, Inc. company (Nummi), Dye has been exposed to both traditional American and contemporary Japanese managerial styles. Nummi is the newly established joint venture of Toyota and General Motors and all personnel are expected to "work Japanese" at its California plant.

Roscoe Dye summarizes his feelings about American managerial styles from his experience (Chira, 1984):

Upper management treated you as a lower grade of people. If you didn't have the education to communicate with those people, they wouldn't bring themselves to talk with you.

By contrast, the introduction of Japanese-style managerial policies increased Mr. Dye's morale and sense of corporate family:

But we found that the upper management is now willing to talk to a common working person like myself. I'm the bottom of the group. If I can have anything to say, and they'll listen to me, I'll feel like I'm being appreciated.

Scientific Management is American in its assumption that lower-level workers are both stupid and a threat to management. They must be controlled and supervised by managers and taught to be submissive. The rejection of this managerial ideology by the Japanese has one consequence that has significant implications.

By assuming that workers are worthy and capable, Japanese managers also believe that workers are too good to perform low-level, repetitive tasks. Labor should be used for more complicated tasks. That is one reason why the Japanese have enthusiastically accepted the notion of industrial robots (nick-named "steel collars" in Japan). Japan has now more than twice as many robots in operation than the United States.

Akira Kojima (1983) notes that current technology gives industrial robots no more than an IQ of twenty, making robots effective only when the tasks are very simple and repetitive. According to the Japanese, no one should have to perform such low-level work. Aside from any gains in productivity and profits, robots are seen as freeing workers from tedious work they shouldn't have to do in the first place! The use of robots in Japan is motivated by more than the search for profits.

The acceptance of robots (or any other ways to increase productivity) in Japan is made easier because corporate workers replaced by robots never lose their employment. They are retrained for more complicated work or transferred to other divisions. Since workers are viewed as intelligent, Japanese managers assume that workers can work smarter if asked to do so and given the opportunity.

The response to automation in America is to fire whoever was stupid enough to have performed any tasks that can be automated. Otherwise these workers would have been talented enough to do something more complicated in the first place. In the past, and tragically often enough today, management would see these workers as probably too stupid to be retrainable.

3.6 Thinking vs Doing

Another feature of Scientific Management still with us is the belief that, if the worker is basically stupid, then his role is to be passive and to obey. The best he can do is follow to the letter the instructions others give. Management "thinks and orders" while subordinates "do and obey."

Not only is the worker stupid, Scientific Management continues, but he is also unmotivated except for his greed for money. All he wants is his wages. There is no need to ask a worker for advice on how to improve his work, even assuming he was intelligent enough to make a contribution. He is both too ignorant and too apathetic to offer worthwhile suggestions. To the followers of Taylorism, the worker becomes the machine he operates.

The Japanese have a different view. They try to make the job more humane rather than reducing the worker to the level of the machine. Soichiro Honda strongly believes that not only are workers intelligent, but that they should also work together. In a speech given at the Michigan Technological University while receiving an honorary degree, Honda said that (Sanders: 1975:11):

No matter how much progress and development is made in science and technology or social structure, it must not be forgotten that it is men who operate them. And this cannot be done by one person alone. It takes a heart-to-heart unity of purpose of many people if they are to become "masters" who effectively operate machines and social structures and thus contribute to mankind. It is with this thought in mind that I tell young employees of my company: "Don't be used by the machine, use the machine."

The above statement highlights one of the major differences between Japanese and American management. The Japanese corporate manager assumes the lower-level worker is intelligent and interested (and loyal) enough in his work to contribute to higher efficiency.

I have mentioned some negative results when too much competition is encouraged. Below is a summary of other disadvantages from competition.

They might seem one-sided and overly pessimistic, but the Japanese strongly believe that person-to-person competition is not the best strategy to motivate workers. There are other ways to convince employees to become better workers, among which is to encourage pride in workmanship, the enjoyment of challenges, and pride in teamwork. Japanese senior executives are firmly convinced that competition – while never completely absent – entails too many costs. Here are a few:

*For every winner there are one or more non-winners. Those who lose in any contest become bitter and angry. They sabotage the winners or take their hostility out on the organization.

*Those who become non-winners may decide never to compete in the future. They will form groups of malcontents who criticize those with ambition to compete. These workers will develop work restriction practices and expect others to also restrict their work.

*Ambitious workers may feel forced to compete against each other. They will refuse to share information or help one another. Production and morale will decrease as trust and sharing decrease. Such competition is common on the group, departmental, or divisional as well as the individual level. Competition decreases cooperation everywhere.

*Work becomes oriented to competition. Workers refuse to become involved with tasks that are unglamorous or which do not lead to promotion. The competitors become enthusiastic only when their work is noticed or important.

*Work is downplayed unless it yields immediate, short-term rewards. Long-range results are viewed as not being visible enough. A competitor expects to be promoted and moved before a long-range plan is completed. Someone else may reap its benefits and rewards.

*Competitors may decide to operate in the safe, traditional manner because experimental efforts may end in failure. The result is the tendency to reject innovation and follow already-established guide-lines. If an experimenter fails, the promotion may go to someone who has done little but who has not failed. The system in the long-run rewards the timid.

3.7 The Japanese Helping Ethic

There are other reasons why helping behavior is more common in a Japanese work setting than in its American counterpart. Americans who need help hesitate to ask for help even when it is available. This reluctance exists because a person asking for aid is acknowledging his own inferiority. To ask for help implies that someone else is more capable. Pride keeps a worker from asking a supervisor or a co-worker for advice; few of us want to look less than fully capable to a foreman or friends. Even when asking for help is officially encouraged, many workers – especially newcomers – would rather learn by trial-and-error than to ask outright for aid. No one wants to appear stupid.

Receiving help, then, gives the recipient the feeling he has been debased for asking for help. The same principle applies to automobile drivers who are lost but refuse to ask for directions.

Most of us are too embarrassed to ask how our work should be done. Many males are so ego-involved with the mirage of male superiority that they don't like to ask female co-workers or female superiors for help or advice. They don't want to admit that a woman knows more. The same problem exists when older workers need to get help from younger ones.

Americans don't like to acknowledge that they are so inexperienced or so ignorant that they need help. In Japan, where pride is more important, it is easier to disguise the fact that someone needs help. When help is offered, aid is given not to help the individual but to the work group. This facade is maintained because the Japanese individual is working to help the group produce; he is no longer the target for aid because the recipient of help is the work team. This also encourages senior workers to volunteer instructions on how things are done without the fear that the recipient will be embarrassed.

Helping another entails obligation. George Homans (1974) has pointed out that people normally feel obligated to return a favor or gift. This obligation creates a tension until the debt has been repaid. Such a tension exists because receiving help (or a gift) makes a person feel inferior until an equivalent exchange has been made.

The receiver feels obligated as well as inferior when a gift or help cannot be returned. People feel guilty or angry when they receive a gift which cannot be exchanged for one having equal value. This explains why those who receive charity seldom feel very grateful.

The same problem exists in any work situation. Few workers can offer equal value when a superior gives them aid. Usually all a subordinate has to offer in exchange for help is indicating that the donor is superior through profuse thanks and flattery. Superiority is easily assumed because when helping someone automatically shows that the donor knows something the recipient does not. Otherwise help would not be asked for. This makes the receiver of help feel less capable in relation to the other person. Such feelings of inferiority make workers resentful instead of grateful after receiving help. Workers avoid asking for help unless they think they can somehow repay the debt. A lesson from this is that superiors can help their subordinates too much. Too much help will make workers feel resentful and inadequate. It makes us feel dependent, as if we were children again.

A consequence of this universal sense of justice is that the lower-level workers are more likely to seek help from other lower-level workers. It is easier to repay a debt owed to co-workers than to superiors. There will always be an opportunity in the future when a co-worker can be helped in exchange. A worker can always offer an equal a free meal or a few drinks.

Japanese executives encourage workers to exchange help and favors. This is made easier by making sure that workers interact often with each other. Japanese workers find themselves members of several teams, and it is easy for Japanese workers to develop a large reservoir of past favors. Over the years, workers build up large accounts of "credit" with one another. It becomes easy to ask for help from another worker, whether a superior or a co-worker. It is understood that all workers owe obligations for past favors. Today's favors will be repaid tomorrow if no debt is already owed.

People become friends when each can repay each others' favors. Repayment for help continues an on-going exchange of aid among equals. Fritz Heider (1958) found that series of equal exchanges among receiver and giver bind them into positive bonds of friendship and respect. Capable supervisors try to encourage workers to exchange favors and help among themselves and with the supervisors. These exchanges tie workers together and encourage a greater unity of interests. This is how consensus develops among individuals and across groups. Naturally, competitors are not likely to want to exchange favors, since the other's gain may be your loss. The setting must encourage an equal and profitable exchange for all parties.

Japanese workers develop such a web of mutual debt and obligations that they feel forced to cooperate with one another. To refuse to ask for help from a co-worker would mean refusing the other person the opportunity to pay off previous favors. Japanese corporate policy, again, encourages mutual exchanges of favors among workers. This practice makes Japanese workers more likely to feel that they owe a debt to other workers and to the company as a whole. As a result, Japanese workers are more likely to want to help one another and to feel loyalty to their superiors.

Japanese workers also feel that the company owes a debt to its workers. An obligation is developed when an employee works for a company and helps it meet its production goals. This is why a Japanese worker faced with a personal crisis will seek help from his employer before going for help elsewhere. After all, the worker assumes that if he has done more than the minimum for his employer, then the latter owes him favors beyond a salary. Co-workers may also feel obligated as a unit to offer help to a friend, whether it involves finding him a good wife, doing his work when he is ill, or listening to his problems after work hours.

On the other hand, the supervisor and co-worker feel that asking someone for a special favor merely continues the system of mutual exchange of favors. A foreman will feel free to ask someone to work overtime without extra pay because this allows the worker the chance to repay past favors. A machinist doesn't mind paying extra attention to the quality of his output because this gives him the opportunity to work off an obligation.

Japanese employers believe that workers owe their company extra consideration. They are careful to give employees more than wages so that feelings of obligations develop. A worker who, after ten years, leaves to work elsewhere for more money would be considered ungrateful. If this worker leaves because he feels no gratitude toward the company, he will be criticized for being too selfish. On the other hand, if he can show that the company itself is selfish and officers did not return the favors he had done for the company, then the company is at fault. It can receive a bad reputation for being an unfriendly and unfair employer. No Japanese executive wants this type of reputation for his company, for then it will become harder and harder to recruit good personnel.

Workers also believe that their employers owe them more than current wages. That is why workers would feel cheated if they were fired after being replaced by robots. The company owes them the obligation to keep them on. After being good workers for years, it would be unfair to fire them when they're no longer needed. The employer is being ungrateful. Managers make sure workers can be retrained before automating their jobs.

When a continuing system of exchange of favors exists, colleagues feel free to ask for cooperation and help. It also means that employee-employer relations are more harmonious than in the United States. No greater reform could be made by American managers to increase productivity than by developing more exchanges of "gifts" among workers and employers.

The exchange of favors, however, must be seen as equal, or one party will feel cheated and morale will suffer. I am not advocating wholesale corporate handouts. Workers must be able to repay these favors. Or better yet, the company repays the workers for above-the-call-of-duty activities. When an accountant comes to work on Saturday in order to help finish Monday's audit, the company should reward him in exchange. The supervisor could let this accountant off the next Friday or take him out to supper as a gesture of thanks.

3.8 American Individualism

Americans are happier when individual effort is rewarded and when individuals stand out from the crowd. Through independence and individualism, success is achieved alone and without someone's help or favors. This is why piece rate as a system of reward was developed in the United States but tried and rejected in Japan.

The successful American is often pictured as the one who has either used others to his advantage or who has cooperated until he no longer needs the others. These aggressive individualists are the ones promoted and rewarded. Workers defined as too dependent on others stay in subordinate positions. Team playing is often necessary, but staying a team player too long is dangerous for an American's career. To describe a person as a "self-made man" is to praise him in America but not in Japan.

The Japanese seldom acknowledge that a person can be a success without the help and cooperation of others. Corporate executives in Japan continuously and personally thank workers for their efforts and loyalty. Even when they exhort workers to work harder and to contribute more, they always make sure they thank them for past successes. They will also, as expected, hint that higher productivity will be amply rewarded. The company, it's implied, repays its debts.

There are ways manager-worker cooperation can be encouraged in an American company. Workers are intelligent enough to know when managers give the harmony ethos only lip service; they know when they are being conned. The adage that "you can't fool all of the people all of the time" still holds true. Managers and supervisors should be alert to any corporate actions that advertise the fact that workers – no matter what is being said – are not in the same class as higher-level employees. Signs of management superiority which workers notice and comment on are the following:

*Discrimination in terms of automobile parking. Do line and floor workers park farther away from plant entrances than do white collar workers or those in the managerial/executive levels? Data General Corporation in Massachusetts has no privileged parking slots. Dividing a company's parking lots into prestige areas reinforces manager-worker divisions. Noticing that some persons have privileged parking does not encourage a worker to begin the workday in a cooperative mood.

*Do all workers eat in the same cafeteria? Do managers eat in the same dining hall as secretaries, file clerks, and everyone else? Sharing food is a sign of equality and acceptance. Or are some workers expected to eat in the back while others enjoy reserved tables in a well-lit area? Irrational though it may seem, workers feel a closeness to superiors who share the same food and general eating location. I do not advocate executives sitting at the same table with a group of metal punch operators, though complete equality is ideal. All that is necessary is visual proximity. A senior-level manager might also stop by a few tables while leaving the cafeteria to ascertain morale. Imagine the pride when a blue collar worker can tell his friends he shared a few words with a vice-president, "and I told him about the dust in our work area." The vice-president in question must listen carefully and investigate all complaints, of course.

*Do supervisors attend office parties, birthday celebrations, and the like? Staying too long may inhibit a party's informality, but a few minutes' visit is appreciated by the guest of honor and the host.

*Many American males have difficulty expressing their softer emotions. It's easy for a man to curse or hit the desk when angry. But this same man will be unable to say, "Thank you. That's a good job. I'm glad you're working here." If he can't learn to express positive emotions, he might show approval and gratitude physically: a hand shake or an actual pat on the back. If nothing else, a personally-written note is always appreciated. Thanking someone should be done in private. It's also easier to praise someone and receive praise in private.

There are many American companies that de-emphasize differences among workers in order to increase morale. Eastman Kodak Company follows such a policy. Kodak is described by Paul Kuzniar (1982), president of the Kuzniar group management consulting company, as reflecting the best elements of Japanese corporations. Kodak, not surprisingly, is also listed by Robert Levering and co-authors (1984) as one of the one-hundred best companies to work for.

Decisions at Kodak are based on consensus and from the bottom up. Decisions develop through compromise and extensive meetings. Blue and white collars cooperate and make joint decisions. Kodak's suggestion plan was begun in 1898 and workable ideas reward those who offer suggestions. Around a million and a half dollars are given annually to employees for submitting useful ideas. Like Japanese companies, workers receive large bonuses based on a share of Kodak's profits. In 1982, workers received an average bonus of $2700.

Kodak's social and welfare programs are as extensive as any Japanese company's. There are recreational and entertainment facilities, leaves of absences, a subsidized stock purchase plan, company-sponsored ski, radio, and chess clubs, and more. The employees have available to them a 2,500 seat theater as well as a bowling alley.

In the Japanese fashion, Kodak offers night school programs to up-grade occupational skills and also promotes from within. It is obvious that Japanese style worker-management harmony and *wa* can be adopted in America. In the case of Kodak, the "Japanese" features described above were developed long before Japanese managerial styles were discovered by Americans.

3.9 Walk-Around Management

The closeness existing among workers in a Japanese company has developed a number of interesting administrative policies, one of which is the practice of walk-arounds. Walk-around is a technique used to decrease the feeling of separation which exists between manual and non-manual levels. It also illustrates the Japanese belief that all workers are part of a "family."

Walk-around management is, as the term implies, the practice of high-level officials walking among the workers and talking to them, usually while they are working. The superior talks informally with each worker in turn, asking about family and other personal matters, as well as about work. Walk-arounds are informal and little extended conversation goes on. This is not a time to lecture a machinist on quality control or to discuss why young people today are not like the young of a generation ago. Don't give a lecture about long hair style on men during a walk-around.

Valuable information does get exchanged in a short time, and an executive can use walk-arounds to gauge morale and work satisfaction. He can get a feel for whatever workers are concerned or worried about. Technical topics can also be discussed, though there are better techniques which encourage workers to suggest productivity improvements. Walk-arounds are better used for non-technical matters. Their utility operates on the emotional dimension rather than on the technical. Walk-arounds allow workers to know some higher-ups by sight. The hierarchy thereby becomes less mysterious to workers and makes the company more of a personal entity what workers can relate to.

Some Americans have used this practice, especially those who have developed their own companies and who enjoy the technical side of the enterprise. Henry Ford, until the later years of his life, kept in touch with his skilled craftsmen and knew many of them personally. He would pass by on his rounds and stop to talk, remembering personal facts about workers. An engineer himself, Henry Ford enjoyed mingling with workers. Before 1913, Ford's automobiles were essentially custom-made. Many parts were unique to each automobile and not yet mass-produced. This demanded skilled workers who could almost hand-craft a car. Henry Ford relied on James Couzens to handle the financial side of the company; Ford concentrated on the production side. Until the labor force reached a thousand or so, Ford knew most workers personally and talked to them on an almost daily basis.

Walk-arounds are still used today in America. John C. Teets of Greyhound spends at least one day a week talking to supervisors, clerks, and drivers. Robert W. Glavin of Motorola regularly spends a half day in a factory talking to workers in the halls, at the cafeteria, and in the laboratories. The examples above show that walk-arounds provide an added source of vital information for Americans.

Naoto Sasaki (1981:37) presents in his book *Management and Industrial Structure in Japan* the career plan of a bank employee destined to become chief of the Foreign Exchange Department. The time from first joining the bank and becoming chief is roughly thirteen years. But the first five years is spent as a cashier, bookkeeper, deposit operator, loan section clerk, and customer relations clerk. This job rotation ensures that he becomes familiar with a wide range of duties and employees. When he becomes chief clerk he will be able to talk with junior clerks and understand their problems from their own perspectives.

Walk-arounds are especially useful wherever skilled workers are at their machines. These operators get a chance to show off their skills before the boss and get a little praise. Some walk-arounds can be led by a foreman who can show off the best workers and give them some recognition. A walk-around in a small company allows a senior executive to learn personal details about some or even most workers. Successful executive have already developed a sharp memory for faces and personal details of those they meet; this skill can be used to get to know lower-level workers as well.

Walk-around management is used as an opportunity to evaluate morale and to receive complaints and suggestions from line workers. Walk-arounds can also be used to respond to already-made suggestions, praise exceptional workers, and the like. Apple Computer, Inc. is another American company whose managers practice walk-around management. This is made possible because its small size (less than 5,000 employees in 1981) in one major location makes personal contact easier than it would be in a larger, geographically dispersed company. Also, Apple is a relatively young company, and many employees have been with Apple since its beginning. Corporate small size and youth make informality easier to achieve and maintain.

Then too, many of Apple's employees and managers are highly educated engineers who are familiar with one another's work problems. Apple managers can better understand the technical and personal problems faced by subordinates as they carry out their rounds than at larger companies. Because of such morale-building practices as walk-arounds, Apple's employee turnover rate is around one percent, as compared to an overall turnover rate in California's Silicon Valley of five percent.

Walk-arounds are not the only reason for such Apple's high employee retention rate. Another reason for this loyalty is that many of the most senior (in employment) employees were given the options to buy Apple stock during its first public offering. The success of the stock has made at least forty employees paper-millionaires. These and other stockholder-employees are motivated to make Apple even more of a success. As in Japan, worker participation in profit sharing plans enhances group loyalty.

Japanese middle and higher level managers spend considerable time in walk-around activities to become highly visible to the line workers. This develops familiarity between management and worker and encourages a feeling of mutual involvement in a company's success. The company becomes more than an employer; it becomes family.

This sense of identity with a company on the part of the Japanese workers is illustrated by how an employee, when asked about his occupation, seldom answers that he is in a specific such as "I'm a lawyer," or "I'm a mechanic." His first response is to mention his company. Being part of the company at any level is more important than what a worker does. His identification is not to a profession or occupation. Nor would he first mention his division or department. He defines himself as belonging to the company as a whole. An American is more likely to declare speciality or division before announcing corporate employment by name.

Chapter 4
Japanese Leadership and Authority Systems

The emphasis on the importance of *wa* places the leader in an ambiguous position. He represents the group and is personally responsible for its actions. He must also lead in such a way that group harmony prevails. He gives orders, developes group consensus, and maintains high morale. These expectations force any Japanese leader to be very much concerned with the limits of power. As he leads, he must not become too different from the other members of the company, nor too authoritarian.

But he dares not let the group wander without direction. He must tread a very fine line between being too lax and too harsh. This balance is harder to maintain in a Japanese group than an American one because Japanese authority is less-well defined. It's hard to know exactly when a leader has ceded too much authority or gone beyond its acceptable limits. By contrast, American executive are better protected because there are more rules in an American company which define better the limits and scope of authority.

There is another complication to being a leader in a Japanese corporation. Whoever has the most official power is also older than most other employees because it is bad form to promote younger persons over those who are older. The rule of seniority demands leaders be older and respected because of their age.

But because of the responsibility to maintain *wa*, he dares not abuse his authority. He may have the organizational and personal (due to seniority) authority to impose his will on subordinates, but he must not use his full power. If he does so, the subordinates will cease to cooperate and the organization and his prestige will suffer. The leader has to be careful not to abuse the power he in theory has. In many ways, it's more difficult to be a leader in Japan than in the United States. Japanese leaders are forced to hide their own powers and work instead to gain their subordinates' acceptance. Japanese leaders are more manipulative and less dictatorial.

There is also the danger that subordinates will agree with a senior because he is older and holds a respected position. This does not encourage initiative and creativity, and leaders try hard to determine what another person's agreement really means. If someone doesn't care much about an issue and its consequences, it is usually easiest to agree and end the discussion. After all, a superior does have prestige and agreement pleases him, as it does anyone.

A Japanese leader must be very careful in not pushing for automatic agreement. This is most commonly done in Japan by not taking a position or indicating favoring one proposal or another. The subordinates are then freer to make up their own minds. Not knowing what the chief has decided, if he has, keeps subordinates from taking the easy way out when making a decision. It's hard to automatically agree when you don't know what the boss is thinking.

Japanese leaders do not always know why subordinates agree to a proposal. Even asking for serious criticisms doesn't usually work. The fact is that the Japanese avoid openly disagreeing with someone, especially a superior. Resistance to a direct order almost always take an indirect path in Japan, the most common is one form or another of passive disobedience. Subordinates carry out passive disobedience by being slow to follow instructions and asking many questions. It's easier for a Japanese to say "yes" and do nothing than to say "no."

It's the responsibility ot the leader to gradually and eventually discover if others really disapprove a plan he favors. If he orders that a certain course of action be taken, he might miss the messages that disagreement exists until it's too late. By then morale will have plummetted and the plan in question is almost certain to fail.

One solution to this dilemma of seeking agreement as well as disagreement is to give more responsibility to subordinates. Let them know if they agree to a plan that they will be responsible for its success. Japanese leaders give subordinates large amounts of independence and responsibility. Otherwise they will either develop into yes-men or be ineffective.

By contrast, American business leaders are less concerned with the social dimension of their power; their positions give them the authority to tell subordinates what to do and order them about. Because power in America is less personal, those with authority need not be so worried about what their subordinates think.

But power in Japan is more ambiguously defined and leaders receive power from other people as well as from the organization. These subordinates can always threaten to take away a leader's moral authority. This is called the legitimacy of power. In Japan, followers can always retract their personal loyalty to a leader. They will obey only when they want to or not at all. A Japanese leader can easily lose the respect of his own superiors if his workers decide he is no longer a worthy leader. This can be done by assistants hinting that a superior has destroyed a group's *wa*, and by subtly refusing to agree to his "suggestions". Or they delay following orders by saying the commands were too vague or one-sided. Since rules are fewer and vaguer than in America, it's easier for Japanese workers to ignore or "misunderstand" orders. Matters go smoothly in a Japanese office only when subordinates voluntarily accept direction.

The difference in how leaders in Japan and in the United States use authority and power is based on each country's different view on the source of a person's ability to tell others what to do. As I show in the next section, Americans believe that most power comes from the position a person has and from his ability to use the resources of the organization to reward or punish. The Japanese emphasize another dimension of power, one that is personal and emotional.

4.1 Leadership-by-Designation

Traditional American practice assumes that leadership is primarily a matter of position, or what is called leadership-by-designation. Leadership in this case is a matter of giving a person a position with the company's authority to give orders. The subordinates are told to obey a leader because they have been formally ordered to do so. In this context, the best leader is the one who is stern and is able to use his formal authority as much as possible. If things are not going as well as expected, the American reaction is typically that the leader needs more power. The Japanese reaction would be that more superior-subordinate agreement is needed.

This approach emphasizes that leadership is the prerogative of a person's official position in an organization and that followers are hired to obey the leader. The subordinate is seen here as a passive person whose option is either to obey the superior or mulishly refuse to obey and pay the penalty if caught.

The manager who believes this will be unpleasantly surprised because few workers are in reality so passive; nor do most workers see their major role as being one of obeying unquestioningly the one in charge. This is the authoritarian ideal: that an order given is an order obeyed. Many Americans emphasize this power dimension of their positions. This gives leaders a false feeling of power.

The leadership-by-designation philosophy is a common one in the United States. We place great store in the assumption that being in a leadership position gives the holder the power to issue orders and influence others. A common reaction in America to an administrative problem is to say, "We need a stronger man in that post. Give him more authority to act and he'll be able to straighten things out." If asked why a problem exists, the average American executive would respond, "The workers are at fault. They need to be told what to do." By "told" is meant "ordered." When things go wrong, the typical American reaction is to ask for more power to order subordinates.

Leadership-by-designation is the classic way of establishing a hierarchy and is based on the notion that someone has to be in charge or there would be chaos. But there are three reasons why leadership-by-designation is a very unstable type of leadership. Workers resent authoritarian demands. We do not enjoy feeling as if we do nothing but obey: forcing persons to act like automatons is the surest way to develop unhappy workers. Morale and work satisfaction suffer when authority becomes too strict.

Authoritarianism is successful only when the subordinate has no choice but to obey. Slaves, convicts, children, drafted military recruits, and other powerless persons can be forced to obey unquestioningly if the punishment is harsh enough. But they won't do their best; they will only do what they have to and probably manage to do a lot less. Even the persons above have ways of resisting authority, such as going AWOL, throwing a tantrum, or revolting in some way. At the very least, unhappy workers can always call in sick. Workers who dislike their jobs can always find an excuse to avoid going to work.[1] Even real illnesses are more common among workers who dislike their work. Ignoring those who pretend to be sick, the authenticated sickness rate is higher than normal among those who take no pleasure in their work.

The second weakness of leadership-by-designation is based on the fact that the world contains too many surprises; reality is too complicated for us to be able to predict all the decisions we need to make. Similarly, few jobs or projects are so simple that enough rules exist to take into account all that needs to be done. There will always be a grey area where a worker will need to use some initiative and self-direction. Otherwise the work would be automated and the human element taken out.

Any leader who insists on complete control will find himself inundated by unforeseen events and details. In fact, subordinates will enjoy asking their leader to solve the pettiest of problems. All they have to say is that they don't have the authority to make the decision; maybe something as petty – and time-consuming – as deciding who will park where in the company's parking lot. The red flag indicating a leader demands too much power is when a subordinate says, "I'm not being paid to think here. I just do what I'm told." Workers will not react to challenges or unexpected problems if they have been told that their job is only to obey. They will wait for orders while the corporate ship sinks.

---

[1] Kurt Lewin and Ronald Lippitt conducted a series of now-classic experiments during the late 1930s. One of their findings (1938) was that workers in authoritarian groups stopped work when the leader left the scene. One of the costs of authoritarian leadership is the need for increasingly more and more supervision and control. The cost of administration increases since more supervisors are needed.

Japanese managers search for ways to make workers adaptable and responsible. In high-tech and other "modern" industries where competition is intense, equipment can become obsolete very quickly. State-of-the-art machinery changes almost overnight. These machines demand high capital investments. How can both workers and machines be used most efficiently? One way machines can be most productive before obsolescence sets in is to operate them twenty-four hours a day, seven days a week. A Japanese technique recently adopted is the long night shift. Sankyo Seiki is the world's largest maker of music boxes, accounting for seventy-five percent of the market. The company established in 1982 night and day shifts which are eleven and a half hours long.

Workers on these shifts, a minority of Sankyo Seiki's force, work three days and take the next three days off. Pay on the long day-shift is twenty-five percent higher than wages on the normal day shift. Those who work on the eleven-hour night shift – they call themselves the "owl troops" – receive a wage forty-five percent higher than the base pay.

What is distinctive, however, is the "owl shift" workers supervise themselves. The work at Sankyo Seiki is highly automated. The work involves primarily inspection and quality checks (*The Japan Economic Journal*, August 7, 1984:7). Quality performance would fall during these eleven-hour shifts unless the workers were especially dedicated and willing to solve immediately whatever problems emerge. The eight workers of Sankyo Seiki's long nightshift cannot wait for the morning until a repair mechanic comes to correct a production hitch. The night shift solves its own problems.

The third weakness of the leadership-by-designation type of power is that employees judge leaders and one another in terms of what is known as "expert power." "Expert power" is based on being recognized as having knowledge or expertise in a given area. This type of leader has the reputation of being an expert.

An employee may be recognized as being an expert on lease contracts. If this person were to tell friends that a vice president's leasing plan was stupid and ill-advised, the plan would probably fail. People would expect its failure and the plan would fail merely because now no one has any faith in it, aside from its intrinsic weaknesses. The leader-by-designation doesn't have the reputation of being capable, and others are prepared to be critical of any expertise he might assume. Being designated as the boss doesn't include an instant reputation as an expert.

Positional leaders get into trouble because their authority is constantly challenged by "experts." If ignored, these experts will become jealous and resist any plan involving their areas of expertise. They are prone to complain behind a superior's back and resist cooperating. The best strategy to use when challenged by "experts" is to co-opt their talents. Let them have limited authority over their area of expertise. This flatters them and makes them your partners, as well as allows them to use their talents.

American leaders-by-designation usually find the above policy too threatening to their ego and authority. This sets the stage for intense power-struggles, even if they're muted by being kept behind the scene. Japanese leaders have little difficulty with subordinates who are also experts. The Japanese give them full responsibility and expect them to use their talents for the groups. Giving responsibility to others doesn't reduce your authority; you are being a good leader who knows how to maintain the group's *wa* by delegation.

A good leader constantly develops the web of mutual obligations through favors given and received that is common in Japan. An expert can be trusted to do his best because he personally owes management, company, and co-workers a number of debts. Taking responsibility and supporting the superior is the way an employee repays debts owed.

Leadership-by-designation develops too much centralization of power and authority and becomes increasingly inefficient. The natural response to this situation is to insist on more power and rules. The logic behind this situation is that if a little power is good, then more power is better. This leader doesn't have the respect of others and he rules through fear. The only advantage this leader has over subordinates is the authority given him by the organization.

Since power is useless unless used, this type of leader, call him an office holder, is on a treadmill having to issue more and more orders, make more and more decisions, and become increasingly dominant. The problem is that no one person can be so dominant and still be effective. There are many issues that should be better be solved by others.

Another problem with centralization of power is that subordinates are forced to become more and more passive: they are told to obey the rules and pass all unusual problems to the superior. They become reduced to paper shufflers. Their unwillingness to take the initiative results in more and more decisions being passed on. This increases the work overload of the superior. The superior ends up by doing everyone's job as well as his own. But then, he's asked for it.

4.2 Leadership-by-Influence

The second type of leadership is called leadership-by-influence. This type of leader is obeyed because others want to follow his lead rather than because they have to. They voluntarily accept his leadership. Subordinates and equals give this leader the right to give them orders.

Such a leader holds power over others because of personality more than official rules. This makes his authority much more flexible. He in fact may ask subordinates to work longer hours than called for in the rule book. But he will nevertheless be obeyed as long as he is accepted by the others. They will not mind ignoring the formal rules. For this reason, leaders-by-influence are more efficient during the times of crises, when rules no longer apply.

Rules being secondary, the leader-by-influence can ask followers to act without rules, that is, independently. He can say "Do whatever is necessary. Find a way to solve this problem." The followers are asked to use their own initiative. To put it another way, workers can make rules as they go along. Obviously this type of leadership can be very effective when solutions are unclear. This is the type of leadership associated with creative behavior.

A leader-by-influence may also emerge because of being liked as a result of personality. This person is liked because he establishes emotional rapport with others. Being liked is also the result of what is called favorable (or positive) interaction. Apart from an emotional rapport, we enjoy the result of having a relationship with someone, perhaps because the other person is sympathetic, does favors, or helps when there's a need. The Japanese, as expected, are masters at doing favors and at helping friends. These acts develop the web of mutual debts Japanese leaders try to establish.

A person becomes a leader-by-influence in another way – by being recognized as an expert. The Japanese encourage this type of leader. They are willing to use all talents someone may have. A subordinate who has a skill will be given as much responsibility as necessary to use it advantageously. He becomes a leader-by-designation in one area of expertise.

The formal leader relies on this specialist to work for the group and not for his own advancement. There is no real danger of direct competition. This expert – or leader-by-talent – can take on more responsibility because Japanese authority is vague. He will make his decisions in his area of expertise only after consulting with others and developing a consensus.

A minor but negative consequence of this power ambiguity is that it's hard for outsiders to know who is really in charge. A division chief is the formal head, but a specific project may be handled completely by an assistant. The division head will be unwilling to make a decision until he's talked to his expert.

Ideally, the leader-by-influence is also the leader-by-designation, though this seldom happens in Japan. If he is, he has a well-motivated group of workers and he has the company's authority to make things happen. Most readers have been in situations where the two types of authority were not held by the same person. In this event, there is conflict over who will be obeyd and work usually grinds to a standstill. As shown below, the Japanese have learned to use this potential conflict to their own advantage.

An example of this type of conflict is a wildcat strike. The leaders-by-designation such as managers and labor union representatives may not want a strike, and both sets of officials may even forbid it. But a leader-by-influence emerges and others follow and a strike follows in spite of the official leaders. A recent example of the type of leader who gained much personal influence for a time is Poland's Lech Walesa. He was able by the force of his personality to forge a labor union and lead a near-revolution in opposition to all formal sources of power.

Another person who "rules" by influence is the Pope of the Roman Catholic Church. He has little power except through personal influence. Carrie Nation was another with charisma. She was able to energize large numbers of prohibitionists even if destroying saloons meant going to jail. Joan of Arc would be another leader-by-influence who motivated followers when no officially designated leader could.

The leader-by-influence may have been democratically elected; he may have become accepted gradually and tacitly; or he may have been appointed from above. The characteristic of this type of leader that stands out is that authority is voluntarily given to him by the members of a group. In this case the leader's power travels from the bottom up rather than being imposed from the top down, as is the case for the leader-by-designation.

The Japanese believe that leadership-by-influence should be as widespread as possible. Leaders-by-influence are supported by the group and reflect the maintenance of *wa*. These worker-selected leaders offer others the feeling that they, too, have the power to influence their destiny, since it's a matter of personal quality rather than the job held. This encourages them to take the initiative whenever the work calls for it. The danger is that this type of follower can reject a formal leader. Japanese history has many examples of generals who switched sides during a crucial battle because they had rejected their leaders.

For the Japanese, the officially-designated leader must have the influence to lead as well as the formal authority to do so. That is why acceptance by others is the major criterion when someone is being considered for a position of authority. Aside from the question of technical skills, the major consideration is whether he will be accepted by members of the group. Often, sociability is preferred over technical skills.

Acceptance develops the leader-follower relationship into a partnership to which both parties must contribute. This partnership maintains the all-important *wa* of the group. This relationship also makes the Japanese hard-working and productive. Imagine how productive a work team can be when every member feels equally responsible for higher production. Workers follow orders, of course, but they are also willing (or eager) to make suggestions to the foreman how to speed up work. This is the Japanese advantage over Americans. More Japanese than American workers want their superiors to succeed.

Japanese executives are more likely to promote someone who is emotionally compatible with others than someone who is only technically capable. Given the choice, the Japanese prefer to advance an expert in public relations who gets along well with everyone over someone who does the work well but isn't well-liked. Technical know-how is likely to be sacrificed for popularity. The value of a manager is based on how many contacts he has developed over the years rather than on technical skills. Technical problems are solved at the lower levels by younger workers. Managers who have collected "debts" and have developed systems of mutual obligations and personal relationships are the most respected. Good leaders will get the most out of their technically-talented subordinates.

The Japanese want to work with people they like. That's one reason why Americans dealing with Japanese find that business negotiations take much more time than if only Americans were involved. The first stage in any negotiation has the purpose of developing a personal relationship. To Americans, negotiations begin by an exchange of contract conditions and other technical matters. To the Japanese, negotiations begin by developing personal ties so that each party can "respect" and accept each other.

The typical Japanese leader enjoys seniority through age over the members of his group. And he has also been given the official authority to lead by the subordinates. These conditions result in the curious – to Americans – fact that Japanese corporate leaders enjoy tremendous power and influence, though much of this source of power lies outside the formal authority system of the corporation.

The prerogatives of authority are vague because once given the authority, either officially or informally, the leader becomes the figurehead for the group. To disobey the group means that an individual is being selfish and individualistic, whether one is the leader or a follower. Once subordinates accept a person as a leader, they are obligated to obey. The leader in turn must take into account the feelings of other members. There is no hint of anarchy in Japanese work groups, though it might seem so to an outsider.

The loyalty workers give the informal leaders has negative as well as positive sides. On the positive side, workers feel obligated to work hard, to use their initiative, and to generally see that the work gets done well. They also follow the wishes of the leader without being forced to do so by rules and penalties. They work hard so the leader won't be embarrassed.

On the negative side, Japanese workers may feel obligated to obey completely those they accept as leaders. Leaders are so respected that no one would be so disloyal as to criticize or question an order. The result is too much conformity. There may be enthusiasm in working, but enthusiasm should not be confused with effectiveness and creativity. When there is a conflict between pleasing a respected superior and rejecting a faulty decision, the Japanese worker is likely to opt for doing whatever supports the group's *wa*. Efficiency takes second place to morale. How is this done?

Employees do so by trying to outguess their leaders to discover what they want done. Kenichi Ohmae (1982) points out that Japanese junior managers follow the strategy of *Jyoi-Katatsu*, a concept which means that the unstated will of the leader should be understood and followed by the junior members. Subordinates try to anticipate what the leader's preferences are and then present these preferences as their own. Obviously not many creative suggestions are presented when all parties are trying to conform to what they think (hope) the others will accept.

This second-guessing the boss is found in the United States, as was shown in an earlier quote from John De Lorean's GM experiences. Part of office politics involves trying to decide in advance what will be acceptable to a superior. Even when a leader genuinely wants new ideas, he may be offered only what others think he prefers.

An example of this tendency to second-guess superiors is for the subordinates to deliver only positive information. It is always preferable to avoid telling someone bad news. What is being done is that someone has decided that pleasing the boss is more important than efficiency and truth. The Japanese are more prone to follow this practice than Americans.

The practice of *Jyoi-Katatsu* gives senior officials more influence than they might seem to have on the surface. They lead without seeming to do so. In fact, Japanese leaders may merely hint that a certain policy is desirable for it to be accepted by others. To do otherwise might threaten the group's *wa*. Harmony comes first even if it might mean agreeing with the leader when there's little cause to do so.

What looks like initiative on the part of middle management may in effect be unrecognized delegation: subordinates know what the leader wants done without being told. Japanese leaders can influence policy even when they think they are being non-directive and democratic. The danger of this situation is obvious: a division head may believe he's encouraging lower-level initiative when in fact subordinates are successfully reading his mind.

There is a feedback cycle of influence in the Japanese authority system. Leaders must be accepted by their subordinates as well as obeyed by them. This makes both parties cautious in how each handles the power/influence available: the subordinate is expected to "know" what the leader wants done, and the leader must be able to convince others to use their initiative. Obviously everyone learns to compromise.

The result of these attempts to maintain the group's *wa* is that, while reaching a consensus is very important to all members, leaders can exert considerable influence on both general policy and specific activities. They are in charge while seemingly not to be in charge. This at times confuses even the Japanese. This is even more bewildering to foreigners dealing with the Japanese. The Japanese need to talk over every issue to make sure everyone agrees instead of conforms.

Another complication in understanding the Japanese use of corporate power is related to the periodic emergence of temporary (expert) leaders. Once a consensus has been reached on a certain matter, it's assumed that those who are the experts can be trusted to complete the task. Once agreement has been reached, all workers are supposed to feel enthusiastic about the project. The next step is for leaders to delegate the task and allow the workers to take complete charge.

There are a large number of projects being carried out in any Japanese office which are not being closely supervised. The subordinates take on the responsibility for the various projects and are more or less independent. The supervisor will keep track of the progress but will not interfere unless asked.

The older division or department head assumes younger temporary leaders will be too group-conscious to be individualistic and try to become stars. These leaders-by-influence can be trusted, in turn, to complete their projects. When a project is completed the temporary leader becomes a team member again while someone else becomes responsible for another project. Leadership in Japan is a matter of the group's needs and rotates on an informal basis according to talent. A subordinate becomes a temporary leader if he can help colleagues achieve the team's goals by taking the initiative.

The leader-by-designation is expected to defer to this temporary leader-by-influence. When the problem is solved, the leader-by-designation again takes charge. To outsiders he has always been in charge. This non-leader gains prestige by allowing the assistant the freedom to complete the task on his own. The work is done and *wa* has been maintained. That's the major task of a Japanese leader-by-designation.

It becomes hard at times for an outsider to determine who is the current working leader of the group, since actual leadership and task responsibility change according to talent and circumstances. But this flexibility allows younger workers to take the initiative when an older, less capable employee is nominally in charge. They also gain experience before they have the formal responsibility to carry out a task. Tasks are delegated and the official leader allows assistants to take charge according to talent.

4.3 Good Leadership in America

An example of how workers become totally involved in their work duties is found, surprisingly, in the United States. We must not forget that Americans are capable of a great amount of cooperative work effort. After all, the work ethic is still an important value in America, nor are most of us complete loners. The problem is that many managers have failed to encourage and reward cooperation and initiative.

Samuel Neaman was once chairman of the board of the McCrory Corporation, a conglomerate composed of department and variety stores (Barmash, 1976). Neaman took control when the McCrory Corporation was losing money. He soon turned the company around, and it became a major source of income for its parent holding-company, Rapid-American Corporation. Neaman's talent was the ability to infuse enthusiasm and pride in workers.

One of his first policies was having every McCrory district – roughly ten to fifteen stores – develop a model store. Each model store was to be a working example of a district manager's professional best no matter the cost. This was the chance for the manager and staff to show off their professional retailing skills and expertise. Good retailing ideas could then be tested "in the field" to determine if their costs could be scaled down or met by higher sales.

Neaman gave employees the freedom to use their experiences and insights. Workers were expected to contribute ideas and suggestions. Each proposal was discussed by everyone and changed if necessary. Neaman assumed that those on the scene and working with customers every day would have developed valuable knowledge. It was merely a matter of asking employees for opinions.

Neaman found that McCrory employees had never been asked for their suggestions, even though all had considerable experience in dealing with the public. If nothing else, they could evaluate store policy from a customer's point-of-view. Potentially useful ideas were put into practice in Neaman's model stores. Those which were profitable were copied by the other stores in the district. Having their ideas adopted became a great source of pride to the employees.

Some of the suggestions presented by Neaman's employees were simple; others involved remodeling, refurbishing, and the like. What was interesting is that the necessary remodeling in Neaman's showcase stores was done by the employees themselves in the evenings and weekends. Without being aware of it, the personnel were copying the Japanese long before it was fashionable to do so. On Sundays the store's restaurant provided free food and beer for the volunteers; the remodeling sessions became parties as the employees became enthusiastic about their work. The model store became a symbol of their talents. The fact that this remodeling could be done by the sales personnel themselves means that many of these improvements did not demand complicated equipment.

The suggestions also brought the employees closer together. They discussed each other's ideas and improved on them. Imagine the pride when your co-workers accepted your idea, added an improvement, and then made it a reality for all to see! If an idea was modified by others, more persons became proud of themselves and of each other.

Samuel Neaman received an extra benefit which would have been unexpected under the previous management. Ordinary clerks and sales persons became so involved in their district's model store that they volunteered suggestions for improvement. Before, no one had thought they had much else to offer but their labor. Suddenly, messages flowed from the lower administrative levels to the higher ones. Samuel Neaman had made line workers part of management.

When asked how he was able to achieve this high morale without drastic labor turnover, Sam Neaman answered by giving his philosophy of management (Barmash, 1976:54):

[Good management is] taking your people and encouraging them to do the best that they have. That's the maximum you have in your organization – the sum total of your best work in one place in a concentrated form and let them produce a finished product so that they can enjoy the fruits of their action.

Too many managers want their subordinates to obey rules without allowing them the freedom to do their best. By contrast, the Japanese have been able to develop a corporate structure which encourages workers to do their best.

With imagination and courage, Americans can, like the Japanese, motivate workers to increase their performance. American management has other Sam Neamans in its ranks, and I will later present a number of other examples. Many American workers have the potential to be better workers. But this potential can only be achieved by changing our managerial styles of those that challenge workers and give them more autonomy.

An example of managerial flexibility is found at Gulf Oil Corp. In 1982, Gulf initiated a "universal equipment" policy whereby workers were expected to ignore job classifications whenever necessary. Maintenance engineers were to help machinists if they had nothing else to do. This policy kept workers from sitting and doing nothing while waiting for their turn on a project. Painters could help carpenters until that phase was completed.

At Gulf, workers are promoted to the "skilled" category and given a pay raise when they can perform seven other jobs. This gives Gulf a more flexible and skilled labor force and keeps the degree of forced idleness low. This "universal equipment" policy encourages workers toward maximum skill development and to cooperate with others by transcending traditional work specialization. Every worker becomes an expert in a number of skills.

The Japanese have encouraged skill upgrading for decades through formal vocational training and updating. Central and local governments provide subsidies to smaller and medium size companies and offer loans if larger companies wish to establish their own training centers.

After post-school training, graduates take standardized exams which measure their skills against national standards. Those who reach a specific level are officially certified as "skilled workers" (*Ginoshi*). Most corporations give pay raises to those who become designated as "skilled workers" in any of seventy-four different trades.

Corporations often prefer establishing their own training centers for new and senior workers because, to the Japanese, occupational training involve more than the development of technical skills. Having their own training centers allows for greater control of what is taught. Training in Japan consist of technical and spiritual (*seishinteki*) elements. Corporations want their employees to develop a "fighting spirit" and a corporate loyalty and identity. But the same corporations are very willing to have more and more of their workers nationally recognized as "skilled workers."

4.4 Achievement and Authority in Japan

The Japanese are as achievement and work-oriented as Americans. But the Japanese are taught to work within a group, while Americans typically are not. A number of studies (De Vos, 1973; McClelland, 1967:200 and 226) have shown that Japanese and Japanese-American children are socialized by their families to value achievement as well as to need to be part of a group. The successful Japanese manager learns to emphasize his dependence on others, not to decrease it.

Pascale and Athos (1981a:12), who have studied how Japanese corporations are organized, note that the successful and respected Japanese manager is recognized by others as being cooperative. His effectiveness lies in being able to cooperate and in not feeling that he has to compete against others, including his equals. The loner in a Japanese group threatens the *wa* and is encouraged to be cooperative. The Japanese reliance on mutual dependency is reflected in the Japanese language, which has no word for "privacy".

Japanese authority is seldom absolute, and corporations can not establish detailed guideline on the rights and duties of employees. This would make leader-subordinate relations too inflexible, and the Japanese prefer authority to be more situational. Vague guidelines allow executives the luxury to compromise without losing face. When a senior official accepts a good idea from a subordinate, he does not have to admit that he has ceded power to the younger person. Instead, he is merely being a good leader by allowing his assistant the freedom to work toward benefiting the group or the company.

This sharing of authority involves a sharing of responsibility. A leader cedes authority to workers who in turn become responsible for the team's success or failure. This creates psychological tensions, because a lack of hard work means letting down the group. There is no individual failure in Japan! Failure is shared by family members or by members of a work group. These group pressures force members to be attentive to whatever needs to be done. A subtle leader can use this group pressure to encourage better individual performance.

Such leaders and workers have a power technique that channels group pressure to the individuals. This is the "silent suffering" treatment, used successfully by Japanese mothers. When a son or daughter doesn't act properly, the mother does not need to yell or shout. Instead, she will act solicitously as usual. But she will also sigh and suggest that her son's actions sadden her. If this doesn't work, she may become "ill" and take to her bed. What son wants to be responsible for his mother's illness?

The Japanese leader can also manipulate subordinates by adopting the "silent suffering" technique. He doesn't yell or shout at a worker whose quality performance is below standard. But he can call everyone together and mention how much the current low quality output saddens and shames him. He may apologize to the group because, after all, he is responsible for the crew's performance. He shows how hurt and concerned he is. This action should make the low quality worker feel ashamed even though the criticism was indirect.

The Limits of Japanese Authority

When the Japanese think of democracy, they do not mean that a majority of fifty-one percent is needed to decide policy. Democracy for the Japanese is a process through which total agreement – a consensus – is achieved. Those deciding an issue will consult with each other. They will compromise and adjust their differences. Group democracy in Japan is not having everyone vote and establishing a majority; it means being part of a consensus.

This creates a problem for the leader. He cannot force his policies on others or he'll be "undemocratic". He must convince others that agreeing with him is the correct choice. This limits his power over others and forces him to cultivate a personal relationship with his workers.

This limitation of leadership is a relative matter. The Japanese are group-oriented and would rather agree than disagree. And they also respect leaders. Those in leadership positions command respect, in part because they are older. Followers are predisposed to agree with a leader, especially if he obeys custom and consults and compromises.

Leaders are careful to develop personal ties with team members. They treat them on a personal level to weave over time a web of mutual debts and obligations. Good leaders perform favors for subordinates; workers then will "owe" debts to be repaid through hard work, quality performance, and so on. Good leaders know the limitations of the subordinates' influence as well as their own.

Another limitation to power in a Japanese context is the respect given to older persons and seniority. The two are almost synonymous, since promotion in Japanese corporations is based on age. The highest person in authority is also the oldest.

Age as a limitation to authority may seem as a contradiction, given the description above. But the (older) leader must prepare the next generation's leader. He must groom assistants for future leadership. A leader allows others to "borrow" his authority. If he does not he is being selfish. Though age gives him respect and authority, age also forces him to cede responsibility to younger managers. It is ironic that just as a Japanese achieves a top rank – such as chief executive officer – because of his age, he is expected to become less of a leader and more of a figurehead. He now become the morale leader rather than the task leader. Those who are younger are groomed to take on more responsibility.

Future leaders develop their own webs of relationships and mutual debts and favors. By giving assistants more initiative than is common in the United States. Such a practice necessarily reduces the authority and dynanism of the older leaders. They have to allow younger workers the scope to make many important decisions. That is why Japanese authority systems are so blurred. Many coporate employees take for themselves authority formally defined as belonging to older persons.

Based on the seniority principle, members of a group must work their way from the bottom up until seniority makes one the leader. If the leader has not prepared someone to follow in his footsteps, the others may reject the new leader as inadequate – even if he achieves highest seniority. Such groups will disband because the new leaders are not accepted by members.

The leader cannot use all of his power when he achieves seniority. He must cede some authority to future leaders. There are many possible future leaders in a corporation, and all must be prepared for one leadership position or another.

Forcing acquiescence – and corporate executives have the formal authority to tell subordinates what do do – would threaten group harmony. Senior executives would be more likely to spend time convincing someone to accept an idea rather than unilaterally telling plant workers they have to accept a policy. The minority should be convinced rather than coerced.

On the other hand, it is bad taste (too individualistic) to disagree with a superior: the search for *wa* is a two-way street.[2] The loyalty a worker has for his company is easily translated into the respect for its executives. Junior executives try to go along with their superiors. Refusing to join the majority is interpreted as selfish individualism and suggests that the person in question is not part of the group's *wa*.

Japanese subordinates spend much effort trying to discover a superior's position before they will commit themselves. If all parties refuse to state their own positions clearly in order not to seem to be too arrogant, time will be spend shadowboxing until everyone has a least "suggested" their preferences. Then the compromise process begins. From an American point of view, too much time is wasted during preliminary meetings. Americans feel that a simple statement of preference and a short "yes" or "no" by those in charge would simplify matters and waste less time in deliberation.

Deliberation is lengthy in Japan precisely because agreement among parties must be developed and maintained. Only then can *wa* continue. Once total consensus has been reached, however, the decision will be quickly and easily carried out. After being accepted by everyone, the new policy does not create resistance and conflict.

The ambiguity of authority faced by the Japanese has one advantage, though it would be dangerous to depend on it. Though authority has few concrete limits, subordinates themselves also do not know when an order has transcended the limits. A request may be illegitimate or not, and it may be hard at times to know how a request will be accepted. This very ambiguity allows superiors to ask more of their subordinates. Managers can ask employees to do whatever needs to be done. If the workers disagree they can always "negotiate" an order's legitimacy.

This ambiguity is a problem when Japanese employ non-Japanese, such as in Japanese foreign subsidiaries. Most foreign workers are used to strict job demarcations and clear limits on authority. Non-Japanese have to learn that Japanese managers see little utility in strict work divisions. Foreigners also

---

[2] Agreeing with someone and supporting his idea places the other in your debt as an exchange for your support. He owes you a favor you collect when you want him to support a proposal of your own.

have to learn that Japanese are willing to discuss their orders (Trevor, 1983). A worker who thinks an order is illegitimate or has gone beyond acceptable limits can always demand (politely) an accounting. Since it's to a supervisor's advantage to get orders obeyed that may not be legitimate, Japanese workers stay alert for such transgressions. The checks and balances between superior and subordinate are vague in Japan; they need to be continuously negotiated and discussed.

4.5 *Wa* and Career Security

The search for *wa* has other advantages for subordinates. Leaders are responsible for the actions of their subordinates. In classic days, a failure on the part of one's samurai might mean the lord would be expected to commit suicide as an apology to his own lord. Today's foremen are similarly personally responsible for the actions of their line workers, though no one expects them to commit suicide if a production quota is not met. On the other hand, production goals are seen as personal goals. A foreman would feel personally at fault when his crew fails to reach the highest standards. He would personally apologize to crew and superiors for his failure. This responsibility keeps a foreman from angering his subordinates. If he demands too much, they might slow their work and make him into a failure. *Wa* forces a balance on the demands people place on each other.

All relations in Japan are personal. There are few ways you can blame "the system." That was why some foot soldiers as well as officers committed suicide during the last months of the Pacific War: they felt they had to atone personally for the war's loss.

The same principle applies to modern Japanese executives. They must encourage the best efforts from their subordinates or else lose face. Leaders make the work environment as supportive as possible.

On their part, subordinates are responsible for the quality of their work. They even feel free to innovate. They assume the boss will protect them if they make mistakes. He also gains credit when his subordinates become successful, and they will share in the glory and rewards as a team.

Ambiguities of Japanese Leadership

The power Japanese managers enjoy can be effectively exercised only when the subordinates give superiors the legitimacy to give orders and to direct behavior. Forcing one's authority disturbs the group's *wa*. There is always the potential – no matter how remote – that subordinates may refuse to obey. This can be accomplished by being absent from meetings, "forgetting" to forward needed information, or refusing to agree without openly disagreeing.

When the Emperor of Japan wishes to reject a decree which displeases him, he will repeatedly move the unwanted bill to the bottom of the pile of bills which he, by law, must sign. The Prime Minister can legally force the Emperor to sign a specific bill and make it official, but that would bring to the surface mutual conflict. To avoid this the Prime Minister removes the unwanted bill and reconsiders its contents.

In the same way, samurai followers would disappear from a battle rather than support a disliked feudal lord or tell him that he was in the wrong. It is bad form (and ultimately futile) to force one's authority on unwilling subordinates. Modern Japanese executives hesitate to give orders which might not be what the subordinates want to do. Before giving an order, Japanese managers, through consultations, make certain that subordinates will accept the commands they wish to make. This is why superiors consult extensively with subordinates before making a decision or before issuing an order.

Another example of the Japanese ambiguity of authority is in the practice of giving the emperor full respect but no power. During the Shogunate, effective power was wielded by the shogun rather than the Emperor. All government action was done in the name of the Emperor, but he was unable to initiate and carry out policy. Like the modern British monarchs, the Emperor reigned but did not rule.

Such ambiguities in American organizations would be defined as power vacuums and demand additional rules and regulations. To an American, the Japanese corporation seems like a formless debating society in which no one is in charge and nothing seems to happen until somehow the long-awaited consensus emerges as if by magic. To Japanese, the American corporation gives the impression of being a rules-ridden machine whose members are forced to be competitive and where success is based on being able to skillfully ignore the rules to one's advantage; the American corporation is defined by the Japanese as mechanical and executives as hypocritical and competitive.

Japanese leadership is seldom absolute because the Japanese view time as a series of cycles. Having authority is also part of nature's cycles. Just as spring follows winter, older leaders will eventually cede to the younger generation. Junior executives should prepare themselves patiently until it is their turn to be senior executives. Promotion by seniority is an example of cycles in life: everyone has a turn.

Being part of a cycle, a Japanese accepts his destiny. This person prepares for his future even though there exist events outside his control; at the appropriate time he must be ready for his turn at whatever fortune offers, irrespective of whether the future holds bad or good fortune. There is a sense of balance in one's own life, and the individual prepares for fortune's inevitable changes. This does not mean fatalistic acceptance of whatever the future brings. The Japanese are very achievement oriented and work hard in order to achieve a certain goal. No one can describe the Japanese as passive. They are highly goal-oriented and driven to achieve their ambitions through group consensus.

Instead, fatalism to the Japanese means being able to accept a situation after he has done his best. The future does not unfold automatically and you have the responsibilities to work to change ongoing events. Japanese fatalism is stoic: you accept the results of your efforts even when unforeseen events interfere.

No matter how tradition-bound the Japanese are, acceptance of the world is a matter of choice. This makes the Japanese very adaptable: they can reject those parts of the status quo which no longer offer any advantages. Japanese fatalism is not a passive acceptance of events. You struggle until either you are overwhelmed by the odds and by bad luck or until you are successful. You accept those events outside your control and try to change the rest. This philosophy encourages the Japanese to adopt selected foreign ideas and practices when profitable. The sense of fatalism is related to their belief that events occur in cycles. No situation is permanent because everything changes. Some things can be influenced by personal effort and others not.

This explains why leadership positions are seen as temporary and why senior executives do not permanently "own" their positions. Leaders will have to vacate their positions of power someday. This sense of cycles obligates Japanese corporate leaders to encourage their subordinates to upgrade their skills prior to their possible promotion. The senior executive only temporarily occupies the leadership position. Eventually, he too will have to step down and allow another to hold the post. The holder of power who does not prepare his successor is being selfish and individualistic. This view also explains why Japanese workers can afford to be so patient; time will reward patience and hard work. By contrast, Americans are less patient; they want short-term, immediate rewards.

The Japanese enjoy a long-range view partly because they recognize that they are part of a very long heritage. Their awareness of the past complements their view of the future. An example of how the Japanese relate themselves to the past and the future is found in the history of Mitsui and Company, one of the largest and the oldest of Japan's trading companies, called *zaibatsu*. These trading companies are a major reason for Japan's successful import-export policies. The founder of Mitsui was born in 1622. The company was officially incorporated in its present form in 1876. Depending on your viewpoint, Mitsui is either over one or three hundred years old.

The official corporate biography of Mitsui (Mitsui and Co., Ltd., 1977:12) emphasizes with pride how Mitsui was able to survive changes in government, earthquakes, a world war, industrialization, and much else. The senior management is also alert to changes in economic trends and the stifling effects of age. As the company's biography states, "It is not uncommon for a business enterprise to lose its vitality after two hundred years, and to fail to respond to changing circumstances". As a response to this philosophy, Mitsui plans decades ahead.

Such long-term interests are guided by past loyalties. During the 1970's, Mitsui officials were faced with having two zinc smelters, one of which was four times more productive. One proposed solution was to close the less efficient smelter. Then-president of Mitsui Mining and Smelting, Shimpii Omoto, rejected this alternative, stating that (Roberts, 1973:497-8):

Their [employees'] grandfathers and fathers have been working for the same mill, and we must respect such personal relationships. It is a social reality that labor cannot be considered just as an element of cost, or a commodity. It is our fate to expand facilities to support the labor force, and thus the productivity of Japan has grown enormously ... We cannot reduce the labor force, so we [must] increase per capita producitivity.

Japanese leaders do not see themselves as "owning" seats of power since power is a shared condition and eventually slips from one's fingers. American leaders believe that, having "won" power, it is theirs until taken away. This sets up a competitive system in which power is the trophy rather than the culmination of hard work, dedication, and especially patience. The Japanese view of the need for leaders to share their power with their fellow workers is illustrated by Soichiro Honda's advice to senior executives (Schnapp, 1982):

It is wrong for executives to act like feudal lords and not know what is going on below them. What is most important in the process of democratization is for the upper people to come down. And that is where the sense of equality is found.

4.6 Avoiding Direct Confrontation

Richard T. Pascale (1983) notes that Japanese managers use ambiguity to maintain *wa*. Using ambiguity allows a superior to avoid making direct criticism while hinting to a subordinate that he is unhappy with a proposal or action. Pascale explains that when a superior says he wishes to: ". . . reflect a bit further on your proposal," he really means, "You're dead wrong and you'd better come up with a better idea." This ambiguity communicates disagreement while it protects the subordinate's pride.

Pascale (1983:513) also presents two concepts useful in this context. The term *omote* (in front) means public display and behavior. This is behavior which is aimed at making everyone happy. It consists of agreements, praise, and public support. *Omote* behavior takes place in front of an audience. In such a situation, a leader does not want to publically criticize someone. This makes both of them look bad and embarrasses third parties. Superiors will criticize subordinates and yell at them, but this will be done in private. Public behavior (*omote*) maintains a pretence of group harmony. The opposite of *omote* is *ura* (behind the scenes). This refers to private talks, informal discussions, and tentative agreements.

Omote and *ura* behaviors allow for experimentation and give-and-take. It is easier to achieve accommodation when affairs are discussed in private and no one is publically embarassed. This makes the Japanese corporate structure flexible. Behind-the-scenes (*ura*) activities are going on which test for possible changes in policy. But no one will admit these discussions – or actions – until everyone agrees they should be done.

Omote behavior is not hypocritical. It's rather that *omote* behavior avoids the shock of change and public censure. There will be no announcement of any major change in policy in a Japanese corporation until everyone is convinced that change was necessary. The *omote-ura* distinction, and there are other similar dichotomies in this book, makes the Japanese cautious. Public announcements may be reflections of consensus. But they also may be political statements that have no substance. A good leader makes sure subordinates know when *omote* behaviors are to be taken at face value or not.

4.7 Foreign Machines and Japanese Spirit

The Japanese are more than patient; they are also very adaptable. The fact that Japan became a major world power – by first winning a war against Russia – within sixty years of being "opened" to western influence is proof of adaptability.

Modern technology, to the Japanese, is culturally neutral – machines are tools anyone can use. But their use must not disturb a company's *wa*. The Japanese view is that any technology is appropriate as long as its adoption does not destroy human relations. That is why the Japanese adopt western technology so easily. Technology is a means to greater ends: company profit, national survival, and public service.

In the same way, automation and more efficient machines are welcomed in Japanese factories. The Japanese are also willing to invest more per worker when these machines result in higher work satisfaction and production. This is one reason why Ford requires twice as much labor hours to assemble a car as a comparable Japanese competitor (Davidson, 1984:19).

The Japanese are very concerned about the use of ever-newer machines to decrease labor costs and increase productivity per worker. That is one reason why industrial facilities in Japan have an average age of roughly ten years, half the age of the same equipment in the United States. To be more specific, over two-thirds (69%) of metal working machinery in the United States was ten years old or older in 1970. The corresponding figure for Japan was thirty-nine percent.

One reason for Japan's high growth in productivity in the last few decades is due to the Japanese willingness to invest in newer, more productive machinery.

Advantages of the Japanese Leadership Style

The Japanese leadership style offers a challenge to American businesses. Aside from the mutual penetration of each other's national markets, Japanese and American companies compete for third-world country markets. These third-world countries offer a test of which managerial style can best cope with foreign cultures. Whether or not Americans and Japanese can export their leadership and authority styles will determine each nation's relative success in capturing international markets. How well each country does in foreign countries is a major challenge and a measure of future economic survival.

Whether American and Japanese authority systems can be exported can be tested by comparing the relative successes of American and Japanese multinational corporations in countries with developed and less developed economies. Such a study has been made by Anant B. Negandhi and B.R. Baliga (1979 and 1981).

These two researchers found that Japanese managers operating multinational corporations (MNCs) follow the same service, wa-oriented philosophies stressed in Japan. Japanese MNCs in America and in other countries follow policies of worker-management equality, concern for the total worker, and of giving workers as much responsibility as possible.

Expatriate Japanese managers also showed greater concern in being accepted by local communities. Not surprisingly, Negandhi and Baliga (1981) found that American MNC's executives experienced more conflict with their host countries and citizens. Americans also exhibited a short-time perspective and a superior attitude which angered the local nationals. This arrogant view is reflected in the following quote by an American managing director:

We came because they need us. We can help them. This little country (Malaysia) and her little people need help, but they must be reasonable, otherwise we will get out of here.

The typical – and more cooperative – Japanese attitude is:

We came here as guests, and our nation is small and needs natural resources, as well as foreign trade and investment to survive.

The above quotes (Negandhi and Baliga 1981:77) illustrate why American MNC directors felt they were experiencing more conflict with local nationals than did their Japanese counterparts. Americans reported almost twice as many perceived conflicts with nationals than did the Japanese. These conflicts were also twice as likely to be defined as high in intensity. American MNCs were also found to have three times as many breakdowns of relationships than did Japanese MNCs (Negandhi and Baliga, 1981:101 and 197).

I add one economic note to support my position that American managerial styles encourage more conflict and inefficiencies than management in the Japanese manner. Americans want to dominate foreign partners and dislike feeling as if national locals control the destiny of American MNCs. U.S. firms do not enter into joint ventures as readily as do the Japanese. Roughly two-thirds of U.S. foreign subsidiaries are wholly-owned in contrast to one-fourth of Japan's subsidiaries.

Moreover, sixty percent of Japanese foreign subsidiaries are joint ventures with foreign majority investment. Only nine percent of U.S. MNCs operate foreign subsidiaries with less than fifty percent ownership (Tsurumi, 1984:244). Japanese MNCs are more willing to accept a minority interest when they invest overseas than Americans.

This might be caused by the fact that American MNCs are larger and wealthier. They certainly can afford to invest larger amounts in their foreign ventures. Yet there is also a cultural reason. MNCs from the United Kingdom and France are also more likely to accept more minority control in their foreign investments than do Americans.

The answer to this Japanese-American difference lies in the fact that contemporary Japanese corporate philosophy emphasizes harmony and cooperation at all levels rather than American-style conflict. This includes foreign partners and business associates. Moreover, Japanese MNCs, with their greater involvement with local nationals, experience fewer conflicts. Japanese leadership style, with its emphasis on cooperation, is adaptable to foreign cultures.

All Japanese managers "say" they are in partnership with workers. This could be paying lip service to the Japanese cultural emphasis on cooperation without a corresponding action. But there is more to this than rationalization and lip service. The cooperative nature of the management-worker relationship can be measured in objective terms.

First, profit margins are very low in Japan. Most American executives would be replaced if they achieved Japanese-level profits. The average return on investment among Japanese manufacturing (except in petroleum products) companies was four percent during 1980. In commerce and trade, the profit ratio was 2,7% (Shiina 1984:45). American companies in Japan enjoy profit-to-sale ratios twice as large or more as domestic Japanese companies.

Second, wage differentials between executives and corporate workers are much smaller than in the United States. Pay differences are less. Workers receive bonuses that reflect corporate profit: in a profitable year, workers receive larger semiannual bonuses. Excess profits do not go predominantly to stockholders or executives. The question of wage differentials will be discussed in a later chapter.

How do Japanese companies profit from their investments if not by a high profit-to-investment ratio? The Japanese strategy is to increase investment returns through market growth rather than high profit margins. High profits are seen by the Japanese as selfish and noncooperative. Instead, the guiding philosophy, as stated Sanae Inagaki, former president of IBM Japan, Ltd., is (Shiina, 1984:45), "Achieve business growth by making the pie larger."

4.8 *Amae:* Emotional Dependence on Others

There is a Japanese term with no English equivalent which illustrates the importance of group acceptance. This term, *amae*, denotes the psychological condition of dependence on other persons' kindness and goodwill. The term is used to describe a child's attitude and expectation toward his/her parents as well as the relationship between two adults of unequal prestige, such as worker and his employer or superior (Doi, 1974). It also describes the dependence of the adult to the group as a whole.

The usage of this concept indicates the subordinate position of an individual vis a vis an authority figure, in this case the group's leader, or the group itself. But *amae* is not a one-sided emotional dependency. While a working adult is a child in relation to the leader of the group, he also expects an emotionally close and supportive environment. Leadership must be flexible enough to adjust to the specific needs of each individual. In this situation no leader can be too authoritarian or else he will violate the *amae* state. As important, *amae* places a debt on the one being "loved," since this warm relationship must be repaid. Sanaharu Oh, one of Japan's greatest baseball players (over eight hundred home runs) had his mentor in mind when he described *amae* as (Oh and Falkner, 1984:174):

Amae is ... affection, softheartedness, tender feeling. Without it, life is false and hollow, and yet it must be struggled with so that you are able to move. *Amae* warms your heart. It also enables you to work twice as hard to overcome all those siren songs of laziness.

Rules and regulations are necessary in American organizations: they insure a uniformity of treatment while everyone in the same position is treated equally. The Japanese authority structure is made expressly vague so that leaders can take into account the complete individual. As an example, corporate pay is partly based on whether you're married or not, and how many children you have. It seems natural to the Japanese that a bachelor should receive less pay than a married man. The latter has more responsibilities.

From an American point of view, *amae* results in a policy of "maternalism," where the employer is concerned for the worker's emotional as well as economic needs. This is partly true. Most authors describing Japanese corporate philosophy define it as "paternalistic." The term "maternal" better describes the employer-employee relationship in Japanese corporations, if by this is meant a concern for emotional satisfaction. Essentially, the Japanese want to be accepted, even "loved" by others. What might seem to smothering for an American is comforting and protective to a Japanese.

Amae can develop to a harmful extreme, as can any emotion. An abnormal manifestation of *amae* results in a personality which is too dependent on others and has a corresponding lack of independence and self-volition. The danger of too much *amae* is that someone grows to expect too much from group members and leaders. This results in timidity and dependency in adult workers.

This overdependence is found between the oldest son and his mother. In America, children – especially males – are encouraged to break their dependency on parents by developing their own identities and life goals. Americans encourage children to test the limits of their parents' authority. This is why parents view their teenage children as being difficult. We encourage them to challenge our authority for their own good. The Japanese do not encourage the development of personal independence. One Japanese cultural idea is the male child who remains loyal and obedient to his parents throughout life. Such ties may be stronger than the husband-wife relationship.

The Japanese mother's dominance over her son is especially strong when she is distant from her husband. She reacts to loneliness by investing all of her emotional closeness upon a son who will in all likelihood inherit the family's leadership. He will be expected, as the next family's leader, to support his mother after death of the father/husband. The wife, finding her husband authoritative and emotionally cold, emotionally smothers her young son and makes him overly-dependent. He may later have difficulty acting independently of others as he seeks to continue the warm mother-child *amae* relationship in his work. The company becomes his "family". This is made easier because to the average middle class male worker, the company has to be his first loyalty.

Amae does more than bind a member to group and superior. *Amae* also binds the leader to the group. The superior also seeks acceptance and emotional support from others. Superiors depend on their subordinates for approval and the reverse. This mutual dependency forces the Japanese superior to consider the feelings of the subordinates. They have the power to withdraw their emotional support from their leader and make him feel alone and isolated (Monroe and Sakakibara, 1977:6).

Superiors seldom dare use all their official power to impose their authority. They can convince, persuade, and encourage subordinates to accept a certain plan, but they do not decide on a policy by unilateral fiat. Independent action would anger subordinates and threaten the group's *wa* if the leader no longer provides *amae* support. They would obey because they have to, and they would go through the motions of following whatever orders have been imposed. Whether the instructions would be followed correctly is another matter. By contrast, Americans do not expect as much emotional support from others, especially from superiors. The American manager would typically say, "I may be a bastard, but I'm the SOB in charge and you'll do what I say!" The result is lower morale and an underground type of resistance avoided at all costs in Japan. The Japanese see American business relations as "cold."

Faced with an authoritarian leader (and this happens), a Japanese would act "colder" and more formal. He would subtly indicate that he's obeying orders unwillingly and gradually withdraw emotional support and friendliness. The boss has then lost the *amae* of his subordinates: he has been rejected and he's now unloved and alone. Most Japanese executives feel very uncomfortable with this situation. In order to avoid this sense of isolation, anyone having authority over others in a Japanese company works to gain "love" and emotional support. The end purpose is getting workers to want to follow your lead rather than having to impose your legitimate authority.

A too well-developed sense of *amae* results in feeling so insecure and helpless that a person needs a superior or group offering continuous direction and leadership (Hsu, 1974:102). If he finds himself alone he becomes insecure and focuses his anger at authority figures. This reaction develops because "they" have deserted him. While many Japanese are willing to work hard to gain acceptance, they hesitate to innovate or be creative. Innovation means criticizing past procedures and doing something others (the group) have not done. Creativity demands individualism, and many Japanese would rather conform to the group than be different. Being different might result in a loss of *amae*.

Because of the need to maintain *amae* relationships, the Japanese demand much more group support than Americans. While the Japanese have recognized the dangers of such extreme dependency, most would accept the belief that *amae*, if balanced, encourages group consensus and discourages a destructive and competitive individuality. The Japanese would say Americans lack *amae* because they are too competitive and individualistic.

The Corporation as Family and Village

The modern Japanese corporation has replaced the rural village and even the family as the major bonds linking the individual to the general society. Before modernization, all Japanese lived in very restricted social worlds offering a secure place for everyone. Even beggars and thieves in classic times had their own brotherhoods with their own leaders and loyalty oaths, making them part of a larger "family." No one in traditional Japan could be called totally free from group ties except for a few outcasts, and these were very few. All Japanese were members of tightly-knit communities which expected *gimu* – duty – to other members. Now that most Japanese work away from the ancestral farms and live in impersonal urban neighborhoods, employers become the source of social anchorage.

Amae is now obtained through a person's employment. This is why Japanese workers become so attached to their corporations: they are substitutions for the lost closeness and support experienced during their childhood. Many Japanese see nothing unusual in working from nine in the morning to eight or later in the evening, six days a week. They offer their total loyalty to their jobs; they receive *amae* in return for their total devotion.

Younger Japanese never experienced this close support from village or large family. Japan is now highly urban and families are more scattered. Many younger workers wish to become free of what they consider to be old-fashioned ties. They are beginning to question the expectation that one's work is the most compelling part of one's life. Western ideas, urban living, and economic success are forcing the Japanese to become more independent from village, family, and now employer. The demand for *amae* is disappearing among the younger Japanese. They increasingly wish to be free of its smothering effects. This will make the average worker relatively more independent of his employer. But there will still be a high degree of employee-employer cooperation in the near future. The corporate *amae* will disappear only very gradually.

The problem faced by those younger Japanese who want more independence from corporate employers is that these corporations do smother employees with attention and favors. Japanese corporations offer as many benefits as possible to employees, so that changing jobs results in material disadvantages as well as feelings of guilt.

These "favors," Americans at times call them organizational "love tokens," encourage employee loyalty for two reasons. These "gifts" are pleasant to have and not found elsewhere. A worker would hesitate to lose receiving them. And these "gifts" entail debts owed the company. The typical Japanese feels guilty if he couldn't repay the debts he owed to someone, even an employer. Suppose an employer helped find you a wife, helped pay for your wedding, and the foreman became your child's godfather? These are all debts hard to repay. They can only be repaid by being a good worker. Any other action, especially leaving for other employment, would be regarded by all parties as disloyal as well as unfair behavior.

How do corporate employers develop this sense of debt in their employees? The answer is that they will go to any lengths. Take a young man just hired after graduating from a university. He can't afford decent housing near his workplace. But the company maintains dormatories nearby for married and single employees. The rent is low because it's subsidized by the corporation. The apartments are small and plain, but they are bargains as well as convenient. In addition, these apartments are used by co-workers. This provides a new employee with instant friends. Otherwise, a young couple would be surrounded by strangers and be residentially isolated. Because housing forms a major part of a young couple's budget, subsidized company housing allows the couple to enjoy consumer goods years before others can do so. Instead of paying more for less comfortable housing, a Toyota employee in his late twenties can afford skiing vacations and a car (Swartz, 1983).

Male employees are expected to wear dark suits, coveralls, or some type of official uniform. To ease any financial strain these rules might entail, companies maintain stores where such supplies are sold at discounts. Young corporate employees can afford cars, vacations, and other expensive goods because much of their living and consumer expenses are either subsidized or completely paid for by employers.

Corporations also own larger apartments for married employees who are saving for a down payment on a future home. When an employee does buy a home, the company will help the buyer get a mortgage with a lower-than-average interest rate.

The list of "favors" corporations offer employees is much longer than indicated above. The lesson is that workers and employers are entangled in a complex web of mutually exchanged debts and favors. The relationship works to the advantage to both parties, as well as supporting the traditional *amae* relations enjoyed and looked for in Japan. This mutual dependency pattern is one of the foundations for Japan's economic success.

Amae in America

The *amae* or family feeling which I have described is not as foreign to Americans as it might seem. A large number of American corporations encourage the American equivalent of *amae*. Texasgulf, Inc. is a company where the family atmosphere has been deliberately encouraged (Gibson, 1981).

At Texasgulf, all employees are salaried. This makes benefits more uniform and reduces the class distinctions which usually divide wage and salaried workers. One benefit all Texasgulf employees enjoy at certain plant locations is free lunches. This encourages a shorter lunch hour, because employees do not spend time looking for a restaurant away from their work place, but this is a minor consideration. More important is that a common cafeteria reduces rank differences among employees. There is also the hope that free lunch creates a sense of obligation in workers and encourage loyalty to the company.

Texasgulf has initiated other programs to encourage a sense of togetherness among employees. The company offers college scholarships to employee's children to indicate the interest Texasgulf has in the employee's family. The company also encourages second-generation employment. One message the company stresses is that all employees are working for and building a company their children would be proud to work for when grown. By contrast, how many Americans in general would actually encourage their children to work in the same place as their fathers or mothers? For most blue collar workers, the figure would be a definitely low percentage.

Texasgulf also gives employees shares of the company's stock at various points of tenure, and a permanent employment policy exists in which few workers are dismissed. These two practices encourage a sense of proprietary interest in the company at a relatively low cost while encouraging worker loyalty. These policies encourage the feeling that the employees and Texasgulf have common, long-range objectives.

The Japanese have a saying "to eat from the same pot," meaning all workers – irrespective of their position – gain or suffer in common from a company's successes or losses. Everyone eats well or starves at the same time. American executives who convince workers that they do not have interests opposed to their company's will enjoy some of the advantages Japanese have over American companies.

Donnelly Mirrors, Inc. is another American company which has developed "Japanese" characteristics. Workers are divided into teams. Members decide on their team's goals and are given near-complete autonomy to achieve these goals. Below is how Donnelly Mirrors' president introduces the company to new employees:

We expect a great deal from you as an employee. For example, we expect you to take responsibility for your work, to help identify and solve problems, to set your own goals, and to help create and maintain a climate where the importance of people is recognized and supported. We also expect you to share in the ownership of the problems facing the business, be committed to high goals, and to work to build supportive and cooperative working relationships between individuals and teams . . .
As an employee at Donnelly you are a member of a work team. All of our work is coordinated and accomplished through these teams. Your work team provides an opportunity for jointly establishing goals and then uniting your energies and talents to accomplish your team goals in a highly effective and efficient manner.

Donnelly Mirrors has established a bonus plan with an average of ten percent of base pay, a liberal medical plan, and a democratic authority structure. Employees, for example, are allowed to come to work late if their work is done by team mates. There are no time clocks to punch at Donnelly. In case of death of a close relative, Donnelly employees are given up to three days of time off with pay.

More important, leaders are "invisible" at Donnelly in that workers, through their teams, are expected to solve their own production problems and improve their productivity. Below is the way the Donnelly Mirrors, Inc. (1983:2) describes how new workers are expected to fit into close, semi-autonomous work teams:

. . . You are not being hired to do just one job, even though you will be assigned a primary job and classification. Rather, you are joining a group of workers, called a work team, who share the responsibility for a part of the company's work.

. . . You are responsible to your team members to help them reach the excellent goals they have set for themselves.

You will help determine the goals of your work team. You will help set, plus meet these goals . . . You will help solve problems of production and scheduling, engineering, and quality . . .

It is obvious from the above quotes that Donnelly Mirrors expects workers to become "leaders-by-influence" and independent. While each work through a team and with an immediate supervisor, Donnelly workers are supposed to be enthusiastic and cooperative. Soichiro Honda would feel comfortable at Donnelly Mirrors.

Other American corporations, too, have hearts, though not to the extent of Japanese companies.[3] Rosabeth Ross Kanter, in her book *Men and Women of the Corporation* (1977), recounts the humane actions of the senior personnel in Indsco, the company she studies. In one instance, a manager had died while on

---

[3] Robert Levering, et al. (1984) have published short descriptions of the companies most pleasant to work for, from a perspective of employees in their work *The 100 Best Companies to Work for in America*. Most of the companies listed have very strong *amae* policies.

a business trip. The president attended the funeral while a vice-president personally made certain the widow received whatever insurance she was entitled to as quickly as possible. A third executive had flown to the site of the death to handle all funeral and transportation details.

Every American organization has a number of "charity" cases: less-than-capable employees who are kept on instead of ruthlessly being fired. A worker may be an alcoholic or someone not able to adjust to technological changes quickly enough. He may be working below expectations because he's going through a divorce or an extended illness. These problem workers are kept on because those in charge offer each a second chance even though a second chance is not a contractual agreement. Pity the poor person who works for a company which has recognized no slack or extenuating circumstances! How much company loyalty will workers develop when a friend is fired because she missed work to stay home when her child was ill?

Rules in Japanese companies, when they exist, are more flexibly imposed. If all members of a company depend on each other for mutual support (*amae*), no leader dares to be too dictatorial; he will need his subordinates' unlimited loyalty in the future.

Americans, by contrast, feel their individualism would be threatened if they "give in" too much to the demands of others. That's why we like well-defined rules and regulations. They tell us exactly what we should do and not do. For the Japanese, being dependent on others or a company means that they can be counted on during an emergency. Naturally, this turns into a debt which will be repaid in the future. The help-debt-repayment-help cycle is part of life's changes. The Japanese worker sees nothing wrong in seeing himself as dependent – without strictly-defined limits – upon his employer. Debts owed will be repaid eventually, through unpaid overtime, company loyalty, higher productivity, and so on.

This is not to say that American managers do not recognize their dependency on others. But Americans view this dependence as unmanly and threatening. We hold the value of individualism in the same mold of John Wayne-the-hero: a real man is independent of everyone else. He dares not depend on anyone else; their weaknesses might destroy him. The Japanese define dependency on others as a natural state and not as temporary misfortune. Dependency is mutual. If you owe a debt, the chances are that the other person owes you something in return.

The American Management Association sponsored a survey to discover what were felt to be the major criteria for advancement on the part of a sample of American executives. Half (52%) believed promotion was based on arbitrary and subjective standards rather than objective ones. A majority (82%) answered that "pleasing the boss" was most important for advancement (Fisher,

1977:72-3). This survey shows that Americans, like the Japanese, believe that being accepted by superiors is the major way of advancement. The Japanese recognize this fact and use it for the advantage of the company.

This view that subjective standards are used for promotion is officially ignored in America although it's probably an accurate image of reality. Pretending that everyone follows the official rules creates ambiguity because no one is certain how to act. This separation between official and actual policy forces employees to see every official statement as being a lie. They believe personal feelings guide the behavior of superiors while official policy says no. This ambiguity causes conflict because it's impossible trust others when standards are unclear. The result is that workers decide they can rely only on themselves and that everyone else is a dangerous rival.

American companies are arenas for far too much conflict and worker-to-worker antagonism. The task for American businessmen is to reduce these conflicts when they result in inefficiency and when they impede economic success, as conflict usually does. Too many workers – including executives – would rather indulge in personal recriminations and run roughshod over others than to make peace and eventual profits through compromise. There is also the importance Americans place on being in control. Those in power at times allow a personal need for power and dominance to hinder progress. Managers need to be reminded than an *amae* relation is not a sign of personal weakness. *Amae* is one way workers can be motivated to work together for the common good.

Amae at Data General

There are many accounts of how high consensus and cooperation resulted in economic successes in American businesses. Unfortunately, these are acclaimed because of their rarity, while instances of successful worker-management cooperation in Japan are assumed to be normal events. One such example of American near-perfect participative management and worker cooperation is the experience of Data General Corporation in developing its Eclipse MC/1800 computer. Tracy Kidder (1981) has recounted what must seem to Americans to be the heroic efforts taken to build a new generation computer as quickly as possible.

The mastermind of Data General's success was J. Thomas West. West selected a team of young engineers by asking them, "Are you prepared to sell your soul to the machine for as long as it takes to get the job done?" He was asking, in essence, for unlimited loyalty and willingness to work at any task no matter how long it might take. He wanted no clock watchers! Those who answered "Yes" were accepted as members of the team. After being hired, Eagle's (the proposed computer's code name) thirty-member team worked up to eighty-hour weeks with no overtime pay for eighteen months. During this time all obligations – such as family or outside personal interests – were sacrificed to work demands. Not all members were prepared to work so hard or be so dedicated, and a few dropped out.

West's managerial policy was to establish general work goals to be achieved by a number of autonomous teams. These teams were then allowed near-complete freedom to select the means of achieving these goals. Team members were expected to develop their own ways of working and the strategies needed to achieve their goals. One team was given the task to produce simulation programs of the computer's functions. This simulation tested the model on a theoretical basis to see if, in fact, the plans were feasible. Such a project generally takes eighteen months or more to complete, but the Eagle team finished the simulation in a stunning six months. One reason such progress became possible was that the personnel felt guilty when they worked "only" sixty hours per week.

It may be surprising to many readers that the completion of the Eclipse MC/1800 took place in America with the involvement of American workers. This account of total company loyalty is expected of the Japanese.[4] But such motivation and morale are not as impossible in America as it might seem, though the above example is an extreme one. Few Americans would accept such long work weeks, though the Japanese come close in the matter of company loyalty. But many Americans are capable of such dedication.

The lessons are clear. Non-engineers will improve productivity if they are motivated to support the goals of their employers. Motivation and involvement can take place if management gives the workers the freedom to make decisions and become involved. This can be achieved only when they feel that they are part of a larger consensus. Full participation emerges voluntarily – not through force or bribes – although workers have to feel as if their extra efforts are worth doing.

The non-contractual, vague relationship which exists between a Japanese worker and his corporation is seen in the employee's creed which Matsushita employees recite every morning:

Progress and development can be realized only through the combined efforts and cooperation of each member of our Company. Each of us, therefore, shall keep this constantly in mind as we devote ourselves to the continuous improvement of our Company.

---

[4] Most Japanese today would unwilling to work as hard as did the Eagle's team members unless there was a great sense of crisis.

Amae Means Never Saying No

The emphasis on *wa* and *amae* creates a number of problems when Americans deal with the Japanese. One problem is the Japanese reluctance to state disagreement for fear of hurting the other party's feelings – thus violating the *amae* relationship. The second problem faced by Americans doing business in Japan is that *wa* demands a large amount of time for deliberation before action can begin.

Masaaki Imai (1975 and 1981), founder of a consulting firm for foreign companies wanting to sell in Japan, was only half-joking when he noted there are sixteen ways to avoid saying "no" too directly in Japanese. The actual number is much greater.

Japanese officials are usually too polite to chance hurting the feelings of others. Being too blunt causes disappointment and resentment and destroys a developing *wa* relationship. It is better to be ambiguous and let the other person break off negotiations in a gentle manner. A direct "no" may be taken as insulting, or as acting in too individualistic a manner. "No" is noncooperative behavior. It certainly does not encourage an *amae* relationship. Few Japanese are willing to say "no" to someone.

One common equivalence to "no" is to say, "This is a very difficult request. There are many problems with meeting your conditions." To an American this answer means that an agreement is feasible in principle; there only remain agreements on delivery schedules, prices, quantities, and other details that need to be negotiated. To a Japanese manager, this response is a gentle hint that the deal is off. In other words, even "maybe" can mean "no" in Japan (Imai, 1975:76).

This reluctance to being too blunt is common among the Japanese themselves, and often even they are unclear as to what an answer really means. No one wants to disturb the group's *wa* to such a degree that he is willing to say "this idea is so stupid, I'll never be able to agree". A worker may hesitate to tell a foreman that a request for overtime is unwelcome and that he would rather go gome early for once and relax in front of his TV set. The need a Japanese feels for the group's acceptance and support (*amae*) makes him avoid direct personal conflicts as much as possible.

A good leader knows how to exploit *amae* without going too far. A foreman can ask for overtime work and then later host the workers to supper as a way of showing appreciation. He must be sensitive to when a subordinate's "yes" is really a "hell, not again!" Ignoring unspoken dissent eventually destroys both the shift's *wa* and the supervisor's career.

At the very least, a good supervisor in Japan develops personal relationships with workers. He should know a considerable amount about their private lives and be very sympathetic as well as solicitous when they experience problems. While *amae* means caring, being sympathetic is not enough. The supervisor in question is also expected to solve these problems. This may mean spending time listening to long tales of woe and giving advice. There will also come a time when the supervisor will be expected to do something concrete to solve a personal problem. Unless the company gives him the freedom to grant special favors, he will fail to live up to his responsibility to support the *amae* relation.

The existence of rigidly followed rules interferes with the responsibilities of *amae*. Superiors must be ready to meet unanticipated demands caused by the problems of the workers. Here again is a reason why authority is ambiguous in Japan. No one can predict what workers will demand of you. Unusual favors have to be repaid in unusual ways, and these tie a worker all the closer to the company.

The Japanese insistence on maintaining *wa* and *amae* results in time-consuming negotiations. Few if any corporate decisions in Japan are unilateral. Decisions are hammered out through a process of achieving group consensus rather than through one person's taking the initiative to make an individual judgment.

Americans believe that negotiating with Japanese takes too long since most of the time is spent on seemingly irrelevant consultation. Every decision in a Japanese company necessarily involves a large number of parties. *Wa* and *amae* demand group-level agreement and a proposal must be discussed by everyone. A consensus will eventually emerge and a decision made which will be supported by all. The process through which this is achieved will be discussed in a later chapter.

Some of this time is taken up by personnel trying to discover what their colleagues really think of a project. Not doing so threatens *wa*. A manager doesn't want to state an objection to a proposal and then learn that everyone else is in favor. Then he may lose the group's *amae* support. Reaching a decision takes a long time, even for the Japanese themselves. Once a decision is made, the achieved consensus will make completion of a given proposal a simple, non-stressful matter.

Large amounts of negotiations are necessary for another reason. Every Japanese wants to be "liked" by the others in a group. Not to be "liked" means being rejected from a warm *amae* relationship. Being too independent and competitive result in the others' rejection. Any threat to the group's *wa* must be met, even if this threat is the leader or colleagues.

The Japanese term for the dangers colleagues pose is "*yokoyari*," meaning interruption (literally, "side spearing"). Each member of the group must make certain everyone else is happy and satisfied before they become a threat to one's emotional security (*amae*). Cooperation among leaders and co-workers is a necessity to Japanese.

The stomach represents the inner self among the Japanese. It is the center of the emotional self. To say that someone "has a clean stomach" means that he is honest and trustworthy. The opposite ("he's got a black stomach") means he is sneaky and treacherous (Masatsugu, 1982:52).

Someone who is being logical ("using his head") and rational may be hiding his true thoughts. The term "*haragei*" ("belly talk") means a conversation which is honest ("from the stomach") and emotionally true. *Haragei* also means intuitive communication. Understanding someone on the "belly" (*hara*) level demands a knowledge of a person's foibles and character. The art of *haragei* is knowing the other person so well that a message is understood even when the opposite is being said. *Haragei* is another reason why the Japanese prefer to establish personal relationships. Only those who know each other well can communicate on the *haragei* level. Otherwise you may not know when the truth is being said expressed.

4.9 The Invisible Leader in Japan and America

The ideal Japanese leader is someone who seems to be less active than the subordinates. He should give the impression that his assistants are continuously taking the initiative. His role is to maintain *wa* through group morale and consensus.

Leaders have another major function, one that can easily be ignored. Corporate CEO's in Japan have the responsibility to guide company policy in a general direction for the long term. They decide what the company will be like in twenty, thirty, or even one hundred years. Senior executives are not supposed to concern themselves with day-to-day minutiae though many cannot resist doing so. Administrative detail is the responsibility of those in the lower ranks.

A corporate president might decide, after consultation, that his steel company needs to get involved with plastics. He might also decide that the company should develop an expertise in plastic manufacturing by establishing joint ventures with American and British firms. Middle level managers will then begin to search out specific foreign partners. How they do so, and who they end up with will develop over time. But the general policy has been set in motion by the top level senior statesman.

From this point of view, senior executives see themselves as elder statesmen or philosophers involved in long-term planning. They establish the general guidelines and goals and allow others to develop the detailed means of achieving these goals. Lower-level managers in Japan are also less intrusive in their subordinates' work than in the United States.

Japanese workers dislike a leadership vacuum. There must be direction. But leadership direction should be in the direction of harmony (*wa*). There cannot be *wa* if the workers do not know what they are expected to do. Before a policy is made official, however, workers expect to be consulted on future policy and changes in policy. Workers need to be reassured that leaders support an action or policy. There is no "do your thing" in a Japanese workplace even for the owner or chief executive. The leader becomes invisible when he is certain that subordinates support him and agree to follow an agreed-upon plan of action (Rohlen, 1975:193).

The Japanese leader is never absent when subordinates need emotional support and work-related direction. He is expected to be easily available when encouragement and even criticism are needed. The leader has seniority as well as experience. He is the only one a subordinate should go to when a matter needs interdepartmental negotiation or the approval of a superior who occupies a higher organizational office. The leader is quietly omnipresent because he has developed a web of mutual debts through favors, advice, and help given to assistants. He must be an active, very supportive, leader, but never dictatorial or arbitrary.

Nor is the leader invisible after hours. Superiors are expected to socialize after work with subordinates. After visiting a few bars, a supervisor may be as happily drunk as his assistants. Late downtown Tokyo is full of colleagues and work teams weaving arm-in-arm down Tokyo's alleys searching for one more bar before the last commuter train leaves for the suburbs.

Leaders will always be visible when a worker needs a personal service. If a worker has a problem which the company will not alleviate, then the supervisor, especially of white collar workers, will most likely help even if he must pay the costs himself.

An interesting comparison of how leaders are more "invisible" in Japan is found in corporate anthems. Below are selected portions from verses from the IBM and Matsushita Electric anthems.

IBM Anthem

We're bound for the top never to fall!
Right here and now we thankfully
Pledge sincerest loyalty
To the corporation that's the best of all!
Our leaders we revere, and while we're here
Let's sing, men! Sing, Men!

Matsushita Anthem

For the building of a new Japan
Let's put our strength and mind together
Doing our best to promote production,
Sending out Goods to the people of the World
Endlessly and continuously,
Like water gushing from a fountain.

Yoshi Tsurumi (1976:231) has noted that the IBM anthem stresses reverence for the leaders of IBM. The verse suggests personal loyalty to the leaders as well as IBM. The Matsushita anthem, in contrast stresses patriotism, consensus, and group harmony. There is no mention of the founder or senior executives. The anthem stresses service to customers. The IBM anthem's first line accepts the notion of competition in order to reach "the top." Matsushita's theme deals more with group effort. Other Japanese company songs and mottos stress that workers are the most important element of the company, and that corporate success can only come about when harmony prevails.

IBM is one of the most Japanese-type corporation in America. This is due in part because during the 1950's, when the Japanese were looking at American corporate practices to copy, they selected IBM because of its high level of success (Drucker, 1983). Yet even IBM, in a totally opposite spirit from the Japanese, developed a personality cult around the Watsons. Below is another IBM song. Note its near-idolatry:

Our voices swell in admiration;
Of T.J. Watson proudly sing;
He'll ever be our inspiration;
To him our voices loudly ring.

Saying that a leader should be "invisible" at times does not mean total non-involvement. Managers are supportive rather than authoritarian. This managerial principle forms the foundation of Japanese managerial philosophy.

Americans have also found this principle to be valid. A source of support for this principle is found in an article published in the *Harvard Business Review* during 1967. This article, written by H. Edward Wrapp (1984), was recently re-published as an "*HBR* classic." The article could have easily been written by a Japanese corporate chief executive instead of a professor and associate dean at the University of Chicago's Graduate School of Business.

Dr. Wrapp lists a number of principles followed by successful executives. Among them are:
*Keep well informed
*Make few decisions
*Limit the number of objectives you're personally involved with

*Work through key personnel
*Provide the company with a sense of direction
*Do not make policy
*Be flexible
*Have few rules

These principles are completely Japanese even though they were developed before Americans became conscious of modern Japanese managerial styles. H. Edward Wrapp's article is proof that sound managerial principles are available to Americans. The fact that many of these principles are "Made in America" should encourage us to explore our own managerial repertoire as well as Japan's.

The first two principles listed above are especially Japanese in character, yet Wrapp recommends them highly. He emphasizes that subordinates should be trained to locate and solve problems themselves. In the Japanese fashion, Wrapp believes in a bottom-to-top decision flow, whereby subordinates say, "Here is a problem; here's how to solve it."

Top managers don't have the time or expertise to make every decision that needs to be made. It is better for a manager to spend more time listening to others and collect information and less time giving orders and making decisions. When the balance is reversed, the manager makes too many decisions based on too little information. He becomes isolated and threatens the company's *wa*.

Chapter 5
The Individual and the Work Group in Japan

5.1 Introduction

Consensus depends on maintaining group harmony. Members of a group must be willing to cooperate. They must also want the respect of others as well, or else disharmony will develop. Having common goals is never enough for group harmony. There will always be issues when honest disagreements are possible. Two persons can both want a group's actions to succeed, and still strongly disagree on how a common goal should be achieved. In the same way, parents can disagree on how to discipline and raise their children, though they both want them to succeed.

Along with a sense of common destiny, there must also be pressure for the members of a group to cooperate. This pressure forces co-workers to discuss their differences and reach a common decision, usually through compromise and exchanges of favors. Workers need to feel that compromising will be repaid in future exchanges. When Japanese executives meet to discuss a controversial topic, they assume that past favors will be remembered, and that now is the time to repay. Those who gained favors in the past will want to cooperate in turn and continue the favorable relationship. Group pressure is effective when the members of a group want to please one another either because of personal friendships, past debts, or because they want the relationship to continue.

In the same way, members of a military unit fight best when no one "wants to let my buddies down." Soldiers seldom think of their patriotic duties at the front. They will be courageous and self-sacrificing when there is high group morale. Soldiers are seldom effective in battle unless they feel loyal to a group. Otherwise each will be thinking only of his own safety.

The same principle applies in civilian life: the attitudes of workers toward each other are as important as how each feels about the group's goal. There are always individual goals (wealth, prestige, promotion, security, etc.), but no team will function well unless each member wants the respect and success of the others.

Imagine a Japanese team gathered to consider a proposal. If they cannot arrive at a common solution, the members face three alternatives. The leader can insist that a common decision be reached as soon as possible, and a discussion now begins with each member presenting his solutions and the reasons for them. As each succeeding person has a turn, the others gradually see where compromise might be possible and a give-and-take session begins. Hopefully, members will alter their positions so that one solution emerges that pleases everyone, or at least one that no member totally dislikes. This round-robin series of presentations is a common practice when Japanese who don't know each other well must decide on an issue.

The second available option when consensus cannot be achieved is for the leader to end the meeting and adjourn. He will then talk to the members singly or in small groups in informal settings, such as a bar, and privately continue the discussion. He may hint that agreement can be reached if certain compromises are made by one or another party. He may then make a personal plea for an agreement, or else suggest subtly that a few persons are resisting consensus and that he is worried about the group's *wa*. When enough individuals change positions and develop an agreement through this gentle arm-twisting, another meeting can be called and the consensus made official.

The third alternative is that there may be a few stubborn holdouts at this point. This is not likely in Japan, since minority members usually change their views just to avoid seeming to be individualistic. If there are some members who nevertheless strongly object to a specific solution, then the proposal is likely to be dropped and rejected. A decision may be delayed until everyone realizes a consensus cannot be reached, and the plan is filed and forgotten until changing conditions make agreement more likely.

The leader, no matter the outcome, is respected because he has not used the power he has to reach an agreement. He has been willing to compromise. He becomes known as a good team member and receives the trust of subordinates when he does so. The next time there is disagreement, many members will agree just to show their gratitude and respect for this leader. They will reason that, if such a good leader favors a specific option, then it's probably the best and one that does maintain *wa*. The disadvantage to this is that disagreement may be so muted that bad ideas are accepted merely because resistance displeases the others.

The Japanese leader, like any successful manager anywhere in the world, has favorite projects or ideas he wants accepted. He uses his influence to "encourage" a certain outcome, although he dares not become too forceful and impose his will too strongly. He would rather consult and convince subordinates. Should he force his views on subordinates too often, the others will gradually reduce their cooperation, begin to complain to others, and generally indicate their displeasure.

Japanese subordinates have a number of alternatives when a supervisor or district chief continuously insists that his own pet policies must be adopted. The subordinates can merely clench their teeth and accept the boss's ideas. The disadvantage with this strategy is that it's assumed by others that administrative decisions are made by the group. Those who dislike a policy will be given partial credit (or blame) irrespective of their original positions. In the Japanese company, a decision or plan is not linked solely to its originator. Once made official, a decision is identified with the group. This reinforces the sense of group unity so important to the Japanese. Those who disagreed and did not speak out must now live with the supposedly group decision. It is easier in the long run to tell others when disagreements happen and then hammer out a compromise.

Because of this stress on group unity, subordinates will somehow find ways to indicate disagreement with their superiors. The first signs of disagreement may be very subtle: someone stares out the window or looks embarrassed when questioned about a proposal. The superior has the responsibility to then gently discover whether or not there is any disagreement. He must encourage the others to present their criticisms. If he is persistent he will eventually find out how subordinates really feel.

A leader who is too enthusiastic about a proposal may not recognize the cues of disagreement his subordinates are giving; if he doesn't actively seek disagreement or at least presents his plan in a neutral manner, the chances are that everyone is too group-oriented to offer criticism. A bad plan gets accepted while morale suffers because the others feel that they had no choice but to agree.

If subordinates continue to feel that their leader is too dictatorial and that poor policies are being pushed, they can always ask for a transfer. Too many transfer requests are red flags that the group's *wa* is weak. A supervisor who receives more than the average number of transfer requests will be seen as a poor leader by his own superior. The threat of transfer is effective in a Japanese company. In the traditional Japanese culture, the ultimate threat to leave a group was to threaten or to commit suicide. This is no longer considered necessary, although modern Japan history contains a number of instances where suicides were committed as acts of protests.

There are other ways subordinates can influence their superior's actions, but again, those who are unhappy have to be very circumspect when showing their disagreement. Because the supervisor is older and holds higher rank, a subordinated can't be too direct in showing displeasure with administrative actions. Doing so is to be disrespectful and too individualistic.

A common strategy available to make disagreement known is the use of a third party to transmit honest feelings. In this way criticism is made indirectly without anyone losing face. Mediation works this way: an employee visits a friend with the same age and seniority and voices his complaints. The friend in turns tells his own superior. The latter is obligated to either investigate the rumor or pass on the complaints.

Someone who wants to complain can always personally seek out one of his boss's superiors or equals, someone who graduated from the same university or who shares a common tie with him, such as membership in the same club or interest in the same hobby. It's easy to informally suggest you're unhappy with your boss during a game of *go* (the Japanese equivalent of chess), after a fencing match or golf round. Meeting outside the office makes the setting less formal and it's easier there to complain without seeming to be someone who threatens a department's *wa*.

In these situations, the subordinate hints that he is unhappy. Or he might present a hypothetical situation without clearly stating who's involved, though it's no secret. In any case, a "bad" leader soon finds that his colleagues and superiors are concerned about rumors that his division lacks *wa*. There is nothing so threatening as when a fellow alumnus and division head says to you, "I don't believe this, of course, but I hear that some of your assistants feel you're not listening to them enough." This will be enough to make him very worried about his reputation as a leader.

There is another way to make a complaint known. Office heads frequently invite their workers to parties and bars to spend an evening drinking. The Japanese believe that no one should be held responsible for what is said or done under the influence of too much alcohol. After a few beers, a junior member can carry on a private conversation with the head and suggest obliquely that something is wrong. On the surface, this message can be ignored or laughed away, since the setting is informal and no one has to take seriously what is said in a bar. A good Japanese manager will listen carefully to whatever is said. Also, a little alcohol can make a person talk more openly than he ordinarily would. Bar talk is an important source of information in a society which insists on politeness and circumspection.

The importance of what is said during a party or an evening of bar hopping should not be underestimated by an American doing business in Japan. The Japanese see bar talk as an extension of what is said in more formal settings. Much can be said in an informal setting that can not be passed on officially.

Americans should listen carefully to what is said to them in informal settings. There are instances of the Japanese continuing negotiations by presenting a list of points which had been discussed during last night's party. To say one thing between toasts at a bar and the opposite the next day at the negotiation table cause the Japanese to distrust the speaker.

5.2 Group Consensus Encourages Trust

The emphasis on group consensus gives freedom of action to subordinates. The leader can trust them to work for the good of the group rather than for their own individual profit. In Japan, where it is assumed that all members of a group are working for the good of all, a senior manager allows his assistants substantial initiative. He trusts them not to attack his policies or undermine his authority. Any new idea a junior member presents is discussed and accepted by all members before it will be put into action. Once an idea has been accepted, the originator has the freedom to carry out the plan as he sees fit. This encouragement of trust allows younger members of a group to use their expertise. They will not be held back by their more conservative elders even though seniority in Japan is so important.

The pressures to conform to the group and to remain anonymous keep an assistant from becoming too independent or from becoming a "star". This protects both co-workers and superiors. No one fears that giving complete freedom to a worker who takes responsibility will result in shaming others or in loss of control. A young manager working on a project will keep others informed, and will continuously ask others for input, though he may not expect much. When he finishes the project, he will "give" the project to the group and offer them partial credit. This gives the person a reputation for being both a good worker and a good team member. And now the others owe him a favor that he expects to collect in the future. This may result in him being the only one recommended for an especially exciting position. In this case, his friends would refuse to be considered for this post, though they may have wanted it for themselves. Past debts can now be repaid by helping the friend receive what he wants. He now owes his friends a favor, of course! The cycle continues.

The Japanese superior does not fear bright and more knowledgeable subordinates. To Americans, capable assistants are potential threats (Pascale and Athos, 1981a:156), since they may be able to take your job away. Middle-level American managers face a dilemma: capable assistants make the division or office more productive; but these same assistants can threaten your job security as well as your pride since good assistants can make you look bad. Further, the sharing of power with subordinates may be seen by others as a sign of weakness. After all, a successful subordinate might be given his superior's job if the latter is seen as not being able to dominate and control assistants. This type of conflict is unlikely in Japan and would be considered as unethical behavior.

There are times when university faculty members feel threatened when interviewing a superior applicant because this person makes others look bad. Many professors would rather hire someone who is mediocre and less threatening. The result is that mediocre universities, their administrators, and their faculties stay mediocre. The same principle operates in the corporate community, or in any large bureaucracy for that matter.

The Japanese executive, by contrast, gains when he cedes authority and independence to his assistants because their success is also his. Those equal in rank do not fear superior colleagues since efforts are group efforts and all members are rewarded. It would be un-Japanese for one person in a team to claim more credit than others. The superior colleague is envied less in Japan and is rewarded more when he's a useful worker as well as a good team member. He has successfully maintained the group's *wa* as well as helped everyone. Someone who is successful outside of the group's influence is defined as selfish.

In the same vein, the superior is praised when subordinates do well. It's to his advantage to encourage assistants as much as possible. The better they perform, the higher his prestige. The successes of his assistants give him prestige. The conflict between supervisor and subordinate is transformed by the concern for *wa* in a mutually-rewarding partnership.

The leader acts as if he's in charge in order to maintain his pride, and he receives partial credit for whatever subordinates do. The fact is, however, the typical Japanese leader does very little that is practical and detailed. This does not mean he's riding on the coat tails of his assistants. He's busy maintaining *wa* and seeking consensus when necessary. Workers are given the freedom to work on their own projects or to develop new ideas because the results of these actions are "given" to the leader and the team.

This view of workers as partners forces corporate authority to be ill-defined. Though Japanese culture in general is bounded by rituals and strictly defined modes of behavior, corporate authority is very fluid and even ambiguous. A result of this flexibility is that younger, less senior assistants make business decisions which in America would be decided by senior members. Even when junior members use a polite subordinate-to-superior form of address when discussing a business problem with superiors, they are actually making suggestions and using their initiative with the assurance that they have the authority to do so.

Always polite and humble, junior workers nevertheless can put pressure on superiors to adopt the plans they favor. But then, they are expected to do so. *Amae* means that the leader expects to receive as much support from the group as the other members. In a way, the group as a whole is in charge: everyone shares authority and responsibility. All share in the glory when the group succeeds.

This ambiguity of formal authority allows Japanese workers the flexibility to quickly change their work behavior because there are few rules and regulations to get in their way. When Americans discover a profitable procedure, they make a rule to make it formal. A rule gives the secure feeling that this procedure will be correctly carried out in the future.

But conditions in the real world change faster than rules, and a worker can find himself expected to follow procedures that are no longer effective. The problem is that situations change faster than regulations. Rules can quickly become handicaps when they were once useful guides. When this happens, rules set up to facilitate work become nightmares of red tape. In Japan, members of a group can quickly decide that a certain rule has become counterproductive. This rule is now ignored and a more efficient procedure agreed upon.

The problem faced by both American and Japanese workers is that the presence of rules in a cooperative venture, such as a company, can lead to inefficiency. Although necessary, regulations tend to be followed even when they become ineffective. A rule is a statement of how someone should act in a specific situation. This statement was made official because it was understood to be efficient and productive. Procedural rules allow for cooperation and planning. They guide behavior.

Rules are followed when those who obey them are rewarded, and organizations set up reward systems which reward those who obey. The dilemma is that workers lose sight of the fact that the rules are only the means to a goal – higher quality or meeting production schedules. But what happens when rules no longer guide productive behavior? There is usually a lag between the time when a rule becomes a hindrance and when it's recognized that it should be changed. This rule has now become a ritual. People conform to it because of tradition and because they are rewarded for doing so. Following the rules become more and more important than getting the job done. Anyone who has dealt with a government bureaucracy (or any large organization) remembers the feeling that there was movement but little progress.

The Japanese are usually – thought not always – able to avoid this type of bureaucratic rigidity. Members of a group can change the rules – or ignore them – if it's recognized that they endanger the group. This makes the Japanese flexible when change is needed. The Japanese work together to help the group rather themselves. Rules are easily changed if it's understood that new rules will help the group's *wa*. Americans rely on rules too much instead of each other, making large corporations rules-ridden and conservative.

This decreased reliance on rules does not allow the Japanese to act in any way they wish. That would be too individualistic. When a company's rules are ignored, a worker does so because his work group will support the new procedure. The final decision to innovate rests with the group rather than the individual. This group dependency is a brake on too much innovation, and many cause as much conservatism and inefficiency as too many rules. But the possibility of change is there. When (and if) the group decides change is needed, then change is rapid.

The flexibility that Japanese companies exhibit takes unexpected twists. Nippon Gakki is a leading manufacturer of musical instruments. In 1965, Nippon Gakki received a shipment of fine wood to be used to make pianos (Woronoff, 1982b). The wood was found to be of inferior quality and could not be used for pianos. The problem was what to do with this expensive supply of unwanted wood.

The decision was to use this one shipment to make a limited supply of furniture. The wood had been paid for and workers with the skills to build pianos could also construct furniture. This batch of furniture was a success, and the company decided to continue making furniture. Workers in the music instrument division were being made redundant by more efficient machinery and needed to be transferred elsewhere. This furniture venture was so successful that Nippon Gakki managers decided to expand their furniture-making facilities. Eventually a separate furniture division was developed and remains an important part of Nippon Gakki today.

This example of corporate flexibility on the part of Nippon Gakki was not an accidental event. The company had been established in 1897 by Torakusu Yamaha as a manufacturer of musical instruments, primarily high-quality organs and pianos (Woronoff, 1982b). When the Japanese society went on a war footing soon after the First World War, Nippon Gakki was ordered by the government to produce wooden airplane propellers. When metal propellers were developed, the company changed from producing wooden propellers to manufacturing metal propellers.

After 1945, Nippon Gakki's executives wanted to return to making musical instruments. But the company had on its hands metal-working tools as well as skilled and experienced mechanics. These could not easily be re-trained to make pianos, but no one wanted to arbitrarily dismiss these workers, even though they had been imposed on the company by the government for war production. The solution was to separate the metal-working facilities from the manufacturing of musical instruments. It was decided that these engineers and metal workers could best produce motorcycles, which were a major post-1946 form of transportation in Japan and in other countries. In 1955, the manufacturing venture had become so successful that it was made into an independent company and given the name Yamaha Motor Company. The two companies still exchange personnel, including senior executives (Woronoff, 1982b).

Some American companies also show as much or more flexibility as Nippon Gakki. However, the typical American pattern is to encourage individual initiative and competition. An successful example of such a policy is found in the 3M Company. Employees in research are encouraged to spend fifteen percent of their time working on their own ideas. When any idea becomes a marketable product, than the developer becomes the product's sponsor and "owner". If this product shows enough promise, the developer can become the manager of a new department where the new product is made. Essentially, inventors and developers at 3M are given a proprietary interest in successful products. They are corporate entrepreneurs.

I mention 3M's corporate entrepreneurial policy because it is a successful non-Japanese strategy which encourages employee innovation. However, 3M's policy works best in its research divisions. In other divisions, 3M's management has adopted more group-oriented means to encourage worker loyalty. In order to listen to workers better and to encourage their contributions, 3M's chairman and chief executive officer, Lewis W. Lehr, visits plants and offices for about an equivalent of six months in a year.

The Wisdom of the Group

The importance Japanese leaders place on consensus and *wa* yields a productivity advantage Americans should consider: high levels of cooperation make each person more productive than if each worked apart from the group. The group is more effective than when the members were acting separately. This is not always true, but there are many work situations where workers would be more productive if they cooperated and worked together.[1] Taping this reservoir of talent demands that leaders believe that workers are, in fact, capable of better effort through cooperation. On their part, workers must also be convinced that cooperation is more advantageous to them than the opposite. Japanese leaders achieve workers' cooperation by rewarding cooperation more than selfish behavior.

American managers generally hold the view that members of a work group are less intelligent than they really are. At the managerial level this attitude is translated into the concept of "group ignorance." That is, workers are assumed to be ignorant individuals. The natural reaction to this state of mind is to tell workers how to do their work. Subordinates are treated as if they were children incapable of intelligent self-direction.

The term "group wisdom" does not mean that the individuals necessarily perform better in a group setting – though that is usual in small groups. The term also reminds that members complement each other. One member usually knows something the others don't, and members of a team can help each other

---

[1] An advantage of cooperation is that, when members of a group cooperate, they are not acting *against* one another. The opposite of cooperation is sometimes conflict rather than noninterference or indifference.

reach a collective decision. The simple sharing of information makes arriving at the best possible decision easier than if each person worked alone.

Thomas Gordon (1977:38), whose books on leadership and human interaction contain useful and practical advice, finds that leaders achieve more when they use the resources of all of the members. Different members at different times can contribute to a group's search for solutions, so everyone should be encouraged to contribute. Each member brings to the group a slightly different perspective and body of knowledge. An engineering problem which three electrical engineers cannot solve may seem easy to someone trained as a mechanical engineer. It's a matter of making sure that everyone is motivated enough to contribute instead of waiting for orders.

Persons working together stimulate one another so that a common solution becomes more likely. If nothing else, it's only human to enjoy finding an answer before someone else. We all like to show off our skills in front of an audience. The good leader trains and prepares subordinates to support each other instead of being competitive and secretive. They will cooperate when they feel trusted and when each believes that helping the others means helping oneself. This is the major key to why the Japanese have been so productive in recent years.

The Personality of the Group

A group which exists to achieve a goal is more than the sum total of the skills and talents of the members. They should not be seen as merely individuals who happen to be working together. This view ignores a fundamental fact: people who are together form personal bonds. How these bonds are formed and what they are like when developed has major implications for productivity. American leaders ignore the fact that workers form social units. They see workers as socially isolated units, or individuals.

A group begins as a collection of isolated individuals. They each have ideas of how to act at work, how much effort to make, what are "unfair" demands, and so on. This individuality soon begins to erode. Fellow workers become friendly; they discuss their work; and they gradually develop common values and behavior patterns. They will merge their beliefs on work as each becomes more like the others.

What happens is that the members become a group. At the same time, they begin to think of themselves as partners in a common endeavor. In this way raw recruits become Marines and a newly hired university graduate becomes a dedicated IBM salesperson. Anyone who has seen a draftee become a soldier recognizes the process by which an individual becomes a group member.

Imagine a newly hired worker. Before joining he had developed a negative attitude toward work and was satisfied with doing a minimum amount of work. He was content to daydream while working. He believed that quota restricting was better than quota surpassing. But now he finds that his new co-workers enjoy what they are doing. They talk about their work during breaks and brag about the quality they've achieved. They also expect the new worker to be as enthusiastic. The chances are that the new worker will change his work attitudes. His views will gradually become more like those of his new friends.

The same personality shift can be seen by any parent who sends a child to summer camp or to college. The returning child is suddenly a new person with new personality traits and habits, some probably negative ones from a parent's point of view. We all change to a degree when we change groups.

This phenomenon is called by social psychologists the *choice shift*. "Choice shift" is the phenomenon that individuals, when they join a group, shift their behavior and attitudes to better conform to the view of the dominant member or members. Usually a new member adopts the attitude of the majority rather than that of any specific person. At times though, a trainee will copy the attitudes and actions of the person located at the next desk or machine. In this context, wise supervisors place a new worker next to the best worker. This trainee is likely to adopt better working habits and attitudes. Place a new worker next to a chronic complainer and you'll soon have two chronic complainers!

The Japanese search for group loyalty and *wa* encourages a choice shift which supports the company's goals. Supervisors are evaluated primarily in terms of the extent their groups have loyal and enthusiastic "tones." Their workers must be gung ho! In America this is left to chance. We are often so individualistic that we ignore the pressures group membership places on members.

Leaders have the responsibility to make sure that the group as a whole does not develop unproductive attitudes and habits. Such negativism can become so compelling that new members quickly adopt the group's view. A recruit can be enthusiastic and wants to work hard. If he's placed in a group whose members are complainers and work avoiders, he will begin to complain about work and will exhibit low morale. He's adopted the group's values and the choice shift is completed. The best thing to do with this group is to disband it completely. Separate the members and disperse them to different groups with more positive attitudes.

The Risky Shift

Groups develop more than various degrees of loyalty and enthusiasm. A good leader can also encourage the development of an attitude of daring which leads to increased creativity. A leader can manipulate the group's atmosphere so that its members become more dynamic and adventurous. This is done by convincing members that creative contributions are expected as well as welcomed.[2]

Research shows that, under certain circumstances, persons will act in a more daring manner when they are members of a group than when alone. This happens when this type of behavior is encouraged by others, otherwise the group becomes conservative.

There is the tendency to behave with less caution when with others than when alone. An example of this phenomenon would be an executive faced with a difficult problem whose solution has no precedent. A common reaction is to delay making a decision, or else accept the most conservative alternative. But this same person will choose a more daring solution after talking over the problem with colleagues.

Why does this change of heart take place? One explanation is that group discussion encourages (Russell Clark 1971) diffusion of responsibility among members. Getting advice from others places some of the responsibility for the final decision on their shoulders. No one now has to pay the full penalty for failure. Success also has to be shared now, but most persons would rather take the chance of sharing a possible success with others rather than failing alone. Those who don't want to share success or fear failure are entrepreneurial types and work best by themselves. Most persons don't fit that mold.

The risky shift is only a tendency. A shift of attitudes will always occur as individuals join new groups, but the direction can be either toward more daring or toward more conservativeness. The leader sets the tone.

A way to tell whether or not a risky shift has taken place is to listen to the first reactions to a proposal. If the first comments of the members are negative ("This can't be done; shouldn't this be the responsibility of another department?") and conservative, then a risky shift has not taken place within the group. The leader must now change the group dynamics so that a risky shift takes place. Encouraging more participation and changing the reward system or some of the personnel are possibilities.

One strategy is to insist that a new solution be delivered and to make all members participate. When members realize all have to contribute and that no one will stand out when doing so, the group's climate will become more positive. Reject all past solutions and insist the group as a whole arrive at a new solution.

---

[2] Creative behavior is more likely when few rules exist. The lack of rules give members more freedom to act or think in unconventional ways.

Japanese leaders are generally quite successful in developing a group atmosphere in which the workers become willing – even eager – to work hard for the group. This spirit goes along with that culture's emphasis on groupism, cooperation, and the values placed on *wa* and *amae*. But this spirit does not automatically encourage creativity. Workers may be so concerned with reading the boss's mind and supporting group consensus that ideas become conservative and timid. The Japanese work hard in general, of course, but the same group atmosphere which encourages this type of enthusiasm can also encourages conformity; a form of "me tooism" develops. The major failing of the Japanese ethos is that the choice shift taking place in work groups often takes the direction toward conservativeness and conformity as well as loyalty. But this is not a certainty. The Japanese also can encourage and receive creative behavior from group members. When the leader projects a sense of crisis, Japanese workers easily make a risky shift. This has made the Japanese very flexible during the last 150 years.

5.3 Group Dynamics

Over a hundred experiments have been conducted studying the risky shift phenomenon (see Vander Zanden, 1981). The settings and problems of these experiments vary, but the basic experiment goes like this: a subject is presented with a hypothetical problem with two alternatives – one that is safe but dull, and one which is risky but exciting. The problem might involve having to select the best of two jobs. One job is secure but its pay is low and the work unchallenging. The other job is one which is highly paid, exciting, but offers a high chance of failure. The subject is then asked to state the probability (1 chance in 10, 5 in 10, 9 in 10, etc.) that he would take the more adventurous alternative.

When this is done, he is then taken to another room where he and others discuss the same problem and asked to restate the probability of making the same choice. There is an overwhelming tendency for persons to make riskier choices after group discussion than when alone (see Vander Zanden, 1981:336). The risky, challenging job is more likely to be selected after a group discussion than before.

The risky shift exists because few members want to appear to be less courageous than the others. Even born cowards become heroes when everyone else is brave and looking on. Persons who are very cautious when alone will urge each other on until someone feels forced to act bravely. That's how mobs begin. The same principle applies to small work groups as well.

Being part of a group also gives the members a sense of anonymity. The blame for a rash action falls on the group rather than on each individual. TV viewers have seen the commercial where someone becomes brave enough to tell the boss he has bad breath. The courage to do so comes from the group. Group membership gives the protection to do something a person wouldn't dare do alone. There is anonymity as well as strength in numbers. In a group setting, even Japanese workers become brave enough to present grievances and criticism they would never dare to alone.

The risky shift happens because, if things go wrong, an individual can always say, "It really wasn't me who did it. They made me do it," and the group gets the blame. This diffusion of responsibility discussed earlier is especially common in Japanese corporations. Japanese managers have to encourage the development of a risky shift in their groups because individuals may be afraid to be innovative when acting alone. After all, suggesting work improvement may be seen by others as being too individualistic and as threatening the group's *wa*. Any suggestion implies that the current procedure is not good enough. Someone is being blamed for having not been efficient.

Suggestions are easier to make if everyone is expected to make suggestions. The group then supports behavior that is more daring than usual. The principle of the risky shift explains why Japanese workers – whose culture stresses conformity – can act daringly. Even when they are proposing a radical change they are still conforming. They have the group's support to do so.

Since the Japanese tend to be conformists, managers make an extra effort to make sure their groups develop an atmosphere that encourages innovation. As shown in a later chapter, the Japanese are very successful in doing this. The well-earned reputation Japanese products have for high quality was achieved partly by the creative behavior of the workers themselves.

Innovation vs Conformity

Japanese executives are aware and concerned that once a group decision has been made, workers are likely to blindly follow the plan even if it is not effective. Group loyalty encourages the Japanese worker to tenaciously follow group decisions without question. If the decision was the correct one, then group loyalty increases efficiency. But a sense of *wa* may cause policy to be followed long after it's appropriate to do so (Woronoff, 1982b:71).

Unfortunately, workers in America and Japan develop the habit of following rules if the reward system encourages conformity. It becomes harder and harder for workers to innovate if they are not protected from failures and rewarded for taking chances. Most find that it's safer in the long run to keep a low profile and follow rules. Creative deviations which might increase efficiency are usually frowned upon, at least tacitly. This rulebook mentality causes a group's tone to become increasingly conservative. The end result is that no one is willing to do or suggest anything innovative. A good leader avoids this condition.

Japanese managers, as we have seen, expect their workers to be enthusiastic about work. This means that workers must do more than follow rules or obey orders. Workers are defined by managers as persons who have the talent to contribute ideas increasing work productivity. The choice shift in Japanese teams takes the direction of innovation (entailing more risk). But since all decisions are made by the group as a whole, there are fewer fears than an individual's contribution will make him stand out. The Japanese culture encourages conformity and consensus, but the group dynamics of Japanese corporations also allow initiative. The Japanese manager strives to balance the need for consensus and conformity with the need for innovation.

This balance between innovation and conformity is hardly ever achieved in Japan. Most Japanese would acknowledge that safe, conforming behavior from corporate workers at all levels is more likely than innovation and experimentation. Although many exceptions exist, the problem in Japan is not in achieving conformity and group loyalty; the Japanese culture already predisposes its members to prefer conformity. The problem is to encourage enough individuality to achieve creativity and innovation. This is done by developing the type of group support which encourages innovation.

The situation is the opposite in America. Our culture encourages individualism. Our task is to find ways to overcome this extreme by encouraging Americans to work together in such a way that the risky shift happens within a group context.

This tendency in Japan toward conformity does not always result in increased efficiency. Because conformity to the group is so important, employees ideally place their own needs second to the company's even when it's neither necessary nor useful. No one dares to appear as if he's not completely loyal to the group. This can result in a facade of looking busy when there is in fact little to do. Japanese office workers often stay late in their office, even if this means extending the work day without extra pay. This practice would be expected to increase the work being done. But work productivity does not necessarily increase.

The reason for this seeming contradiction is that Japanese office workers consider themselves to be part of a team. All workers in a department will stay late until everyone has finished the day's work. Leaving the office before anyone else would shame those who are still working, and may be seen as disloyalty and even laziness. If someone can't finish by five o'clock, then perhaps the others are not doing enough work. The result is that many Japanese white collar workers feel obligated to stay at their desks longer than necessary. Workers will stay in the office in order to appear to be working long hours when in fact they are not doing anything constructive.

Arthur Golden, who has lived in Japan, gives the example of office workers who stay at their desks until their supervisors leave, even when they have nothing to do (Golden, 1982). They sit at their desks and act as if they were busy. Probably the supervisor also stays longer than necessary because he too wants to make a good impression. That not all Japanese office workers are super-achievers is reflected in the saying, "Go to work early; leave work late; but don't do any work." At least some of the busy-seeming atmosphere in a Japanese office is pure sham.

The same happens in America and in other countries. The Australians have a respected fictional hero, called a "bludger." The bludger is someone who seems to be accomplishing a large amount of work while actually doing very little or nothing (Renwick, 1980). As long as they don't stand out, many Japanese office workers are probably "bludgers" at one time or another.

5.4 How the Group Rewards the Individual

The picture I have drawn so far of the Japanese emphasizes their preference for conformity and group dependence. This is a true reflection of the Japanese, but it is not a complete one. Stressing only the value of conformity would result in seeing Japan as a nation of sheep. But the dynamism of the Japanese society clearly shows otherwise. The Japanese are capable of being innovative and of adjusting quickly to changing conditions.

The reason is that while the Japanese worker must work through the group, he must also show through his initiative that his personal goals support the group's. Edward Norbeck, an anthropologist who has spent a number of years in Japan, describes (1976:10) the lives of members of several Japanese urban and rural families. He also notes that personal ability is highly valued in Japan. People are expected to work hard to improve themselves and their environment. But the context of all of this effort is through one group or another. A farmer works long hours in paddy fields and vegetable gardens to support the family and to be able to afford to send one or more sons to college. An assembly line worker in a Toyota plant aims for higher quality to help his group achieve a higher bonus.

Hard work is valued because it helps the group as well as the individual. For a person to work hard only for himself would be seen by others as almost as bad as being lazy and unproductive: both situations harm the group. Westerners have the same negative feelings toward a miser. The miser works hard to amass his hoard. But hoarding as an end in itself is to Americans useless and self-defeating. Scrooge is pitied more than honored for his wealth. The Japanese also evaluate a miser as morally unsound. A miser is scorned because he is too individualistic: his actions does not support a group, whether family, friends, company, or nation. If he were to spend his wealth on his family, though, he would receive honor and respect.

Edward Norbeck (1976:78) offers a striking picture of how the individual relates to his group. He describes the life of Jiro, a university graduate working for a large corporation. Jiro was well-liked by his co-workers and his supervisor, Mr. Kodama. Jiro accepted the company's rules, helped his colleagues, and was willing to work overtime whenever necessary. He was known as a reliable, cooperative worker. A few years after joining the company, department head Mr. Kodama "suggested" that Jiro pass the government's examination to become licensed as a patent lawyer. This request was essentially a command and refusal would have destroyed his career. Jiro, knowing that only one out of every twenty applicants passed the patent law exam, studied hard during nights and weekends for ten months.

During this time, Jiro noticed that Mr. Kodama was friendlier and acted more informally toward him. His co-workers noted that Jiro now had a sponsor. It was clear that Jiro was being rewarded for the extra efforts he was devoting to the company. Even his colleagues showed him more respect. Jiro continued studying until the time he took the patent law exam – studying until the early morning while doing his own work during the day. He lost weight and gave up any thoughts of enjoying his evenings and having any social life.

Jiro passed the examination and became certified by the Japanese government as a patent lawyer. Mr. Kodama, as a sign of his approval, then took his charge out to lunch at the city's finest hotel. During the meal, Mr. Kodama obliquely mentioned that he had a niece who had reached marriageable age. Since it was also time for Jiro to settle down and marry, would Jiro be willing to meet his niece? The upshot of all this was that Jiro and the niece married each other a year later.

This story illustrates how individual efforts made on behalf of the group are rewarded beyond contractual obligations. It's a matter of exchange: the group rewards extraordinary effort with extraordinary benefits. And since groups are powerful in Japan, the individual finds it easier to gain advantages for himself by working for the group. The rewards a group can offer are usually greater than what a person can receive through his own efforts. The Japanese reward personal ability and effort only when they benefit a group.

This cooperative view extends to a company's customers and clients. The Japanese prefer to see company-customer relations as a mutually-profitable exchange rather than purely commerical behavior. The Japanese like to sell their products, of course, but they feel more comfortable when they believe their company's products provide a valuable service. The customer is a partner and as much a part of the company as workers and executives. Sato Kiichiro, employed in a Mitsui subsidiary, summarized this typically Japanese view when he said (Roberts, 1973:493):

My idea is that big corporations have some social responsibility. They have to serve customers; they have to take care of their employees and shareholders; and their business as a whole should be for the good of the nation.

Bringing Talent into the Company's Family

Traditional rules of inheritance offer insights on how the Japanese manager balances the demands of group versus individual needs. I have already noted that employees and employers form a family. The same was true in the past. Many managerial practices Americans see as strange or unusual are reflections of the fact that each Japanese company is seen as a family. The differences between an American and a Japanese work environment partly come from American managers viewing workers as individuals with no other tie to the company than a contract. Japanese managers see themselves as parents and older brothers to subordinates.

We saw how a young manager, Jiro, was rewarded for his extra work not only by increased prestige, but by marrying his supervisor's niece. He now enjoys a tie with his superior through marriage. There is no reason to doubt that uncle Kodama-san will help his new in-law's career. Jiro had already shown that he was a superior worker by passing his law exam. Kodama now owes Jiro a work debt as well as a family debt.

This practice of multiplying ties – whether friendship, school, or marriage – within a work context is common. Jiro and his new uncle were following established custom. The Japanese have been able to absorb modern practices within a traditional framework. There is much in a contemporary Japanese corporation that is very old.

Before the age of industrialization, Japanese businesses were family concerns led and operated by family members. Some of these businesses became quite large even by modern standards and continued to be dominated by the founder's family for generations. This longevity is remarkable since genetics does not insure that the second, third, or fourth generations will have the business skills equal to the founder's. Nor is there a guarantee that sons and grandsons will have an interest in working for the family's firm. These are problems faced by business families in any country, including the United States. No one can predict whether the inheritors will have the intelligence and drive of their ancestors, or the interest in following in their footsteps.

The continuation of family control in family-owned businesses was of great interest in traditional Japan, where family identification and loyalty were all-important. Japanese business and merchant families solved the problem of inheritance by developing an ingenious but effective policy: the adoption of superior workers into the family.

The practice was simple to enact. Family businesses face two general problems: the continuation of quality management and family control. The solution to both problems was to evaluate carefully the younger members of the family. If none seemed talented or dedicated enough to eventually manage the family's business, some sons were given symbolic but powerless positions in the company. Others were encouraged to devote themselves to other occupations and might become monks, scholars, or respected higher-level government bureaucrats.

Then the members of the family council carefully evaluated their employees to see which ones showed above-average intelligence, character, and business skills. These would be trained for future advancement and promotion. Their background would make no difference. Such marked employees might be ambitious and hard-working peasant's sons or apprentices from poor urban families.

The best of these future executives would later be adopted into the owner's family, given the family name, and treated as natural sons. They would worship their new family's ancestors and in all ways take part in family activities. If there were an unmarried daughter in the owner's family, she would be married to the adopted son at the same time as the adoption ceremony. This cemented further the ties between the new son and his adopted family. In this way a promising worker would be adopted, married into the familiy, and declared the heir all in the same day. The head of the company gains a superior heir who will benefit the company; he marries a daughter to a promising young man; and he ties more closely a good employee to the company.

This Japanese adoption-marriage practice shows how individual initiative and achievement are rewarded through group membership and group dependence. The superior worker is rewarded and the group – in this case the family – gains a valuable member. A balance between individualism and group interests has been achieved.

5.5 Corporate Structures Supporting Group Consensus

A number of structural features in Japanese corporations reflect the need to maintain harmony (*wa*) among members. By structure is meant any way of organizing human relationships so that behavior is channeled into a specific pattern. Structure can be physical, such as the number of members in a group. Smaller groups make it easier for members to become friends. Larger groups need rules and regulations – a bureaucratic structure – to organize the behavior of the members.

Another structural variable is time, and how we define time influences behavior. One of the most frustrating experiences Americans working in foreign countries have is how non-Americans define time. Americans use time very precisely and expect others to do the same. But in a Latin American country, a meeting called for ten o'clock will seldom start "on time." To many Latins, "on time" means a half hour or more later. The Japanese see time in a much larger context than Americans. The Japanese are able to plan for longer periods; their time horizon is larger. This makes the Japanese more patient and willing to wait for long-term profits. Our time horizon is much smaller and makes Americans impatient.

The Use of Space

The use of space is another structural factor of the human condition (Brooks and Kaplan, 1972). The individualistic value held by Americans encourages the belief that space should "belong" to some person or another. Owning space means sole use of an area, whether it concerns a private bedroom, a private parking space, or a private office with a door keeping others out (Becker, 1981). In America, the more privacy a worker has the more power he holds and the higher he is in the company's hierarchy (Dean, 1977).

Because of the insistence that group identity is more significant than individual identity, an individual in Japan is less likely than an American to be alone. Few Japanese enjoy the using of space on a private basis. They prefer group activities.

A distinctive use of space radically different from American practice is the near-total lack of private and semiprivate offices. Only the president and a few other senior executives have private offices to themselves. Few other persons have their names on their office doors. Placing a nameplate on a door or desk marks them as "belonging" to that person. It's a brand of ownership that would be seen as too individualistic. Some Japanese corporations allow no private files or records. All are placed in common file cabinets. This practice makes it easier to replace a person who is rotated elsewhere or who is temporarily out of the office.

Giving a Japanese manager a private office separates him from fellow members and isolates him from his work group. Americans give a worker an office as reward and as an indication of higher prestige. The Japanese view this situation as punishing the ones who did not receive this reward and as dividing those who need to work together. A private office threatens group consensus and creates possible divisions among members. Peers and their superiors are expected to work together, and there is no need for artificial divisions such as private offices.

Most Japanese companies, even the largest, have private offices only for their presidents. Executives are given space next to their assistants and subordinates. Supervisors are housed in large offices with desks arranged in two rows for their assistants and staff.

A section chief or department head can see what everyone is doing because an open office allows the head to keep track of the work flow. Open offices also make it easy for work to be passed on to the next desk or station. This is the equivalence of the Just-in-Time system in the office!

If someone is ill or away on a vacation, a colleague at the next desk can easily take over, answer the telephone, and continue the work. The use of communal office space in this way encourages workers to become interdependent. One key employee cannot block the work process.

The lack of private offices has another benefit, one that is secondary but still important. Open, large offices reduce costs. The absence of separate offices economizes on the space needed, and office building costs and rents are less. There is less duplication of equipment, less space devoted to walls and dividers. Density means economy.

Communication is face-to-face when people work in view of one another. There is less need for memos, paper shuffling, and the personnel to type and store them. Open offices also make group loyalty and worker-to-worker cooperation more likely. For subordinates, open offices make superiors more accessible. It's easy to catch the eye of the division chief when he works a few desks away. In addition, it becomes harder in an open office to keep secrets and hide information since relatively few things belong exclusively to one person or another. Telephone conversations are overheard, files are kept in common cabinets, and dealings with visitors are visible to co-workers. In this environment, few activities can be kept hidden or monopolized. This encourages cooperation. If you can't keep a valued customer secret, you might as well share the work with co-workers and receive credit for doing so. They will find out what you're doing soon enough.

Even department chiefs in Japan have desks alongside their subordinates. This makes the socio-geography of Japanese office space different from that of American corporations. Offices are large and contain desks and work space for every member of the department. All workers are visible to each other and interaction is easily accomplished. Desks are lined up in clusters or in double rows, so a worker sits side-by-side with two others and can look directly at another colleague straight ahead. Department chiefs and section supervisors have their desks at the end of these rows and are visible to their subordinates.

On their part, the supervisors can oversee everyone and watch over them. This keeps the workers working since they are easily visible to the supervisors. At least they learn to look busy. White collar workers have many ways to look busy when they are not. Many can also pretend to have to visit clients and then disappear into a coffee house for an hour or so.

Meetings in a Japanese office take place in a common area. Offices contain a cleared area with couches, chairs, and a coffee table. Meetings take place in this open area which is visible to everyone else. If more privacy is needed, a meeting can always take place outside the office, in a coffee lounge or a bar. Many restaurants in Japan stay open all day although food is served only at specific hours. Coffee, tea, and snacks are available throughout the day. It's common for groups of employees to leave their office to spend some time in a coffee bar.

Like the French, the Japanese enjoy going to small cafes where primarily tea and coffee are served. Because openly staring at strangers is un-Japanese, there are no sidewalk cafes where customers and the public are visible to each other. However there is an ample number of small coffee houses in Japan. Since Japanese offices tend to be noisy as well as crowded, Americans conducting business in Japan should cultivate the habit of frequently visiting the same coffee houses and taking their Japanese colleagues there. Having the personnel recognize you and make an extra fuss over you impresses others. Much business during working hours is conducted in small coffee bars.

The combination of large offices and the love of going to coffee houses has one distinct disadvantage: it becomes difficult to locate someone quickly. Middle-level managers spend as much as one-third of the work day away from their offices, with the result that most are not easily available without appointments. Coffee shops become extensions of the office.

American office space is so partitioned that there is relatively little public area. By contrast, Japanese work areas tend to be mostly public in nature. There is no need, as there is in an American office, for a distinct lounge or water cooler where neutral space is available for sociability and informal consultation. Japanese managers do not have to leave private offices and congregate in public areas when they wish to be with each other. There are so few private areas in the Japanese office that workers can interact with each other with ease.

Americans are more likely to separate their private lives from work. But the Japanese do not. Co-workers take vacations together, drink after hours together, and develop close personal ties. Japanese spend more time with co-workers than with their neighbors. This is partly due to long working hours, but there are other reasons, including the fact that employment means "family."

The result is that the divisions between private and public work areas in Japan are blurred since so few working Japanese are ever alone. There is no need for much "non-work" space as is found in America. A salaryman – the Japanese term for any businessman – would think it strange to find office areas set aside for leisure or private use. Co-workers use their desks as places to take breaks and to consult with one another. When an office becomes too hectic, the Japanese can always escape to a coffee bar.

The Use of Titles

The emphasis on the cohesion of the group results in another corporate structural contrast between America and Japan. Just as there are few private offices in the Japanese company, there are also few individual positions in the corporate organizational table. Each employee is a member of a work group or division and seldom holds a specific, individual position. The only exceptions would be the highest level officials.

The American bureaucratic structure, following the German-European model as developed by Max Weber, contains a specific designation for every member in an organization. The bureaucratic structure organizes the relationship among all persons within each division and department and smaller subunits. A table of organization based on the classic European bureaucratic model defines every person's position and his relation with others. It is possible in such a model to draw a diagram showing the organizational position for each employee and to trace each person's superiors, peers, and subordinates. Every person has a "box" defining his relation with everyone else in the organization. This is his "private" space.

This specificity allows for comprehensive planning and coordination among all members. There is a place for everyone and all workers are easily located in relationship to other workers. A superior knows from such an organizational structure how each worker fits into the whole and exactly what his duties are. When a person is hired, he/she is necessarily hired for a specific position with clearly defined rights and duties. Promotion means leaving one position and obtaining another. Consequently, the American bureaucratic structure is both individualized and hierarchical.

Japanese tables of organization do not give an individual a specific position. A table of organization defines divisions and departments but does not descend to the individual level. There are no organizational "boxes" for individuals as there are in American companies. Just as there are few private offices and individual rewards, the Japanese corporation has few individual positions. One can find listed the accounting department of a Japanese corporation, but no organizational chart will indicate to the outsider who is the junior accountant, third level. Nor is there a nameplate which indicates that a specific desk belongs to the third administrative assistant of the department of Research and Development. The organizational chart does not descend to the individual.

Job descriptions do not exist in Japanese offices. New workers are assigned to a division or department and given whatever tasks come up. With no job description available, office workers have much more freedom than their American counterparts on how to complete a project. Since most tasks are group projects, a new worker can easily get advice from others and learn by copying. Different persons handle paperwork differently, and there is little effort to standardize procedures. This adds to office chaos. No one can predict how something will get done, how much time it will take, or even who's responsible (Woronoff, 1982b:28). But this works for the Japanese.

Aside for the concern for group consensus and support, Japanese office workers are saved from complete inefficiency through the Japanese concern for details. The Japanese work from one detail to another and avoid vaguely-defined grand schemes. While Japanese offices look like chaos, the fact is that projects are being advanced detail by detail. The Japanese are thorough and work gets done.

The Size of Groups

Masumi Tsuda (1977), in his analysis of one hundred large Japanese firms, found that most departments were relatively small. Tsuda found that two-thirds of the departments recognized within the corporation contained ten persons or less. Only ten percent of the departments had a membership of over thirty persons. Such small size encourages group identification and loyalty among the members.

It's easy for members of an office with less than ten employees to go to a weekend retreat or to give one another office parties several times a year. Members of a small group can conveniently go together to a coffee shop, a restaurant, or a bar for several hours after work. White collar workers and managers go together to a bar several times a week as a general practice.

Members of a department would be unwilling to leave the office at the end of the work day until everyone else had finished the assigned work. Then they might all visit a bar for several hours to relax and discuss the day's events and office politics. It's at this time that workers, under the guise of inebriation, feel willing to voice their complaints. The division manager would be present at some of these occasions. He is available, in an organizationally neutral place, to listen for indications of low morale and for whatever gossip would be difficult to transmit during work hours.

The small size of each division allows easy access to superior as well as encourages the workers to work together. Small group size also allows workers to interchange duties. Since the organization does not allow the individual worker a specific niche, it is easy to vary activities. This gives workers a varied experience.

A disadvantage of such task variablility and ambiguity of position is that an outsider has difficulty discovering who is responsible for a specific task. He must discover the appropriate individual through a personal search because duties are so vaguely defined. To an American in Japan, the process of discovering who is in charge of a particular project and whom to talk to can be very frustrating as well as time-consuming. Generally, division heads do not concern themselves with the day-to-day activities of their personnel. They may not know exactly who is doing what at a given moment. Lower-level employees are given responsibilities without being given an official title.

Small groups have a number of advantages over large ones. In a small group, members are guided by the personalities of the leaders and the members themselves. As groups get larger, increasingly more rules are needed to coordinate activities and make sure all members work. Large groups are more likely to have "free riders" as members (see chapter nine). These are members who don't want to work or who refuse to cooperate. It's easier to hide in larger groups and "free riders" are more common in larger groups than in smaller groups. More formal rules are necessary in larger groups. The result is bureaucratic rigidity.

Japanese corporations need fewer rules than their American counterparts because each company consists of many interlocking smaller groups. This makes the employee-corporation relation very personal. Managers can personally ask workers to perform a task instead of pointing to some rule or another. This leads not only to more positive worker motivation, but also to higher work satisfaction.

Small group size also leads to more productivity. I have already noted that it's easier to hide in a larger group. Small membership forces everyone to contribute more equally. For most tasks, member productivity increases until group size reaches ten or so (Slater, 1958; Steiner, 1972). After that size is reached, some workers feel free to coast on others' efforts. At the same time, the better workers realize others are "free loading" and decide to do less.

Because smaller groups are guided by the emotional makeup of the members, smaller groups are more cohesive than larger ones. Members of small groups are more loyal to one another as well as more supportive. This leads to greater commitment to company goals.

A Japanese corporation is in actuality a mass of small groups organized around personal loyalty rather than rules. This forces members to discuss business matters extensively to develop personal relationships with one another. All this is emotionally exhausting and very time consuming, but the result is organizational flexibility.

An American wanting to do business with a Japanese company should remember that authority and responsibility are not the same in Japan. Someone responsible for a project may in fact have little formal authority to be in charge. The Japanese manager officially responsible for a project dares not make unilateral decisions because he may not be completely familiar with a project's details. He would meet with subordinates as well as superiors before announcing a decision. The American who insists on seeing "the one in charge" in order to demand an instant decision will be disillusioned when dealing with the Japanese.

5.6 Turning the Recruit into a Team Player

Corporate recruits, whether college or high school graduates, are given intensive indoctrination to develop them into loyal employees. The first few months after being hired are taken up with training rather than with work per se.

Recruits spend the first two or three weeks at the company's training center. Aptitude tests are given in order to have some criteria for future placement. But most of the time during this period is taken up with "personality development."

This includes large doses of lectures on the company's history and purpose. The recruits learn company's songs and are introduced to senior officials. The training centers have dorms and other living facilities, so recruits are isolated from the outside world. This isolation forces new employees to rely on each other and begin to develop friendship ties with co-workers.

If the recruit had been hired by Japan Air Lines, he would learn the following company song:

There! See the star-like craft,
Rainbow-colored lanterns shine in the magic night
High above all the storms and clouds upon the earth,
Onward, peacefully, the silver bird of hope.

Not all Japanese companies have corporate songs, though most do, and not all companies expect employees to sing them even when they exist (Lee, 1974:479). Many are poetic, as is Suntory, Ltd.'s poem to Red Light, one of the distillery's wines:

What a manly name Red Light is,
Shaking the axis of the earth.

The sun rises with a roar at dawn.
Our company, beloved company,
With its bright future rising.

The development of company identification and co-worker friendship ties are encouraged by group activities, group projects, athletics, and classroom discussions. For future salesmen in a Japanese automotive company, each group disassembles and reassembles a complete car. They learn to work together as they learn about their products. YKK (Yoshida Kogyo Kaisha), the world's largest manufacturer of zippers, is privately held and the president is a dominant presence in the company. Yet YKK stresses that workers form a "family". All YKK employees are called "members" to reinforce this sense of togetherness.

Becoming a "company man" involves more than learning occupational skills. These corporate training centers also offer courses on how to answer the telephone and how to bow correctly to customers. There are also lectures on how to deal harmoniously with colleagues, how to express one's opinions without offending others, and how to dress correctly. Tailors are sent to the training centers to measure recruits for business suits and shirts which are sold at a discount.

Japanese companies encourage physical exercise and recruits march together, go on long hikes, and do daily calisthenics. The comparison between these centers and military boot camps is not far off the mark. Physical exercises are supposed to develop the employees' "spirit" and personality. If they can endure physical harships, it's believed, they will become better workers and dedicated, as well as more self-assured, persons.

Other companies send new employees to a Buddhist temple for a short course in Zen meditation. This type of program has the purpose of supposedly fortifing the personality by teaching self-discipline. During the temple stay, the students clean their own living areas and live very austerely and simply. Zen courses are also made available to more senior workers who feel a periodic need for a quiet retreat. Many companies send experienced employees to various camps and temple courses so that they can recapture their early enthusiasm.

This strong company identification is encouraged by all large Japanese corporations. Even self-made entrepreneurs who have developed their own companies accept the value of togetherness among their workers. Post-war Japan has been the stage for a large number of iconoclastic self-starters who broke away from large companies to become independent. The expectation is that these entrepreneurs would have developed an individualistic outlook. But this has not happened. The successful independents accept the ideal of corporate "family" and mutual dependency.

An example of this reliance on corporate consensus by "self-starters" is Nidec's president and founder Shigenobu Nagamori. As an engineer, Nagamori worked for several large companies and earned the reputation of being brilliant but too independent. He finally quit and started his own company with three other engineers. He first worked out of his home and would travel around Japan and later the United States to show his company's wares. Now Nidec produces almost ninety percent of the world market for hard disk motor drives with total sales of over $36 million (Kotkin and Kishimoto, 1984).

In spite of his independent character, Nagamori spends up to one-third of his time recruiting and training new personnel. He has also written a small book describing the ideal "Nidec man". This ideal employee is someone who is enthusiastically loyal to the company and concerned with quality production.

Japanese entrepreneurs who have rebelled against large corporate familism nevertheless encourage *amae* and *wa* in their own companies. The model of the contemporary corporation as family is a strong and all-pervasive one, even among those who have successfully rebelled against it.

The Japanese Godfather

In order to give Japanese workers the feeling that their company is smaller and more personal than it is, large corporations have instituted what in America would be called a sponsorship structure: a senior and higher-level employee is assigned a new worker (Monroe and Sakahibara, 1977:50). The sponsor has the responsibility of teaching the junior worker how he is expected to act at and off work. He becomes a "godfather" or mentor to the recruit. This mentor is expected to help his younger charge with both career and personal problems.

The "godfather" structure has been described by Peter F. Drucker (1971). Drucker, one of the major proponents of Japanese style participation management, is also one of the early popularizers of Japanese managerial styles to Americans. He recommended Japanese managerial structures long before it became popular to do so. In many ways, Drucker is both mentor and godfather to those who wish to understand and bridge American-Japanese managerial differences.

As Drucker points out, the Japanese godfather is in reality a sponsor who helps to develop and guide the godson's career. Senior middle-level managers are expected to devote a large amount of time helping the godsons for at least the first ten years of their careers. This godfather is given a number of young employees to watch over. A senior manager skilled in human relations devotes most of his working time to his godsons. He is in essence an informal part of the company's personnel division. This is networking with a vegeance!

The godfather has no direct authority over the younger man. The link between the two is usually geographic or educational. The godfather can presume to "adopt" a managerial recruit because they both were born in the same village or province, or because they graduated from the same university and had studied with the same set of professors. Having this type of linkage makes the relationship more natural.

The godfather sees his charge frequently. He gives him advice on how to dress and what hobbies to have. He takes him out after hours to show him how to entertain. He also guides his career. The godfather listens to complaints about work and superiors, and can informally pass these complaints on to the right parties if warranted. He also passes on the criticism and praise the godson needs to hear. A supervisor may find it difficult to openly criticize an assistant for exhibiting a negative attitude or for not contributing enough effort to maintain the department's *wa*; the godfather can do so more easily.

The godfather structure makes the organization more personal to those at the lower ranks. The system also makes it possible to give information otherwise too embarrassing to pass on. By developing this sponsorship tie, the newcomer automatically has support which will help and protect him. Once again, the Japanese corporation has features which make it more like a family.

5.7 Delegation

"Management sits; it does not do" in Japan. Senior executives develop general policies, maintain consensus, and concern themselves with their group's *wa*. All of this is made possible because subordinates are expected to want to work for the good of the department or division. The means to achieve this goal are through extensive delegation. Decisions and the responsibility to carry them out are given to persons who are at the lowest possible level in the organization. Essentially, those who perform a job are given enough responsibility to do so correctly. Decisions are made at the level where workers are the most affected by such policies. This can only be done through extensive delegation and consultation, and Japanese leaders delegate more extensively than their American counterparts.

The early training of new employers is concerned with two general developments. First, workers are expected to become loyal, enthusiastic, and cooperative members of the company. I have already discussed this concern. As important, workers are also expected to gain a general understanding of the corporation as a whole and how work is performed over a wide variety of departments. Extensive rotation and adult education programs develop mutiple skills in the worker. As that happens, the worker can accept more and more responsibility. If he is capable, he is delegated more and more duties and decisions. Workers believed to be superior are constantly challenged with more and more responsibility. Delegation in the Japanese company is a common way of testing workers.

American executives view employees as hired for specific purposes – an accountant is hired for his present accounting skills, and so on. Persons in this context are purchased services to perform specific duties. Japanese executives, by contrast, see new employees as human resources to gradually develop. The value of a new worker is not based solely on the skills he has at present but the skills he will have in the future. New members of a company are investments instead of expenses made necessary by current needs. That is why Japanese workers are expected to develop additional occupational skills over the years.

Japanese management firmly believes that the worker needs increasingly more and more responsibility if he's to develop his talents. Future growth demands delegation of work responsibility. Only by being delegated more responsibilities can someone develop new skills and gain varied experiences. Delegation is the way Japanese managers train and develop (or improve) their human resources.

Lack of delegation in America is due to more than the way we view power and in the limited extent managers trust subordinates. There is also the matter of how managers classify lower-level workers. Workers can be defined either as persons who have a limited potential or as persons who, if given the opportunity, will develop their talents and skills. The first view is a static one which assumes that workers have already achieved their potentials once hired. If they had the potential for a better position, this argument continues, the worker would have already developed the skills needed. He would have applied for a better position in the first place.

This view encourages an American to seek a new employer when he thinks he can perform the duties of a job that demands increased skill. He has already been typecast by the current employer. In short, Americans become disillusioned with their employers because no one appreciates or expects their development. They are not given the chance to do more than what they have been hired for. Without delegation, superiors are slow to realize when workers are ready to be promoted.

The second view, more common in Japan, assumes that all workers can upgrade their current skills if motivated enough. Present skill level is seen as temporary. Workers are encouraged to take on a wide variety of duties to gain more experience. The Japanese also believe that anyone can do better if he has the spirit (courage) to want to. Success in anything is a matter of personal determination. Japanese executives hope that they can motivate workers so that they will want to achieve greater and greater goals. These motivated workers are then given the opportunity to achieve these goals.

Americans hire employees not only to fulfill specific tasks, but primarily to obey. When we evaluate a prospective worker, we are often more concerned with the unstated question, "Can this person take orders?" than with the stated question, "Can this person do the work correctly?" Americans assume that working for others involves obedience. This is another reason why American corporations contain so many rules; we need rules because we are so concerned with making certain that superiors have the means to make others follow orders.

The typical Japanese company has fewer rules and regulations than its American counterpart. Workers are trusted to be so motivated that they will do anything that will help the company. Japanese companies have rules, because coordination is necessary when a large number of persons work together. Rules promote coordination. Japanese employers also expect that employees are motivated and capable enough to do whatever needs to be done, irrespective of whether or not a rule covers a specific problem.

Because of this trust, Japanese managers assume that workers want to do their best for the company. As a result of this expectation, Japanese executives and foremen delegate to subordinates responsibilities to a much greater extent than is found in America. A major lesson American managers can learn from the Japanese is that delegation of authority can be greatly extended without loss of productivity. Giving workers more freedom does not necessarily mean giving them a license to do less work. The opposite instead will happen: workers with more freedom will become harder and more creative employees.

The Advantages of Delegation

Delegation makes work more challenging. People are motivated in part by money, but hope of a financial reward is not the only reason people work. Money does not make a dull job more pleasant, and most dull jobs are low-paying to begin with. Better performance can be achieved not only by offering money but also by making work more challenging and its environment more socially pleasant.

Dr. Teresa Amabile has noted that creative activity is more likely when a person is faced with an interesting problem. Research found that creativity occurs when people are motivated, not only when there is the expectation of a material reward. Motivation happens when there is an intrinsic pleasure of trying to solve a problem (Hunt, 1982). We work better when we are challenged than when the task is dull. In the same way, managers can boost productivity by delegating more responsibility and giving more interesting work to their subordinates.

The limited view American management has of workers is seen in the automobile manufacturing industry. Car production demands a high amount of specialization in which many duties are highly repetitive and therefore boring. Many assembly line functions last two minutes or less and the worker repeats the same work motions twenty to thirty times on hour.

The most popular job on Detroit's assembly lines is the one which requires the worker to jump from job to job to relieve workers during their rest periods. At Chrysler's plants, this rotation is called the "tag-relief" system. Workers consider these the best jobs on the assembly line because they offer variety in addition to a ten-cent an hour pay increase. This increase is too small to make much difference in a paycheck. The chance to perform a variety of tasks makes the "tag-relief" system a success (Simison, 1982:19).

Most assembly line workers would enjoy taking part in the "tag-relief" system even without added pay. A greater variety of duties makes the work day more interesting. There is no feeling more dismal than waking up every morning knowing what you're going to do all day. Workers should be offered the opportunity to exchange work duties with one another whenever possible. Morale would increase and cause decreases in labor turnover and absenteeism.

Management's complaint is that workers may not be skilled enough to perform more than one duty at peak efficiency. This lack of trust is based on the assumption that most assembly line work is so complicated that each task demands a long period of training before it can be performed. This is false and most assembly line work can be learned in a very short time. If management feels that assembly line workers are too stupid to learn a larger number of work duties, a worker could be rotated among a limited number of work stations. Sweden's Volvo has adopted such a policy. Workers are split into groups, and each team has the responsibility for a small number of different tasks. The members of the team decide who will be doing what. This allows the workers to distribute the day's work among themselves.

Managers in both Sweden and Japan define the worker at any level, whether manual or non-manual, as more trustworthy and intelligent than do Americans. This distrust results in a lack of delegation and does harm to the workers as well as the economy.

What are the consequences when managers do not delegate responsibility? Studies how that employees who have dull, repetitive, routine tasks tend to also restrict their production. After all, if the work is uninteresting, few workers will feel motivated to work harder and they will do no more work than is absolutely necessary. Workers react to boredom by exhibiting high absenteeism, labor turnover, and low product quality. Judson Gooding (1970:70) reports that absenteeism:

"Has doubled over the past ten years at General Motors and at Ford ... It has reached the point where an average of 5 percent of G.M.'s hourly workers are missing from work without explanation every day ... On some days, notably Fridays and Mondays, the figure goes as high as 10 percent. Tardiness has increased ... there is more turnover. The quit rate at Ford last year was 25.2 percent ... Some assembly line workers are so turned off ... that they just walk away in mid-shift and don't even come back to get their pay for the time they have worked."

Similarly, many workers quit as soon as they learn how boring assembly line work is and that there is little chance to change work duties. Chrysler reported that half of new workers during 1969 did not complete their first ninety days at work. One Ford plant during 1969 was forced to hire 4,800 new workers in order to be able to maintain an already established a work force of 5,000 (Braverman, 1974:33). This is an annual labor turnover of almost one-hundred percent!

A high rate of unemployment will reduce these dismal symptoms of low worker morale, though the low morale will remain. The fear of unemployment will not make the typical assembly line work more pleasant; nor will workers be motivated to increase their efficiency or the quality of their work. The above examples may seem extreme, but many workers other than those on the assembly line dislike their jobs so much that work performance is impaired. Widespread delegation and job rotation would ease some of these problems by providing more variety.

Delegation also has an advantage for higher-level workers. Simply stated, delegation gives managers more time to do more important work. The Nineteenth Century sociologist Vilfredo Pareto proposed that most of the time spent by members of a group is spent on trivial matters while more important items are given less time. A law derived from this concept goes like this: the less important a problem, the more time is spent on it.

The same principle applies to modern managers: managers spend more time on relatively trivial matters and less time on the more important ones. One reason why this is true is that less significant questions are so much more numerous than those which are vital. Another reason for this discrepancy on the effort spent on important matters as opposed to those that are not is that the latter are housekeeping duties. These must be taken care from moment to moment if a department is to run smoothly. These housekeeping problems need to be solved as quickly as possible or morale and work in general will suffer. To those involved, housekeeping issues take on an inordinate importance way beyond their actual significance.

This is why a corporate officer may spend as much time deciding who will park close to the office as deciding who will be promoted. He will be forced to expend as much energy and time ending two workers' bickering as he will wooing a potential client. These seemingly petty matters are important.

Morale suffers if someone gets a nameplate while others do not; a manager cannot delay deciding who will be given a larger office.

The examples above may seem trivial, but they become major problems if ignored. Many of these problems are essentially unsolvable because no one decision can satisfy all parties. No executive can promote all who deserve to be promoted; nor can all junior executives each be given a private secretary. These problems take up too much of a group leader's time because the best solution is going to be an imperfect one. These problems cause much more anguish and tension than next year's budget because they cannot be solved to everyone's satisfaction. They are also numerous.

A general rule of thumb is that important problems are one-fifth of the total number. The remaining four-fifths fall in the trivial category. More important, these issues take up four-fifths of a manager's time but produce one-fifth of worthwhile results. The typical manager is inundated with a large number of trivial issues which do not contribute very much to a company's profits. The four-fifths principle has been illustrated by Robert Heller, whose works on how to improve managerial functions are always instructive. Robert Heller (1981:60) offers these examples of Pareto's principle:
1. 20 percent of the items in any inventory account for 80 percent of all movements in and out.
2. 20 percent of the customers provide 80 percent of sales.
I add the following:
3. 20 percent of executive duties take up 80 percent of his time.
4. 80 percent of an executive's duties could be better performed by subordinates.
5. 80 percent of absenteeism is accounted for by 20 percent of the work force.
Imagine being able to get rid of the minor duties which take up eighty percent of the time! Any manager should be happy to be able to spend more time on the more important problems waiting on the desk. In addition, the "trivial many" taking up four-fifths of a manager's time do not arrive in a block all at once. They arrive at the desk at all hours, and all of us find ourselves constantly interrupted while trying to deal with one of the more important "vital few" problems (Juran, 1981).

The way to dispose of these numerous but minor problems is to delegate them to others. First the manager trains subordinates to handle these problems either individually or together. If he expects them to solve these burdens, he can then devote more of his time to the "vital few" problems. Those who cause many of these problems themselves are forced to find their own solutions. There is no greater satisfaction than to force those who are to blame for a situation to solve their own messes.

The advantages of such delegation are obvious. The manager now has more time to devote to more significant problems and he thereby becomes more effective. As important, delegation also makes others responsible for these irritating problems. One of the major advantages of the Japanese managerial system is that Japanese senior managers delegate most or all of these "trivial many" problems to subordinates. They can use their skills and time to plan ahead or to solve the more significant problems which can be solved only at their administrative level. Delegation only asks managers to avoid those tasks which can be done by others; the manager then has time to do what the subordinates cannot do and what only he has the authority to complete.

American managers in the middle levels tend to believe that, since they are "in charge," delegation means losing control. According to this view, the one in charge has all of the responsibility and she is accountable to her own superior. Giving another the independence to complete an assignment means delegation results in loss of control. But delegation is necessary if an executive is to be able to complete her own work. The question is not whether or not the manager should delegate, but rather how much to delegate.

The answer, following the Japanese, is that a manager should delegate as much as possible. In spite of the fact that someone has an imposing title and office, most of the work-time will be spent to trivial matters. He can feel secure that most of the duties he delegates will not be spectacular ones. On the other hand, delegation will improve the efficiency as well as the quality of his own work. He now can turn his attention to more important matters.

From the perspective of those who are given more responsibility, delegation forces them to act more responsibly. It is natural for people to avoid manufacturing problems they are expected to solve themselves. Delegation keeps many problems from ever developing in the first place. Subordinates are more likely to consider the consequences of their actions when they know the superior refuses to get involved in low-level problems.

A good policy for any supervisor is that problems should be handled where they originate. Americans working for Japanese often have to learn that the Japanese expect a person who sees a problem to also solve it. If you're smart enough to recognize a problem, you're also smart enough to find the solution. Whoever is part of a problem is forced to be responsible for the solution.

Since the Japanese are group-oriented, each individual feels responsible to maintain group harmony and to help his fellow employees whenever possible. On the other hand, he is delegated enough authority so that he has enough power and resources with which to use his own initiative. In the same way, American executives will find that delegation develops a greater sense of responsibility and esprit de corps among subordinates. They will be forced to work together more.

Delegation of responsibility to subordinates also increases the likelihood that decisions will be of higher quality. It is a common fallacy that superiors are all-knowing and all-wise. Many administrative problems originate at lower levels and subordinates are more familiar with such issues and their solutions than superiors. They are on the scene, and they may have even caused a specific problem themselves. When two persons are quarreling over increased office space, the superior does well to encourage them to solve their differences themselves. Why make an enemy unnecessarily?

This policy encourages workers to solve problems before they are blown out of proportion. Following the Japanese principle that the person who does the work also knows more about it than any outsider, the participants themselves should arrive at a solution to any problem they've caused. Problems are best solved by those who are directly involved.

As important is the fact that delegation offers administrative experience to subordinates. The delegation of even minor problems gives subordinates the chance to develop their managerial skills without the possibility of doing great harm if they fail. Remember that most of these problems are minor if solved quickly enough. A wrong decision at this level is less costly. As the workers gain more experience in problem solving and in using their own initiative, they can be given more and more responsible tasks. The work becomes meaningful and more interesting.

Adopting a policy of delegation gives a manager the chance to train his personnel to replace him. This is a plus because delegation allows the manager to devote himself to more important affairs; he then, like his subordinates, becomes more promotable. As his subordinates become better workers, he becomes recognized as a better manager.

A foreigner dealing with Japanese managers first experiences confusion as to who is in charge of a certain project because of the custom of extensive delegation. I have noted that leaders delegate most of their daily responsibilities of younger associates. This delegation causes confusion to outsiders because lower-level Japanese managers make many more decisions and have more responsibility than American counterparts.

To an American, the lines of responsibility and authority in a Japanese office become tangled. But the work gets done; the subordinates become experienced; morale stays high because of involvement; and the leaders have the time to devote themselves to more important matters. Such a system of delegation was partially developed by General Motors in the 1940's, but few American corporations have followed GM's example.

Managerial delegation in America should be greatly expanded at all levels. The advantages of delegation as shown by Japanese and some American corporations are clear. Delegation demands that the workers are trusted enough so that they are given the responsibility to use their own initiative.

Managers on a powertrip will be unwilling to give workers the independence delegation demands. This lack of trust is one facet of the "American disease" which threatens our international primacy.

5.8 Tolerating Mistakes

There are two major elements of delegation that the successful manager does not ignore. A manager, by definition, deals with subordinates. This seem obvious, but many managers forget that they are dealing with humans and not automatons. Remembering this, a manager must be (a) patient with the mistakes of others and (b) control his own emotions when mistakes are made. Subordinates will make mistakes and superiors need to be prepared to handle them.

All persons make mistakes. The superior who is unwilling to allow mistakes is being unrealistic and expects too much from subordinates. The cost of most mistakes is less than the benefit gained from the worker's learning experience. Since most activities in an organization are relatively trivial, the good superior shouldn't mind a few mistakes from an inexperienced subordinate.

In practical terms, a manager should not criticize personnel so that they become afraid of further experimentation. Undue criticism destroys morale and trust and turns workers into extremely conservative bureaucrats, whether they are manual, staff, or white collars workers. Workers who have experienced criticism are likely to reject innovation and become permanently conservative. Once they have discovered the "safe" way to act they will avoid any change in work procedures.

On the other hand, past mistakes should not make the manager afraid to delegate. Managers often become impatient with the slowness or the errors of others. At times, there is the temptation to decide, "I'll do the job myself because no one else can do it as well as I can". The manager may think that he has regained control of the situation and now he can show workers how to do a given task. What has actually happened is that the subordinate has delegated work to his superior so that the manager is now a highly paid flunky. What does the subordinate have to do if his manager is now doing his work?

The Japanese reverse this direction of delegation. Whenever possible, the subordinate is given responsibility for completing the tasks of the boss. The worker works to maintain the group's *wa* and will be rewarded for doing so. As for the superior, there are enough other projects to do.

If a manager gets the impression that a subordinate seems to be continuously in a state of urgency, he should suggest that the subordinate delegate more of his work. Following the Japanese, American managers should delegate their authority and responsibilities as much as possible. An office managed in this way gives the impression of calm efficiency rather than being the center of a storm. An office which seems to be in the middle of a whirlwind indicates the holder is disorganized (and therefore inefficient), is not delegating enough (and is therefore also inefficient), or both. All of that hot air rarely fools anyone.

The supervisor does not abdicate his responsibilities when he delegates, nor does he become totally removed from the activities of the subordinates. Delegation should be seen as a strategy of on-the-job training (Engel, 1983:159). The superior should be ready to offer advice and direction; he becomes an instructor rather than a dictator. Employees have to be prepared before delegation of responsibility and then watched over. When the delegated task is finished, the superior should evaluate the performance and inform the employee how well he did. Then he can delegate more tasks.

Chapter 6
Practical Examples of Japanese Cooperation

6.1 The Ringi Decision-Making System

The concerns Japanese have for group harmony and smooth social relations result in what to Americans seem like unique practices. One of these most distinctive administrative practices is the ringi decision-making technique. Decisions constantly have to made in a corporation. The challenge, to the Japanese, is that decisions be made so that they do not threaten a group's *wa* but instead reinforce group consensus and harmony. In order that decisions are accepted by the workers, decisions are carefully discussed by everyone before they are made official. Naturally, a Japanese executive cannot always predict if a proposed course of action will be accepted, nor if a idea will eventually be developed into an acceptable working proposal and placed into action.

The Japanese manager is faced with a dilemma: a correct decision may be viewed by others as too individualistic if the decision is unilateral. The problem, then, is how a Japanese chief executive or foreman can develop new programs or give instructions without seeming to be so dictatorial that he is willing to ignore a group's *wa*.

The solution is the ringi system,[1] through which new ideas in the Japanese corporation are presented in such a way that workers do not feel resentful. The ringi system is based on a written statement which proposes an unorthodox plan of action not covered by ordinary procedures. This plan is then presented to others. Through compromise and consultation, the proposal is altered until consensus is reached. When this has been done, the proposal can be officially announced and put into action. By forging a compromise, an executive has introduced new ideas to subordinates and supported group harmony at the same time.

The ringi decision-making system operates in the following way. A plan or proposal is prepared in the form of a document *(ringisho)*. This document states a problem and outlines the solution. The *ringisho* is drawn up by a member of middle-level management and usually originates from that level. At times, a senior executive may "suggest" to a lower-level manager the need

---

[1] The term "ringi" is not italicized because its usage in the English language is now common. I have also omitted the pronunciation marks of Japanese words used in this book. These are useful only for Japanese speakers.

for a specific ringisho, but the initiative generally originates at the middle levels of the corporation.

The reason for this specific organizational level of origin is that the Japanese believe that planning should involve those who carry out the plan since those on the scene are most familiar with a situation. And, since they will be the most affected by the plan, they are the most motivated for it to succeed. No plan can succeed without the cooperation of those involved. The Japanese ensure that the cooperation is a enthusiastic as possible by making those involved co-sponsors and partners in the new enterprise.

There is an important psychological principle involved here. Getting the input and eventual acceptance of those who eventually carry out a project results in the feeling that this project becomes "theirs." People are more likely to be loyal when they have participated in the planning stages. Early consultation encourages workers to identify with a proposal.

Early consultation also makes those involved responsible for a project's success. If a project fails, it is becomes the subordinates' fault that they didn't see the plan's weaknesses. They had been consulted and given a chance to contribute. In America, where those in charge are likely to deliver unilateral orders, subordinates can explain failures (maybe due to disinterest) by pointing out no one had given them a chance to study a plan before it was ordered into motion. Failed policies are always someone else's chestnuts.

The ringi system encourages subordinates to use their initiative and participate actively during the planning stage of any project. Japanese executives strongly believe that a person capable of following orders is also capable of making those orders better in the first place. The ringi system is based on the assumption that workers should be allowed the initiative to develop the plans they will have to carry out. The Japanese clearly recognize that nothing is easier than to issue orders and then sit back while others try to make sense out of vague or inappropriate directions. This is not the way *wa* is achieved.

Senior officials in Japan rarely involve themselves in day-to-day decisions. These are formed at lower levels by those with the responsibility to implement them. The major functions of senior executives are to plan ahead and to maintain company-wide morale (*wa*). The ringi system is a procedure which allows senior executive to avoid spending too much time on matters better left to subordinates.

Even very dynamic managers believe that higher management should encourage subordinates to take charge. Konosuke Matsushita founded Matsushita Electric in 1935 and this organization and its allied companies now form one of the largest and most aggressive worldwide conglomerates. Yet the founder quit school when nine years old and came from a poor farming family. This entrepreneur typically reflects the Japanese value of managerial harmony even though he built his own company. Konosuke Matsushita summarizes his philosophy as:

The top executive should quietly sit back when things are going well. He should interfere as little as possible in the day-to-day operations. But if serious difficulties arise, he should firmly take personal command (Gould, 1970:38).

Not stated openly in the above quote, however, is that Matsushita employees are expected to solve their "serious difficulties" themselves. Nor should "difficulties" be allowed to become "serious." Matsushita electric and its subsidiaries are legendary for the decentralization of their decision-making process. Decentralization is common at Matsushita Electric even though Konosuke Matsushita is a self-made man. He was twenty-four years old when he, his wife, and brother-in-law founded the company. He voluntarily chose semi-retirement when a still-hardy seventy-nine years old.

During his retirement, Matsushita wrote a number of books presenting his ideas on how to correct Japan's current problems and reform the society. His most common theme is that the Japanese people need to trust each other more. In his book *Japan at the Brink* (1976:52), Matsushita wrote:

Everywhere in Japan today there is dissatisfaction in the midst of plenty, and this dissatisfaction tends to make people distrustful of anyone they feel to be depriving them of what they want. Distrust creates dissatisfaction, and dissatisfaction breeds distrust – it is a vicious circle. Spiritually, we are probably worse off than we were in the period immediately after the war.

In order to encourage the spirit of *wa* in Japan and in the world in general, Matsushita founded the PHP Institute for social research to increase understanding among people. Many Japanese corporate leaders retire before they need to in order to become elder statesmen and to devote their time to philanthropic projects.

The Ringi System in Action

The written plan, or ringisho, is first submitted horizontally to one's peers within the middle management levels, within one's department, and across divisional and departmental lines. The *ringisho* is shown to members of all departments potentially affected by the ringisho's contents. A production foreman may draw up a ringisho suggesting quality improvements of a product. This *ringisho* will be sent to the foreman in charge of distribution and storage; to the engineering division; to the accounting department; to the head of the local labor union if a change in work procedures is anticipated; anyone else who needs to be kept informed.

All personnel in departments potentially involved are shown the *ringisho*. These persons accept the *ringisho*, suggest modifications, or reject it. At each level there are numerous general discussions. Whenever a suggestion is added the *ringisho* is shown again to those who have not seen the modification. This is obviously a time-consuming process.

There are two advantages for passing out a *ringisho* at this stage. First, Japanese workers who are equal in age, status, and seniority work better together than with seniors or juniors, and a *ringisho* is less threatening when presented horizontally to equals. One doesn't lose "face" when interacting with and criticizing peers. There is also less pressure at this stage because the *ringisho* is tentative in nature and therefore is safe to criticize. One can view the incomplete proposal with a more critical eye than if it were a superior's favorite project.

The *ringisho* also travels horizontally across divisions from one department to another. This encourages managers to interact with members in other departments and decreases the tendencies in all organizations toward departmental secrecy and isolation. Middle-level managers are forced to discuss common problems with staff as well as line workers. They have to deal during these early stages of planning with technical specialists.

Ringishos give younger managers the chance to gain visibility as well as experience. This feature encourages managers to become generalists rather than specialists. *Ringishos* also force managers from different parts of the company to interact and become familiar with one another. Since extensive interpersonal skills are prerequisites for a future executive, going from person to person to discuss a ringisho and negotiate various changes provides valuable experience.

The Japanese do not feel comfortable dealing with strangers and would much rather avoid such situations. The temptation is to stay in one's own departmental offices where everyone is well known to the others. *Ringishos* force younger workers to deal with the widest possible range of colleagues. It would be easy for a specialist patent lawyer to stay in his office most of the time. But a *ringisho* spelling out the need to build a new automated factory would eventually reach the patents division of the company. The *ringisho's* proposal might involve new machines, the adaptation of older ones, or at least the study of recently published patents.

The senior patent lawyer would not want to deal directly with the (younger) originator of this *ringisho*. His assistant would then be asked to recommend it or not. This assistant would be forced to talk to a large number of co-workers in the accounting department (for budget considerations), the engineering staff, etc. This person would know a large number of other workers throughout the company after a few years of handling *ringishos*. He would also have developed a number of mutual debts with others after being forced to compromise on a number of *ringishos*. These workers now owe each other a number of favors which form the basis for compromises and cooperation in future ventures.

When all middle-level managers have seen, modified, and finally accepted a *ringisho*, the document is shown to and evaluated by more senior officials. One of the major duties of senior officials is to evaluate *ringishos*. Top officials and chief executive officers seldom get involved in day-to-day operations, and reviewing *ringishos* offers them a general view of future operations and allows them input on on-going decisions. Though senior managers "sit," they are never ignored by younger managers.

By the time a senior official sees a *ringisho*, it has been accepted by a large number of lower-level personnel and it would be hard to reject such a *ringisho* out of hand. This would be too individualistic and authoritarian. An executive who strongly objected to a specific proposal would have already seen to it that his displeasure would be well known during the earlier stages of development. No one is going to present an important *ringisho* without being certain no senior officials obviously object. Senior executives would already have a general picture of the contents of any *ringisho* long before it reaches their desks. There is little secrecy or ignorance in a Japanese company!

Ringishos also help to break down the differences between organizational levels. A senior official who hears of a *ringisho* that interests him will want to talk to the originator. He might "accidentally" meet this younger manager and his superior somewhere away from the office, in a informal setting. A negative response at this time would "suggest" that the *ringisho* in its present form is doomed. The three might spend several hours at a bar discussing on a informal basis why the senior manager opposes the *ringisho*. This would be the time to either accept changes in the proposal or convince the executive his objections are groundless or selfish.

Gradually, the ringisho travels vertically until it reaches the managing director or the president of the corporation. If accepted at the highest levels, the ringisho is then returned to the originating work group, where it is implemented.

Advantages of the Ringi System

The major advantage of the ringi system is that all relevant employes are allowed ("forced" might be more appropriate) input during the early stages of a proposal. Those who would be affected by the proposed plan are expected to interact with others during a discussion stage when criticism is easier to make.

It becomes more difficult to find fault with a completed plan after large amounts of time and effort have been invested in a *ringisho*. Once a plan has been accepted, everyone is morally obligated to follow official policy. A *ringisho* during the early stages is unofficial and viewed as a tentative statement of policy. Criticisms and amendments of a *ringisho* are positive contributions rather than disruptive, noncooperative activities.

The ringi system allows for criticism in a cultural system which emphasizes conformity. A ringisho also prepares workers for coming changes by informing them that a certain change is being considered. Many officials insist that they see a *ringisho* over which they have little formal interest; they want to be kept informed of what is going on. In Japan, proposed reforms are carefully evaluated before being accepted. After potentially-involved workers have accepted a *ringisho*, all have had the opportunity to make contributions and all have been kept informed on possible changes in the company. Change does not need to disrupt the company's *"wa."*[2]

Another advantage of the ringi system is that, once accepted, there will no longer be any opposition to a plan. There is complete acceptance when it is time to put a specific plan into action. If total agreement had not been achieved, the *ringisho* would have been altered or rejected earlier. The *ringisho* system allows for criticism and for full access to vital information about proposed changes and their effects.

More than a generation ago, Coch and French (1948) found that change in work procedures among American workers was associated with hostility toward supervisors and a high rate of labor turnover; many workers would rather quit their jobs than alter their work habits, even when work change is accompanied with increased pay. The ringi system decreases the resistance and hostility which often accompanies changes in the work place when workers are unprepared for it.

Likewise (Patchen, 1970:181–99), employee participation in decision-making increases workers' identification with the company and its goals. Participation in work changes gives the workers the feeling that change is not being arbitrarily forced on them. Joint consultation among managers and workers before a change is introduced reduces tension and resistance to change (Coch and French, 1948). By contrast, attempts to introduce change without prior consultations result in workers' resistance. The ringi system expressively enhances group identification through employee participation and consultation.

A *ringisho* is the Japanese managerial counterpart to the American practise of participative management. Both encourage the widest range of worker in-

---

[2] This type of cooperation also operates at the national level. Proposed changes are carefully analyzed to see if any pose a danger to "Japan, Inc." Little legislation is passed in the national assembly unless the civil service and corporate leaders have had the chance to evaluate and support a specific bill. See Vogel (1975) for several examples.

volvement at the lowest possible organizational level. The ringi system, however, is more systematic and allows more freedom of action. It's hard for even the Japanese to know when a "yes" really means "no", and the ringi system encourages junior managers to develop extensive friendship and information networks which allow criticism and open (honest) discussion. Since superiors see a large number of *ringishos* pass over their desks, they have to rely on their assistants to tell them which ones are acceptable. This involves subordinates in important decisions of a scope not allowed in America. The development of a *ringisho* also encourages middle-level management to interact on the organizational vertical and horizontal interdepartmental levels. At the same time, personnel gain experience in dealing with those outside their own work groups. This is an advantage to the senior officials who expect subordinates to become familiar with operations throughout the corporation and develop company-wide ties.

The ringi system is also used as a training device for junior executives. This practice forces them to develop plans and new systems as well as to develop new skills.[3] A senior official in marketing may ask a subordinate to react to a *ringisho* from the accounting department which proposes the purchase of a new computer system. The latter would have to learn about this new system, interact with accountants as well as computer specialists, and decide how this new computer can be used to the advantage of both the accounting and marketing sections.

The junior manager in marketing, on his part, has extended his knowledge of computers, he has had any errors in his *ringisho* corrected, and he has been asked by the accounting section to take their interests into consideration. He has been informally criticized if his plan is incomplete or inadequate without being officially reprimanded. The junior manager has been forced, in the interest of company-wide consensus, to become a generalist rather than a specialist. This process is excellent training and testing for future senior executives. Even someone eventually transfered to a "child company" gains from this experience.

The ringi system also allows less talented superiors to save face when talented subordinates indicate superior knowledge. Younger personnel can exhibit their updated knowledge when the superior is not completely familiar with the intricacies of a specific proposal. By making minor suggestions and taking some initiative, a superior can take partial credit for a successful *ringisho* as long as he trusts the abilities of his assistants. The system insures that younger workers can innovate without threatening the prestige and self-respect of

---

[3] The ringi system is also used to encourage Japanese managers and staff to be creative and innovative. Drawing up and developing a consensus for a *ringisho* forces younger personnel to come up with new ideas.

upper-level managers. Middle-level managers are usually the real initiators and change agents in Japanese corporations.

An approximation of the ringi method in America is found at General Motors. GM encourages a consensual committee process whereby decisions are hammered out informally, a practice developed when Peter Estes was GM president. Many decisions were made during daily lunch meetings of the executive committee. As Estes states concerning a major decision made over lunch, "We had a committee meeting later, but it was just to make sure nobody had any objections" (Burck, 1981:50). Had these informal sessions involved lower-level employees, GM executives would have had adopted an equivalent system to the *ringisho*. The process works best, though, when personnel from different levels interact. Otherwise, a meeting may be less constructive and merely convened for agreement purposes.

An American reader might be confused at this point as to the benefits of a ringisho for a specific, middle-level employee. This person does most of the researching, negotiating, compromising, and reassuring until a *ringisho* is accepted by all. The *ringisho*, as it becomes accepted by others, also becomes their instrument. The originator does all the work while others seem to receive partial credit if any at all. The Japanese see the benefits differently.

Good ringi decisions are credited with more than one author. Everyone naturally wants to be known as an early sponsor of a successful proposal. Ideas likely to be accepted are more quickly passed around. Many informal meetings take place so that a "pre-consensus" agreement can be reached. On the other hand, rejected *ringishos* disappear and, as would be expected, no one volunteers to be remembered as their sponsors. This process is common in American companies as well. Administrative failures are orphans in every country.

The originator is remembered for a least his efforts, and a successful originator receives partial credit while a failure is shared by all. Like his American counterpart, the Japanese manager hopes to protect himself from possible failures and to be recognized for his successes. The Japanese manager achieves this balance through reliance on his work group. Sharing credit is a small price to pay for the group's protection.

In addition every favor given in Japan entails a debt, and the Japanese keep a very careful accounting of all types of favor exchanges. Being known as an ingrate is something a Japanese wants to avoid at all costs. Giving someone partial credit will be repaid in the future. The ringi system is one way fellow employees repay favors and develop mutual debts to be cashed in the future.

It is possible for Japanese managers to try to take advantage of someone else's successes. This is especially true for an immediate superior. The respect a worker owes someone who is both older as well as in a superior position makes it hard to voice complaints. Complaining is be seen as being too selfish and individualistic.

A department head or a foreman can make life impossible for subordinates he doesn't like. A department head can ask for overtime, rush work, and can place a negative report in a worker's file. He can also start a rumor that someone is uncooperative and too individualistic. Another ploy a supervisor has available is to assign a worker demeaning or unpleasant tasks. A senior accountant who has displeased his superior can easily be "asked" to perform a simple audit a newly-hired co-worker can do.

A factory foreman can publicly criticize a worker's "spirit" and attitude. This complaint is vague enough to be hard to answer. After all, complaining back will be seen by others as a proof of the charge. Caught in this no-win situation, this worker is better off swallowing his pride and becoming friends with the foreman. Accepting "unfair" assignments quietly places the foreman in his debt. Not treating the worker fairly in the future in turn makes the foreman look selfish and unfair. He has to show friendliness and fairness in order to maintain the work team's *wa*. The team members themselves will begin to complain if one of their co-workers is treated unfairly. Workers in Japan are group-oriented because they are expected to be so and because they rewarded when they support their superiors' and the group's *wa*. The saying "to get along, go along" is accepted to an extreme degree in Japan.

Rewarded for being group-oriented, Japanese workers are not completely helpless when they feel they are being exploited. The Japanese have a very strong sense of what is right, and they resist being caught in what they see is an unequal exchange. If a manager's supervisor were taking unfair advantage of an assistant, the junior could ask for a transfer, or complain to age peers and former school mates in other departments. They would pass the gossip on to their own superiors who would be disturbed by this indication of low morale. The guilty supervisor would quickly be questioned in a subtle and unofficial manner about the lack of *wa* in his division. Since *wa* is a feature of good management, this supervisor would be motivated to quickly change his practices. He would probably invite his workers out for a few drinks and gently try to find out why morale was low. He might feel obligated to apologize to his workers for his past actions and promise to be a better supporter of the group's *wa*.

On the other hand, satisfied and productive subordinates are positive measures of superior management skills. Giving credit to subordinates and protecting their failures enhance the prestige of the executive. Encouraging subordinates to develop and later gain credit for developing successful *ringishos* aid both the superior and the subordinate. There is no greater praise than telling a Japanese manager he has the best work team. His subordinates' successes are also his. In the same way, a good *ringisho* reflects credit on the superior. It shows he's encouraging the best effort from subordinates.

Disadvantages of the Ringi System

The completion of a *ringisho's* rounds is time-consuming. A large number of persons must be consulted and many compromises made to please all parties, each of whom considers the political impact of a *ringisho* on their division and prestige. Then there are always the busybodies who are curious about a *ringisho* though it involves nothing in their areas of responsibilities. They will want to make comments just for the sake of seeming to be involved. They can't be ignored though they add little to a proposal. But these persons have to be talked to and their support gotten. You have to touch all bases if you want your ringisho accepted. A seemingly uninvolved person may have the contacts and influence needed to influence a third party's agreement.

Each leader consults with his own staff and colleagues to obtain everyone's support. Officials displeased with a *ringisho's* contents may delay a decision or voice vague disagreements. Those unsure on which position to take make noncommittal statements that are so ambiguous that no one can understand their intent. It takes patience as well as tact to be a Japanese manager.

Officials also evaluate a *ringisho* in terms of whether or not they feel their superiors like the proposal, since these officials will also have to judge the *ringisho*. Not wanting to disagree with a superior, there is the temptation to reinforce the status quo. This fear of contradiction can make a middle lever manager very conservative and conformist. The danger implied in a *ringisho*, a danger apparent to many, is that subordinates will try to predict their superiors' reaction and act accordingly. A *ringisho* in this context reinforces existing biases rather than initiates changes.

There is also a snowball effect pressuring for conformity as more and more officials accept a *ringisho*. The more a *ringisho* is accepted, the harder it becomes to criticize or reject it, since doing so gives the impression that one is not a team player. To sign may be easier than to criticize. Critics of the ringi system call it a system of collective irresponsibility.

A *ringisho* can be used to avoid personal responsibility and risk-taking in another way. A timid manager can originate and distribute a ringisho on a matter which is trivial but which he fears may be controversial; the ringisho in this case is a means of passing the buck.

The Future of the Ringi System

The Japanese are aware of the drawbacks of the ringi system. During the 1950s and 1960s when the American managerial system seemed better than their own, the Japanese established a number of study groups to see which American practices could best be incorporated into the Japanese system. It was decided that the ringi system was too central to Japanese managerial philosophy to be totally discarded, though some adaptations of the system were recommended. Too slow a decision-making technique, the ringi system is becoming an information medium through which comments, advice, and suggestions are asked. The ringi system is still preferred for medium-range and long-term proposals effecting large parts of a company.

Toyota Motors Company uses the ringi system primarily for situations involving contracts, court cases, expansion projects, and any proposal involving large sums (Furstenberg, 1974:66). It is also used to give junior managers experience by exposing them to a large number of the same documents being evaluated by superiors. This practice follows the belief that all employees, since they are part of the same company, should have as much information about their work as possible. While this may result in too many memos and other forms of communication, at least no one can complain that he lacks information.

Some Japanese organizations have limited the number of hierarchical levels and higher officials a *ringisho* must pass through. The search has been to make the *ringisho* system more efficient rather than to find a replacement for it. Its ability to promote group cohesion and interdepartmental communication makes the ringi system too valuable to discard completely. In America, interdepartmental memos, company newspapers, and in-house publications, including "president's messages" are all attempts to achieve some of a ringisho's utility. These, however, support or announce unilateral decisions and seldom encourage communal loyalty among workers.

6.2 Japan's Lack of Lawyers

The differences between American and Japanese societies are nowhere so clear as in the difference ways each country uses its respective legal system. The essence of these differences is that the Japanese are reluctant to resort to lawyers to solve their disputes. The Japanese values of supporting harmony and *wa* encourage the Japanese to seek mediation before seeking litigation. Bad debts, accident claims, inheritance disputes, tenant-landlord disputes, and the like are likely to be resolved rather than being formally presented in a law court (Chapman, 1981).

The reason for such a strong reluctance to seek legal redress lies in the Japanese belief that disagreements should be solved through compromise and eventual consensus. As in a corporation, quarrels among neighbors or business associates should be discussed until they are resolved. In the same way, suing a neighbour would be considered as an attempt to impose a solution by one party over another and consequently disapproved. Obviously, group harmony would be threatened by a lack of mutual agreement.

This preference for person-to-person solutions to disagreements results in Japan being the modern, industrialized nation with the lowest ratio of lawyers to its population. There is one lawyer per 10,000 person in Japan, as compared with 18 lawyers per 10,000 in the United States. The corresponding ratios for France and West Germany are two and four per 10,000, respectively (Tanaka, 1976:266). The relative unimportance of lawyers in Japan is illustrated by the fact that there are at least 35 certified flower-arranging teachers for every Japanese lawyer (Chapman, 1981).

There is more at work here than an unwillingness to seek legal ways of redress, since the postwar period was a litigious one. At that time, the Japanese were quite willing to sue and go to court. And, in fact, Japanese lawyers keep very busy today. There is no shortage of activities for today's lawyers.

But there is a shortage of lawyers. One reason for this is that the number of lawyers in Japan is kept artificially low by the government. To become a lawyer one must take two years post-university training at the government's Legal Training and Research Institute. To be accepted as a student as this Institute, essentially Japan's only law school, applicants must pass very rigorous entrance examinations. About as many Japanese per capita take these exams as Americans take the bar examinations. The difference is that less than two percent (1.5%) of applicants pass in Japan while most (74%) Americans do so. Japan could easily have as many lawyers in a decade or so as America if most who applied eventually got accepted (Upham, 1981b:151).

Even so, lawyers are less likely to be used in Japan. Business negotiations tend not to involve many lawyers, especially during the early stages. When Japanese businessmen deal with Japanese rather than foreigners, the chances are that lawyers will seldom be called on. Japanese corporations will employ persons trained in the law, especially for patent and tax matters (which are distinctly separate specialties needing specialized training), but many will not have passed the formal examinations necessary for licensing.

There are many Japanese who act as lawyers without being officially counted as such. While there are an estimated twelve thousand practicing lawyers in Japan, there are probably slightly over one-hundred thousand others doing legal work in one related way or another. This figure includes judges, government legal advisors, real estate specialists, and tax attorneys (Clayton, 1984).

Formal litigation is used so seldom by the general public that more trials take place in the state of Ohio than in all of Japan. Incidents which would almost automatically become court cases in the United States are settled informally, if not necessarily amicably. In a study of Tokyo taxicab companies, two cases were filed out of 2,567 accidents involving physical or property damage (Upham, 1981b:150). One reason for this lack of legitation is that, on the average, the plaintiff will usually lose a court case. Japanese legal thought is often concerned more with societal *wa* than with the protection and promotion of individual rights. A person suing another person or a company usually receives little sympathy from the presiding judge.

Plaintiffs are often blamed by the Japanese public for being greedy and for exhibiting a selfish lack of *wa*. In addition, Japanese courts are notoriously slow, and few Japanese have the financial resources and the patience, as well as the social support of friends and neighbors, to sue. They are practical as well as cultural reasons why there are one hundred times the number of litigations in America than in Japan (Tsubota, 1984).

When a civil conflict exists, the first step is usually to select a mediator who is respected by both parties. Hopefully, this mediator is able to develop a compromise acceptable to both parties. This is the likely result. For one reason, if an agreement cannot be amicably reached, then the mediator has failed; he loses face. The blame for this failure will also be placed in part on the party who refuses to compromise. If the mediator is someone respected by both parties, they are under great pressure to reach a consensus.

I do not want to picture the Japanese as a people who always solve their differences in a mutually satisfactory fashion. But the legal system is not organized to handle a case load as large as found in America.[4] Getting satisfaction through the Japanese courts is more time-consuming than in America as well as more expensive. It's usually easier to settle through extralegal means (Tsubota, 1984).

There is an illustrative as well as amusing story illustrating how the Japanese view law and the legal system. A man lost a purse containing three gold coins. A second man found the purse, and by reading the owner's name on the purse,

---

[4] Japanese judges are notorious for relying on the spirit of the law rather than on the strict letter of the law. A plaintiff may have the law on his side and still lose because a moral "right" supported his opponent. While the Japanese legal system looks very similar *on paper* to those of western European countries, the spirit interpreting these codes is altogether different (see Upham 1981a and 1981b). Japan adapted extensively as European law codes were used to modernize the society (see Gould, 1984).

located the owner and presented him with the purse. The owner, ashamed of having lost valuable property, refused to acknowledge his loss or that the purse was his. The second man insisted that he had found the purse, that he wanted to hand it over, and that he expected a reward for his honesty. In the Japanese fashion, the two parties agreed to present their case to a local judge renowned for his wisdom, He was asked to mediate their quarrel.

After hearing both arguments, the judge took a gold coin from his pocket and added it to the three in question, making four coins in all. He then gave two coins to the original owner and the two others to the finder. The judge then pronounced his judgment. Because of this disagreement, he said, the owner now has two gold coins instead of three; the finder has two coins instead of three had he kept his find. And the judge himself was out one gold coin. Because of this disagreement, all three had lost one gold coin, and the two fools before him had better not appear in his court again!

Japanese who want to make sure a legal matter will end to their advantage can hire members of the *jidan-ya* (compromise makers) profession. These are essentially bill collectors, evictors, and the like who are willing at times to use violence and physical intimidation. This is patently illegal, but some Japanese are willing to use these quasi-gangsters to shortcut the time that formal compromises and judicial processes take. Lawsuits involve expenses as well as time, so it is no surprise that, if a compromise doesn't seem likely (court costs and filing fees are very costly in suits involving large sums), the aggrieved party might be tempted to use extralegal means to gain satisfaction (Tanaka, 1976:285).

However, the ideal among the Japanese is for conflicting parties to try to resolve their differences personally or through a mediator. Most Japanese feel that a search for a formally legal "justice" might cause more conflict and more disharmony. It is better to compromise a little than to insist on the strict letter of the law. Like Americans, most Japanese prefer receiving mercy rather than relying on a strict interpretation of the law.

Takeo Shiina, chief executive officer and president of IBM Japan Ltd. recommends that American exporters, to be successful in Japan, must realize that Japan and American cultures contain different legal systems. He points out that IBM Japan has been active in Japan for nearly sixty years (Shiina, 1984). IBM Japan was able to grow into a company with 14,400 employees by paying close attention to the Japanese legal as well as business culture. IBM Japan is now regarded by university graduates as one of the most prestigeful companies to work for.

Part of this distinctive Japanese business culture, Shiina advises, lies in the fact that to the Japanese, law is appealed to only as last resort. There will be personal appeals, private meetings, and attempts to negotiate any differences between business associates when they disagree. Laws, to the Japanese, are legislative actions performed by bureaucracies. Thus, laws are imposed upon parties because of politics, specific interests, or immediate interests that may not be valid in the future. Custom and tradition are more important to the Japanese than laws.

By contrast, Americans see laws as legislated by the Congress or other legitimate representative of the people. For Americans, bad law is one which does not originate from the people or which does not protect one individual from another. Laws are "sacred" to us. To the Japanese, custom, tradition, and harmony are sacred. Americans tend to rely on the letter of the law: a law is what it says. By contrast, the Japanese search for the traditions and group harmony a law should support. If it fails to do so, then they are quite willing to ignore the law; or else they will "interpret" its meaning until it does fit present needs.

Suing for breach of contract or insisting on the letter of the law uses abstract principles to take advantage of individuals. This reluctance to sue is a trait similar to the pressure faced by managers to develop group harmony and consensus among co-workers and subordinates. The importance of the group and the avoidance of open conflicts are keys in the understanding of the Japanese society. The Japanese who cooperates is living up to a very pervasive cultural trait.

6.3 The Japanese Contract

Another example of the Japanese reliance on cooperation is the way contracts and agreements are viewed. Contracts tend to be vague and contain ill-defined clauses because obligations, the Japanese believe, should be guided by personal relationships. The conditions directing these relations may change faster than impersonal legal documents. Relations, whether business or otherwise, should be ruled by guidelines that allow for mutual adjustments. Rules always exist and must be followed, but the personal dimension should also never be forgotten. Because of this attitude, the Japanese find it difficult to deal impersonally with others. Every action is taken "personally." There is a disinclination to separate the personal from a "business is business" approach.

A well-defined contract is necessary only when strangers have to deal with each other. Only those who distrust each other, according to the Japanese, need a detailed contract. Mutually-dependent friends who trust each other have no need to be so formal. Those who have formed personal relationships should be willing to act on the spirit of an agreement rather than on its literal nature. Stressing the letter of the law disturbs the harmony two partners have formed.

The Japanese establish personal relationships when dealing with others. A written contract is an aid to one's memory rather than a straightjacket binding those concerned. Japanese exporters had to learn to their dismay that foreigners expected detailed and very formal trade agreements. They also learned that foreigners – Americans in particular – were quite willing to sue and seek legal redress whenever they thought this would be profitable.

Nowhere are cultural differences so evident as how Japanese and Americans view the nature of a contract. Americans see the signing of a business contract as the final stage of negotiations. All that is left to do is for each party to carry out a contract's conditions and clauses.

The traditional Japanese view of what constitutes a contract is quite different from the above. The word is translated as *keiyaku*, defined as an agreement to form a business relationship (Clayton, 1983). It does not legally bind both parties to specific courses of action. Instead, a *keiyaku* documents a willingness to work together. Details will be agreed upon later as well as change when future conditions change.

This contractual vagueness exists because the Japanese believe that personal ties, not laws, should guide long-term relationships.[5] Asking for a detailed contract enforceable by an impersonal third party (the legal system) is understood as a lack of trust. A person's integrity and sense of honor are questioned when there is an insistence on a detailed accounting. The same principle is found in the United States when two persons achieve an agreement and shake hands as a sign of mutual trust. Shaking hands is based on the participants' sense of honor; a contract can be signed later if needed. This approach works when parties know each other well and are connected through a system of mutual obligations. It works less well when strangers begin to develop business ties.

The *keiyaku* is vague because the Japanese realize that external forces and unanticipated events can make contracts invalid. The Buddhist heritage also emphasizes that fate intervenes in human affairs, and that the individual can often do little against these forces. Contractual parties should adjust their obligations toward each other when conditions change radically.

Most Japanese now understand that the western concept of a contract is not the same as theirs. However, as negotiations proceed, and contractual relations become more and more specific, it's wise for Americans to ask their

---

[5] This same conception of the nature of contracts is also found in China. Chinese contracts contain clauses which are statements of hopes and expectations rather specific conditions (Bennett, 1984). Foreigners wishing to export technology into Shenzhen, a duty-free zone established for foreigners, must agree that, among other conditions, this machinery will produce "remarkable economic results" for China.

interpreter whether the Japanese negotiators are thinking "contract" or *"keiyaku."* If the latter, they fully expect that details will be flexible and negotiable even after an agreement is signed. The *keiyaku* is a document which will change as the demand for *wa* changes. It is more of a token of friendship than a rigid document.

The emphasis of people over laws parallels the Japanese distrust of lawyers and legal nitpicking. Lawyers traditionally have been given low prestige in Japan. It is best not to include legal representatives during the early stages of negotiation with the Japanese. Lawyers get involved only after the parties have agreed to agree.

Japanese businessmen who deal with Americans see the latter as almost eager to find loopholes in an agreement in order to seek an advantage. By contrast, Japanese business relations are seen as forming a new group which binds the participants through some type of general loyalty. This American willingness to break a contract in order to gain a short-term monetary advantage confuses the Japanese. Customer and business relations are seen as long-run and are not limited to contractual conditions. Japanese manufacturers establish permanent relations with suppliers and customers whenever possible. They become part of the company's "family" in the same way employees become family members of the corporation.

Business agreements with Japanese take time to conclude because both parties want to understand each other as completely as possible. This way each participant gets a feeling for each other's special needs and preferences. Fewer disagreements will later develop when this is achieved. The Japanese are willing to agree to ignore certain conditions of a contract if this ensures the relationship's *wa* and a profitable future partnership.

Suppose a supplier has agreed to deliver a certain number of parts over a period of time at a specific cost as stated in a contract. Suddenly the suppliers's costs go up due to a large increase in fuel prices. This makes the agreement no longer as profitable. The supplier's senior management would likely ask for a new agreement involving higher returns. The manufacturing managers, unlike their American counterparts, might very well agree to a higher price. The assumed and unspoken agreement is that the supplier would return the favor in the future. This could be done by later offering the buyer lower prices when costs decrease. The supplier might also be expected to increase deliveries at the same prices, even if this means added costs due to overtime and sheduling changes. The idea of going to court to evade contract conditions or to force the other party to live up to the letter of the agreement is not the Japanese way.

The non-contractual understandings in a business agreement force potential associates to learn as much as possible about the other parties. It's for this reason that formalizing an agreement takes up so much time when dealing with the Japanese. They want to make sure they understand clearly all contractual and non-contractual obligations. This way to understand the latter is for all parties to meet informally under social conditions so that a wide range of topics can be explored and discussed.

The subjective (emotional) expectations while negotiating are as important as the objective (impersonal) ones and must be agreed upon before an agreement can be finalized. But the former are difficult to understand. It is relatively easy to agree on prices, delivery schedules, or specifications. That can be done at the office in a businesslike environment and is a straightforward process. In Japan, such matters will be left to subordinates. The subjective, extra-contractual agreements demand establishing a personal relationship. An employee dealing with potential clients must entertain. This allows business discussions to develop on a personal basis in a friendly atmosphere.

The corporate employee who entertains customers receives an entertainment allowance, often larger than his own salary. Many of his evenings and weekends will be taken up with entertaining at the company's expense. This activity is so extensive that more is spent on business entertaining than on the national defense budget (Graham, 1981)!

The purpose of so much entertainment is two-fold. Those involved develop personal feelings toward each other. They form a new group based on a feeling of harmony and *wa*. As important, though, is that this entertainment also allows each party to understand and know the other. These personal relations, it's hoped, will make misunderstandings less likely in the future. This leads to less legal litigation as well as greater interest in business partners.

The Japanese have an envious reputation in being honest and reliable business associates. When a contract is finally agreed upon, the Japanese are certain they can live up to all conditions both spoken and unspoken, and they are willing to do so. They bargain hard, but an agreement, once reached, will be followed as agreed. If the American partner feels that a clause is not being adhered to well enough, or that some change in the contract is needed, he should do the following. Hint that you're not completely satisfied, and call for a face-to-face meeting. Preferably, offer to go to Japan (see chapter ten).

Before leaving for Japan, make comprehensive preparations. Be prepared to give extensive reasons why you are unhappy with your Japanese partner, with ample proofs. These will be passed on to a large number of specialists who will go over the specs very, very carefully.

Once in Japan, talk honestly with your Japanese counterparts. Don't yell, threaten, or insult. Camly state your grievances. Don't threaten to call in the lawyers. The Japanese know this will be done as a last resort anyway. Keep the discussion friendly and low-key. The Japanese will listen carefully and consider very seriously what you have said.

6.4 Wages, Bonuses, and Gifts

In order to decrease person-to-person competition and jealousy, Japanese wages are primarily based on group rather than individual characteristics. In addition, Japanese wage differentials tend to be smaller than in the United States. There is more equality of reward in a Japanese corporation.

Many Japanese have criticized American executives for being paid too much. It's true that in contrast to Americans, Japanese managers are grossly underpaid. As important is the fact that the differences between higher and lower level members in a Japanese corporation are small when compared to American pay schedules. In terms of basic pay (though not expense accounts), Japanese corporate workers' wage levels are very equal. While wages for all are relatively low, they are also more equal in Japan. This real fact of equality reinforces the Japanese sense of "family." The group ethos of the Japanese operates to keep wage differentials at a minimum. There is less chance of feelings of relative deprivation among Japanese corporate employees.

In the Chiyoda Chemical Engineering and Construction, Ltd., male blue-collar wages were ninety-two percent of male white-collars, though virtually all of the latter had university experience and the former had not (Davis, 1982: 425). Nor does Chiyoda emphasize educational achievement when retirement benefits are considered. Imagine that a Chiyoda employee was to retire after thirty-one years of service. When a university graduate with a master's degree is given a retirement bonus of 100, an employee with a bachelor's degree receives 91, a senior high school graduate receives 77, and a junior high school graduate receives 60. There is not much difference in how workers are rewarded when seniority is taken into account.

This company deals in highly technical products, and employees' graduate degrees would all have been in technical fields. Yet an employee with two years of high school would be given a retirement bonus sixty percent as large as the one received by a college graduate with the same seniority. The same income differences exist when wages are considered. A fifty year old male with a senior high school degree receives a salary that is ninety-one percent that of a university graduate of the same age.

Another way of looking at wage differentials is to compare Chiyoda employees with thirty years of experience. Given equal seniority, a senior high school graduate earns seventy-seven percent that of a university graduate. But a university graduate with only ten years seniority earns sixty-three percent of a senior high school graduate with thirty years of service, and forty-eight percent of a university graduate with the same thirty years (Davis, 1982:428). It's clear that length of service is highly rewarded at Chiyoda, as it is in all Japanese companies.

Younger workers, from this perspective, are underpaid, especially those who are well educated. Their reward at this stage is not financial. Instead they receive job security, being able to join a "family," and many fringe benefits. This policy of rewarding seniority rather than formal attributes (education, experience, etc.) also places at a disadvantage those who make mid-career changes in employers. Although older, their seniority at their new company is non-existent. It would be unfair to pay a new, older worker on the basis of age only. The solution preferred by Japanese corporations is to hire only younger workers and reward primarily on the basis of seniority.

Japanese executives earn salaries not much different from average workers. There is a smaller range among pay levels in comparison to wage differences in the United States. This occurs on the national as well as the corporate level.

When considering the total national income, the Japanese wealthiest twentieth percent of income recipients received 37 percent of Japan's total income. The corresponding percent for the United States, the United Kingdom, and West Germany was 47%, 37%, and 47% respectively (cited in Keidel, 1981:129). There is more income equality in Japan than in the United States. While this is a recent, postwar phenomenon, this lack of high income differentiation certainly contributes to the Japanese view that all workers gain or suffer together.

In 1979, a typical corporate president earned roughly eight times the salary of a first-year employee. In the United States, the same difference in pay is about twenty times (Gibney, 1982:66–7). Take-home pay of corporate workers in Japan does not vary much from one level to another, except in terms of seniority. The lack of large income differences among workers at different levels encourages a greater sense of common loyalty.

Another difference in incomes received between Japan and the United States is that Japanese executives are not paid as much as their American counterparts. Promotion in Japan is rewarded by prestige and honor rather than financial gains. The average pay for top executives in the United States during 1981 was around $ 1,500,000. In Japan, presidents of the largest companies received an average of roughly $ 400,000. The tax bite for those in the higher income brackets is also higher in Japan (Gibney, 1982:66).

Relatively low salaries as well as low intra-firm salary differentials make it easier for a Japanese executive to claim that all workers are part of a family and still be believable. Japanese workers can see for themselves that they share profits in common, and that improving productivity does not result in higher pay for executives only.

Bonuses

A significant part of corporate pay is based on semiannual bonuses averaging three to six months or more a recipient's base salary. These bonuses come from two Japanese traditions and are given out in December and July. The first custom is the midyear visit to ancestral cemeteries and places of family origin. Visiting both relatives and cemeteries involves certain expenses. A son may want to pay for a shinto rite at the grave site or for a grave marker; these are very expensive when elaborate. The rites can also be especially expensive for the recently dead. For the truly devout, the first two or three years after a parent's death involve a number of expensive Shinto memorial rites. Most younger Japanese, especially those living in cities, are gradually abandoning these customs. It's more pleasant to go skiing or to visit Hawaii than to spend a vacation visiting relatives and cemeteries.

Visits to relatives necessitate gifts, often expensive ones. Distant relatives keep up with each other through a series of seasonal gifts. A farmer might send a box of fresh vegetables to a city cousin or brother. Such gifts, of course, must be repaid eventually. The midyear visits offer a city dweller an excellent opportunity to do so. The Japanese need extra money during this time to be able to afford gifts to friends, neighbors, and family members, as well as customers. Business relations also give each other gifts at this time. Many, though not all, of these business-related gifts are paid by the employer.

The Japanese also believe that no one should start the new year owing debts. The December bonus is used to buy year-end presents (*o-seibo*) and pay back minor debts. This is a very festive season and there are festivals, parties, exchanges of gifts, and more parties, all of which entail expenses. Unlike Americans who celebrate the coming of the New Year, the Japanese celebrate the end of the old. Parties are attended to help everyone forget the old year and to forgive any animosities which might have developed over the past year. All companies and most voluntary groups and associations hold a series of year-end parties to encourage co-workers to forget past slights and rededicate themselves to the group's *wa*.

The significance of these bonuses for corporate workers is that they are based on the company's profitability. A good financial record results higher bonuses for everyone, while the opposite results in lower or no bonuses. Workers receive periodic reminders every six months that better work is rewarded. These bonuses are company-wide in that permanent workers receive them, so there is also the reminder that everyone gains when the company prospers.

Workers receive smaller bonuses during depressed periods. Usually, higher executives experience larger pay cuts than their subordinates. This is a not-so-subtle reminder that leaders depend on their followers and must take the responsibility for the company's welfare.

The largest part of these bonuses is standard and does not change from year to year except during periods of economic crisis. They are written in union-management agreements and, barring an economic disaster, can be counted on from one season to another. Usually, though, these bonuses are larger than the minimum. This makes these semi-annual windfalls more like delayed payments than bonuses per se. They are cushions keeping the company's finances flexible. During a period of economic depression, a company can reduce its payments every six months instead of laying off valuable workers. These bonuses offer companies a way of regulating labor costs to fit sales curves and investment programs.

These bonuses arrive every six months and can't be used to plan a family's day-to-day budget. Japanese budgets are organized around non-bonus income and the bonuses are seen as "extra" pay. A corporate housewife, for example, can't always predict what a future bonus will be, and daily expenditures can't use windfall income received months later. These semi-annual bonuses make it easier for Japanese families to save a large proportion of their total incomes. This savings rate – three times larger than in the United States, makes more money available for capital investments and economic expansion without the pain of inflation.

According to a 1984 survey of Japanese housewives (*Look Japan*, 1984:28), ninety percent of Japanese families give gifts in July *(o-chugen)* and December *(o-seibo)*. Counting these two types of gifts and for other occasions – births, weddings, etc – Japanese families buy an average of seventeen gifts. Each gift usually involves a return gift, so gift exchanges are an important source of social cohesion.

The same degree of exchanges of favors and gifts usually (drinks and meals) goes on at work. While many workers enjoy limited expense accounts, most accept un-reimbursed business-related expenditures as normal. The Japanese believe that a team's *wa* cannot be fully developed after hours and on weekends. There are also parties and banquets, especially during the end of the year, which must be paid for and attended by all employees. These semi-annual bonuses are important because social expenses – business related and otherwise – increase during July and December.

Social pressure does not allow the Japanese to keep all of their bonuses. On the contrary, a part of these bonuses, in addition to gift buying and party expense, is used for irregular purchases such as appliances, automobiles, or clothes. About sixty-five percent of bonuses are spent on shopping and gifts. This gives the economy a boost twice a year instead of once a year as in the United States. American department and jewelry stores, for example, count heavily on sales made during the christmas season. Japanese stores enjoy Christmas twice a year!

The year-end bonuses provide a surprise for American tourists visiting Japan in December. The Japanese have adopted Christmas decorations and music with a zest that belies the fact that only one percent of the population is Christian. Christmas lights and Christmas trees decorate department stores. Christmas jingles play in public places and reindeer decorate the walls. Even the life-size statue of the Colonel standing in front of each Kentucky Fried Chicken outlet sports a Santa Claus suit in honor the season!

On a more serious level, bonuses are visible rewards of workers' loyalty and productivity. They are also tangible tokens of the company's gratitude. They represent the successful achievement of worker-management *wa*.

6.5 The Education Rat Race

The value the Japanese place on education is another major area of difference separating American and Japanese societies. The Japanese are very much concerned with how knowledge is to be transmitted and what will be taught. These concerns are responsible for much of Japan's post-war recovery. Education is highly respected in Japan, and is often a lifelong quest. Many Japanese continue to take various classes throughout their adult years. The Japanese, for example, read more newspapers and books on a per capita basis than Americans. While some of this reading time is devoted to adult comics with pornographic scenes and plots, the Japanese neverthless are serious readers.

The Japanese nation is one of the best educated in the world, and illiteracy is almost unknown. This literacy has been achieved in spite of the fact that Japanese script is highly complex and difficulty to learn. Students in Japanese high schools are still learning to read and write the basic 2,000–3,000 characters (of words and concepts) needed to be considered literate. A specialized vocabulary – for a profession or occupation – demands the Japanese become familiar with a greater number. Even for everyday use, the Japanese reader must become familiar with a two very different alphabets plus a larger number of Chinese characters.

In spite of this difficulty, the quality of Japanese education is high. In standardized test after test, Japanese children have scored higher on the average than children from other nationalities, and far above the American averages. This includes math and scientific subjects as well as problem-solving abilities. In terms of mathematic achievement, Japanese thirteen year olds have an average score almost twice that of Americans taking the same test (Husen, 1967). All students learn a foreign language as well as the basic skills for playing wind and keyboard instruments. Their knowledge of American and European history and geography is at a par with the average American high school graduate.

A reason for this high quality is that the Japanese take education very seriously. The Japanese government leaders during the second half of the Nineteenth Century realized that to survive the western colonial threat, the population had to be educated along modern lines. The Japanese accepted the fact that western technology could easily overwhelm Japan. But unlike the Chinese at this time, the Japanese felt confident that they could learn European knowledge and adapt it to their use. Even today, education has a patriotic dimension: learning helps the nation survive.

Another reason for the high quality of Japanese education, especially in the primary and secondary levels, is that Japanese do not hesitate to push their children to work hard. Japanese children are spoiled when very young. Infants are rarely punished and young children are, from an American perspective, pampered and spoiled. All this stops when the child reaches the age to go to school. From then on, his major responsibility in life is to prepare for adulthood through education. This also applies to girls, though to a somewhat lesser extent. The standard school week is five-and-a-half days of class, with frequent Saturday afternoon outings for cultural events. The school year is long (240 days vs. an American 180 days). Homework takes one to two hours a day in the primary schools and up to two and one-half or more hours in high school (Christopher, 1983: Chapter 4).

Children who do not take their school studies seriously are not living up to their filial duties. They are not showing proper gratitude to their parents. Failure in school is a familial (and a patriotic) as well as a personal failure. This motivates Japanese children to work long hours on their school subjects.

Nor is this all. For reasons to be explained below, most middle-class children aged of nine or ten and over attend private tutorial schools *(Juku)* three or four times a week. The *juku* prepares good students for the entrance examinations which have to be passed in order to attend the better high schools and universities. *Juku* sessions are all taken up with the memorization of knowledge useful for entrance examinations.

This intensive effort begins before reaching high school.[6] In Japan, high school attendance is based on aptitude as well as residence. Whenever possible, each school system operates a number of schools ranked by difficulty and expectations. Children will attend a high school because of aptitude and test performance rather than neighborhood residence. In one sense, all high school students in Japan are bused. Every large city supports a number of high

---

[6] The best description of the high school environment in Japan is found in Thomas P. Rohlen's *Japan High Schools* (1983). This book contains excellent analyses and descriptions of Japanese high schools and their cultural environment. Both the strengths and weaknesses of Japanese education below the post-high school stage are described.

schools, each at a different level of difficulty. Elementary school students must take a high school entrance examination before being accepted. The better qualified students attend the more demanding and better respected high schools. The less motivated or intelligent students go elsewhere. Private high schools exist, but they too require prospective students to take entrance exams, and each is ranked in terms of its difficulty, discipline, and the degree of success of its graduates to be accepted by the better universities.

School rankings are important because the major purpose of a high school education is to prepare students to pass the entrance examinations of Japan's colleges and universities. High schools are ranked in prestige in terms of how many of their graduates are accepted by the top-ranking ten to twenty elite universities. Even private high schools are similarly ranked. No privage high school expecting to be respected would accept only wealthy students who cannot meet the standards of the school. All elementary school children must pass very difficult exams in order to be accepted to the best high schools and into universities.

The major responsibility of mothers with children in high school and lower schools is to see that they do well in school. A mother is expected to encourage her son to study and to help with homework, if possible. She becomes the child's driving force, since the father is seldom at home until late at night. He expends all of his energies at work.[7]

We see here major values of the Japanese culture at work. Education, like developing exports, is a patriotic matter. A businessman can feel he's an ancient samurai when he has conducted a successful piece of business which "helps" Japan (and the group). Students are also seen as front-line warriors on whose shoulders the future of Japan's prosperity and cultural survival.

There is, in the educational system, no support for individuality. Students are not encouraged to develop a strong sense of individuality. While of high quality, Japanese education is based on already-established guidelines determining what a student should learn. Individual interpretations of topics and speculations are not welcomed. The Japanese child learns very early to conform intellectually as well as socially.

---

[7] A mother's concern for her student son can be manipulated to his advantage. A student might demand special foods and treatment to make studying easier. A "good" mother often cooks two suppers, one containing the favorite dishes of her son and another for her late-arriving husband. The latter would probably be a simple supper of rice and vegetables if he's had a snack with co-workers before getting onto his commuter train. The son's preferred menu would be more western.

The Education of an Elite

This emphasis on hard work and rote memorization exists because an individual's primary educational goal is to enroll in one of Japan's best universities. All work in high school is focused on passing the entrance examinations of the high-pretstige universities. A student who is accepted by a major university is assured of getting job offers from the best government ministries and the most-respected corporations. Few who hope to rise to the top levels of Japanese society can do so unless they are graduates from one of the "best" universities. There are exceptions to this, but they are very few.

Becoming a student in these high-prestige universities requires passing very competitive entrance competitions. On a national average, roughly four applicants take university entrance examinations for every opening (Rohlen, 1983:84).[8] Most students have either give up their aspirations or try again. According to Thomas Rohlen, one-third of those accepted by universities have taken the yearly entrance exams at least one other time. Roughly 200,000 Japanese high school graduates (called *ronin* or wandering samurai) are studying at home to prepare themselves for next year's round of examinations.

Nearly all Japanese leaders are graduates from a handful of Japanese elite universities. Over a hundred and fifty years ago, education was seen as a major means toward national survival, and the Japanese established a number of national elite universities. Those who graduate from these – Tokyo University (called Todai) and Kyoto University have the highest prestige – are guaranteed success in life. Nearly all of Japan's political, national bureaucratic, and corporate postwar leaders are graduates of Todai or the next ten highest ranked elite universities.

The exceptions are few and dramatic in their scarcity. For example, 557 of the presidents of Japan's top 993 corporations are graduates of Todai, Kyoto, and Hitotsubashi universities (which are public) and the private Keio and Waseda universities (Woronoff, 1981:211). It's easy for Japan's elites to develop a sense of togetherness and identity: most have graduated from the same few schools.[9] A recent survey of Japan's one hundred major companies found that one-fourth of all chief executives were Todai graduates (Rohlen, 1983:38).

From one point of view, Japan's society is an open one: anyone who graduates from an elite university is assured a leading position in life. And in point of

---

[8] This is a rough estimate and includes repeaters and those who apply to more than one university. In addition, an applicant must be accepted by a specific department as well as by the university. Medical schools, elite universities, and elite departments have as many as twenty-five applicants for each opening (Bedford, 1981).

[9] Given the rigidity of the educational system and the fact that all of these elites have passed the same entrance examinations, they have roughly the same knowledge and outlook in life.

fact, Japan's elite contains a greater proportion of upwardly mobile members than does America. Family inheritance means less in Japan than in the United States. But the costs of private tutors and *juku* attendance as well as other types of cram schools and examinations trials are prohibitive to many families. The poor, or those who live in isolated rural areas, cannot offer their sons the elite primary and secondary education needed to pass the entrance exams of the best universities. Some families are able to bribe university officials through "donations" to accept their children, but that too takes above-average wealth.

Unlike America's elite schools, most of Japan's are public rather than private. While some of the highest-quality universities are private, most are government-supported. To bribe one's way into a lower-prestige university does not make up for not being accepted by an elite institution. Private universities are also ranked in importance by the general public. They must restrict admission to only the best that they can attract to maintain their reputation. The admission examinations of the best-ranked private universities are as difficult as those found in public universities.

The Examination Hell

How is membership into the elite determined if family prestige and/or wealth are secondary as criteria for selection? The answer is selection through examination.

There are roughly ten applicants for each opening at the dozen top-ranking elite universities and a five-to-one ratio for the two dozen universities considered to be ranked in the second prestige tier.

Applicants hoping to be accepted into a top ranked university must first take a one-day general exam. Those who qualify then take a two or three-day series of test on as many as eight different areas. Virtually every high school student wanting to attend an elite university attends a *juku*! There is the Japanese saying that "more than four hours sleep means failure" for anyone hoping to pass a university's entrance examination. Applicants are expected to spend the last months before university "examination hells" preparing all of the time for these exams. This preparation means memorizing answers to past and possible future questions. In Japan, pre-college education, except for vocational programs, is oriented almost completely toward the university entrance exams.

Those who fail to get accepted to their first choice can take other examinations at lesser universities, study for a year or more and retake the exams, or lower their career expectations. As stated earlier, roughly 200,000 students take these exams for the second or more time. And a small number of applicants who fail commit suicide each year in disappointment (Woronoff, 1982a:118). Of the 398 suicides during 1976 of those under twenty-one years old, one-third did so because of school-related reasons (Rohlen, 1983:330).

The Four-Year Rest

What happens after this grueling initiation into higher education? Surprisingly, universities are lax compared to high school. It is assumed that anyone able to pass these rigorous exams "belongs." They are no longer rigorously tested. Tests and make-ups tend to be easy and attendance is not usually required. At any rate, it's easy to be excused from class or to take re-examinations. Except for technical fields (i.e. engineering and medicine), university coursework is not overly demanding.[10] Some students take their last two years of residence seriously, but many others do not.

Japanese university courses are easier to study for than their American counterparts (Christopher, 1983:92). Once membership in a university has been achieved, students become part of close, supportive groups. Graduation is almost certain. Students take a two to four-year rest from their "examination hells."

These university years are times of relaxation and maturation. For the first time since twelve or so, Japanese youths have the time to join clubs – often sport or politically oriented, develop new friendship, and generally enjoy Japan's prosperity. This is the freest period of life. There are few social and other responsibilities at this time and many have considerable amounts of money to spend. Once they graduate from the universities, former students shoulder their family and career responsibilities. Undergraduate enrollment offers successful Japanese students the chance to mature, develop their personalities, and in general explore their world. Their high school years were too oriented toward rote learning to allow much leisure for personal interests, intellectual or otherwise.

Seniors from the elite universities are interviewed and most are also be given additional examinations by prospective employers. But the fact that they are graduates means that, if their characters and personalities "match" a company's or a government bureau's personnel profile, all will be employed by the most prestigious employers. Group membership is more important than individual characteristics, and an elite diploma leads to corporate acceptance.

---

[10] Similar to graduates from the best European college-oriented high schools programs, Japanese high school graduates have achieved an education comparable to two years of a good American college or university. From this perspective, perhaps Japanese college students deserve a rest.

6.6 The Japanese at Play and Work

The Japanese Way of Baseball

How the Japanese emphasize cooperation and group membership is illustrated by Japanese baseball. Baseball is an American game and baseball as played in Japan follows the traditional rules developed in the United States. Americans have no trouble following a game or even playing professional baseball in Japan.[11] The Japanese have modified many of the behind-the-scene-aspects of the game. The formal rules are the same, but much of the atmosphere is different. Japanese baseball players can be easily compared to corporate employees. They have many characteristics in common with Japanese workers in general.

Robert Whiting (1977) has spent over ten years in Japan and has written excellent descriptions of Japanese baseball. Much of the discussion below is based on his accounts.

The Japanese are baseball-crazy. *Besuboru* stars are as famous as movie stars, and baseball stadiums are almost always filled to capacity. Each team has its fanatic and loyal fans, and fans can watch a pro-baseball game every night on TV during the season. For those who wish to attend a game, there is sake, broiled eel, *hotto dogu* vendors, cheerleaders, double-headers, and pageantry.

The most important principle of Japanese baseball is that the player must be a team player. Victory goes to the team which has the most group enthusiasm (spirit). Individual records are less important than the team's win-lose record. Winning pitchers, for example, are used as long as they do well on the mound. An American pitcher would insist on rest long before a Japanese because too much pitching might hurt his arm and shorten his career. The Japanese pitcher stays on the mound as long as he can. In one series, the celebrity Kazuhisa Inao started five of the seven games and pitched 47 innings. During his career, Inao appeared in half of his team's games and pitched an average of 345 innings a year (Whiting, 1977:69).

Spring training officially begins in February, but players are expected to report a week or two early to show enthusiasm. Players also come early for normal practice and stay late. Players train together and follow the same schedule. Four-hour workouts are common, and all players arrive at the stadium hours before a game for group exercises (Whiting, 1984). For a night game, many managers expect their players to be at the stadium by noon for an afternoon of practice.

---

[11] Each Japanese professional baseball team is allowed two foreign players. This is another instance of the Japanese being willing to learn from foreigners. Some Japanese have suggested that they will soon not need Americans to teach them how to play baseball.

Tatsuro Hiroaka is manager of the Pacific League Seibu Lions, Japan's 1982 baseball champions. A national hero known for his authoritarian regime, he once kept his players busy for 120 consecutive days without a day off. This included six to seven hours of training per day, plus evening lectures and lessons (Whiting, 1983). No wonder professional baseball players are seen in Japan as samurai!

Players who perform badly apologize to their managers and teammates. A player in a slump withdraws to a week-end retreat to meditate on his weaknesses and lack of team spirit. He would consider how he can help the team regain its *wa* and winning record. Bad performance of any kind is defined by the Japanese as a failure of will as well as skill. Failure is the result of a lack of effort, spirit, and group loyalty. In the same way, corporate managers ask workers to learn new skills and assume that developing talents is a matter of will and determination.

Another American-Japanese difference is that each baseball game in Japan lasts a half hour longer than in the United States. Japanese pitchers will stare (meditate? gather one's strength?) at an opposing batter for several moments or more. This is the Zen moment of calm and of gathering one's forces. After a few moments of concentration, the pitcher will "attack" the batter with a pitch. The contest of will and spirit between batter and pitcher begins. After a pitch, the pitcher spend a few minutes consulting with the coach and fellow teammates. Japanese baseball resembles Kabuki theater as well as a competitive sport.

Players live in a dormitory during the practice and playing seasons. They attend mediation sessions together, eat together, and take vacations as a group. After losing a game, all members of the team will bow to the crowd in apology for their loss.

The relationship between worker and group is duplicated in Japanese baseball. On both the baseball diamond and in the factory, individual effort can be measured in home runs, balls caught or missed, production quotas, parts rejection rate, etc. Tetsuhari Kawakami was manager of the Tokyo Giants. His baseball philosophy is described by one of his players (Oh and Falkner, 1984:196–7):

Play with greed for victory . . . We (the players) had an obligation to the team, but this obligation was best fulfilled by learning to use ourselves individually to the limit . . .

The above spirit of dedication to group goals is the same spirit managers and supervisors want to instill in their workers. The individual does his best to make the (work) team victorious.

The way baseball has been translated from an American to a Japanese game illustrates how much the Japanese value group harmony and consensus. Just as the game of baseball has been adapted to better fit Japanese cultural values, so do Japanese business practices reflect Japanese social traditions. The most important value distinguishing the Japanese employee/employer from Americans is the Japanese emphasis on the importance of the group. Even Japanese baseball, a game so typically American, reflects this emphasis on group consensus and *wa*.

The 'Forget-the-Year' Office Party

Members of any group develop petty (and not so petty) jealousies and interpersonal irritations. It's normal for people who are together most of their waking hours to blame their frustrations and boredom (there are as many boring jobs in Japan as in the U.S.) on one another. The same is true among the Japanese. They experience personal frictions to the same extent as Americans. Such negative feelings are avoided at all costs in Japan because they are seen as unworthy and antisocial. Workers should enjoy being with another and feel motivated through company loyalty to give employers a full and dedicated work day. What happens when this ideal is not achieved?

One strategy is allowing workers to let off steam through a safety valve called a "forget-the-year" party (*bonenkai*). These year-end parties are gigantic binges with the purpose of clearing the air and end frustrations, disappointments, jealousies, and tensions related to work and follow workers (Young, 1983).

Attendance is unofficially mandatory. Any co-worker who does not attend becomes suspect: he is obviously acting too independently of the group. Most companies pay half or more of the costs of these parties, so they can be considered as official events. The new year period is one when parties occur, and a company which did not support these occasions would appear to be stingy and ungreatful. It would be as if a New Orleans company refused to let employees leave early to attend a Mardis Gras parade. Every member of the office or work team is expected to be present. They may not stay late, but attendance for a short while is the usual pattern. After the ceremonies and some socializing, the younger employess might split off on their own for more contemporary entertainment. A group of younger males may go off to visit a disco or wild west bar. Few male employees would leave early and go home.

Each *bonenkai* party begins with a formal toast and short speech by a senior official, making the gathering official. He thanks those present for their efforts and dedication to the company, and asks for the same loyalty and enthusiasm in the coming year. After a few more toasts, the senior executive quietly leaves the party. His absence gives the subordinates more freedom to act and feel as they wish. He may also want to get down to serious drinking and partying himself but doesn't care to act like a fool in the presence of so many subordinates. He can let his hair down later among his own equals without losing face (Young, 1983).

The party gives co-workers another chance to become friends by loosing inhibitions. The party becomes a setting where insults may be given and arguments begun. "Being drunk" is an excuse to forgive and forget any offensive behavior that might take place during the evening.[12] Group loyalty is reinforced while *wa*-threatening feelings are harmlessly vented and excused as caused by too much alcohol. Co-workers become friends again.

The Japanese at Work

The enthusiasm for work that workers exhibit is remarkable when compared to other countries. Simply put, Japanese workers are at their posts when they are supposed to be. Absenteeism is almost nonexistent in Japanese corporations. The United States Bureau of Labor Statistics has reported that absenteeism in the United States is about *twelve* times the rate of Japan (Richmond and Kahan, 1983:69). This figure is based on excused and unexcused absenses, as well as abseenteeism due to illness.

One reason for this lack of absenteeism is the union-management harmony the Japanese enjoy. The reasons for this are discussed elsewhere in this book, but the fact is that company-wide *wa* is seen as the responsibility of organized labor, the workers themselves, and of management. The proof of this is the low absentee rate among Japanese workers. During the 1970s, Japan lost an average of 1.1 man-days of unexcused absenses per ten employees, as compared to 5.1 lost man-days in the United States (Shimada, 1983), on an annual basis.

There have been periods in Japan's recent history when labor strife was as explosive and distruptive as any experienced in the United States. Japanese culture makes labor-management harmony possible, but not automatic. Contemporary Japanese have worked hard to achieve the harmony they now enjoy. West Germany has a man-days lost statistic about as low as Japan's. The Japanese man-days lost figures were as high during the 1940s through the 1960s as America's are now.

An important study comparing how Japanese and Americans feel about their work during 1960 and 1976 has been sponsored by the Japanese Institute of Labour and conducted by Shin-ichi Takezawa and Arthur M. Whitehill (1983). This survey shows how the work attitudes of Japanese and American workers both differ and have changed from 1960 to 1976. The authors also show that,

---

[12] This is the time when a co-worker can suggest that another is too aggressive or argumentative. The party can also be used as an occasion to apologize to fellow workers for any social errors committed during the previous year. The purpose of an American Christmas party is similar to a *bonenkai*. A naval tradition – crossing the equator – similarly offers sailors the chance to "get even" with officers and develop a sense of *wa* with shipmates.

for some attitudes, the two national sets are not as different as expected. Below are some of the findings from Takezawa and Whitehill.

A major difference between the two national work forces is that the Japanese show much more respect for superiors and managers. To the 1976 statement "If my immediate supervisor enters a crowded bus on which I am riding," the answers "always offer him my seat since he is my superior," and "offer him my seat unless I am not feeling well" were selected 45 percent of the times by the Japanese and 4 percent by Americans.

The question "If you feel your rate of pay is unfair, the best way to get satisfaction in the long run is to ..." was answered "show patience and confidence in management by not voicing your complaints" or "ask a senior worker to serve as a go-between to voice your complaint" 34 percent of the times by the Japanese sample and 6 percent by the Americans. Americans were much more likely to say that would use their union representatives than the Japanese (Takezawa and Whitehill, 1983:103).

More telling are the answers to the statement, "I think it is most desirable for my co-workers to work at maximum capacity ..." Forty-nine percent of the Japanese agreed with this statement, as compared to sixteen percent of the Americans (Takezawa and Whitehill, 1983:69).

One more finding from this excellent work. When asked to agree to the paraphrased statements, "I think of my company as having a greater or equal importance than my personal life," 73 percent of the Japanese agreed while only 21 percent of the Americans did so (1983:59). One-third (37%) of the Americans said they completely separated work from personal life (47% of younger workers). A low one-tenth of the Japanese agreed (14% of the younger workers). Japanese management has created a great deal of work harmony and support among workers.

Automation in Japan

I present one more example of how the attitude of Japanese and Americans workers differ, to the advantage of Japan. Although robotic technology was invented and developed in the United States, Americans are slow to take advantage of this technology. There are now roughly two hundred firms in Japan manufacturing robots at one level of complexity or another. Most (80%) of these automated work procedures are sold in the Japanese market. Why is this so? Why has the introduction of robots been so easily done in Japan?

One reason is that Japanese workers do not fear automation. Work duties tend to the unspecialized, and workers are expected to develop a number of skills. At this time, robotic technology is relatively primitive. Robots can perform only very simple, repetitive tasks, such as spray painting, spot welding, or etching microchips. The loss of one type of unpleasant task is welcomed rather than resisted. Japanese workers realize that they can either do something else or else be retrained. Workers in Japan rotate work duties much more often than American workers. No one will lose his factory job when only one task is automated (Ishii, 1983).

Workers develop friendly feelings toward their machines. This is due to the Japanese culture as well as the way workers are treated when new machines are introduced. Japanese workers give their machines names, offer them rice wine during New Year's celebrations, and generally endow them with human characteristics, just as many rocks and geographic features (such as Fujiyama) are given sacred characteristics by the Shinto religion. This love of machines would not develop if there were the danger that machines would replace workers. Since this is not so in Japanese corporations, workers can afford to see robots as helpers which increase bonuses and corporate *wa* (Ishii, 1983).

There is the story, probably untrue but recounted often, of workers programming their machines to perform mid-morning exercises along with them. The sight of a line of workers and their machines performing the same arm movements must be impressive.

This acceptance of machines used to increase productivity is another indication that the work place in Japan has been made into a cooperative one. Management, since the 1950s, has redesigned work relations of all types so that workers are more likely to be supportive rather than antagonistic. This has demanded changes in work practices, reward systems, supervisory techniques, and much more. The lesson for Americans is that the Japanese have been able to revolutionize the work place in a mere twenty to thirty years and that America can do the same. Given the American genius for improvisidation, we can adapt to new, more democratic-consensus types of managerial styles.

6.7 Rewarding the Japanese Way

What can Americans learn from the Japanese? I have suggested many practices that can be adopted by American management and will continue to do so in later chapters. One general strategy that can increase American productivity is to treat workers as valued members of an enterprise. Achieving the potential benefits of company loyalty depends on encouraging cooperation among workers and managers. Bonuses for faster workers or for higher individual productivity will not achieve their intended goals if they encourage workers to compete against each other. Like the Japanese, Americans must learn to cooperate for the good of the company instead of competing against one another.

Surprisingly, learning from the Japanese is not as impossible as it might seem. Americans do not have to "become Japanese" in order to enjoy some of the advantages Japanese businessmen have over Americans. The Japanese have successfully exported many of their managerial techniques to their American factories and workers. Americans have found that they enjoy working for their Japanese employers in the Japanese manner.

The Japanese have been forced to adapt many of their traditional work practices by copying from the United States and Europe. The Japanese were willing to learn Nineteenth century technology from foreigners and continue to do so. We can do no less.

A major advantage the Japanese have over Americans is their emphasis on cooperation. Americans managers can benefit by rewarding cooperation. Like the Japanese, Americans know when someone is taking advantage of them. The problem, then, is to develop strategies which encourage cooperation instead of competition. The way to do this is to reward individuals when they cooperate and help the group become more productive instead of rewarding successful competitive behavior.

It would be easy for most Americans to adjust to less competitive and less individualistic forms of management and rewards. Many reward systems used today are so competitive that production is restricted rather than enhanced. We have already seen that workers at all levels will restrict their own and their co-workers' production in order to reduce competition. Very few work groups or teams have ever existed which did not establish some production-reduction quota of one sort or another.

The purpose of studying the Japanese ways of work is to introduce a new set of values, a new way of managing, and to force Americans to rethink how to manage and work together. The problem is that Americans find it hard to change the way they feel about human nature. Americans are individualistic while the Japanese are not. Americans assume that a work group will be productive when each member is happy. That is, make the individual happy and the group will run smoothly. In essence, we believe that groups exist for the benefit of their members and that individuals are the building blocks of groups. In Japan, the individual exists for the good of the group, not the reverse.[13]

---

[13] Involved in this expectation is the emphasis on duty. Group members receive satisfaction partly because they are working to achieve group goals and because they have been hired by their organizations in the first place. Monetary rewards are additional to the satisfaction of doing one's duty. The closest Americans come to reflecting this value is in volunteer and charity work and those who choose a military career for patriotic reasons. I would also add to this list religious workers, especially roman Catholic nuns, and those who teach any of the first ten grades in public schools.

In spite of these cultural differences, the Japanese group approach can be successfully adapted to the American setting. This will demand a careful rethinking on what is the ideal relationship between individual and group. But it can be done. The axiom American managers must accept is that all managerial behavior should tie individual interests to group interests. No one is to be rewarded unless others also benefit. This is a principle which has been used in the United States, but only on an infrequent basis. Americans don't appreciate enough its utility. The value of studying how the Japanese cooperate is that Americans can profit if we learn how to cooperate.

One example of group-level reward is found in the U.S. military. Drill instructors at Marines' boot camp give every member of a barrack a week-end pass when everyone passes inspection. On the other hand, every recruit is restricted to the base if one Marine has a badly-made cot or unpolished boots. Everyone is punished for the mistake of one member.

The outcome is easy to predict. The goldbricker is going to be punished by his buddies. They will want him to know that his failure has cost them a leave and that this makes them unhappy. They will make sure all cots and boots are G.I. before the next inspection. As a side benefit, these Marines learn to depend on one another. The lesson is that a good marine looks out for his buddies. This feeling is commonly found among Japanese workers and should be encouraged in America.

I present below two general rules of reward based on the Japanese model of management. These rules do not ignore individual advantage. They reflect the Japanese view that although individuals must be served by the group, they in turn should be motivated to help the group achieve its goals (Alston, 1982).

The First Rule of Reward

The first rule is never reward only the individual. Few workers develop innovative ideas solely by themselves. They learn from more experienced co-workers and receive advice and support from others. The major portion of a bonus should be awarded to a worker's total work unit rather than to an individual. This policy recognizes that most work is the result of the success of more than one person. This rule assumes that the work being rewarded is group-oriented because few of us work alone. There are exceptions to this, of course. Salespersons and waitresses, for example, may depend on their own skills for success or failure at work.

Most American workers work with others as part of a team of one type or another. But we still look at workers as individuals rather than as co-workers whose productivity can be increased through cooperation. The dictum that rewards be shared when work is shared recognizes the cooperative element of most work situations.

This principle holds true even if one member is obviously responsible for the group's success. In Japan, all irregular bonuses are given equally to all members of the team, division, or department which proposed the innovative idea. This group approach may be too radical to adopt completely in America; I suggest that the originator be given slightly more than the co-workers. The principle, however, remains: rewards should be as equally distributed as possible, and be given to the group as well as to one member. While wages in an American corporation can never be as equal as in Japan, there are ample ways of rewarding members of small groups equally.

The Advantages of Group Rewards

The purpose of group rewards is to achieve cooperation. Cooperation, in turn results in team workers helping each other and supporting the goals of that group, whether company, department, or shift. Since most workers expect to be rewarded when they support a company's goals (that's why they're working there), the problem is how to reward in such a way that cooperation rather competition is encouraged. One strategy is achieving cooperation through what social scientists call "equalization of reward".

The term refers to rewarding members of a group as equally as possible. If rewards are equally distributed, members cannot be jealous of one another as they compare their rewards – such as pay – with what others receive. There have been a number of experiments and studies dealing with the effects of differential rewards. Research has found that productivity is higher when group members are rewarded equally (Miller and Hamblin, 1963:778).

A number of patterns develop when rewards are not equally distributed. First, less well rewarded members become "free riders." They increasingly decide that those whose pay is greater should do more work. Becoming jealous, they decide they are being cheated if they work as much as those who receive greater rewards.

Second, jealousy and discontent cause less-rewarded workers to decrease their cooperation with those who are rewarded more. Why should they help someone who's getting more than they do as a result of cooperation. The result of unequal reward is (A) less production on the part of the less-paid members and (B) less cooperation among workers.

The way to avoid these productivity blocks is to reward equally. Most of us work with others, and rewards must be equally distributed if cooperation is a factor leading toward higher production. A question always exists as to who contributes most or the least. The Japanese avoid this dilemma by stressing that *every* contribution is worthwhile, even if it's relatively minor. All parts of an engine are necessary if the car is move. Some parts may be more complicated or expensive, but all are necessary. Even Japanese janitors will be personally thanked by a senior executive when they present a way of making themselves more productive. They will also be thanked, again by a senior executive, for their loyalty at a year's-end party.

Equal rewards give persons a sense of distributive justice. Distributive justice is the feeling that the distribution of rewards is fair. Those who work together should also be rewarded together in an equal manner. Miller and Hamblin found in their experiments that equal rewards make it less likely that co-workers will be jealous of one another and try to block each other's productivity.

There are situations when it's clear who's the best worker in a group or who's the most important member. This person stands out. Any supervisor can point out the key members of a work group, as can the workers themselves. The American tendency (and practice) is to reward this "star," either by a pay raise, a promotion, or both. This is individualistic and not the Japanese way. This super worker may not be exerting more effort than the others. He may simply be more talented than the others or may be using the talents of others. Or this person has been trained by the company to develop skills others don't have. Rewarding this person even though he contributes more makes the others jealous. Though they contribute less, they are still important.

The Japanese reaction would be to reward everyone as well as the hero. The others can offer this person *amaeru* (love and affection). He receives the "love" of others because they have all benefited from his actions. On the other hand, group reward places a debt on the less productive members. They don't completely deserve a bonus made possible by the group's star. They should feel obligated to work harder or at least thankful to this hero. At the very least, they will not slow down the best worker.

The Support of Group Harmony

Rewarding co-workers equally makes them partners for future ventures. They are less likely to maintain a policy of secrecy since secrecy and non-cooperation cause everyone to lose. Workers are motivated to seek each other out to exchange ideas and to evaluate each other's proposals. Rather than punishing the rate-buster, group-level rewards encourage workers to punish the laggard, as in the example of the Marines' boot camp. Non-cooperation is seen as harming the group. Cooperation, by contrast, tests whatever ideas workers have developed; ideas are more likely to have been more carefully prepared before being offered to management when they have been discussed and cooperatively analyzed by co-workers.

Group rewards encourage intra-group harmony among the members. Being rewarded as members rather than as individuals, group members become supportive peers rather than potential competitors. As an added bonus, group rewards encourage the worker to express aggressiveness against outsiders rather than toward members of the group. The Japanese are formidable competitors because of their intense in-group loyalty. They compete well against outsiders because they cooperate on the group level (Ozawa, 1980). Non-members are outsiders to whom insiders owe no loyalty. On the other hand, a Japanese who feels some kinship with someone will be very supportive and loyal.

Not motivated to compete against fellow workers for individual rewards, the employee can more easily see co-workers as a "family" in which all, no matter how they differ in talents, can be trusted to help one another. That is why Japanese workers are not as passive as might be expected. Each is willing to work hard so that the group, not the individual, is successful. This makes the Japanese very achievement oriented as well as competitive (De Vos, 1965). This enthusiasm is group-centered rather than individualistic.

There is another advantage when intragroup trust and enthusiasm are achieved. Collective rewards allow for greater group autonomy as well as individual initiative. This may seem contradictory, but it is not. Group rewards encourage group loyalty by encouraging a greater sense of duty on the part of the members. Less supervision will be necessary because members want to help the group. Loyalty demands being willing to exhibit initiative for the good of the group. Outside interference is seen as an expression of a lack of confidence by higher officials (Rohlen, 1974:114) and is resented by the workers.

This is why Japanese executives can expect a high degree of voluntary participation from their lower-level workers, whether they are initiating cost-saving proposals or developing Quality Control circles at the shop-floor level (See for example, Knoz, 1979; Juran, 1978). Another advantage of this trust is that Japanese companies have fewer rules and regulations than American companies, especially at the shop floor. Japanese workers can be trusted to do whatever needs to be done and to do it in a cooperative manner. To do otherwise would show disloyalty to the group.

At the same time, because supervisors and managers of a group are rewarded for their group's innovations, supervisors encourage workers' experimentation by making available needed resources and advice. The supervisor becomes a close member of the group when he expects to receive an equal share of any possible bonuses. Jealously is decreased because the supervisor is no longer threatened by the initiative of subordinates; he is rewarded by their successes.

The Second Rule or Reward

The second rule is give the group a group reward. Just as all members of a family enjoy a new oven or television set, team members are expected to enjoy certain rewards together. In Japan, a crew achieving the highest production record during a given period will be photographed for the company paper. A plaque with members' names can also be hung in a "hall of honor."

When a group is rewarded, each member enjoys individually the first type of reward: a cash bonus or watches given to everyone. By contrast, the recipients of the second type of reward enjoy the reward together. This is a common Japanese practice. American managers are so individualistic that they have difficulty rewarding group members as a unit. The Christmas office party is often the only group-level reward employees experience together.

A typical example of a group reward is an occasion where workers and spouses are given a supper by the company. Here, all celebrate together. The company, in addition to individual bonuses, can offer to partially or completely subsidize a group picnic or other outing, just as companies partially support employees' athletic teams. Or, as was done during the Second World War, award an honored group a special symbol – such as a flag to be hung in a public place. In Japan, a company bonus will be used by a group of families to take a vacation together at the company's expense. A testimonial dinner and an office party are examples of group rewards used in America. These should be used more than they are.

An advantage of rewarding the group as well as individuals is that the members develop a group memory. Members to remember (and exaggerate) what "we" did together; a group mythology is born. After sharing several such events, the members become symbolically bonded together; they now become "family." Such bondings unite the workers, thereby encouraging them to cooperate and support one another in the future.

Group Rewards in America

Group awards are given by American industry. The Scanlon Plan is based on the notion of group reward. Both management and workers are rewarded when there has been any cost savings or productivity improvements. All personnel involved are motivated to help improve efficiency rather than feeling competitive.

Other examples of group rewards are found in the petroleum drilling industry. Drilling is dangerous work and safety in the field demands teamwork as well as individual caution. In order to motivate workers to "work safer", American petroleum companies have developed ingenious combinations of group and individual rewards.

Blocker Drilling Company was cited in 1980 as the drilling company with the best safety record in the industry. Blocker gives individual gifts to workers with perfect safety records; these include belt buckles, caps, and diamond rings.

For individual rewards, rig crews with one month of no accidents (defined as no injury which keeps a worker from work the next day) are given twelve pairs of work gloves. Three months of safety results in the men receiving coveralls. One year of safety is rewarded by a jacket for each crew member. A $ 500 ring is awarded to each member of the crew with two years of accident-free work. More than one crew works at a drill site so these bonuses are visible to other workers. An accident on the part of one member causes the whole crew to lose, so individual crew members benefit when all cooperate to maintain safety standards.

There are also rewards given to the group as a whole. Every year Blocker hosts a picnic for workers and their families, complete with contests, prizes and free food. Each rig crew is encouraged to take part in a chili cookoff. In Texas and Oklahoma, being a member of a prize chili team is a matter of great pride. For 150 accident-free days at a given drill site, the company throws a barbecue for the crew members and prints their names and announcement of the event in the local paper.

In the same way, Spartan Drilling, Inc. rewards both the individual and the rig crews as a whole. Individuals receive duffel bags (for 200 accident-free days), leather coats and bronze medaillons (350 days), and watches and silver medallion (500 days). After 150 safe days each crew member receives a knife; at 200 days each person receives free work gloves. For one thousands days of safety the worker is personally presented by the president of Spartan with a diamond ring, a set of tools, a television set, and a platinum medallion.

Group-level awards consists of a "crew of the month" citation with the members' picture published in Spartan's magazine. A wall plaque citing the crew's safety record is set up in a prominent place at the drill site.

Limitations of Group Rewards

Group rewards work best when there is little labor turnover. They are not effective in departments, such as sales, when members are forced to compete with each other. Nor would group rewards be useful when workers fulfill their functions independently. However, most work done today demands interdependence. Workers in these settings would benefit from some kind of group rewards.

Although a plurality of the Japanese reward systems is too group-oriented for Americans, many Japanese strategies can be adapted to the American psyche. Americans, like the Japanese, will cooperate when they see that it's to their benefit to do so.[14] It's a matter of understanding what is done in Japan, and then deciding which practices would be accepted by Americans.

---

[14] It is important to remember that, although the Japanese are group oriented, they seek individual rewards like everyone else. Few Japanese today would suffer personal privations unless they believed they would be eventually rewarded by the group.

Chapter 7
Permanent Employment

The central feature encouraging worker loyalty in Japanese corporations is the practice of permanent or lifetime employment. The word "lifetime" is a misnomer since Japanese workers are not expected to work up to the day they die. The phrase instead means that selected employees expect to work for one employer from their first day of employment until retirement. Even after retirement, many continue to work for the same company for as long as they wish. The term "permanent worker" is given to employees who have been given a lifetime contract.

Permanent workers have total job security except under very extreme and unusual conditions. The company's bankruptcy is the most likely circumstance which would invalidate permanent employment agreements.

The Japanese logic underlying the nature of lifetime employment is best described in contrast to the American model of employment. More individualistic, Americans define themselves in terms of occupational skills rather than where they work. A nation of specialists whose skills "belong" to the persons, Americans define themselves as doctors, teachers, mechanics, or administrators. Being a welder, say, means someone has welding skills. These form part of that person's self-image.

This individualistic identification of skills is less common in Japan. Japanese identify themselves more through their group memberships than by their individual characteristics. Americans feel their individual skills belong to them, and it is an easy step to view employment as a series of stages where skills are increasingly rewarded. Since they are personal properties, it's rational to see these employment skills as integral parts of a career involving different employers. Occupational skills belong to the individual and should be used to maximize a person's rewards.

By contrast, Japanese workers see occupational skills as belonging to a group more than belonging to the person. A skilled worker in America is a welder who happens to be working for Ford. His Japanese counterpart would define himself as a Honda employee who happens to be a welder. If new skills are needed then this Honda worker would be willing to be retrained.

This difference in viewpoint is an important one. In America, individual talents belong to the person. He has the right to use his talents anywhere and anyway he wants. In Japan, work talents belong to the group, such as an employer, as much or more than they belong to a person. Lifetime employment is a response to this view. The learning of a skill entails a debt which cannot be repaid except through a lifetime of loyalty. Receiving a skill and then leaving for another employer is considered as selfish behavior.

On the other side of the agreement, working for a company for a few years places an obligation on the employer. The employer should not, on a moral level, discard a worker when he's temporarily no longer needed. The existence of the lifetime employment concept fits the Japanese cultural ideals of group loyalty and of group-individual exchange of favors which develop into mutual dependency.

This policy of permanent employment is one of the most different from current American practice, and the one least likely to be adopted in America. Yet many of the advantages as well as disadvantages Japanese companies enjoy over their American competitors are traced to the ideal of lifetime employment.

It is difficult to understand how Japanese corporations operate without considering the fact that some employees enjoy lifetime employment while others do not. There are no important features of Japanese corporations which are not influenced by the presence of lifelong employment, whether it is the nature of fringe benefits workers receive, the organized labor movement, or the loyalty employers expect from employees. Even that part of the labor force not enjoying absolute job security is influenced by its availability to others. At the very least, knowing others have permanent employment encourages workers to work for and hope to eventually achieve the same. The ideal of lifetime employment is such a strong one that even temporary workers act as if they are permanent employees.

Not all Japanese workers enjoy permanent employment. This practice is found only in large corporations, and only for a minority of their employees. Companies with less than one thousand employees generally do not offer lifetime employment. A large number of workers in larger corporations are defined as "temporary." These are the unskilled who are often hired for the month, week, or even by the day. Many already-retired older workers work for previous employers or new ones. These are classified as temporary workers no matter how long they work for the company. Some unskilled and semi-skilled workers are classified as temporary though they may work for the same company for years. A janitor of a bank, for example, would be considered as temporary even though he might never be replaced.

Even those who are not lifetime workers are influenced by the ideal of this practice. For one thing, a temporary worker might show enough promise over the years to be given a lifetime contract. Workers who exhibit enthusiasm for their work or who seem especially loyal to the company will be recommended by supervisors for permanent employment. This gives workers the motivation to do their best.

The ideal of lifelong employment permiates all sectors of the Japanese society. In 1958, the Tokyo District Court ruled on a case involving four Honda Motors strikers. These four union leaders had occupied the roof of Honda's executive headquarters and disrupted non-factory related operations. They had been consequently fired by the management on the basis that their behavior had been excessive as well as illegal. The strikers sued to regain their jobs. The court ruled that, although their behavior had been illegal, dismissal was too extreme a punishment and ordered the four re-instated.

Temporary workers do not receive the fringe benefits that lifetime workers enjoy, and a permanent contract becomes a great financial advantage. Also, in a country where pride and honor (face) are so important, to be known as a temporary worker is demeaning. Workers would rather act as if they were permanent and be treated as such. And, in fact, the ideal supervisor acts as if all subordinates are permanent by encouraging a "we" feeling to sustain company loyalty and an interest in quality work.

Lifetime employment is such a strong ideal in Japan that many employers feel ashamed when they dismiss workers. They will try anything first before firing excess labor. No company wants to earn a reputation for being a revolving-door even for temporary employees. Temporary employees are treated as if they were an integral and permanent part of the company as much as possible.

Managers are quite willing to hire free-lance specialists on a temporary basis. Even these are re-hired regularly and employed at intervals over a period of years. I know of a self-employed maritime lawyer who helps importers cut through the red tape involved in importing goods into Japan. His knowledge of maritime law and his personal relations with government officials makes him invaluable. His command of English also makes him a valued translator/ interpreter. But he prefers to work only with a limited number of companies to which he is loyal. As a favor to the travel company which hired him as a guide when he was a university student, he also serves as a tourist guide once or twice a year. He considers himself disloyal if he does not help his former part-time employer during the busy tourist season. The travel agency would feel embarrassed if it did not ask this free-lancer to work for them at least once a year. Although the ties are tenuous, he is part of the corporate family.

7.1 The Nature of Permanent Employment

Lifetime employment means more than a reluctance to dismiss employees. Many American companies have policies which use dismissal of workers only as a last resort. Lifetime employment has two dimensions in Japan: an individual and a social component. The individual element refers to the fact that, once hired, a worker will not be dismissed even if he does not match early expectations. No one will be fired for being inadequate in a relative as an well as absolute sense. This worker will not be dismissed because someone else has proved to be better. Under the lifelong employment system, no one competes with others to see who will be able to stay with the company. No one is fired for failure.

In practical terms, the company has the responsibility to find the optimum use of a worker's talents. The inadequate worker is rotated from one work area to another until a place is found that is compatible with his aptitudes. Or this worker will be sent to a school to develop a skill the company needs. Permanent workers have no fear that work failure will result in unemployment. It becomes the company's responsibility to make workers profitable in one way or another when their skills become obsolete. Lifetime employment endures through technological change and changing markets.

On the other hand, the person who is hired permanently has essentially been hired on faith. The company is saying, "We trust you and believe you are the person we need for the next forty years." This places the onus of debt on the worker. He now feels that he's receiving more from the company than he's as yet given. He's motivated to seek ways to repay this debt. This might take the form of working harder or by being concerned with high quality performance. Permanent workers also feel obligated to take evening or weekend courses in order to become more valuable to the company. Permanent employment places an obligation on the worker which goes beyond contractual obligations.

This sense of obligation is found among American as well as Japanese workers. Tenured university professors, who are essentially permanent workers, are much more willing to become involved in committee work than those who are untenured. Ask any senior professor why he spends time as a member of one or more committees. He will first tell you what a waste of time and how boring committee activities usually are. But then he's likely to say that he feels as if he should help manage the university though he gets no extra reward, except maybe daydreaming time. Many tenured professors are loyal to their university and are willing to spend extra time and effort to ensure its success. Many Japanese workers feel the same way about "their" company.

Thomas Peters and Robert Waterman, in their book *In Search of Excellence* (1982), find that the major feature of "excellent" American companies is a management that is people-oriented. The managers care about people, whether employees or customers. This same concern for individuals is encouraged by the policy of lifetime employment in Japan. If your workers will be with you for years, it's only natural that you will be very concerned about their morale and productivity. Colleagues will also be especially helpful and supportive of those who will be together for decades. Lifelong employment forces all concerned to treat others as long-term valued resources.

The earlier chapters of this book pointed out that the Japanese dislike person-to-person competition. Lifelong employment supports this push for harmony. At least workers now don't have to compete against each other for a limited number of jobs. Supervisors of permanent workers can enjoy the luxury of personal relations with subordinates. No one wants to become friendly with someone who may soon have to be fired, since to dismiss a friend is a painful experience. The reaction to this possibility is to maintain social distance by being as formal as possible. Being impersonal allows you not to get emotionally involved.

Military officers are not supposed to fraternize with the enlisted ranks partly because, aside from feelings of snobbism, it's hard to order into danger someone you like. In the same way, it's hard to become friendly with someone who may be gone soon, either because of being fired or because of a better offer. In these situations, it's easier to avoid becoming too emotionally involved or dependent. By contrast, Japanese workers can afford to treat one another personally and informally, and in fact are forced to do so. Lifelong employment makes it necessary as well as encourages closer working relationships. No wonder Japanese corporations seem so people-oriented!

The Company-Worker Ties Based on Permanent Employment

Who should benefit when a company experiences a very profitable period? What should be done with excess profits not needed for capital investments, repayment of debt, and the like? The American answer would be most likely to reward the shareholders through increased dividends, offer higher bonuses to senior executives, or both. The workers would be ignored because their relation with the company is strictly contractual They have no claim on the company's treasury except what is stated in contractual agreements. The workers will receive no less than what has been agreed on; they certainly will get no more.

The Japanese response is different because lifetime workers are considered to be more integral than any other segment of the company, even stockholders, and maybe even the president himself. Their satisfaction is considered first, since the long-term profitability of the company rests on their shoulders. This is one reason why corporate lifetime workers in Japan are paid so well and are given so many fringe benefits. They are the aristocrats of Japanese labor.

The surplus profits in question would be distributed to all permanent employees as well as management in the form of a bonus. Stockholders in Japan are not considered as part of the corporate "family." They may hold company stock but they have not really contributed to the company's success. Permanent workers, however, have both directly contributed to the company and are its future. Lifetime workers are given this excess profit in the form of bonuses.

This perceived importance of lifetime workers operates both ways, and they are expected to suffer when the company does less well. Permanent workers receive smaller bonuses, or even pay cuts, when their company is in financial difficulties. In contrast to American custom, however, Japanese lower-level workers would receive smaller proportionaly pay cuts than higher officials. The reasoning is that higher-level managers are both wealthier and in charge, and it's reasonable and fair that their pay cuts be larger. They are hurt less by larger decreases, and larger pay cuts is one way senior managers can "apologize" for the company's lack of economic success.

The lower-level workers would suffer more by larger pay cuts, and they must be protected as much as possible from economic disasters when the company's profits decrease. In times of economic recessions, the relationship of position to pay reduction is direct in Japan: the higher the office, the larger absolute and percentage pay decrease received. This philosophy, unfortunately, is reversed in the United States. Who knows the damage in morale and loyalty this causes among workers? GM's chairman Roger B. Smith, in 1981, announced that all of the company's white collar workers would have their salaries reduced in order to proportionally reduce the price of GM's cars. However good Smith's intention had been, his own salary reduction under his proposed plan would have been $1620 out of a yearly base income of $475,000. This reduction, needless to say, impressed few workers.

Permanent employment offers workers security from economic cycles and change. This operates in two important ways discussed below. The first advantage is that the company refuses to lay off or dismiss workers when demand for a product decreases. The worker becomes immune from seasonal swings in the economy or consumer demands.

The second advantage lies in the fact that lifetime workers cannot be dismissed when they are replaced by more efficient labor-saving and more productive machinery (or more productive workers!). The introduction of labor-saving and procedures, such as robots or more productive ways of manufacturing, are tied to the retention and retraining of permanent workers.

Let's take these points in greater detail. Weak markets occur in any economy, often on a regular basis for certain industries. It's been a practice of American automobile manufacturers, for example, to temporarily lay-off workers to re-tool when changes in styling or the introduction of new models are necessary. The Japanese permanent worker knows that economic forces cannot make him redundant either temporarily or permanently. Permanent workers will be given other tasks if a part of the company shuts down or decreases production.

Permanent employment completely protects the labor force from economic change even if keeping a worker becomes a losing proposition. There would not be a lay-off when a factory is shut-down while machinery is being replaced or repaired.

There are no sunset industries in Japan in the American sense. A company faced with a declining market gradually diversifies and seeks to develop new lines before product "dogs" become completely non-profitable. Nor would plants or offices be suddenly closed down. The old facilities would not be discarded until new opportunities within the company were developed. The permanent workers would gradually be assimilated into the company's new sections while older sections were being replaced.

Workers replaced by machinery are transferred or retrained, or most likely both. This policy reduces the worries about becoming unemployed due to automation or increased productivity. When a Japanese company invests in a new machine which allows two men to produce what four previously produced, two workers will be transferred rather than dismissed. The two extra workers can alway be kept to increase production on another new machine. To permanent workers, increases in productivity result in increased pay for all rather than redundancy for some.

Decreased demand for goods in America usually demands a decrease in the labor force, since no American executive wants to maintain idle workers indefinitely. After all, American executives reason, one major source of savings available during an economic downturn is being able to dismiss workers who are no longer profitable. When the economy rebounds, the company can rehire former employees or else train new workers. The point, though, is that while some Americans may work for the same company for their working lifetimes, few enjoy complete job security. As the saying goes, "If you can be fired, you're part of the working class," and most of us fall in this category. The Japanese response would be, "if you can't be fired, you're part of the company; be loyal to it."

Hiring Once a Year

An interesting and unique aspect of the lifetime employment ideal is the practice of hiring once a year. Japanese corporations interview and hire new members only during Spring. There are a number of reasons for this annual hiring. The first reason has to do with the available supply of younger job seekers. There are more younger Japanese looking for work right after their graduation from high schools, technical centers, or universities than at any other time. This being so, the better-than-average graduates would be hired first, and the less capable later. It is more convenient for companies and job applicants if all hiring is done at the same time. This is when applicants have just graduated and need employment. All companies and all applicants compete together during a shorter period and on a more equal basis.

Executives know that the complete pool of applicants is available at one time. Applicants are not tempted to extend their search beyond a certain limit after which all openings have been filled. Applicants at another time of the year are either those who have quit other employers, those who are very hard to please, or those who are too independent. Companies would rather not offer these types of persons permanent employment.

Since the time most Japanese look for work is after graduation, hiring is done after the end of the school year. Seasonal workers, part-time workers, casual laborers, housewives, and retirees returning to work would be the only ones being hired throughout the year. Everyone else is already working or in school.

In order to decrease corporate competition and the pressures of finding work, Japanese corporations are by law forbidden to recruit students except during the Spring. Then there is a frenzy of recruiting, testing, and interviewing. The tension is necessarily great because the most attractive job seekers will be offered permanent contracts. Since it's bad form to change employers, those who already work don't interview. If a company doesn't hire the university graduates it needs by June, then it has to wait another year to fill its positions.

Another reason for what can only be described as an annual hiring frenzy is the value the Japanese place on seniority. Seniority is the basis for most of a worker's pay raises and promotions until age fifty or so. Only after that time will merit play a more important – though not a complete – part in promotion.

Because hiring is done once a year, workers in each class have equal seniority. A university graduate who joins Honda in the spring of 1986 will have equal seniority with all others hired at that time. They all begin at the same trainee level, receive the same pay, and are given the same fringe benefits (housing, meals, etc.). The 1986 recruits will be senior to those who join in 1987, 1988, and so on. Since everyone joins after graduation, they will all have about the same age. On the average, 1980 recruits will be five years older than 1985 recruits.

Since early promotions are all automatic, all superiors are older and enjoy more company of seniority in comparison to all subordinates. The power of holding a superior position is reinforced by the age and seniority of the senior office holders.

7.2 The Permanent Worker's Responsibilities

Lifelong employment involves more than an employer's categorical promise to never dismiss an employee; it is also understood that the worker accepts certain conditions. The lifetime contract is a two-way agreement.

There is the assumption that the worker will stay with the company until retirement rather than leave at the first opportunity. The employer can count on a stable labor force. An applicant can be hired with the expectation that he is a permanent fixture. This allows for long-range planning of personnel allocation and development.

Management need not fear that valuable, knowledgeable workers will be recruited by competitors after they have been expensively trained. Their skills now "belong" to the company. It would be dishonorable for a worker with a permanent contract to develop a skill and then join a competitor. While there are no laws baring permanent workers from changing employers or going out on their own, it is considered of questionable taste to do so; the worker, at the very least, is acting in a selfish manner.

By the same token, companies hesitate to hire someone who has quit a former employer. This person shows he is undependable and may turn out to be unworthy of the benefits of permanent employment. Such an applicant would have shown too much individualism. Younger formally permanent workers who leave employers usually start their own companies and become self-employed rather than work for other corporations.

Permanent workers are not given the opportunity to idly enjoy their work security. Companies do not expect their permanent workers to become drones, though no doubt some do so. Instead, the ideal is that, in exchange for work security, workers will continuously adapt themselves to meet changing corporate needs.

If a given task is no longer performed, the worker is expected to re-train himself in an operation or skill where he is needed. Permanent workers are hired as employees in the most general sense. What each do will be continuously re-negotiated by management and workers over the years. This necessarily demands job rotation to fit the needs of the company as well as the interests of the worker. Permanent employment demands that the worker will do whatever is needed, rather than what interests the worker at one time or another. Eventually, though, the worker will find the work he wants to do.

Pay for permanent workers is based on seniority and level of entry (manual, managerial, etc.). A thirty year old machinist who becomes a welder will be paid what all high school graduate, manual level workers with ten year seniority are paid. Given this perspective, what a Japanese factory worker does is not important in terms of rewards.

Japanese factories need few job classifications tied to pay differentials. An employee performs the tasks he's asked to perform as needed without worrying whether work changes are demotions, associated with pay changes, or violations of his contract. If he has the skills, a welder is willing to operate a milling machine when there's a need. To this worker, pay, bonuses, and fringe benefits are related to seniority more than the work performed.

A disadvantage to this situation is that persons doing the same task or working together would be receiving different levels of incomes, based on age, seniority, type of employment, gender, and the like. Aside from seniority, it is customary for corporations to differentiate according to need. A single worker would be given a raise when he married even though work remained constant.

Americans feel uncomfortable being hired for non-specified work duties. We prefer knowing more exactly what is expected and what our duties are. This ambiguity is one cost of permanent employment: the worker's employment is secure but his duties may change at any moment.

The effect of internal change in Japanese companies has been carefully studied by many scholars, notably Robert E. Cole (1979), as reported in his book *Work, Mobility, and Participation.* Cole compared an American and a Japanese automobile company. He found that job changes within the Japanese company was relatively common, though these changes were not necessarily accompanied with changes in titles or pay. The changes often considered of job redesign. An assembly line worker might be taught techniques of quality control or machine repair without a corresponding change in work classification. Cole's term "career enlargement," or better yet the term "job redesign," best describes changes in work responsibilities in Japanese corporations.

Japanese employers assume that permanent workers will up-grade their skills whenever asked to do so. They must become more valuable to the company overtime. New workers are "blank paper" who will become more and more useful to the company as their pay automatically increase. Younger workers at all levels are expected to enroll in evening and weekend courses in order to develop a wide variety of skills. Manual workers also take evening courses on quality control, machinery maintenance, or programming. Non-manual, white collar workers take courses in accounting, automation, or administrative procedures. Supervisors and foremen continuously enroll in human relations and leadership courses.

Permanent workers are also expected to take a long view of their careers. They should be willing to temporarily take on boring, unpleasant tasks with the expectation that such sacrifices will be rewarded later. Frequent rotation makes being stuck permanently in a bad job less likely. The policy of automatic promotion makes it certain that unpleasant duties will eventually be transferred to those with less seniority. Unpleasant jobs are considered as more like "paying ones dues" than punishment. Unpleasant tasks may also be important ones; doing them for a while gives the worker wider experiences as well as prestige.

Another responsibility lifelong employees accept is to be good workers. For the Japanese, a "good" worker means more than someone who works hard, makes suggestions on how to improve productivity, and so on. A good worker is also someone who supports others and works well with colleagues. Cooperation is respected more than individualism. A good worker is a team worker.

People who expect to work together for decades have to learn to accept each other's foibles and idiosyncracies. When this is impossible, a worker has to accept an unpleasant situation. Japanese workers who are known as unfriendly and uncooperative can always be transferred. This is only a short-term solution since perpetual job rotation is both impossible and unproductive. A non-cooperative worker in one setting will usually continue to be disruptive elsewhere. The end results is that workers are forced to accept unfriendly work mates and "reform" them if at all possible. There will be pressures to teach such workers that non-conformity entails hardships, such as loss of group support and friendships.

Since Japanese workers spend much of their leisure time together, not liking your colleagues is hell indeed. A disgruntled American worker can seek another employer or avoid those he dislikes after the work day. In Japan, few well-paying positions are filled through mid-career changes. All corporate promotions are in-house and automatic. If you're not hired by a large, well-respected corporation right after graduation, you're never going to join.

Permanent workers who do not contribute to a team's *wa* or who cause conflict cannot be summarily dismissed. Nor can such disharmony be quietly ignored in the hopes the person responsible will leave or reform. Such tensions must be quickly eased before morale suffers. Then too, a work group with a lack of *wa* reflects badly on the leader. The result of these pressures is that the offender will be dealt with quickly by colleagues and supervisors until harmony is re-established.

The introduction of this aspect of Japanese work ways would be resisted by Americans. Most do not want to change their personalities and personal habits because they displease others at work. American individualism conflicts with the intense group demands defined as normal in Japan.

Few Americans would accept such solicitude and pressures to conform from their co-workers. There are many examples of how intensely personal Japanese management can be. The two examples below are typical. Soichiro Honda's concern for quality work caused him to watch workers very carefully. One story, now part of Honda Motor's mythology, recounts that when he once saw a worker tighten a bolt incorrectly, Honda rushed over, re-tightened the bolt himself, and hit the worker lightly on the head with his wrench saying, "You dammed fool. This is how you're supposed to tighten bolts (Sakita, 1982:72)." In another instance, a Matsushita Electric manager was sent a letter by his superior telling him "to control your quick temper and don't drink too much (Gould, 1970:49)."

The two examples above illustrate the range of conformity expected of permanent workers. No facet of work and personality is ignored by Japanese management or immune from criticism. Such concern would be defined as extreme and a violation of personal freedom by Americans. But personal feelings must be submerged to group demands in Japan. Japanese managers are seldom reluctant to act (Americans would say interfere) when they feel individuals must change for the good of the group. A vice president of Matsushita Electric once summarized the company's managerial philosophy as (Gould, 1970:79):

We believe people can be trusted, and should be allowed to go on their own as much as possible. But we closely supervise in case of ruinous mistakes . . . Everything depends on the innate capability of the individual executive. But we can also speed up his performance.

Because of lifetime employment, an employee cannot replace another permanent worker and take his job. This decreases competition and inter-personal rivalry, a policy the Japanese favor because otherwise harmony would be more difficult to achieve. The Japanese are not idealists. They realize that cooperation among workers is not automatic. It must be carefully encouraged. Groups are carefully structured to achieve cooperation and *wa*.

A negative factor of permanent employment is that an employee may at times have to work for someone who is less capable or disliked. The first situation is especially prevalent in modern and high-tech industries. Imagine a Japanese computer specialist joining a company as a lifelong employee. He finds that his superior, ten or fifteen years older, is out of touch with more recent technical developments. This supervisor cannot be demoted or fired, and the younger engineer has to learn to accept the situation. He will diplomatically try to "educate" his boss.

The senior manager on his part is encouraged by company policy to give bright subordinates as much freedom as possible, but younger workers usually have to give in to their conservative superiors when they disagree. To do otherwise and insist that you're always right when someone who is older is wrong would disturb the group's *wa*. This is frowned upon. The younger engineer learns to be diplomatic; the older supervisor learns to listen to subordinates and give them the freedom to use their more modern expertise.

A recent multi-national survey of workers 18 through 24 years old asked respondents how many times each had changed employers. Seventy-two percent of the Japanese sample answered "never," while only one-fourth of the Americans did so. Notice that the sample is made up of a fairly young and restricted age group. Nevertheless, three-fourths of the Americans in the sample had experienced more than one full-time employer, and one-fourth admitted to four or more job changes after graduation. Only one percent of the Japanese admitted to having four or more different employers (Sasaki, 1981:3).

The same survey contains another interesting fact. The Indian sample, like the Japanese, exhibited a very low level of job mobility. The job mobility figures were lower in India than in Japan. Eighty-five percent of the respondents in India said they had never changed employers. Lifelong employment is only one aspect of Japan's labor scene and it is not unique to Japan. While an important consideration, labor immobility cannot by itself explain the post-1945 Japanese economic miracle. Other countries have a relatively large part of its non-agricultural workers in employment situations we Americans would consider as permanent, or near-permanent.

No one assumes that the lifelong employment policy in some parts of the French industrial sector or in many of the Scandinavian countries makes their economies as dynamic as Japan's. The same is true in most of the Communist block countries, where labor is relatively immobile. In Russia, for example, job security in the industrial sector is still accompanied with alcoholism, absenteeism, and low quality work. Japan is unique in that it teaches that lifelong employment, even when it's only an ideal, can be a very effective policy when attached to other procedures.

Lifelong employment does not increase worker loyalty and enthusiasm unless it's also linked to bonus and promotion plans, as well as continuous skill up-grading, ill-defined job classifications, and few salary differences. The policy of lifelong employment becomes counter-productive unless workers are allowed to rotate their duties and rewarded when they up-grade their skills. For lifetime employment to work successfully, permanent workers have to become increasingly valuable to the company. They will receive higher incomes as they age; the employer needs greater productivity over the years.

From an organizational point-of-view, such rotation is easily done. Pay is based primarily on seniority, and wages differentials are not based solely on the work done. The Japanese do not encourage extensive work categorization since there is little need to do so in terms of wage or promotion. The typical Toyota auto plant has essentially seven work classifications; a corresponding Ford plant has two hundred.

William Ouchi (1981), James Abegglen (1958), and other analysts of Japanese corporations feel that the pattern of lifetime employment is the most central feature of the Japanese economy which enabled Japanese corporations to produce the post-war "Japanese miracle." I do not believe that lifetime employment is the dominant reason for the Japanese economic success in the last decades, but it is central along with other elements.

I discuss below the major features of lifetime employment and its positive consequences for a corporation. I then discuss exceptions to this pattern and some of its more negative features. Lifetime employment offers great benefits for employees, but it also results in disadvantages. Imagine not having the opportunity to change employers when the chance for higher pay or more interesting work is available. Lifetime employment can be very restrictive to the employee.

Lifetime employment is more of an ideal than a reality to most Japanese workers. Less than half of the Japanese labor force works for establishments offering a lifetime contract. Not all corporate employees have lifetime status even when it's corporate policy.

Employees with lifetime status are under no legal obligation to remain with the company if they wish to leave. The agreement is an extra-legal one based on each party trusting the other. Anyone who wants to change employers is legally free to do so. He will be viewed as disloyal and extremely selfish (or individualistic), but he can legally change employment. Few other companies would offer a lifetime contract to someone who was base enough to "desert" another employer. There are few headhunters in Japan luring mid-career employees from one employer to another.

Employees can be dismissed, but the reasons for dismissal are more social than economic (Abegglen, 1958). Workers who create friction with others, who refuse to obey safety regulations, or who encourage union-management conflict (Clark, 1979:172) will be encouraged to resign, especially when these have not yet been given lifelong employment.

There are ways of placing pressure on unwanted workers who have permanent status. Foremen who wish to get rid of workers can demand excessive unpaid overtime work or give them unpleasant duties. Few workers will be dismissed outright, but many are "encouraged" to leave. Lifetime employment remains an ideal that is not always achieved.

Chief executives are very reluctant to dismiss unproductive but loyal workers, especially those in the managerial levels. Those who don't seem to be loyal to the company are encouraged to work elsewhere. Someone who has displeased an executive can be asked to perform demeaning tasks, such as asking a college graduate to do something usually done by a high school graduate. An engineer might suddenly be asked to inspect the sewers or transferred to a plant in an isolated part of Japan. The last threat is a serious one, since this person may not want to move his family where housing is inadequate and schools are inferior.

While there are many strategies available to managers who want to discourage workers from staying with a company, most are unwilling to use such ploys. One reason is that no manager wants to be seen as being unfair. Observers might not understand that a worker who is treated harshly has deserved this treatment, if he in fact does so. These witnesses would blame a supervisor for acting in a *wa*-threatening manner. This behavior also makes the supervisor look like a dictator. Japanese managers try to reward good behavior rather than punish bad actions. Acting in such a way as to force a worker to leave a company is a sign of that the company is no longer "family."

Lifetime employment is a very compelling moral standard for corporate workers and executives alike. Dismissing someone means the company itself as well as the person has failed. A supervisor who cannot keep workers will be blamed for not being able to maintain the team's *wa*. Nor does a company wish to gain the reputation of being an unpopular employer. Such a reputation will make it harder if not impossible to hire the best graduates. Since permanent employment is an ideal held by most job applicants, rumours that a corporation doesn't live up to lifelong employment standards and doesn't maintain *wa* destroy a company's chances of hiring the best applicants. Few Japanese university graduates would join a company knowing that they might be forced to seek other employment in a few years. Their chances for a corporate career would have been destroyed by then.

Before someone is fired or encouraged to leave, superiors and co-workers will talk to the offender and try to convince him to be a better employee. The supervisor may even talk to the parents of the offender! There will be attempts to change this person's work to see if this can increase his morale. His complaints, if he has any, will be carefully considered. If a worker continuously refuses to obey safety regulations, there will be meetings to discuss with him how his actions endanger himself as well as others. Co-workers will watch him more carefully if that's needed. Dismissal will be done only as a last resort and after very careful consideration. Firing someone, even if he's at fault, can be compared to an American divorce; it should be seen as a very serious and unfortunate situation. Keeping workers is a company's responsibility.

7.3 Hiring Rituals for Permanent Employees

A prospective employee being considered for lifetime employment is evaluated in terms of loyalty and work potentials. Corporate recruiters consider as most important the question of whether or not a candidate will be loyal to company and co-workers. Recruiting officials try to estimate the degree to which a potential employee will accept the company's leadership. They will evaluate whether or not he will be loyal to its demands even if these are unpleasant. Corporate enthusiasm is the quality most looked for in an employee.

There are many unpleasant duties to be performed in a corporation, and employers need to be assured that a prospective employee will be dedicated enough to place the company's short-term demands over his own, even to the detriment of his family's needs. Companies want workers who will accept overtime and extra duties as normal demands. An employee being sent to America as a salesman or as a student would be expected to learn English on his own time and to accept being separated from his family for a number of years. Loyalty to the company is the major expectation in a candidate being considered for lifetime employment.

In addition to exhibiting a potential for company loyalty, candidates must show that they can get along with fellow employees. A recruit would not likely be hired if he were to cause friction with others by being too competitive or unfriendly. A requirement for employment is that the prospective worker will be able to become a harmonious member of the corporate family. To be hired for a lifetime, the candidate must convince recruiters that he trusts the company enough to promise complete loyalty and that he can be a functioning part of a team. An employer is hesitant to hire for thirty-five years or so an applicant likely to disrupt the company's *wa*. As might be expected, there is a lot of crystal ball gazing when job applicants are being considered. Interviewers from the personnel department try to guess what kind of person an employee will be in ten or more years. This concern is made less suspenseful by the fact that the Japanese believe that people can be changed for the better. Corporate managers know that recruits will go through intensive indoctrination. Afterwards, workers will be pushed to become supportive and enthusiastically loyal employees.

Since these candidates are being considered for lifetime employment, it is no surprise that the personnel department is very powerful and influential in a corporation. Members of the personnel department must be able to present to upper management candidates both superior in talent and compatible with others. Personnel directors are highly respected in Japan and given substantial influence and discretion over employment and personnel matters. Since these officials become intimately knowledgeable about the personalities and talents of all hired, they become involved in worker promotion and work rotation. Members of the personnel department remain concerned with those they hire and offer advice whenever personnel matters occur. They will be consulted, for example, when someone is being considered for advanced education or to be sent abroad.

Members of the personnel department in Japanese corporations are also more influential in planning and development matters than in America. Any change in policy demanding changes in work duties or an increase in the labor force necessarily involves the personnel department. Personnel officers help make decisions on employee needs for the next thirty years or so. For example, a decision to expand the robotic division in a plant involves the dilemma of considering hiring new engineers familiar with that specialty as against sending a number of already-employed engineers back to school. Automation also forces all executives to have to solve the problem of what to do with displaced workers. They cannot be dismissed, and others positions have to be found for them.

Personnel directors resist recommending the lifetime hiring of specialists whose skills may not be needed after five years or so. Then too, those already employed may be part of other long-range projects. Sending someone away for retraining means replacing him with another. Personnel problems become complex when projects being considered involve a permanent labor force. Expansion into new fields is done very carefully; limited, short-range involvements are resisted when hiring for a lifetime.

The problem of whom to hire is extremely complicated when an applicant is being considered for lifetime employment. Any mistake will remain with the company for decades. Skilled persons cannot be hired for a short time to see if they turn out to be valuable or not. The Japanese corporation cannot fire its personnel mistakes; it has to live with them. This thought keeps members of the personnel department awake at night.

The same problem is faced by senior executives considering whether the company should expand in new areas. American executives are able to cut their losses by dismissing workers or selling a division that turns out to be unprofitable. But to the president of a Japanese company, the ending of a line, say transistor radios, in order to expand into computers involves the consideration of what to do with redundant or untrained employees. They have to be kept on even when their skills suddenly become obsolete.

Applicants do not choose an employer because a challenging opportunity exists or because one company offers a greater salary than another. Joining a corporation because of a special opportunity is considered extremely short-sighted. An American engineering graduate might join a petroleum corporation because a new exploration team for an off-shore site was being formed. This engineer would consider the experience he would gain, the work to be done, and the salary being offered. When the exploration was completed he easily joins another exploration team of another company. His resume would have another entry, making him that much more valuable to other prospective employers. Each short-term employer becomes a stepping-stone in a career.

But the Japanese candidate considering lifetime employment must worry about more than how his resume will be expanded. He evaluates an employer not for a specific duty, but as a place to belong for his whole working career. This first job is irrelevant when considering a lifetime employer. The major question is how satisfied he will be with the company and future co-workers. Employment is, then, a once-in-a-lifetime decision. Lifetime employment means that once hired, you are stuck with your first and only choice. No other company will want to hire you if your first employment turns out to be a bad choice.

The same dilemma is faced by the recruiter. He must evaluate how the candidate will perform over a lifetime and not just in one set of duties of another. The consequence is that recruits are not hired on the basis of their specific talents. Their general aptitudes and especially personality traits now become very important. Job descriptions for open positions are necessarily vague because no one can predict what will be needed or what someone will want to do in the future.

In one survey sponsored by the Japan Recruit Center and reported by Naoto Sasaki (1981:32) senior executives in a number of Japanese firms were asked what is important when considering a recruit for lifetime employment. All said that they would seriously consider an applicant's references. And all applicants must take a number of aptitude and knowledge tests. These measure technical as well as general knowledge, and include personality stability and profile indices. But personal interviews were considered the most important aspect of the recruitment process. Seventy-five percent of those responding to this survey said the face-to-face interview was the most important part of the recruitment process.

When asked which personality traits were considered most important, Sasaki reports eighty-nine percent mentioned "character and personality." Three-fourths also mentioned "ambition and aggressiveness." The traits "ability and knowledge" were considered as important by a mere twenty-six percent. The Japanese do not hire because someone's technical skills are needed for a project which might be discarded later.

Most Americans would be dismayed at the idea that hiring be done more on personality than on skill. But the Japanese view is that a worker's major need is the ability to get along with others. Given that trait, loyalty to the company and the promise of enthusiasm would be stressed next. A person's "spirit," the Japanese feel, can overcome any technical difficiencies. Educational training and specific talents are ranked last.

Corporate recruiters assume that applicants are hard-working and ambitious, and they must have a reputation for stability and good character. Many companies hire detectives to interview a promising applicant's family members and neighbors. Recruiters assume that specific skills can be developed as the need arises. Given lifetime employment, an employee will be asked to continue training over the years. Traditional Confucian ethics places a great value on education, and respect for education continues in contemporary Japan.

Japan's Optimism

There is one point about Japanese culture which should be emphasized. The Japanese commonly complain that their country is small and resource-poor; that its land is over-populated and its economy weak compared to the major world powers. These complaints are often voiced when talking to Americans. But while the Japanese generally believe what they are saying about their nation's problems, that's only part of the picture. It's a Japanese trait to be humble, and few Japanese want to give the impression before strangers that they are proud. Proper etiquette demands that conversation begin by an apology. The foreigners shouldn't take early disclaimers by a Japanese very seriously. After these first negative expressions, Japanese speakers express glowing optimism about themselves and Japan's future.

It's bad taste to brag, but the Japanese will nevertheless gently hint that Europe and the United States are no longer as dynamic as they once were. The implication is that Japan's sun is rising and ours is not. I mention this because lifelong employment demands a tremendous amount of optimism. Hiring people for decades and agreeing to work for one company also for decades contain the implicit belief that the company's market will expand and that there will be work and increased opportunities. Japanese corporations would not offer lifelong employment unless management believed in future prosperity; nor would individuals accept lifelong employment if they did not believe in their company's future.

7.4 Becoming a Permanent Employee

Lifelong commitment on the part of a new employee and the company begins with the signing of a contract and a ceremony. The new member is welcomed to the company and is at this time formally recognized. He signs a document in which he pledges to obey the rules (whatever they are) of the company. There is no specific list of rules and expectations, just as parents don't expect their new-born to be able to understand the family's rules. The executives on their part recognize the person as a permanent member of the company. That is all, except for a ceremony involving speeches, presentations, toasts, and a formal banquet (Rohlen, 1974).

This ceremony occurs once a year after all prospective employees have graduated from school, been interviewed, taken company examinations, had their backgrounds investigated, and attended a rigorous indoctrination program. They are hired at the same time so each new member has equal seniority with age mates.

The induction ceremony of new members consists of speeches by the president of the company and other high-level officials. Besides moral and patriotic messages and praises of the company, these speeches contain references of the company's importance to the Japanese nation and the problems it faces. There is also mention that employment transforms these recent university graduates into adults. This ceremony is seen as rite of passage from child/student to adult/worker status. The suggestion is that employment bestows adult status and that the new employee should be eternally thankful for this opportunity.

As this induction ceremony continues, a representative of the new employees' parents will thank the company for accepting their sons, and will tell the sons to be dedicated to their company and that family honor demands their being good workers. The above is, essentially, the Japanese version of paternalism, more correctly called familism. The new worker is seen as joining a new family as if he were being adopted. The reader is excused from feeling that I have exaggerated, or that I've emphasized one aspect of Japanese employment over others. But the simple truth is that contemporary Japanese managers take the familial model very seriously.

Below is a representative statement by a Japanese on how his company has always maintained a paternalistic attitude toward its employees. The speaker is Mr. Ishida, past president of Idemitsu Petroleum Company. During an interview for a Japanese newspaper, Ishida said:

The philosophy of Idemitsu is, to put it briefly, application of the Japanese home life to enterprise. Since the first day of our business we have endeavoured to bring our employees up men of good character, because they were left to us by their parents . . . even during the very poor years after World War II we put the priority on the construction of dormitories and company-houses for them. Our company is our home.

Mr. Ishida spoke these words in 1972 but the statement, quoted and translated by Naoto Sasaki (1981:61–2), would be accepted today by Japanese senior executives. The quote stands as an ideal to be achieved: our company is our home. By "home," the Japanese worker means "family." The quote above shows something else about the idea that company means "home and family." Mr. Ishida said "our" when he described the company as a family. He felt as much a part of the company as the lowest-level worker.

Going back to our induction ceremony. The new employees speak after the speeches by executives and parents. A representative of the new workers thanks the parents for their love and parentage, thanks the company, promises that all are worthy of employment, and re-dedicates all inductees to faithfulness and hard work. The ceremony closes with a banquet and more toasts and speeches. The corporate family now has formally accepted its new "sons."

Note the total absence of a list of specific obligations, or rules governing the organization. There are speeches of welcome, toasts, etc., but no description of duties to be performed. The ceremony resembles more a baptism or adoption than a detailed listing of contractual obligations.

The agreements pledged by both sides are implicit rather than explicit and kept deliberately vague. It is now assumed that both parties will be concerned for each other's welfare no matter future problems. Stating minimal conditions and specific expectations would limit this agreement by making it finite. Doing so is insulting, as if no one could be trusted to be fair or honorable. Both parties should have enough trust in each other to be willing to make unlimited commitments.

This is one reason why America has more lawyers and litigation than Japan. We quarrel over one another's contractual obligations. In business, Americans agree to very specific conditions which limit future interaction. To us, a contract should be specific so that all conditions are clearly defined and limited. The Japanese prefer more inclusive understandings. That way there is more understanding for a give-and-take relationship.

During 1982, Hideo Sugiura, executive vice president of Honda Motors, said that there were four "Company Principles" which formed the framework for basic policy. The second principle (Sakita, 1982:20) was:

... that good corporate management must be based on trust. The management and employees should share a sense of pursuing a common goal, so that each individual will play a specific role and the corporation as a whole will be working in unison to achieve that goal. And this thinking is both understood and supported by our work force, as a way to enhance their individual capabilities and *raison d'etre*.

An American business contract states conditions and allows parties to keep their independence in non-contractual matters. This contract states what one's obligations are and are not. For the Japanese, both the employee and the company agree to become mutually dependent upon one another, no matter what might be demanded later of either party.

In American culture, a similar agreement is found in our marriage contract, in which the groom and bride each agree to "love, honor, and obey" the other. This vagueness allows the marriage partners to live up to their wedding vows no matter what situation arises. Since no one can predict ("in sickness and in health") what specific problems a couple will face, the vows need to be vague and all-inclusive.

Loyalty as the Glue for Company and Worker

Rohlen (1974:19) described the Japanese lifelong agreement of permanent employment as an elastic one which is adjustable to the developing needs of the parties. The company does not dismiss its employees since doing so would violate the agreement made upon hiring that no dismissals will occur unless the company is on the brink of bankruptcy. On the other hand, the agreement pledges everyone's loyalty. All parties must adjust their differences together, not just one side. During times of economic depression all workers will receive reduced pay if necessary, and since higher-level employees receive higher pay, they will also be expected to receive larger percentage pay decreases than the lower-level workers. In times of economic prosperity the workers will be rewarded by increased bonuses and greater fringe benefits. In a way, the current optimism in Japan allows management as well as workers to accept blank checks. It's assumed the company and workers will provide the funds.

The agreement between the new member and the corporation is vague and elastic and both parties realize that future adjustments will be necessary as occasions arise. If a worker has a special need such as an expensive medical operation, he will expect the company to help with financial support, a reduced workload, or whatever else is needed. If a problem with alcoholism exists, the company should be willing to send him to a rehabilitation center, perhaps at the company's expense, and at least hold his job open until his return. This familism is so complete that many companies accept responsibility when workers have traffic accidents when going to or coming from work.

On the other hand, during periods of slow business a worker should be willing to do anything needed to help the company: receive less pay, repair and paint buildings if there is nothing else to do, or take the initiative to make the company more competitive. During this idled time workers repair and re-build the machines they use and take courses to upgrade their skills.

A large corporation manufactures more than one product, and if sales for one product slump it is relatively easy to shift one's permanent workers from a less to a more profitable production line. Idled workers are now occupied and their new division does not have to hire untrained, temporary workers to meet the sudden higher production demand. The shifting of idled workers has other benefits. The division experiencing a boom does not have to pay as much overtime, and valued workers are kept busy until a new cycle of demand begins and labor is needed elsewhere.

In point of fact, the Japanese are hesitant to hire temporary workers if permanent labor is available in another part of the company. Not only must permanent workers be put to work, but managers assume that workers will accept any task which needs doing. This may demand longer work days for a while, but workers are expected to be loyal enough to want to help the company. Their loyalty will be rewarded in the long run in the form of bonuses, personal thanks, and better fringe benefits.

Peak work loads present a number of grave problems to Japanese managers. Temporary labor may be expensive as well scarce during a boom period. Temporary workers must be trained and many may not be devoted enough to the company's goals to want to exert the extra attention needed to maintain high quality performance. Japanese executives are also hesitant to hire temporary workers because they are strangers and outsiders: they are not part of the corporate family. Keeping these workers on too long and then discharging them may result in ill feelings and guilt. Management feels guilty when forced to dismiss workers who have been part of the company for a while. Even these temporary workers have placed a debt on the company. Dismissing them when demand lessens makes hollow the company's claim of familial concern for workers.

These misgivings result in the tendency to make do with the workers at hand, even when this means large amounts of overtime. If the shifting of workers from an idled part of the company to an area of high demand is impractical, then the work day will be extended and the worker may or may not be paid overtime, depending on the circumstances. This policy allows bonuses to be later paid to those who were loyal. It is only fair that those employees who remained faithful during lean periods be allowed to share in their company's successes during a boom period. Examples of this type of optimism in a company's ultimate success are the employees who accepted stock in lieu of pay when McDonald's and Apple Computer were struggling companies. In these cases, they have been amply rewarded for their loyalty and optimism.

Lifetime employees are also expected to adopt heroic measures whenever the company's future is in danger. Kyoto Ceramics sponsored an American subsidiary in San Diego, California, called Kyocera International, Inc. After being established, the San Diego plant failed to earn a profit. The Japanese president fired the American engineers and imported Japanese replacements. The Japanese engineers worked seven days a week from 6:30 a.m. to midnight until Kyocera achieved a profit (Bylinsky, 1981). Now financially established, Kyocera has a policy of no lay-offs or firings except for "misbehavior" and idleness. To encourage the work ethic, each Kyocera shift begins with a pep talk by an executive. One custom which has not been imported from Japan to California is that in the parent company workers run, not walk, when making their rounds. But that too may change in the future.

7.5 Advantages of Permanent Employment

Americans see lifetime employment as stifling since the worker would be discouraged from seeking a better position when the opportunity happened. But the average Japanese accepts security and membership over opportunity and individualism. He would say to an American that any corporation offers a complete scope for a worker's ambitions and talents. Corporations are large enough to offer everyone the perfect niche he seeks. Further, the loyalty a worker offers the company is exchanged for the company's loyalty to him. Just as a child needs the protection and care of parents, a Japanese adds that adults also need the protection and emotional support of one group or another. *Amae* is a major component of lifetime employment.

There are advantages for both employee and employer to lifetime employment. This policy, no matter how agreeable to one party, would not continue very long if it did not offer very distinct advantages to all. Career, lifetime employment in the industrial sector is a fairly recent innovation in Japan. There was no such practice until the early twentieth century. The practice would not have developed and continued if it did offer very practical advantages.

One advantage of lifelong employment from the company's viewpoint is that a smaller personnel department is needed. Fewer applicants have to be interviewed, tested, hired, trained, and introduced into the company. Since no senior executives are hired, the personnel department minimizes recruiting costs by restricting its search of new employees to recent graduates from high schools and universities. Because of this lack of labor turnover, the Japanese executives expect to train and develop a smaller number of workers over a period of time. Japanese corporations replace relatively few workers. Instead they add workers as needed for expansion.

This labor permanency also results in an ever increasing skilled force while avoiding the dislocating effects of having to hire periodically new workers who are unfamiliar with their work and their co-workers. Over time, the company's work force becomes more skilled and more experienced. The same workers learn to work together and develop a sense of team loyalty. Those who can't cooperate leave. The rest become increasingly loyal to co-workers and company.

Permanent Employment and Organizational Efficiency

In America the normal reaction to a large number of new workers, irrespective whether the cause is organizational growth or employee turnover, is to increase the company's bureaucratic structure. This is because more rules are needed to guide the inexperienced recruits. Labor turnover demands more paperwork and bureaucrats to direct the new employee's behavior. This adds to the company's overhead. Eventually, the new rules needed to organize new members choke initiative and production suffers.

An example of rapid labor turnover due to both the loss and the increase in personnel is found in the Intel Corporation. After a period of rapid growth the Intel Corporation, a leading manufacturer of microprocessors, found that corporate growth had been accompanied by an even more rapid bureaucratic proliferation. The problem faced by Intel was compounded by the fact that employee turnover was at a very high level through no real fault of the company. Employee loss was due in part to the intense competition for experienced workers in the Silicon Valley, an area where the emerging computer-related industry in America is concentrated. In Intel's California plant, one-third of the six-thousand workers quit each year. Worker turnover was a major problem. This made Intel less profitable than it might have been (Main, 1981).

Intel executives solved part of their problem by asking employees to simplify their own jobs. The results were remarkable! Suddenly Intel workers began to make suggestions on how to cut down on unnecessary paperwork. The members of the accounts payable department reduced the amount of time an account was processed from twenty to sixteen minutes, and the staff needed for processing was reduced from seventy-one to fifty-one. In another area, Intel was able to reduce the number of steps needed to order inexpensive supplies (i.e. pencils and paper) from ninety-five to eight; the paperwork needed was decreased from twelve forms to one.

Intel has not been the only organization to suffer from over-bureaucratization. Most organizations increase their bureaucratic, administrative personnel faster than its productive members during a period of general growth. The U.S. military is a good example of the uneven growth of administrative in relation to "producers." Before 1961, it took thirteen administrative steps to produce a new weapons system. Now it takes roughly four-hundred steps.

Having an experienced and stable labor force allows a Japanese corporation to keep its paperwork and bureaucratic buffers to a minimum. Following the example of Intel, other American corporations can profit by asking their workers how their work could be simplified. The Japanese do this constantly.

The Intel experience teaches another advantage of lifelong employment. The experienced workers stay and become advisors to the newcomers. These more senior workers are familiar enough with the company's procedures to inhibit the growth of bureaucracy and can personally show recruits how to perform. The company remains people-oriented rather than becoming rules-oriented.

While the above statement is difficult to measure in a reliable manner, a number of studies of Japanese corporations have suggested that, in fact, Japanese companies have fewer rules and restrictive work categories than American corporations. One such study was made by Vladimir Pucik and associates (1984).

Their report dealt with a comparison of job mobility patterns among managers in a Japanese and an American automobile company. One finding was that the Japanese company had relatively more technicians and fewer administrators while the reverse was true in the American company. Having fewer rules, Japanese corporations can devote relatively more human resources to technical rather than administrative problems. Permanent employment contributes to this Japanese advantage. Japanese corporations are leaner and meaner.

Lifelong employment, with its vague contractual requirements, supports the belief that each company is so different that efficiency is achieved by workers learning over time to be compatible. Workers' skills are not easily transferable from one organization to another. They can be used most efficiently in only one organization (Taira, 1970:184). Under the system of lifelong employment, each worker is encouraged to develop new skills within the specific context of the company's needs. Not having been hired for a specific job, the Japanese worker learns how he can best contribute to the success of the company. Although each new employee adapts and conforms to the customs of the company, he is also given a large amount of freedom. The company gives him scope to develop his talents and his own place in the company. But the company sets the limits to these talents. These skills are company-specific rather than market-specific.

The average American worker wants to develop market-specific skills. These are skills that are transferable from one company to another, according to the demands of general economic conditions. Such skills allow a worker to accept the highest of many possible bids from different companies. Market-specific skills are well-known and recognizable to potential employers. The company knows what skills it can use.

By contrast, the usefulness of company-specific skills are limited to one company, as when a worker knows the quirks of an old machine or motor. Such talents are not in demand by corporate outsiders. These skills are valuable only in one setting, and companies do well to encourage such talents if they can keep the workers who develop them. They provide in-house productivity advantages. Unfortunately, company-specific skills develop slowly. A company must nurture and encourage this type of knowledge over a long period of time. Few graduates a few days out of college have company-specific knowledge to offer. They have to learn how their new employers operate.

The disadvantage to having only company-specific skills on command is that the worker becomes less mobile as he becomes more valuable to one employer. He learns how to work within one company, and these skills are not adaptable elsewhere. This is one reason why mid-career mobility is frowned upon in Japan. Aside from indicating disloyalty and undependability, a worker's skills may not be regarded as transferable and a company would rather develop company-specific skills in younger workers. Besides making the worker more productive and valuable, company-specific skills keep workers with one employer. A worker who feels his skills could be better used (or rewarded) elsewhere has almost no choice but to start his own company. No one else would hire him.

I have already noted that the typical Japanese corporation is less bureaucratic than an American company. This allows a Japanese employee the chance of fitting the company to his own specifications. The scope won't be large, but the company's structure will be flexible – perhaps ambiguous is a better term – enough to allow a worker to use initiative and to work his own way. Rules are few and alternatives to the status quo are more easily considered by the senior staff. In spite of the fact that Japanese are conformists, Japanese corporations are highly flexible and are quickly able to adapt to changing conditions. The Japanese worker may conform to his work group, but part of this conformity involves using personal talents for the good of the good of the company. Good workers search for new ways to become more efficient and productive. Lifelong employment gives him the motivation as well as the time for this search. To an American worker, being a good employee often means only obeying the supervisor and following orders until a better offer comes around or being dismissed.

Another source of company loyalty derived from lifelong employment lies in how the Japanese worker sees himself in relation to the company. I have already noted that a worker is hired on a lifetime basis because of his general rather than specific skills. Consequently, the new worker must take part in an extensive training program to develop whatever skills the company needs. He feels gratitude because his employer has given him the opportunity to become a more skilled worker.

To the Japanese worker, personal skills are not his own when his talents have been developed through the sponsorship of the company. Leaving after developing at the company's expense new occupational skills would be an ungrateful act. Much like an adult who will not reject his parents after they have trained him, the worker should not ignore the benefits he has received from his employer. These skills "belong" to the company as much as to him. Lifetime employment would not exist if the employer could not trust the worker to stay after the company had gone through the expense of upgrading his skills.

By contrast, American workers define occupational skills as personal property to be used for the owner's advantage rather than the employer's. This is why no one is especially surprised when valuable workers change employers. Many may have even joined not because the firm offers a lifetime of opportunity but because they want the experience of working there for a few years or less. With this experience, the workers will seek greener pastures and incidently add to the problem of employee turnover. The Japanese avoid this disruption by promoting only from within and by not hiring outsiders except at the start of their careers. Mid-career employees use their skills for the company which hired them as their first and only employer. American workers take for granted that their skills are transferable. MBA degree holders, for example, change employers frequently during the first ten years after graduation. They view their first employers as stepping stones.

To an American, a position which does not offer the chance to gain experience useful in another setting would be considered as a dead end and rejected as unworthy of his ambition. It would not add a line to his prospectus, and this position would have to be given to a less ambitious and perhaps a less-skilled worker. Ambitious climbers learn which jobs and which divisions are so employee-specific that they would be useless to company-shifters. If the promotion ladder is a steep one, a worker would not want to consider such a position: he would have nothing to show for his efforts except years in service.

General Motors Corp. is an example of an American corporation which has adopted a policy of lifetime employment for its salaried executives and managers. Two-thirds of GM executives have worked only for GM and no one else. Fewer than one percent of the top executives leave the company to work elsewhere. GM brings outsiders into the executive circles only when there is an urgent need for outside experts and for new ideas (Burck, 1981). These are brought in at the vice-president level and are considered as "new blood" to revitalize the hierarchy when it becomes too consensus-ridden.

An interesting innovation not found elsewhere in America is the GM-sponsored General Motors Institute in Flint, Michigan. The only accredited college owned by a U.S. corporation, the Institute trains future GM managers. The last three GM presidents have been graduates of the Institute, and nearly all graduates (95%) become GM employees. Five years after graduation, sixty-five percent of these employees are still working at GM. The Institute, in the Japanese fashion, provides GM with cadres of dedicated, well trained permanent workers.

The Long-Range Perspective of Permanent Employment

Lifetime employment ensures a permanent labor force for the company. Except for deaths, workers expect to work together until retirement. Since the average Japanese lives almost a quarter of a century beyond the age most retire, work groups will not change unless members are rotated within the company. It is axiomatic in this system that no mid-career senior level personnel will be hired from outside the company. Some may be given more responsible work than others, but the "family" will remain intact over the decades.

This permanency of labor is one reason why graduate education is relatively undeveloped in Japan. Employers would rather hire four-year graduates with a general, unspecialized educational background. Later, superiors may ask him to develop some specialized skills as the need develops. To fill this need, each Japanese corporation maintains its own specialized educational programs to upgrade employee skills.

Lifetime employment enables Japanese corporations to develop a long institutional memory (Ouchi, 1981). An employee expects to receive rewards over the long term. He is secure in feeling that earlier successes will not be forgotten. He knows that, except for death and retirement, superiors and equals are going to remain with the company. They will remember what has been done and reward accordingly. A manager can do favors knowing that they will not be forgotten. Favors given will eventually be returned. Over the years, managers build up a complex web of obligations, favors, and debts with the expectations that they will eventually be repaid.

Japanese managers are also more likely than Americans to avoid tasks which offer only short-term profit because their work will be recognized in the future by those currently in charge. A younger manager does not fear that being temporarily transferred to a minor branch will cause him to be forgotten by his superiors. He knows he will not be replaced by others who have more visible profiles. The company, in essence, can ask a member to perform unpleasant tasks for a while because he will be rewarded in the future. After all, the parties involved will be with the company for at least thirty-five years.

There is nothing more frustrating and morale destroying than the fear that work will be unrewarded because superiors use their offices as revolving doors. The natural reaction to this situation is to do nothing unless it can be recorded somewhere. This forces employees to act only within official guideline and established procedures. The result is increasing bureaucratic timidity and a loss of nerve. Low employee turnover makes it less likely that extra effort and favors will be forgotten as new members come and go. Labor stability also makes it more likely that ancient quarrels and disputes will be remembered.

To avoid this, Japanese lifetime workers have to be very careful not to antagonize colleagues. Who knows if a seemingly temporary dispute will be remembered to one's disadvantage years later.

I know someone who quit a post in anger. Before he left he visited each person he had a grievance with and told him off. This gave him great satisfaction at the time. The problem was that five years later when he wanted return to the company, there were enough of the old guard who personally remembered his tirades and wanted nothing to do with him. Permanent employment forces long-term colleagues in Japan to see their relationships in a long-term perspective. Today's *wa* is maintained in part to avoid future conflict and retribution.

In America, corporate employees must get their superiors' attention as quickly as possible. Lower-level managers and staff personnel must keep in mind that they, their colleagues, and their superiors, will change employers a number of times during their careers. Favors and debts must be repaid quickly before those involved separate.

A superior who is thinking of leaving may not want anyone to know his plans. Rumors spread quickly in any office, and this person needs to keep his options open. He does not want his superiors to know he's looking for a position elsewhere until he either gets a promotion or a firm offer. Nor would this person want to tell his own assistants of his plans, since this will affect their work and is likely start rumors which will reach the wrong persons. So assistants work for a man who might very well leave soon and be unable to return favors.

Suppose that, as in the above story, a supervisor accepts an offer from another company. His replacement may be a stranger with her own assistants. The original subordinates are now faced with having to get to know and impress a new superior while some are necessarily downgraded. Much of the work done for the predecessor is wasted. American companies, because of their labor turnover, have short institutional memories.

There are positions in every company which are recognized as way-stations to promotion. These short-term positions are given to those seen as highly promotable and offer experience to these "water-walkers" as they rise from job to job. These office holders do not remain stationary for long unless they fail and are not promoted.

Master sergeants in the U.S. Army face a similar problem. A career sergeant with several tours of duty in his records develops a perspective which stresses the long-run. He wants to do nothing that might threaten his career and his approaching retirement. His best strategy is to follow the rules and do nothing rash. He knows how the system works. Rotation and promotion in his case are regular; the most advantageous policy he can adopt is to accept the system and wait. There is little he can do that can speed up his career.

On the other hand, a newly-appointed lieutenant has to be noticed by superiors as quickly as possible. First assignments will be short-term as he is rotated from one responsibility to another. The young lieutenant sees his work in a different context than does the older sergeant. An up-and-coming junior manager is more like a shavetail than a sergeant; near-retired foremen and senior clerks are the company's master sergeants.

Office-holders who see little chance of promotion realize that these early career "stars" come and go on a regular basis. The strategy they will adopt is one of maintaining a low profile and minimal extra effort. Few of us want to exert effort which will not be recognized or rewarded. Lifetime employment counters this tendency by ensuring that superiors will always be with the company. Extra work will not be forgotten since the participants remain together throughout their careers.

7.6 More Advantages of Permanent Employment

Lifelong employment, in addition to developing long-term person-to-person systems of obligations and special ties, also encourages a different time perspective than is found when personnel come and go frequently. When office holders rotate frequently, few feel motivated to get involved in projects which will be completed only after current personnel have gone elsewhere.

Ambitious Americans are seldom enthusiastic in projects which will not give immediate results. We are more likely to seek short-range advantages than longer ones. Office transfers as well as changes in employers mean that few persons at the beginning of, say, a five-year project will be on hand at its finish. These changes in personnel cause confusion, loss of recognition, and a hesitancy to become involved in long-range projects. By contrast, life-long employment allows for long-range projects. When you know that you and your colleagues will be together for decades, long-range projects are seen as just another fact of working.

In the same light, lower-level managers feel secure to experiment and test new techniques because failure will not be punished with dismissal. This feature of lifetime employment makes the typical Japanese administrator more flexible than his European-American counterpart.

Under a system of lifetime employment, a company is forced to develop an employee's talents because employees are hired more for potential than specific skills. He will work for the company for roughly thirty-five years or more, and it is impossible to predict what skills will be needed during this time. As he works, the worker's superior and immediate supervisor will be alert for any special aptitudes and interests he exhibits. He will be transferred from department to department to test his interests and be encouraged to take additional training and education. Most white collar employees in their twenties and early thirties take one or more evening courses to upgrade their skills. Workers are defined as capital investments rather than as temporary units, as would be the case in America. During the 1970's, when it was decided that Japan needed to develop a computer capability, those who exhibited talent and/or interest in this area were encouraged to enroll in evening programs or were sent back to school on a full-time basis, some in America.

The greatest advantage of lifetime employment results from the fact that the company has a stable labor force on which it can count. Senior executives can formulate long-range plans and set aside a work group and prepare its members for a project which may not be completed for years. The Japanese executive has a stable team and he knows that these men will remain with the company. The company's investment in developing their skills will not be wasted. If a long-range project is successful, the men involved will be respected and rewarded. They do not fear being replaced after the project becomes a success for a failure.

While long-term employment forces workers to avoid inter-personal conflicts, disagreement at times exists. This seeming contradiction is based on the fact that middle and senior management hold different time horizons. By definition, middle-level managers will be with the company longer than their seniors. This fact causes middle management's time horizon to be longer than their superiors'. It's middle management's responsibility to evaluate each policy in terms of its long-range effects. These workers will not only be part of the company when the effects of policy are felt, but they stand to gain or lose according to long-term success or failure.

This forces middle management in corporations to review the long-term consequences of any plan. Since most new suggestions originate at the middle managerial level, such managers consider any long-term problems which might result from a policy being proposed. This will necessarily involve extensive discussion among middle-level managers before any proposal is offerred to the top levels. By that time, all middle-level managers have met together and achieved an agreement.

By the same token, upper management have to convince lower-level managers that a policy does not endanger future consensus and the company's well-being. They are ready as well as unified when their superiors ask for opinions.

Permanent employment forces middle-level management to join forces and consider the long-range view. The policy also forces them to take the initiative when change is being considered. No wonder Japanese corporations are so quick to adapt new technology and to produce new products. They are forced by corporate circumstance to think more about the future than the present. Few Americans can afford to do so.

7.7 Disadvantages of Permanent Employment

Robert E. Cole (1971:61) estimates that only roughly twenty percent of those fully employed in Japan enjoy permanent employment status. All other workers are defined as "temporary" though they may work for the same employer for years. Permanent employment is more of an ideal than a reality enjoyed by all workers.

Smaller enterprises cannot afford to keep permanent workers during the downside of business cycles. They offer no lifelong employment contracts and few fringe benefits. Management in these concerns are more likely to be authoritarian than familial in their managerial style. Even in companies offering lifetime contracts, "temporary" workers are given few fringe benefits, such as overtime pay, housing and food subsidies, or even free medical programs. The separation between lifelong and temporary workers is as great in other ways.

An important disadvantage of being in the "temporary" category is that labor unions represent primarily the interests of the permanent workers. Union members see themselves as an integral part of the corporate "family," and they exclude temporary workers from many of the benefits of union protection.

These temporary (*ringiko*) workers are usually unskilled and their welfare are not recognized as being the responsibility of labor unions or management. They do not receive semi-annual bonuses or other fringe benefits. They perform the most arduous, simple factory tasks without much hope of advancement or security. At times a foreman may be impressed enough with a *ringiko* to sponsor him for promotion into permanent employee status, but this is a relatively rare occasion.

Women Employees

There is a large number of workers in even the largest firms who are almost never given the opportunity to achieve permanent employment. These are women employees. They account for one-third of all the employees in the manufacturing sector. This category of temporary workers offers Japanese corporations a flexibility in their labor force not usually recognized.

Younger female factory and office workers are expected to work for a few years after graduation, then quit work to marry (Cole, 1971:147). It is a Japanese cultural imperative that all young women now marry during their twenties. They can contribute to the family's income by working on the family farm, in a family-owned store, or perform cottage industry work part-time at home. But the Japanese strongly disapprove of young married women working full-time away from home.

It is understood that women will shift their loyalty from employer to husband and children after they marry. Their major responsibility belongs now to their family. For this reason, women work for a few years until they marry. Some, a very few, work until a child is born, but this rare. Whenever finances permit, married women should be at home full-time and not work at all.

When they marry, women workers are replaced by another group of just-graduated younger girls, or by older women whose children have married. The latter are nearly all from the poorer, lower classes, but they remain an important source of cheaper, temporary labor. This cyclical movement of virtually all female workers offers a corporation a flexibility in the size of their unskilled labor force. This enables management to decrease its least valuable surplus labor when the economy or when the company's sales are decreasing. Other women can be easily hired or rehired when economic conditions become more favorable.

Early Retirement

If left unchecked, the policy of permanent employment would result in a well-paid geriatric management. Given the fact that Japanese male life expectancy is in the seventies, a company's work force would eventually contain a majority of very old workers at all levels. This potential problem is avoided by the custom of early retirement, which allows workers to retire in an honorable manner before becoming senile or feeble.

Japanese corporations officially retire employees when they are roughly fifty-five years old. They are retired, given a retirement bonus, and a small (usually inadequate) pension. Senior-level retirees are offered bonuses equivalent to five or six year's salary. Lower level manual workers are also given a retirement bonus, customarily a month's pay for each year of employment or more.

Some retirees return to the family farm to become part-time farmers. Many others start their own small stores with one or two employees. Although Japan has half of the total population of the United States, Japan has 1.61 million retail outlets in contrast to 1.55 in America (Vogel, 1979:195). Many of these stores are owned by retirees as sources of financial security during old age and to keep occupied.

The lump sum given at the time of retirement, along with savings and loans, can be used by the retiree to become self-employed through the start of a new company or family retail store. Private and public pensions are too small to maintain a retiree's customary standard of living, and most retired persons must continue to work after being officially "retired."

Higher-level retirees often establish companies which are satellite suppliers to their former employers. Many corporations offer loans and guaranteed markets to encourage capable retirees, still in the prime of life, to establish these "child companies" (*kogaisha*). Many of these *kogaisha* are staffed almost completely by retirees (Broadbridge, 1966).

If already established, these "child companies" attract retiring corporate officials although they are paid lower salaries than before. These retirees know their former companies well and have already developed close ties with those who remain. They continue to be defined as part of the corporate "family" and are expected to continue to work for the original company's *wa*. The central company now has a dependable supplier whose officers know the company and its personnel well.

Not all employees leave the company at age fifty-five. There are two other alternatives besides retiring completely (not usually financially possible), becoming self-employed, or working for a *kogaisha* or other company. The first alternative to leaving the company is promotion. When the time for promotion approaches, workers are evaluated as to their value to the company and promoted on the basis of merit.

Earlier promotions are based automatically on the basis of seniority. But at fifty-five, some managers are offered continued employment within the company and promoted according to merit. Some become directors, essentially "elder statesmen," but others are promoted to the top positions of the active leadership. They become the senior managers of the corporation.

Other retirees, both in manual as well as in non-manual positions, are asked to continue to work for the company as temporary workers (Cole, 1971:164). They receive less pay and fewer bonuses and fringe benefits than before, partly on the reasoning that, with their retirement bonuses, older workers need less income.

Through these retirement alternatives, the company retains the workers it wants, sends former employees to sub-contractors, and releases those considered as inadequate in a face-saving fashion. The company also retains a cadre of older skilled workers at a lower pay. Since these are now temporary workers, they can be laid off or given less duties at reduced salaries. The company is able to maintain its (partly fictional) policy of permanent employment by having a flexible work force of older and female workers.

In America, the "last hired, first fired" policy based on the seniority principle forces companies to lay off younger workers, who are essentially the future of the company. The reverse is true in Japan. Companies are better able to keep the younger workers. Corporate employers give them steady employment at a time when they are starting their families and careers. Occupational insecurity is concentrated among older workers who have already established their families, have received retirement bonuses, and can better afford reduced employment.

The policy of lifetime employment offers Japanese corporations a number of distinct advantages. By hiring a person for life, management shows the recruit trust and unlimited support. This entails a debt upon recruits which can only be repaid through loyalty, enthusiasm, and hard work. This debt is so vaguely defined by both parties that it results in a flexibility American managers might envy. Companies can ask workers to change work duties and enlarge their responsibilities without having to re-negotiate pay rates or contracts.

This flexibility makes rules, job demarcations, and specific positions less necessary. Organizational changes are made more easily; workers become more adaptable. Less bureaucracy and fewer administrators are needed, leaving room for relatively more technicians and first-line producers.

Lifetime employment offers Japanese companies a stable, increasingly skilled labor force whole identification and loyalty are total and long-term. Perhaps that's one reason why, according to one study, more than eighty percent of Toyotas being produced have no defects. By contrast, the average Ford has seven or more defects when it comes off the assembly line. If quality is a human as well as a technical problem, lifetime employment contributes to the high quality of Japanese manufactured products.

Lifetime employment solves a number of particularly Japanese concerns. This policy allows for less competition among employees. All are paid and pro-moted on the basis of seniority. Work is performed according to merit, and no one competes against another individual for a position or pay raise. Less-than-adequate employees can be given easier duties without being embarrassed through demotion. This system encourages worker harmony and cooperation. They all work together to maintain the company's *wa*. By the same token, not all corporate workers enjoy this privileged status. Temporary status and early retirement make the corporate labor force less rigid than it might first appear.

Lifetime employment reflects a number of Japanese cultural ideals, notably the emphasis on the importance of group membership, loyalty, and harmony. The system encourages long-range planning, employee upgrading, and reten-tion of valued personnel.

Lifetime employment will remain an important, and unique, feature of Japa-nese corporations as long as the economy expands and skilled workers are in demand. Even the "oil shocks" of the 1970s, with their accompanying higher inflation and unemployment rates, did little to discourage Japan's acceptance of lifetime employment. This practice will continue as long as the Japanese economy remains as it is and Japanese workers remain as group-oriented as they are today.

Chapter 8
Achieving Performance and High Productivity

8.1 An Introduction to Quality Control Circles

Basic to Japan's recent economic successes are the ways Japanese manufacturers produce high product quality at a relatively lower cost. Americans need to understand how these quality-cum-low-cost procedures form an integral part of Japanese management philosophy. Product quality is cooperatively achieved by workers in partnership with managers. The ways this is done are the keys to how the Japanese work and manage. Quality work performance illustrates Japan's success in achieving harmony in the workplace.

The survival of many of our manufacturing concerns depends on their being able to match Japan's quality and cost levels. If Americans can't achieve comparable product quality/cost standards, America will become an economic colony of Japan. We will end up exporting knowledge (hopefully) and raw materials to Japan and importing Japanese finished products.[1]

I show below how some American companies have successfully adapted Japanese techniques to achieve higher quality and lower costs. This has been done primarily by adopting the Japanese technique of Quality Control circles (QC circles). This adaptation can achieve long-term and wide-spread successes only when the social factors supporting QC circles are understood. Before discussing what Quality Control circles are in detail, it is necessary to show why Americans should adopt the Japanese current mania for quality work performance, and what exactly is meant when the Japanese talk about "quality." As would be expected, the Japanese conception of "quality" is quite different from an American's.

Product quality, apart from competitive prices and excellent design, is a distinctive feature of today's Japanese products. Even when Japanese goods cost the consumer as much as their American counterparts and it's obvious that their general designs are copies, Americans and other non-Japanese will often prefer Japanese to American goods. Again and again, Japanese products have fewer defects and higher quality than their American counterparts. This is the major challenge faced by American manufacturers. Americans can develop faster computers and smaller cars. We can even invest in more

---

[1] The number of licenses granted by the Japanese government to import knowledge in the form of patents and procedures has decreased in recent years. Japan is relying less and less on foreign countries for state-of-the-art knowledge.

automation to increase worker productivity, which is already high. But these improvements mean little if the quality of our consumer goods is inferior to Japan's.

Though Japanese goods were recognized throughout the world until the 1950s as shoddy and inferior, they are now as good or better in quality than their competitive counterparts. Even non-traditional, high-tech Japanese goods are respected. How has this come to be? How did the term "quality" become linked with the Japanese? How were the Japanese able to develop quality production techniques in such a short period of time?

There are two related answers to these questions. Japanese manufacturers seee high quality as an integral feature of productivity. Quality and productivity are not defined as separate problems. Quality is not a function of higher costs and extra labor, but rather of design and production. Quality is a built-in feature of any object. Low quality refers to bad planning as well as bad worksmanship and production errors. As important, low quality to the Japanese is seen as the result of inefficiency. A "good" product is both error-free and made as cheaply (efficiently) as possible. The problem to the Japanese, then, is how to produce a product as perfectly and as cheaply as possible. Quality and productivity are facets of the same problem and cannot be separated. One cannot be achieved without the other. A well-made product is nevertheless seen as a failure if it is also highly priced due to low productivity procedures. The Japanese do not accept the widespread American belief that high quality means higher manufacturing costs and hence higher retail prices.

One point should be made. The Japanese view a "perfect" product as one that is error-free. But for something to be definded as "perfect," the Japanese demand that the whole production system should be error-free. It is not enough for any batch to be 99% error-free. While only one item, say a television set, out of a production batch of 100 contains an error, this is not production "perfection" to the Japanese. They are dedicated to reducing this error rate to one in a thousand, and then to none at all. The ideal of error-free production is not a statistical standard where a certain number of errors are acceptable in a specific production batch. To contemporary Japanese manufacturers, error-free production means exactly that; every product can and should be error-free. Pride in their products and in their company demands no less.

How this standard is achieved is another distinctive element of Japanese production philosophy. Simply put, quality production is every worker's responsibility. Workers are expected to be personally concerned with making every product they make better and more cheaply. As would be expected from the discussions in earlier chapters, Japanese managers encourage workers to suggest production improvements. Their model of the worker is based on the belief that everyone involved in making a product help in reducing production costs and in increasing quality. A large part of this chapter is devoted to explaining how and why involvement of the workers in quality control has been so successful in Japan.

The best example showing how workers participate in quality control is found in the Japanese development of Quality Control (QC) circles. If quality production is a major way of successfully competing with the Japanese – and I think it is – then QC circles form an important way to do so (Juran, 1981).

QC circles are teams of workers who meet several times a month or so to discuss production problems. Their goals are to discover how the quality of their work can be improved and how to reduce production costs. As if this were not enough, QC circle members also work together to improve the quality of their work life, including safety procedures.

QC circles encourage non-managerial (including clerical) and staff workers to initiate work improvements. They are asked by management to improve their productivity and work performance. QC circle team members are expected to become so deeply involved in their work that they are willing to take the initiative in making their work more efficient. They become co-partners with managers to improve the company's products; they become change agents; they become part of management.

This situation is radically different from that found in the United States. Most American management believes workers are paid to obey rather than to be co-partners. Improvements at work is assumed to originate from production experts and managers/supervisors rather than from the workers themselves.

QC circles membership demands that workers perform more than the minimum expected. QC circles fail when workers are unwilling to improve their own producitivity without supervision. Workers must want to use initiative and become involved in what they are doing. QC circles fail when workers take no interest in their work. Many jobs can be performed while the operators daydream or discuss sport. To these workers, quality and production quotas are standards to avoid rather than surpass.

QC circles are more than a way to improve productivity. They are also the best example of how Japanese managerial techniques can be adopted by Americans.[2] Over half of America's *Fortune* 500 have adopted QC circles in one form or another. In the last ten years, hundreds of other American corporations have developed QC programs with various degrees of success. QC circles prove that at least part of the Japanese work philosophy can be

---

[2] QC circles are also used in South Korea, Taiwan, and elsewhere in Asia. There are even QC circles in Latin America and Europe.

transferred to the American scene. While QC circles do not offer solutions to all of America's managerial and manufacturing problems, they offer the possibility of lower production costs, higher product quality, and higher work morale.

The term "quality" needs to be defined before discussing the characteristics of Quality Control circles. The focus is primarily on what quality work means to manual workers, especially those directly involved in production. But the same discussion applies equally to plant janitors, those unloading material from a railroad car, or secretaries developing new work techniques. The difference in quality control between the Japanese and Americans is most pronounced on the manual, blue collar levels, but quality improvement can be the concern of all workers.

A word of warning. QC circles, or any other strategy to improve manufacturing quality, will not work if the workers are blamed for the low quality of products. Attending QC circles should not be punishment for presumed failures on the part of workers. Worker involvement in quality improvement occurs because workers are asked to be management's partners, not its scapegoats. As David Cole (1981:117–19) stresses:

Quality . . . is a management responsibility. Any U.S. quality problem is not all the fault of the American worker; some of the best Japanese and German plants are in the United States.

Quality improvements depend on the willingness of American workers to identify their company as "family". They must want to contribute to the company's *wa* and rewarded when they do so.

8.2 Definitions of Quality

Quality has two general definitions. The first meaning of the term is what Philip B. Crosby, former vice president of the ITT Corporation, calls "conformance to requirements." Crosby means by this phrase that a product should be built according to formally-stated specifications (Crosby, 1980:15). Quality is achieved when a product is produced the way it's supposed to be. Quality management guarantees that work will be done the way planned. In this context, quality performance depends on good communication. Orders (requirements) must be clear to those who are expected to carry them out. This is a problem not always understood by those who give directions. The extent directions are understood should never taken for granted. What is clear to an engineer may not be clear (or possible) to the machinist who actually does the work.

Two other points dealing with how high-quality is achieved need to be made here. First, knowing what should be done is meaningless if workers cannot react quickly. As Philip B. Crosby (1984) emphasizes in another book, *Quality Without Tears,* production problems are often uncorrected until an expert arrives or after a shift shuts down. The problem of idled workers is eliminated by giving workers the permission and responsibility to make corrections. Workers are often able to make production changes to solve problems. The question is whether or not they are encouraged and trained to do so instead of expecting to wait for an expert.

The second point I wish to make here is one often ignored. Management is in charge, and quality production is the responsibility of those in charge. When quality production is low or below specifications, the search for the origin of this problem should begin with managers and supervisors, not the workers themselves. What is usually the case is that original directions are either incorrect or not communicated clearly enough, or that high quality is sacrificed by those in charge for other goals.

By directions I mean here both overt and covert instructions. Covert instructions are indirect messages. An example of an indirect message is when a worker is told to speed up production even when this results is more errors. The implicit message being communicated is that quantity is more important than quality.

The above preference of quantity over quality is well established in America. GM's Alfred Sloan established during the 1920's what is essentially a policy of minimum definition of quality. He said that any given product does not have to be better than a competitor's; it only has to be as good. Making a product better than a competitor's increases costs and is wasted effort. It's more profitable to focus energy and material on increasing the production of a product rather than its quality. Quality emerges as a goal only as a response to competitors. The result is the guiding axiom *Acceptable Quality Level* (AQL). In other words, quality is a secondary concern (Cole, 1981a:89) and becomes a major goal only in response to competitors.

The *AQL* philosophy encourages manufacturers to see product quality as less important than current profit-loss statements. Sales, financial, and promotional departments become more important than a company's engineering and design sections. The disadvantage with the *AQL* policy is that a company is forever playing catch-up with competitors, as the American auto industry did when Japanese better-quality imports "invaded" the United States.

Quality as defined so far is a static and very limited concept. This view assumes that a product's specifications are already as good as the can be. If that is so, then it follows that quality is achieved only when workers obey orders to the letter. Any deviation or shortcut leads to errors and should be avoided. Again, quality is achieved in this view when workers obey. They are not encouraged to think for themselves and innovate. The more they obey, the higher the "quality" of their production.

The second definition of quality is that "quality" means both "better" and "cheaper". The term "quality" here involves the idea that any product or process can be made more efficiently (cheaper and faster) and more error-free. Quality does not refer only to how well specifications are followed, but also to the improvement of current production procedures and the specifications themselves.

Quality in this sense is an on-going process. Theoretically, there are always ways to make products cheaper and better. Specifications are temporary guidelines soon replaced by more exacting standards. Workers have the responsibility to be prepared to change their activities as often as necessary when they find a better way of working. They become smart workers rather than only obedient ones.

If specifications are seen as temporary guidelines rather than engraved in stone, who is responsible for making these on-going improvements? The Japanese answer is, "The worker himself". The person at the machine knows best how to improve his or her production. Floor workers may not know everything about production and quality improvements, but they know what they are doing. From this follows the Japanese notion that a major source of ideas on production improvement must come from the workers themselves.

The definition of quality as "following specifications" is an American concept and practice. The second definition of quality ("quality as the search for improvements") is Japanese. The task of American manufacturers is to emphasize the first less and the second more.

The American Concept of Quality

The American definition of quality is obviously a limited one. It derives from the Scientific Management school were high productivity is achieved only when workers perform their work in the way demanded by experts. This approach places a premium on obedience to standardized instructions. Workers, in this view, are paid to be passive and to follow orders. This approach assumes that workers don't know how to work more productively; there is the belief that outside specialists have discovered the "one best way" to perform any routine. The Japanese see "quality" as going beyond these restricted assumptions.

Seeing quality as "conformance to specifications" is only the first step. Philip Crosby (1980) states that existing specifications are the best available, and that workers can offer few improvements. It's assumed here that change at the production level can only harm production and will decrease the quality of the product being assembled. The Japanese, by contrast, encourage workers to make suggestions *before* they have achieved "conformance to specifications".

Philip Crosby realizes that most products and assembly acitivites do not depend on only one person to complete them. In a complicated world such as a corporation or a modern factory, orders are passed on through several organizational levels, duties are highly specialized, and success occurs only when all a product's parts fit together in the way planned. Quality in this sense means that workers follows specifications: they are doing what they are supposed to be doing. Otherwise, chaos results. In this context, there must be a plan, and everyone must follow this plan. This is a bureaucrat's heaven.

Quality here depends on workers following orders which allows for planning and cooperation. Hopefully, Crosby continues in his book, *Quality is Free,* quality work means doing the work right the first time. This zero-defect policy saves on material, re-working and repair, and on the costs involved in recalls.

The assumptions behind viewing quality as "conformance to requirements" demands first of all the premise that the product's specifications are adequate in the first place. Assume that after design, development, and marketing research, a product in question – a television set – is both durable and attractive. Let's also assume that assembly specifications are clear to trained workers. Quality here means that the workers perform to specifications so that production standards are maintained. When a television set is finally assembled, it conforms to established standards: there is no surprise, no shoddy work, and assembly goes well.

The senario is of course idealized. One problem faced by workers is what is meant by specifications: are tolerances to be viewed as minimum or maximum standards? Many American workers view production standards as idealistic and while they might try to approach these specs, they seldom try to achieve them. Or to put it another way, the worker gets as close to performance standards as necessary to please quality inspectors. That's why Japanese manufacturers located in America establish smaller tolerances for their American workers. Americans must be told to do more to achieve a comparable level of quality as the Japanese.

The blame here is usually, and wrongly, placed on the workers themselves. Every reader has heard that "Pride in workmanship no longer exists in America." Or that "No one wants to do good work anymore". Social scientists have no proof that workers today are less interested in their work performance than they were a generation ago. We must not let nostalgia blind us. By contrast, it's important to keep in mind that quality is not magic. It demands hard work and constant attention. Twenty years ago, imported cars had a higher ratio of recalls and customer complaints than did domestic cars. If the Japanese can learn to manufacture higher quality, so can (and must) Americans.

The presumed decrease in quality work assumes that workers are free to vary their work activities. The fact is that many if not most industrial/manufacturing duties are so specialized and mechanized that the typical worker has little leeway in what is being done. Most workers are told to follow orders and to work as quickly as possible. The result of this rigidity is boredom as well as the feeling that quality is not encouraged.

Robert E. Cole (1981a:90) has interviewed Japanese and American automotive officials on the question of quality performance. Cole says:

Poor quality is more a function of management priorities and reward systems than of a declining work ethic. All too often, employees at all levels of the organization get a gentle slap on the wrist for poor quality; but they get belted for failing to meet production quotas. Until some more balance in *that* reward equation is reached, all the management slogans, directives, and campaigns in the world will be ineffective in changing current practices.

Coles goes on to point out that "(Japanese) high production quality derives fundamentally from the application of specific management systems and strategies." He means that managers, supervisors, and workers are all rewarded – symbollically, socially, psychologically, and financially – when high quality performance is achieved.

The Japanese counter negative feelings about quality work by enlarging the scope of work as much as possible, even if this means only job rotation. Going from one dull job to another is better than doing the same dull activity over and over. In this situation, a bad part or assembly once in a while makes the work day more exciting. After doing the same simple operation for several hours, an error makes for excitement.

American workers see manufacturing specifications as maximums for another reason: quality control in America has as its goal the discovery and elimination of sub-standard, low quality products. To the average worker, quality control is the search by someone else for his own mistakes and errors. The natural reaction to this is to view quality negatively, as a threat to one's self-esteem. Achieving high quality means that the inspectors ignore you when you do well; they only react to your mistakes.

In the United States, low quality performance indicates that a specific person has made a mistake; someone is to blame for making an error. This makes workers defensive and nervous. They see quality in a negative way, as a way to avoid punishment. Quality inspectors in this context are necessarily enemies of production workers. They catch mistakes and blame low quality – even when caused by external forces – on the floor workers.

In Japan, quality control is not seen as a way of catching a person's mistakes, but rather as a way to improve performance. Japanese quality control measures are primarily preventive. They concentrated on keeping errors from happening in the first place (McMillan, 1984:162–4). American quality controls focus on discovering mistakes after they are made. Quality in Japan is more than a product's assembly and performance. It also refers to *how* a product is made. Low productivity and low quality in Japan are evidence of system mistakes, or group-level inefficiency. Individualistic Americans see individuals as responsible for low productivity and high error rate. Even when a single person is at fault in Japan, the blame is placed on the group or system. This avoids making personal criticism. In a typically Japanese manner, quality work is a way of supporting the group. Even if you don't care about the final product, you will – if you're Japanese – want to help your team by working better.

The suspicious attitude American workers have toward programs to increase quality performance is well founded. Many workers see such programs as hidden ways to speed up production: quality means "speed-up" work and few workers in America see any benefits coming their way when quality and productivity are increased.

Quality in America is restricted to the product level rather than to the sub-unit and sub-assembly levels. Quality inspection tests the complete product after assembly is completed (Ross and Ross, 1982:17).[3] The Japanese prefer to test for quality at each assembly point whenever possible. The end result is that the completed product in Japan has been inspected more often than the United States. These lower-level inspections are made by the assemblers themselves. Obviously, such a large number of inspections would be too costly if specially trained inspectors were used. Instead, the Japanese expect the floor workers themselves to be their own inspectors whenever possible.

The difference in results between the Japanese and American systems of quality procedures is illustrated in Motorola's Chicago television set plant after it was taken over by Matsushita. Before the sale, Motorola was averaging 150 defects per 100 TV sets. Then the Japanese took over. An American work force using predominately the same equipment and machines as before eventually achieved a defect rate of 4 per 100 TV sets after the introduction of Japanese style quality control.

A similarly ironic event took place during the 1970s when Zenith, then a leading producer of color TV sets in the United States, sponsored a series of ads with the theme, "The quality goes in before the name goes on". Unfortu-

---

[3] The books by Ross and Ross (1982) and Barra (1983) on QC circles are two of the most practical guides on the topic.

nately, Japanese television sets at that time had a defect rate of less than twenty-five percent of American sets. Later, Zenith led a suit petitioning the U.S. Treasury Department that the Japanese were "dumping" color TV sets in America. Zenith asked that increased import duties to be placed on Japanese TV sets. This case was eventually presented before the U.S. Supreme Court and dismissed as groundless. American producers must become more serious about quality manufacturing if they are to match and surpass the Japanese. Many manufacturing sectors in America are more productive than their Japanese competitors when a product-worker ratio is considered. But while Americas can often produce a product more efficiently, this short-run advantage came about by sacrificing quality.

Steven C. Wheelwright (1981) points out that Americans see quality and low cost as opposites. One can be increased only when the other decreases because Americans define these two concepts as mutually exclusive. American manufacturers have traditionally been concerned primarily with manufacturing – through mass production – the cheapest goods in the largest quantity possible. We let other countries manufacture low-batch high quality items while we made life more comfortable for the masses. In a democracy with a very small elite, economic success is based on supplying the masses with cheaper goods. Other countries with wealthier and more stable elites, such as was found in Europe one hundred years ago, could cater to small but wealthy upper classes. The general population at that time was too poor to buy many goods anyway.

The American genius was to see that the general American population could support a growing industrial sector through the expansion of mass production techniques. Goods would become cheaper through mass production because their low cost would encourage a high demand. Henry Ford made the automobile into a consumer object that a large proportion of the middle class could for the first time afford. Along the way to mass production, however, Americans de-emphasized the importance of quality: a product had to be "good enough" for its market, not perfect. Quality was often rejected as an unnecessary refirement because quality meant higher prices.

The Japanese Concept of Quality

Quality first defines how well a product is made. The worker becomes a better worker when the quality of his work improves. Quality in Japan also involves the notion of progressively higher productivity, not only by working faster, but also by working smarter. Quality results in a better and a cheaper product. I will use both concepts to mean "quality" unless otherwise noted.

American management has emphasized quantity over quality performance. Assembly workers today find it hard to believe that managers have made an about-face and now want to emphasize quality first. Workers in this situation naturally believe that pressure to increase quality is another con game. Management has found another way to squeeze workers to produce more in duller jobs.

The average manufacturing worker in Japan has no such fears. Quality helps the group, which in turn helps the members. The result is that Japanese workers take pride in achieving and even exceeding tolerances in their blueprints. The typical Japanese manufacturing product is now as good, and often is better, than what is demanded by engineering and design personnel. Specifications in Japan are challenges rather than threats.

One advantage to this concern with individual quality production the Japanese enjoy is that workers themselves become involved in improving the quality of their work. The individual worker becomes his or her own quality inspector. Because of the involvement of the workers in quality improvement, high quality can be achieved without the use of outside quality inspectors. No longer is quality the responsibility of someone else ("If there's a problem in quality, its 'their' fault; its none of my business"). Fewer inspectors are needed and this results in an obvious economic saving: less personnel are needed when workers accept the responsibility for the quality of their own output. Workers, on their part, feel freer because inspectors are not looking over their shoulders for mistakes they might make.

The American automobile industry uses one quality inspector per seven workers. The Japanese automobile industry uses one quality inspector for each *thirty* workers (Davidson, 1984:10). The ratios differ not because the Japanese ignore quality performance. It's the opposite. In Japan, workers are expected to inspect carefully their own work and to take note when their materials are sub-standard. As a footnote, quality to the Japanese also means zero-defect. Anything less than perfection leaves room for improvement.

There is still another advantage to the Japanese practice of expecting a worker to meet or exceed a product's manufacturing specifications. Most consumer products made today are constructed from a larger number of separate parts and sub-assemblies. If each sub-assembly or part barely meets or just fails to meet manufacturing specifications, then the total product will be inferior: each sub-unit's weakness adds to the total inferiority of the product. A weak or inferior battery, for example, can harm the total electrical system of a car and cause problems even after replacement. This analogy can be expanded to any system made up of separate but interdependent parts. Weaknesses are cumulative.

This principle that component strength is limited to its weakest unit also operates in an administrative system. If the quality of work suffers in the typing pool, the other divisions ultimately also suffer. The Japanese are well aware of the fact that "a chain is only as strong as its weakest link". This may be trite, but much of Japanese manufacturing and managerial concern for quality is based on the view that each detail is important and contributes to over-all quality.

The existence of this principle is one reason such complicated products as television sets or automobiles are often of better quality in Japan than in America: each sub-unit is better made and therefore contributes to the total quality level of a finished product. The American practice of failing to meet a series of specifications may not cause a product to be initially rejected, but after some use, these combined weaknesses eventually result in an inferior and less profitable product, if only in terms of durability, length of working life, brand acceptance, and repair history.[4]

Worker involvement in quality performance offers employers an added, unexpected bonus. This bonus uses self-interest to increase loyalty to the company. Workers allowed to improve their work performance will not always think of the company's problems first. It is natural for persons to make things easier for themselves. Workers asked to discover and solve work-related problems will study problems that bother them personally as well as those that effect the company's profitability and efficiency (Gryna, 1981). These "selfish" concerns create frustrations and lower morale. But their eliminations increase morale, cohesion, and company loyalty.

These irritations are often simple to solve, and they give workers the self-confidence to attack more complex, and important, problems. Workers may suggest that the nearest water fountain is too far away from their work area, or that noise makes verbal instructions hard to understand. Workers also become irritable when their tools are awkward to use or when office equipment are uncomfortable. They are also familiar with safety problems. Meeting these complaints helps the company in the long-run, although they originate out of selfish concerns. Many of these selfish concerns deal with vital company problems. Most workers want to do a good job and become irritated when they are blocked from being more productive. A worker may complain that he waits too long for new batches of parts. Solving this problem makes his job more pleasant. It also, from the company's viewpoint, makes him more productive.

Many situations, of course, are recognized as problem areas but are not easily solved. Some problems may demand extensive re-organization and expenses. Workers who learn how complex some operations can be also learn to respect supervisors and managers more. Many workers have low opinions of supe-

---

[4] The ill-fated Edsell was rejected by the public partly because, in their haste to place the car on the market, Ford officials ignored quality assembly.

riors. Realizing the limits of their superiors' power forces workers to sympathize with them. Perhaps then workers will make more realistic demands on their supervisors. American manufacturers pay a price by not encouraging worker involvement and responsibility in quality performance. This lack of concern is found in all levels of America corporations, and not just on the assembly floor.

Quality as Improvement of Products

The term "quality" in Japan has a second meaning in addition to "conformance to requirements". Quality performance also refers to the belief that any product can be made better, more efficiently, or more cheaply. This view of quality begins with the assumption that the Japanese worker can improve the quality of his work if encouraged and rewarded. Not only are the Japanese expected to meet and, if possible, to exceed manufacturing specifications, but they are also expected to take the initiative to improve their own productivity and that of their colleagues.

Workers in Japan do not disregard work specifications and operate their machines on an independent basis. No Japanese worker would be so individualistic as to want to be that independent, and schedules are too tight in Japanese factories to allow for much unplanned procedural change. Production schedules are strict and don't allow for much individual variation. Any changes in production procedures will be very well thought through before being enacted. Each worker is expected to think about what he is doing and to be alert for possible short-cuts to improve production. An electronics assembler may suggest to her work group and supervisor that a different type of welding machine or screwdriver would allow her to be more effective. Or she might suggest that the addition of a color code would allow her to assemble two subunits together with a lower rate of error.

Essentially, the Japanese view toward quality work is that managers expect each worker to exceed specifications. This reduces errors and results in a product with a level of quality which exceeds manufacturing standards. As important, the Japanese worker is also expected to be actively concerned with the improvement of the quality of work. He is to take the initative in the search for improvements.

By contrast, American workers are expected to obey their work orders and to not take an interest in anything but their formal directions. Traditionally, improvements in production involve an outsider – a supervisor or an efficiency expert – and not the worker himself. American blue collar workers, their supervisors would say, are not being paid to think. Moreover, many jobs are so low in interest that to pay attention to what is being done results in being even more bored than before.

Worker involvement in quality performance is not unknown in the United States. Much of the impetus for quality performance in America uses Japan as the model and is still restricted in scope. While some American companies promote higher productivity by encouraging worker involvement, most do not. The many exceptions are exceptions to the general rule. In the Kearney, New Jersey plant of Easton Corporation, production workers are allowed to repair their own equipment if they wish to do so. Obviously, workers who have been taught how to repair their machines will also know how to operate them better than before. These workers also will develop greater interest in their performance as they become involved in more than their specific duties.

At Easton's Kearney plant, no one punches a clock at the start and end of the work day, since it was felt that clock-punching was demeaning. The success of these and other employee relations practices, as reported in the May 23, 1978 issue of *Business Week,* is reflected in the fact that the Kearney plant has a four percent labor turnover, as compared to sixty percent in an older, more traditional Kearney factory. Absenteeism, which in some Easton locations can reach a high of twelve percent, is a low three percent at the Kearney site.

Japanese blue and white collar workers have not always been involved in the quality of their work. While artisans have traditionally been concerned with the improvement of their skills, such as in pottery-making or in the construction of fine swords, the industrial sectors were not models of work participation and quality performance before 1940.

In fact, most Japanese export products before the Second World War were recognized throughout the world for being cheap and shoddy. Few foreigners would have considered Japanese goods to be potentially competitive with the higher-quality German or American products. Such low-quality goods were at that time a necessity because the Japanese labor force was unskilled and largely illiterate. The advantage the Japanese had in world markets was in having a cheap labor force rather than in having a skilled labor force or more efficient machinery.

After their 1945 military defeat, Japanese corporate and government officials realized that the industrial sector would have to upgrade the quality of its products if it were to compete successfully in the international markets. The nation could not enjoy the dubious advantages of being an underdeveloped country. One reaction to this challenge was to involve both management and blue collar workers in quality control. The average Japanese factory now has one-half the number of inspectors than would be found in a corresponding American factory.

Quality performance is not a cultural trait engrained in the Japanese personality. It is a goal that all workers must be taught to accept. The road to this quality control began after the Second World War. American advisors, including W. Edward Deming and J. M. Juran, travelled to Japan and convinced Japanese manufacturers that it was necessary to develop programs stressing quality and a low rate of product defects.

At this time, the Japanese were very receptive to ideas coming from America. Their colonial empire had been destroyed and Japanese leaders realized that they would have to adopt a more peaceful strategy to revitalize their economy. Instead of imperial conquest, the Japanese would rely on economic success in international competition as a mechanism for the procurement of materials and markets. American foreign policy at this time supported the development of the Japanese economy as a balance against Communist expansion in Asia. It is an ironic fact that we encouraged the rebirth of the modern Japanese economy.

American quality control experts introduced statistical quality techniques to Japanese engineers. Deming emphasized objective methods to develop quality control and product improvement. Juran, in 1954, taught that quality control must be the concern of all levels of management and workers and not just the efficiency engineers and specialists. It was at this time, during the 1950's, that the Japanese developed the practice of viewing quality in its widest sense as the concern of all workers: quality is a company-wide objective shared by all personnel.

How can workers concern themselves with quality improvements? After all, workers have their own duties to perform; how can they develop the skills needed to discover and make these improvements? The answer is typically Japanese. Workers are divided into groups whose specific coals are to improve quality and productivity. These team members work together as a group to discover and solve work-related problems. Any skills needed by these members would be taught by outsiders or by one another. Thus the Quality Control circles concept was born.

8.3 Quality Control Circles in Japan

Deming made such an impression during his 1950 lectures on the techniques of quality control that the Deming Prize was established in 1951 to promote this concept throughout Japanese industry. This prize is now one of the most coveted awards given to Japanese corporations and the annual winner gains great prestige. The presentation of the Deming prize takes place on national television with all the pageantry of a Miss America contest. After very thorough discussion and analysis, American quality control procedures were adapted to fit the Japanese corporate environment. Quality control circles were first introduced in Japan in 1962. It is estimated that roughly one out of eight hourly employees is now a member of one or more Quality Control circle (Cole, 1979:137). No greater contrast between American and Japanese managerial philosophy exists than the latter country's extensive and very successful use of Quality Control circles.

A Japanese quality control circle consists of ten or so manual workers with a supervisor or foreman, all of whom are alert for ways to increase product quality and producitivity. The latter is accomplished by attempting to cut production costs. In contrast to American manufacturers, the Japanese view productivity and quality as essentially different aspects of the same problem. The two are inextricably linked. Members of a QC circle monitor all aspects of their work for opportunities to increase quality and productivity. QC circle members are encouraged to look at every facet of the work environment. At one Yamaha plant visited by the author, members of a QC circle had won an award for developing a series of exercises to be done at home so that the workers could keep in good physical shape.

QC circle members meet formally once, twice, or more a month for sessions which last from sixty to ninety minutes. Participants are first encouraged to present their ideas on work improvements. No idea is criticized, so that a suggestion will not make the presenter feel ridiculous. The atmosphere is positive and supportive. Every member is encouraged to make any suggestion at all, even if farfetched. QC meetings are supposed to pin-point problems and suggest improvements. Their purposes are not to pat everyone on the back and maintain the status quo. Every idea is given some consideration. The team then decides whether or not a suggestion warrants further study.

Problem specification is probably the major responsibility of a QC circle. The first and most difficult step toward work improvement is for workers to recognize and define a problem. Locating a problem refers to more than solving errors. Problems exist when a process is not perfect or error-free. A machine does not have to blow up before a problem is located. A problem exists if a machine is running well but at ninety percent efficiency instead of one-hundred percent. It is relatively easy to find a solution after a problem has been defined, but first there must recognition that an improvement is possible. To find a problem, workers must be willing to criticize the status quo. There must be a strong support for change. This requires worker involvement.

Robert E. Cole, director of the Center for Japanese Studies at the University of Michigan, is an expert on Japanese business practices, including QC circles. He has been a vigorous supporter of QC circles in America for over a decade. While QC circles can raise productivity, decrease production costs, and improve the level of product quality, Cole also warns that QC circles do not automatically usher in a new industrial age (Cole, 1980). He notes that Japanese executives recognize that QC circle members can gradually decrease their creativity over time as members increasingly refuse to recognize existing problems. They develop a loyalty to the groups' status quo, in part because no member wants to criticize co-workers. People also get tired of constantly looking for imperfections.

There must be attempts to maintain enthusiasm for quality improvement. This may take the form of daily fifteen minute meetings to discuss general production plans, as is done at the Quasar plant, the American subsidiary of Matsushita Electric.

Cole notes too that many Japanese companies do not have QC circles. And many that do so find that some circles are ineffective; perhaps as much as one-third contribute little or nothing to a company's improvement. The point is that QC circle members must want to improve their work and must want their companies to succeed. This is not an automatic feeling, even for the Japanese. Many workers want to be left alone and believe that QC circle participation is a form of coercion to squeeze more work for less pay. When workers become enthusiastic QC circle members, however, the results can be astonishing.

For example, members of a QC circle once decided that the blueprints they were working from caused delays because they lacked enough details. Also, the blueprints at times referred to other documents not easily obtainable by the operators. The QC members could have decided that ambiguity in directions was a natural state of affairs, maybe because they were not trained engineers. Instead, these machinists pointed out exactly where their directions were vague or misleading. It was then up to someone else to correct these errors. What was clear to one set of workers was unclear to another group. The workers could recognize a problem without necessarily being able to correct it. On the other hand, the engineers could understand the blueprints and did not realize that a problem existed at the floor level.

Another example of QC circle performance involved a group of inspection personnel who routinely used microscopes in their work. This QC circle decided that the $ 4,000 microscopes being used were less desirable than a $ 1,500 model. The cheaper model was adequate for their intended use and took up less space than the more expensive scope. The result of QC circle meetings was impressive savings that could be made in future instrument purchases. Purchasing agents became more careful in allowing future users to test and evaluate equipment before their purchase (Amsden and Amsden, 1976:11).[5]

---

[5] For a history of Japanese QC circles and their characteristics, see the article by Horoaki Nakazato of the Tokyo University in Amsden and Amsden (1976). This work, sponsored by the American Society for Quality Control, contains detailed descriptions of how QC circles operate in American and Japan.

Recognizing a problem and deciding on a solution are not the only responsibilities given to QC circles. QC circle members should be encouraged to do more than to offer a detailed plan for solving a problem. Whenever possible, QC circles should also be involved in the implementation of the problems they want solved.

Implementation gives workers practical lessons in how problems are solved, offers a reality test for solutions, and increases worker involvement. Merely for QC circle members to write a memo, "X should be changed in this way. Doing so will save ten minutes in downtime" is not enough. Workers should be involved in each stage of implementation.

William L. and Harriet Mohr (1983) offer an example of the benefits when QC circle members implement their ideas whenever possible. Imagine a QC circle in a machine shop. The members decide that new lights should be installed on each machine in the shop. They had found that the shop's machines had been moved after lights had been installed. The lamps were now too far way to be efficient. Bulbs were hard to change and burned out often.

The solution was to install new, more efficient lamps on each machine. A professional draftsman and a lighting engineer were called in to offer advice. Later, the members of the QC circle ordered raw materials, manufactured new brackets and fixtures, and installed the new fixtures themselves.

Not all workers have the skills to implement their suggestions, but QC circle members should be encouraged to implement their suggestions whenever possible. Doing so makes future suggestions more realistic, develops new skills among workers, and shows workers in a concrete way that suggestions are seriously accepted by the company.

8.4 Quality Control Circles in America

The first and major requirement of a successful QC circle is to develop the ability of the members to recognize problems. The next step is for members to be willing to present ideas and suggestions, even if they might seem to be nitpicking or a little silly. Management often have to build up employees' self-esteem so that they will have the confidence to present problems in a QC meeting. This demands not only support and encouragement on the part of management, but also an investment in training to develop employee skills.

To cite one example, Ball Corporation, at its Fairfield, California plant involves selected trainees in as much as 200 classroom training hours (Shepherd, 1980) to give them the knowledge useful in QC circle participation. Many QC circle members are at first too shy to present ideas to a public. Many persons are also unwilling to defend their ideas vigorously enough. Most lack the experience of public speaking and haven't developed the necessary skills to develop confidence when in front of an audience, even friends and co-workers.

Recognition of a problem may come from many sources. At times outsiders may present QC circles members with a problem. In Japan, QC circles members ask customers if they have any complaints. At Toyota, most customer complaints are sent to QC circles to be solved. But the QC circle concept works best when ideas and problems originate with the members themselves.

At the Hughes Aircraft Company, some QC circles are made up of persons from different departments and job classifications. This ensures that members with different perspectives work together. A company with organizational and coordination problems would do well to form QC circles with members from different departments and levels. Once a problem is presented, the members will discuss how this problem will be handled. The customary procedure is for QC circle members to assign to each other various tasks related to a given problem. They meet again later to compare information and possible solutions. If necessary, members meet with members of other QC circles to broaden their perspectives. Many production problems can be solved only through the cooperation of two or more QC circles.

It's amazing how very simple changes can result in large financial savings. Some work arrangements are invisible until these who perform the work are encouraged to think about what they are doing. One QC circle invented a new type of variable voltage tester which eliminated over ninety percent of emergency service costs (Barra, 1983:158). Another saving was made when QC circle members decided that product specifications in one part of a plant were unclear and unavailable when needed. They suggested drawing large wall charts that were visible to all from their work stations. Now workers didn't have to stop work and leave their work areas to check specifications.

The underlying QC circles philosophy is that those who do the work are best able to improve it. This reflects the Japanese belief that management can trust the workers to be concerned with the total good of the company. The popularity of quality control circles is such that an estimated ten million volunteer workers are members of these groups in Japan. Some, but not all, participants are given overtime pay for their extra efforts.

Each quality control circle team is given instruction on quality control, statistical techniques, and problem solving. These sessions take part during both the work day and during the workers' leisure time. When a problem is discovered or a possible production cost cut is suspected, the team meets to discuss the matter. Solutions are then presented and analyzed. If more technical knowledge is needed, relevant engineers and staff specialists will be invited to a QC circle's sessions to offer advice. When a solution is arrived at, a proposal will be presented to management.

At times a group which has been successful in cutting production costs will be given a small bonus for its work, such as a banquet paid by the company, or a banner proclaiming their efforts hung in a conspicuous place in the plant. Symbolic rewards can include such benefits as a visit, a letter, or a commendation from the company's president. Financial rewards given to each member are of course appreciated, but they are not always necessary. Money should never be the only reward.

An advantage of QC circles is that production problems are often solved or prevented at the production line before a product is completely assembled. It is cheaper to correct errors before a product leaves the factory. Many defects are difficult to discover and correct after assembly (Cole, 1980). The manufacturer saves on recall and warranty repairs when errors are discovered during the assembly process.

Quality control in America traditionally involved outside specialists who solve a certain problem or offer advice. These outsiders disrupt normal work procedures, lower workers' morale by threatening to change their work habits, and temporarily increase costs. The improvements they offer are imposed on the workers without the latter's agreement or their understanding the need for these reforms. Japanese Quality Control circles, on the other hand, use local labor and eliminate problems before they develop into major crises.

In Japan, the responsibility is taken on by the workers themselves since all line workers are responsible for the quality control of their own output. There is then less need for efficiency experts; those who exist are seen as having an advisory function helping workers improve their own work procedures themselves. This talent is wasted when American managers assume that manual workers, besides being unmotivated, do not understand the work they are doing. Another counter-productive assumption is that Americans tend to assume workers don't want to be more productive. By contrast, the Japanese believe that any worker can be motivated to become involved in work improvement.

Alvin Gouldner (1954) found that managers and workers in an American gypsum plant customarily ignored selected safety rules which all parties reviewed as unnecessary and irritating. These safety regulations had been imposed on the company by an outside party – an insurance company. The workers felt that certain safety rules were non-productive and useless while others were not. The latter were faithfully obeyed while the others were ignored except when insurance inspectors were on the scene. It was obvious that workers were capable of making decisions about their work.

A QC circle made up of floor workers, supervisors, and insurance officials could have easily determined which safety rules were necessary and which ones were not. Then the workers would have been more motivated to follow the useful rules because they had participated in their selection. At the very least they would have understood the rationale behind a rule's existence. Workers resent having imposed on them a rule they don't understand. Such rules will be ignored unless the company invests in an extensive supervisory system. Company rules in Japan are carefully explained to those who have to follow them. These rules must be accepted by all parties involved. Rules which are misunderstood and rejected by workers will quickly be ignored.

A QC circle becomes the modern, human-relations version of the often-maligned suggestion box. In America, a factory's suggestion box is often seen by management as a way of letting workers express their grievances by letting off steam when they complain as individuals. In Japan, floor workers are expected and encouraged to offer positive suggestions which are listened to very carefully. Hence the prevalence of over one million quality circles in Japan.[6] Where QC circles do not exist in a Japanese company, management will pass out questionnaires asking workers for their suggestions on production improvement and advice on job enrichment. After analysis of these questionnaires, senior executives will establish workshop meetings to discuss in greater detail the worker's suggestions. The Tokyo Gas Company, after distributing a series of such questionnaires, later conducted over 1,000 meetings with workers in order to achieve consensus on suggested work changes.

There are many ways to encourage high quality performance. QC circles make up only one strategy among many. A practice similar to QC circles is the "repair line", found in Teac Corporation, a Japanese maker of audio and information-processing equipment. Taec's newest plant has eight different conveyor lines, each dealing with several different products. Taec produces limited quantities of high-precision products and assembly processes change frequently. The challenge Taec faces is to train its workers to develop a large number of skills so that each can quickly adapt from one small-scale batch to another and still maintain high quality performance. The repair line is Taec's answer to these challenges (*The Japan Economic Journal*, August 7, 1984:7).

The repair line is an area of the factory located near the quality control station, the final manufacturing stage. All products that have failed inspection or

---

[6] This is a rough estimate. The term QC circle in Japan is very specific and those that meet specifications are registered with an agency. There are other groups which functions like QC circles but are not officially registered because they are organized differently. The Japanese continue to experiment with QC circle forms and are adapting them to fit different conditions and work environments.

quality standards after or during assembly are sent to the repair line. There, workers inspect the various products and try to repair them. Note that *all* rejected products go the repair line. This forces workers to develop varied skills. They have to expand their knowledge as they to deal with a number of different products with different defects.

The existence of a repair line has a number of advantages. Workers stationed there gain experience repairing a varied number of products. They learn how all of the plant's products are manufactured and assembled. They can spot systematic errors while they learn. This learning is especially important at Teac Corp., where product life-cycle is relatively short. As they develop skills to repair different products, the workers become better able to adapt quickly to new manufacturing demands. They don't get the chance to become over-specialized. Having a number of skills, experienced repair line workers can better adapt to changing manufacturing specifications, no matter how extreme. They have already worked on a number of products; new work practices are extensions of what they have been doing all along.

These workers also learn to rely on one another as they face new repair challenges. In the Japanese fashion, Teac workers learn to work together. When they form QC circles of their own, they can apply their experience to increase manufacturing quality and productivity.

In the short-run, repair lines are not efficient. They take workers away from normal duties and increase the costs of educating workers quite able to perform other, though limited, duties. After they are trained, however, they decrease a plant's rejection rate. They also become more generalized experts. They can replace other workers, train others, and are better able to spot manufacturing and assembly weaknesses. They become quality inspectors. They repair the faults they now discover.

Americans as well as European companies have imported the concept of Quality Control circles from Japan. Hewlett-Packard boasts of over five hundred Quality Control circles which have been given credit for a twenty percent improvement in production quality. Advanced Micro Devices, Inc. also established QC circles in which the company's employees meet to discuss production, including safety, problems. For the above company, acid burns formed the major cause of accidents. The workers eventually made a number of suggestions which reduced the number of burn accidents drastically. Obviously, the workers would be highly motivated to solve such a problem if given the chance, since they themselves are affected. On the other hand, the reduction of accidents reduces lay-offs and production bottlenecks while morale increases because of a safer working environment. Better safety procedures in turn reduce labor costs. In a similar attempt to increase productivity, Westinghouse has today over six hundred QC circles. There are, in fact, over one thousand American organizations today which have established QC circles.

There is another American company which has been able to use employees not only to test its products but also to become more involved in quality. Apple Computer, Inc. adopted an ingenious strategy to encourage product-interest among its employees. Apple's allows any employee who has passed a company exam to take home an Apple personal computer. This is Apple's loan-to-own program and every employee, no matter the employment area, is qualified to take part. By the end of 1981 roughly 1,400 of Apple's 2,600 employees were participating in the program. The equipment is free and there are no restrictions on the use employees can make of their computers. Those who participate enjoy several thousands dollars worth of equipment at no cost to themselves.

This policy encourages Apple's employees to take an interest in the company's products. Now employees can show their friends and family members their company's products. It is always a morale booster when workers can show to others – especially their children and spouses – what in fact their labor produces. This encourages pride in one's employment. It also de-mystifies the work. An engineer or secretary at Apple may have difficulty explaining to non-specialists what each does during the work day. But a secretary and clerk can point to their Apple PCs and each say, "I help make this machine". Pride comes easier when tangible results of one's work are visible to others. Owning a replica of the machine your company produces encourages a high interest in quality production.

Apple's take-home policy has the additional advantage of free testing and measurement of consumer needs. Many of Apple's employees are not computer specialists or engineers, and their computer skill levels are at the same level as the general public. Their use – and misuse – of computers will resemble that of the average population. The take-home program provides comprehensive consumer testing at a relatively low cost. The problems encountered by an employee are going to be similar to those faced by the typical buyer.[7]

Instead of second-guessing the needs of the potential user, Apple engineers can now learn from employees what additional programs are needed or which ones are too complex to use easily. The take-home policy provides Apple with

---

[7] A similar take-home program is followed by General Motors. GM executives and their family members are allowed to "test" new models by driving them themselves. The official rationale is that family members are normal consumers who will spot construction and design faults under normal driving conditions. Until such cars are offered to other, lower-level employees, G. M.'s take-home program is as much an executive perk as much as a road test of new models. A lottery could be held monthly in which all workers are eligible to win demonstration models to keep for a month or two.

an already-made testing laboratory for consumer motivation analysis and acceptance. Apple employees, for example, can quickly and cheaply tell designers that a keyboard "feels" uncomfortable or that the keys are too small for beginners to use effectively. What Apple has done, of course, has been to adapt the Japanese philosophy that a worker intelligent enough to work on a product is also intelligent enough to improve its production and its design.

Whether QC circles will ever be as useful in America as they are in Japan is hard to predict. QC circles have already improved productivity wherever they have been instituted in the United States. But the Japanese group-orientation and sense of *wa* probably cannot be matched in America.

Robert W. Hall (1983:173–9) is pessimistic about achieving the full QC circles' potential in America. He notes that QC circle participation in a Japanese factory can reach ninety percent and above. In the U.S., a thirty percent rate is considered unusually high. Hall also points out that middle-level managers feel threatened when lower-level workers make suggestions. Suggestions are seen as placing blame on these managers. Finally, Hall believes that most American managers are too impatient and don't want to devote enough time and resources to train QC circles members. Their emphases on the short-term preclude waiting a year or more until QC circles begin to deliver suggestions.

Hall presents evidence that many Americans are too individualistic to be willing to work together in QC circles. Hewlett-Packard Company found that QC circles were less effective than another arrangement. At Hewlett-Packard, workers post suggestions on a bulletin board. The ideas are thereby made public. This encourages workers to think them out clearly before they are presented. The supervisor has forty-eight hours to respond to any specific suggestion. He must reject it or pass it on for further study an implementation. A response to each suggestion is later posted for all to see.

Hewlett-Packard has a tradition of encouraging informality and open discussion. All workers use first names, and management is accessible. The company offers free coffee and snacks twice a day. It also maintains ten recreational areas, some in foreign countries. These can be used by any employee at a low cost. The company also has a policy of lifetime employment (Levering et al., 1984).

With such close interaction, high employee retention, and managerial informality, formal QC circles are not needed at Hewlett-Packard. Hewlett-Packard enjoys the benefits of QC circles without their presence. Each American company has to adjust to the specific type of QC circle which best fits into its own organizational structure. Many can use other forms of employee participation to achieve the same advantages.

The overwhelming evidence is that QC circles have been extremely beneficial when managers are willing to devote time and resources (including overtime pay, bonuses, and rewards) to the development of QC circles. Like Hewlett-Packard, some companies have to transform the Japanese QC circle into forms more acceptable to Americans, but the basic principles remain valid. Perhaps no American company will ever achieve 99 proposals per worker (Fuji Electric) or even 56 (Aishi Electric), but even a much smaller ratio in American would prove valuable (Davidson 1984:54).

The QC circle approach is based on the premise that workers should be given more responsibility and job enrichment/enlargement. A QC circle is only one of the forms this premise can take. While few person deny the advantages offerred by QC circles, there is no agreement as to which type to adopt, nor should there be. Below are two other American alternatives to Japanese QC circles.

At the Livonia, Michigan, Cadillac engine plant, GM divided floor workers into teams of ten to twenty persons. Each team is responsible for a number of functions and members are encouraged to learn the duties for each function in their division. To encourage this learning, GM offers the "pay-for-knowledge" plan. The more functions learned, the higher the hourly pay received.

There were formerly forty-five job classifications, each with its own wage rate (*Business Week* May 16, 1983). Now there are only four wage levels beyond the probationary. Each wage level is based up how many skills are learned. The highest pay level demands that a worker learn the skills of two teams. These teams meet formally once a week to discuss safety issues, production problems, and job rotation schedules. The success of these team efforts is reflected that during 1982, workers' suggestions saved the Livonia plant $ 1.2 million and reduced the scrap rate fifty percent.

Note that the "pay-for-knowledge" plan offers workers immediate and personal rewards. They receive pay raises as they learn new skills, and their work becomes less repetitive and simple. Pay and variety are great motivators.

GM at Livonia has done more than encourage upgrading and team work. The company has also tried to encourage loyalty to the total plant. Managers and floor workers dress almost alike and share the same cafeteria. These policies de-emphasize the traditional blue-white collar divisions. As an added symbol that all workers share a common identity, no individual parking spaces are reserved for individual managers. The closer parking spaces are filled on a first-come basis.

Thomas Watson's QC Circles

No discussion of American QC circles would be complete without mentioning Thomas Watson, Sr. of IBM. Watson wanted IBM employees to be proud of their work and IBM. He insisted that employees improve their own jobs. Watson also adopted a policy of lifetime employment. Foremen became "managers" who helped workers rather than commanded them (Drucker, 1983). Every employee was eventually put on a monthly salary and hour wages were eliminated.

Workers were divided into groups or teams which became the basic units of IBM. In 1935, workers were asked to improve their own productivity, and QC circles were born. Today's IBM employees are similarly expected to continuously upgrade their skills. Workers attend training sessions periodically to "Do better what they are already doing well." IBM gives them the opportunity to take the responsibility for improving their work.

The above practices continue today and, not surprisingly, are found in IBM Japan, the Japanese subsidary. IBM Japan is highly Japanese in character. QC circles are very active. One eight-worker team came up with 122 suggestions for product improvement (Sadamoto, 1982). In a recent survey, IBM Japan was cited as the foreign company Japanese university students most wanted to work for.

8.5 Waiting for the Benefits of Quality Control Circles

QC circles will succeed in the United States only under certain conditions. The first condition is that QC circles must operate under conditions of group consensus. Consensus is easily achieved in Japan and not so certain in America. This consensus must be total – workers, unions, supervisors, support staff, and managers. QC circles will create more harm than profit if any party resists their implementation.

Thorough planning is also necessary. Everyone involved must be fully informed as to what is being considered, and every step must be carefully planned. Detailed plans and schedules are necessary to allay fears and uncertainty. Anything new is usually considered threatening. This is especially true when QC circles are initiated, since workers who are asked to act in new ways are naturally going to be suspicious, Fears of the unknown and distrust are reduced by complete disclosure and depends on detailed planning. It takes time to gain the trust of workers who have seldom been trusted by management before.

The nature of Japanese education as well as their decision making process is to go from one detail to another as thoroughly as possible. Only after a stage has been clearly studied will the Japanese go to the next. Americans tend to rush wildly from one stage to another; details, it is thought, can be taken care of later. QC circles fail unless managers are willing to plan ahead. For one thing, inadequate planning reduces workers trust. They don't know what to expect and will be suspicious of a plan originating from management. Comprehensive planning also reduces the time QC circle participants will take until they understand what is expected of them.

A last point to consider, from a Japanese point of view, is American impatience. Americans like quick, immediate results. The Japanese see Americans as unwilling to patiently work for long-term goals. One of the rationale for the Japanese army's willingness to declare war on a militarily superior United States was the belief that the Japanese people could be trusted to support a longer war than Americans.

The same point is valid for the introduction of QC circles in America. Various Japanese officials and executives worked for years before the QC circle concept became widely accepted. It took that long to convince everyone that their development could be a positive factor. American QC circles take from at least one year to two years before they produce any tangible advantage. A long-term commitment is necessary or the effort will fail.

Management must also develop a "hands-off" policy toward QC circles. This is easy enough to achieve in Japan and much less so in America. That is, American managers should adopt a "wait-to-see" stance and not try to force QC circles in one direction or another. The team must be given the responsibility to define which problems to study. If this freedom doesn't exist then the members will resist what they see as managerial manipulation. QC circle members don't want to do management's work.

The temptation for American managers to interfere is great. This is especially true when QC circle teams turn their attention to what is traditionally defined as quality-of-work issues rather than production problems per se. It's natural for people, if given the opportunity, to want to make their own lives better bevore they attack someone else's problems.

QC circle teams which first enthusiastically search to improve the quality of their own work place should not be discouraged. Even if the improvements suggested help only the workers themselves, the next problems attacked will be more germane to productivity and quality improvement. This is where patience is necessary.

General Motors is an American company which has seriously adopted Quality Control circles. GM executives have also been patient when QC circles do not provide miracles. Toyota Motor receives 17.8 suggestions per employee per year, of which ninety percent are put into practice (Cole, 1981a:94). By contrast, GM averages less than one suggestion per worker, and only a fifth of these are ever adopted. This difference is a startling one, but QC circles at GM are relatively new. A decade ago, Toyota Motor received much fewer suggestions, most of which were not useful. If GM is willing to wait, the volume and quality of its QC circles' suggestions will increase.

TRW Inc. carefully introduced QC circles to its work force (Di Giorgio, 1981). QC circles volunteers attend a six to eight week program before being placed in a group. In the Japanese manneer, productivity increases at TRW directly result in pay bonuses. One half of the savings made by QC circles is given to all workers in the form of semi-annual bonuses, usually worth over five hundred dollars per employee. TRW's management found that many QC circles' suggestions were simple (though effective) enough to be put into effect by the workers themselves.

TRW's corporate aim is to encourage a feeling of "family" atmosphere among workers. There are no time clocks except for probationary employees, coffee and doughnuts are free, and all workers are salaried. Workers are divided into teams, and each team is given the responsibility for arranging breaks and work responsibilities. To formally emphasize that management and labor are working together and that all workers are considered equally important (and respected) to the company's welfare, there are no executive parking privileges and all workers eat in a common cafeteria.

A similar QC circle success story is found at Campbell Soup. Campbell instituted QC circles in 1981. Workers attend an eight-hour program with sessions on problem analysis, idea barnstorming, and data collection (Mans, 1981). The underlying philosophy for the establishment of QC circles at Campbell was that:

... the program recognizes that employees who do the work in the plant are the 'experts' in their particular areas of specialization and provides them with the analytical tools and avenue of communication they need to solve problems they ecounter in performing their jobs.

The above quote would be accepted by Japanese corporate executives and expresses well the Japanese corporate ideal. In the Japanese spirit, Campbell's workers at times made productivity improvements *before* reporting the problems at QC meetings. They discovered and solved productivity snags by themslves. This is worker enthusiasm and initiative with a vengeance!

8.6 Making Quality Control Circles Work

Despite Japanese and limited American successes, the wide-spread use of QC circles in America will not be automatic. A major problem is that there is a temptation for managers to use QC circles as a subsitute for labor unions. QC circles can be used deal with workers' grievances since one set of problems QC circles involve improvements of the workers' work environment. This includes safety procedures, work rules, overtime and promotion standards, and even pay scales. The control of those issues currently covered by collective bargaining will not be easily given up by labor unions.

QC circles can, however, become links between management and unions. In fact, QC circles will be difficult to establish without obtaining the active cooperation of unions. QC circles originated because it was felt that such structures would encourage the active participation and cooperation of the shop-floor workers. Labor unions form an important source of management-worker cooperation, and QC circles can be used to bring management and labor closer. QC circles complement rather than replace labor unions.

The cooperation of the unions can be made more lilely by keeping the local union informed of the purposes/goals of QC circles. If unions participate in QC circles, then they must in all fairness be given the credit they deserve. It is tempting for a supervisor to claim full credit when "his" QC circle suggests an improvement. Such supervisors must be convinced that QC circles must not be used to enhance their prestige. Workers realize quickly when a QC circle is being used to their disadvantage and cooperation will stop.

An obvious reason for organized labor's hostility is that QC circles threaten job description and demarcation. QC circles are more likely to succeed when workers perform more than one function. Members must be free to learn how to become generalists rather than specialists. This policy threatens many union-management agreements because pay is often based on seniority as well as the work being done. QC circles challenge seniority/classification bases for pay. Members have to develop skills beyond their own job requirements. And what happens when a young worker finds a way to increase production by combining his work with that done by an older worker? Labor unions and management need to discuss such potential problems very thoroughly and honestly.

Many QC circle suggestions involve job enlargement, job simplification, or both. Some tasks will become more productive when the worker is given more responsibility and increased tasks. Some suggestions will eliminate non-productive tasks and sequences. Implementing such improvements force unions as well as management to become more flexible. The solution in the QC circle context is that all QC circle activity be overseen by joint management-union committees. Labor-management cooperation has become more common recently in the United States, and QC circles offer such an opportunity for cooperation.

Under some conditions, QC circle suggestions are sent to both management and union officials. Any suggestions which threatens the prerogatives of either party can discussed by both parties. Successful QC circle existence is based on the cooperation of individual workers on the line, customers, supervisors, management, and labor union officials (local or otherwise). Each forms a link whose cooperation with the others is necessary.

Ideas presented by QC circles must be carefully handled, especially when they deal with labor-saving devices. Workers and union representatives must be convinced that no one will be dismissed or downgraded as a result of work improvements proposed by QC circles.

There is also the problem of how to reward those workers who take part in QC circles. Not all QC circle sessions can be held during work hours since that would cause havoc with production schedules. Most sessions probably can occur during the work day, especially during off-peak and down-time periods. But some will necessarily take place after the work day. Company officials have to decide whether these meetings qualify for overtime pay or not. Not doing so can violate union contracts. It is here that union cooperation is vital. On the other hand, managers have to be convinced that QC circle sessions are part of a person's work duties. Many supervisors, for example, will at first see these meetings as a waste of time, since workers are "doing nothing". Everyone involved has to believe that QC circles are worthwhile, even if the short-run benefits are disappointing.

About half of Japan's QC circles meet after the work day, and most participants receive overtime pay. Employers planning to use QC circles must be prepared for increased costs when QC circles are first introduced. There will be either overtime pay or decreased work days when QC circle members meet during the last hour of the day or later.

If QC circle members meet after the work day, managers must be prepared for the fact that some meetings will last more than one hour. Overtime pay will necessarily vary and is not completely predictable. The best technique for getting ideas from participants is to encourage a freewheeling amtosphere where everyone is encouraged to throw out ideas and suggestions (Kim and Lunde, 1982). Members should feel free to brainstorm and present as many ideas as possible. Some circles warm up slowly and meetings may last beyond the official limits. Managers have to learn to accept such variability and expect that more overtime will be demanded at one time than another. This is not the time to be rigid and tightfisted. QC circles will prove to be cost-advantageous eventually.

QC circle members must learn to trust management. The major obstacle to successful QC circles, aside from workers' disinterest and apathy, is cynicism. The trust that the workers need is based on their belief that management takes QC circles very seriously and is willing to support them. Trust and enthusiasm are developed through constant feedback. QC circles must receive reports on the reception of their suggestions as quickly as possible. Workers will become cynical if their proposals become pigeonholed somewhere and forgotten. They are putting forth an effort beyond their normal duties and managers are expected to do the same.

QC circle suggestions should be accepted even if little or no improvements can be expected from their adoptions. Their acceptance provides variety, and they are always sources of pride on the part of members. Managers who cannot accept serious QC circle proposals when they seem trivial are better advised not to develop QC circles in the first place.

Mike Robson (1982) has published a practical guide for the establishment of QC circles in England. He finds that QC circles' proposals are usually acceptable and should not be rejected out of hand. Historically, most QC circle suggestions are low-cost answers to problems and can be easily put into practice. The task, then, is for managers to develop a positive attitude toward QC circles and their suggestions. Managers should be encouraged to accept most QC circle proposals. The chances are that QC circles teams will eventually discover additional ways to improve productivity and the work environment.

The question of how to reward QC circle members for useful ideas must be carefully thought out before establishing of such circles. One practice successfully adopted both in Japan and in America, is the use of Public Symbolic Rewards (PSRs). PSR systems reward exceptional behavior through the use of public recognition. PSRs are useful because workers are not completely motivated by financial rewards. There are other ways of showing the company's gratitude. PSRs recognize fact that most persons enjoy the respect of others. We all like to be singled out for praise, whether this involves a pat on the back, a medal, or a certificate stating the company's gratitude. PSRs are facilitated by setting aside a room or wall – as in a cafeteria or coffee area – where posters can be set up announcing what QC circles have done. Another recognition is to hang up graphs that show the relative productivity increases of various work groups. This type of visibility incourages group-level loyalty and team enthusiasm. A trophy can be awarded monthly to the team or unit which increases its production above all other groups. The members could have their pictures taken and posted. The company's newsletter would contain a feature on each month's winners. These actions develop pride in group actions as well as QC circle competition. Such publicity also informs members of other QC circles have done an idea to improve production in one department might be applicable in another department. As an added bonus, making QC circle contributions visible encourages others to become more creative.

A PSR room containing awards and productivity improvements can also be used to announce safety records and general successes of the whole company. The latter includes announcements of new production levels, completion of new plants, and exhibits of new products. Company teams' trophies and records can also be located in PSR rooms.

Public symbolic rewards are never enough in a materialistic society like America. These material rewards can range from small subsidies for coffee to large cash rewards:

* The company is the host when QC circles meet. The company should offer as matter of courtesy and gesture of appreciation coffee, doughnuts, and other light snacks. The serving of beverages defines the occasion as informal and brings the participants closer together: those who share food become more emotionally linked to each other than before. The familiar rituals of serving and eating food at the beginning of a meeting also calm and relax the participants.

* If time permits, the team's foreman or supervisor might offer drinks and relaxation after late-hours meeting is over. Ignoring problems of commuting and transportation, the leader can be given a small expense account in order to entertain his group. Members will probably continue to discuss work affairs during these quasi-parties, so the expenses will not be wasted.

* Monthly winners should be given small financial rewards whenever possible. These rewards can vary with the significance of the solutions presented. A joint management-union committee can be established to determine these awards. This allows union officials to keep themselves informed on QC circles' activities as well as get them to participate in matters involving morale.

* The company can host annual or semi-annual suppers for the QC circle members and their spouse/guests. These memorial dinners can be used as a gesture of gratitude on the part of the company. The discussion of a team's work and successes over the previous year encourages member loyalty. A visit by senior executives to these events is highly recommended as their presence is a sign of the company's support. Similar functions in Japan always involve a senior official, if only for the first half of the evening. These events are also excellent opportunities for evaluating worker morale.

* Offer points for successful ideas, perfect attendance, increased output, etc. Reward all QC circles in proportion to the number of points won during the last quarter, or six months. Prizes can be cash or goods selected from a catalog. Accumulated points could be used as discounts for buying these goods. The company can use any of the various available discount catalogs to ensure a wide selection.

* If a company or its affiliates manufacture consumer products, prizes for superior performance can include the company's products offerred at a discount. This policy "consumer tests" products in real life situations and allows workers to show families and friends the products they help make. This encourages the development of pride and sense of belongs. Such company loyalty will result in greater concerns for quality work. Which goods are accepted or rejected offers some insight on how the company's products are evaluated by the workers.

Rewards for productivity increases can be given to all employees, irrespective of whether someone is a QC circle member or not. While this strategy rewards the "free riders", it can also encourage them to become more active in QC circles. Such a policy drives home the point that productivity is a major concern of higher officials and that they take productivity improvements very seriously. Fort Howard Paper Company has benefit plans which are tied to personal productivity, as are individual employee bonuses. But Fort Howard also declares a paid holiday to all personnel, called a "productivity day", when economic conditions warrant such a move. Rewarding all employees when productivity increases is a better practice than declaring a holiday when the founder or president dies. At least then the employees are more concerned with productivity than the (hopefully declining) state of health of the president.

The question of attendance and membership in QC circles can be problematic. The major point to remember is that *membership in QC circles must be voluntary*. The rationale for QC circles is that they encourage the enthusiastic participation of personnel in projects and increase productivity and quality performance. These goals will not be achieved if workers feel as if QC circle membership is forced on them.

Some workers will not want to become QC circle members, and no one should be forced to join. In the first place, informal group pressure will encourage many to participate eventually. Unwilling members can become trouble spots at a later date since their low morale can infect others. It is better, when a QC circle program is first established, to allow only those who volunteer to participate. Some of these will drop out eventually, but the dropout rate should decrease and remain stable after a few months. Many other workers will eventually become attracted to QC circles as their suspicions decrease and as QC members receive their material and non-material rewards. Participation will increase over time.

QC circle membership should be looked on as a reward in itself. Many workers will enjoy a circle's activities if only because of the sociability that develops over time. Also, workers have been underestimated by managers in America. Many welcome the chance to search for higher productivity and job improvement: at the very least, looking for work changes lessens work boredom. Two final motivational factors are reward (financial and social recognition) and a sense of workmanship.

QC circles cannot work unless managers and supervisors are willing to give workers the freedom to act autonomously, even if it looks at first as if time is being wasted. Worker initatives take time to develop, and it takes time for each team to learn to operate on its own rhythm. This freedom to innovate and experiment cannot be productive unless supervisors are willing to delegate some of their responsibilities. The Japanese are expert in delegation and we must develop the same skills.

Chapter 9
Meetings in the Japanese Style

9.1 The Necessity for Face-to-Face Meetings

Japanese corporate workers at all levels meet often with colleagues, superiors, and customers. The searches for *wa* and consensus force them to spend more time with others than is the case in America. The dislike of paper communication in preference to face-to-face discussions, the relative lack of rules and regulations, and the familial model of management in Japan all result in formal and informal meetings. Making sure that everyone is satisfied with a project and that everyone who wants to has contributed take time. Then too, the Japanese are extremely social. They enjoy being with others.

The work day is too short for both work and meetings, and Japanese white collar employees expect to meet colleagues and clients in the evening for at least three times a week. It is a rare Japanese manager who arrives home before nine o'clock for more than a few times a week. Weekends and vacations also often involve business meetings, social gatherings with co-workers, and going to weekend retreats with co-workers. Many vacations can be considered as partly work-related. Vacations at times are spent with work colleagues and involve lectures, discussions, and the development of occupational skills.

Long work weeks are a normal practice because the Japanese believe that full consultation and participation cannot be achieved until all personnel have a chance to discuss with each other all matters at hand. This necessitates meeting with others after working hours. By contrast, Americans feel that meetings are often a waste of time and that the manager or executive can generally be more efficient if he make decisions alone. The decision maker can always, it is thought, call a meeting after a proposal has been decided on.

This type of meeting has as its purpose the conveying of orders rathers than establishing a process of collective decision making. The Japanese strongly believe that very few decisions should be made in isolation. By contrast, Americans feel that creative mental activity is primarily a solitary process. The making of a final decision may be a private matter to a Japanese executive but the decision-making process itself demands extensive consultation with others. We are more used to collective action after a decision has been selected and not before as in Japan. American meetings tend to have the purpose of informing others about a decision that has already been made rather than to share information and ideas.

Americans need to learn how to make committee meetings, executive sessions, and any of the many types of situations when people get together more efficient and more concerned with morale building. The Japanese have found that the solutions to these two problems involve the policy that every meeting involve as much participation among all the members as is possible.

American managers should consider making meetings more numerous, not less. But the purpose and the behavior expected in such meetings must change. My belief is that meetings can be made much more productive than is common. When conducted properly, meetings become more productive. In addition, more satisfaction can be obtained from attending these meetings. Americans see meetings as necessary evils and usually a waste of time. But the use of the techniques and organizational principles discussed below will produce more efficient meetings.

Given the negative expectations Americans have toward meetings, it's no surprise that most are in fact either a waste of time or actually increase any conflict existing among the participants. Unless carefully handled, getting people together can offer them an arena in which they zestfully attack opponents and even up old scores. Meetings, however, are necessary in every organization. The trick is to make them more effective in terms of the work done and in terms of increasing motivation and morale.

This chapter shows how meetings can be arranged to make them more productive as well as morale-boosting. Unlike the Japanese, Americans have not paid enough attention to how meetings should be conducted. Japanese managerial behavior teaches one major lesson: meetings are more productive when everyone participates and is allowed to contribute. Aside from making participants more productive, full participation develops higher morale and closer worker-to-worker ties. The previous chapter showed how the encouragement of full and supportive participation resulted in the development of QC circles. This chapter focuses on other benefits of the Japanese emphasis on consensus and participation as well as how to make small groups more effective.

QC circles, however, are only one example how the Japanese are able to make a certain type of meeting very productive and creative. Americans have seldom realized that workers could meet to discover and solve these problems by themselves. Before the Japanese showed us the value of QC circles, Americans assumed workers could seldom meet together in a productive manner. American managers need the sensitivity Japanese have in making it possible to encourage members to want to work for job improvement. Telling people to "do something" for the company is not enough. They must be willing to do so.

The Advantages of Face-to-Face Communication

Face-to-face communication is the most efficient form of communication available when done correctly. When two or more persons meet together, each receives and gives off messages through physical motions, voice inflextion, facial changes, and eye contact. Much more is being understood that what is being verbalized. We can better evaluate a person's enthusiasm and honesty when we can see the other person. Body language helps emphasize our emotional states. The changing of our voice inflection, tone, and even noise level give others an added dimension of communication. Watching a talented Shakespearean actor recite a scene is a much more emotional experience than reading the same material ourselves.

Face-to-face communication is also faster. We talk faster than we can write, especially when we become enthusiastic. Responding to others' communication is much faster by speech. Successful executives learn to rely on written communications only when they are content with a slow pace and when immediate responses are not needed. A written message is also perfect when an answer is unnecessary or when the sender does not want to have to react immediately to the other's response. That is why it is easier to send bad news in a written message than to deliver it personally in a face-to-face situation.

Smaller organizations and work units easily utilize face-to-face communication. The small number of persons involved make them readily accessible for personal interaction. It is easier to meet face-to-face with colleagues when they are fewer and when they work in more restricted locations. By contrast, larger work units need to develop formal mechanisms to ensure that there is as much information-sharing as possible. An active policy of holding a large number of scheduled meetings is necessary, as well as the exchange written communications. For many if not most messages, verbal communication is better than written ones. When oral messages are necessary, a group setting is usually – though not always – the best strategy.

Donnelly Mirrors, Inc. is one of the best American example of consensus management (see chapter eight). All grievances are discussed by a committee which meets once a month. All decisions must be unanimous before they become official. All workers are divided into teams of ten. Each team is responsible for its paperwork, production quota, and operations improvements. The members of each team set their own production goals. This is using meetings with a vengeance!

Members of larger businesses need to hold meetings because larger organizations have more detailed divisions of labor than do smaller companies or departments. The work environment becomes impersonal and divided very quickly as a work unit (company, department, team, etc.) gets larger. Members soon have to rely on rules rather than face-to-face communications. Managers of larger units should make special efforts to bring increasingly isolated persons together before communication breaks down.

Smaller organizations or the sub-units of large systems don't have the resources to allow for much specialization; the opposite is true for larger units. One advantage of organizational size is the company's ability to increase the division of labor through specialization. But organization size also has the disadvantage of making personal communication more difficult. The challenge is for managers of larger work units to search for ways to make the environment smaller and more personal.

Increasing size and specialization both divide workers from one another and cause mutual ignorance and hostility. Workers associate more and more with fellow specialists and isolated themselves from members of other groups. This tendency is enhanced by the fact that American corporations isolate specialized functions in different geographic areas. Accountants are physically located in office space away from non-accountants and rarely meet with anyone other than other accountants. This causes a breakdown in communication. In this situation, memos can only partially decrease isolation. A way to avoid this danger is to initiate inter-department joint projects. At the very least, sending junior accountants to discuss common problems with members of another section breaks down organizational isolation.

As to the size factor, it becomes harder and harder to deal with everyone when an organization becomes larger and larger. Sheer size precludes closeness because circles of acquaintances stay about the same size even as the number of co-workers increases. Doubling the size of a division doesn't means that workers now double the number of close friends they have. Instead, friendship cliques remain about the same size; there are merely twice as many friendship cliques than before. The result is that the "company" becomes defined as one's department or division and loyalty often stops at that limit. A GM engineer working in the Buick Division is not likely to feel any loyalty to the Chevrolet division.

This fragmentation is more likely when different groups, as they always do, compete for the same limited resources. Unfortunately, resources don't usually expand as fast as personnel. As groups get larger, the competition for limited resources – even it's only trying to be first – becomes fiercer. Geographic isolation and competition force ever-increasing members of divisions to divide themselves psychologically as well as physically. A growing sense of distrust hampers cooperation and eventually reduces efficiency. Members from different work units begin to keep secrets from each other, hoard resources, and increasingly refuse to cooperate with "them". At this point interdepartmental conflicts are defined as win/lose situations: whatever "they" get, "we" lose. When this happens, divisions resemble warring feudal king-doms as various cliques emerge to claim the total loyalty of their members in response to the hostility of non-members.

Members of organizations react to increasing group size by increasing bureau-cratic controls. Numerous studies have found that as organizations grow, the number of bureaucrats and rules-keeper increase faster than productive line workers. John Kasarda (1974), in his analysis of the effects of organizational growth on the increase in the number of administrative personnel, found that administrators increased faster than non-administrators. Bureaucratic and administrative personnel grew faster than both line workers and top-level managers as organizations became larger. Kasarda also found that the person-nel concerned with communication – clerks, secretaries, and the like – in-creased faster than managers and executives. As an organization increases in size, there is a greater need for more rules and for persons to communicate these rules to everyone else.

Anyone talking to an "old-timer" will hear complaints that in the old days, when the organization was smaller, there was more personal interaction, the boss knew everyone's name, that people helped each other, and that whatever needed to be done was done without relying on rules or orders. The list could go on and on. The complaints stem, aside from a nostalgia for an idealized past, from the fact that more bureaucratic controls are established as the work units become larger. The one-room schoolhouse differs from P.S. 184 in that the latter involves several thousand students, hundreds teachers, and many non-teaching specialists. The only way to organize so many different types of workers is to increase the bureaucracy and its rules. Spontaneity and creativity both decrease.

Expect more rules and more paperwork as a business or department becomes larger. To offset this increased reliance on bureaucratic control, managers must make special efforts so that people meet face-to-face. Hence the im-portance of developing the correct forms for meetings. Specialists from different areas need to interact, as do co-workers, in a personal way. The exchange of memos is too impersonal and rigid to allow for the free exchange of information needed for creative work.

There are dangers associated with face-to-face meetings, and these are pres-ented below in other sections. But one major disadvantage to direct, visual communication can be discussed now. This problem deals with the difficulty men have talking to women on an equal basis. Women are faced with the handicap that men tend not to listen to women or to pay attention to what they are saying. Take the situation in which a group of male and female staff personnel are asked to develop a plan of action to solve a problem. The crisis demands a creative solution to be arrived through the mutual discussion of all of the member's ideas. What generally happens is that female specialists are likely to be given little credit for their ideas. Men listen less carefully to a woman's statements than to a man's. She is not taken as seriously as are the male members.

A woman participant may present an idea which is at first ignored by the males. Later a male will present her idea as his own, and the men will then seriously consider "his" idea. At this point, many women become discouraged at not being listened to and will decide it's not worth talking during meetings. A leader does well to listen carefully to female subordinates and to encourage them to speak up more often. Group leaders must also encourage males to pay closer attention to contributions of female members. The best strategy to use when such sexism exists is for the leader himself to repeat what a woman has just said. It is a sad commentary on the problems faced by women in business that what they say often lacks legitimacy until repeated by a man.

Women are also more likely to be interrupted by males than when the speaker is a male. Men feel freer to interrupt a woman speaker, ignore what she is saying, and then to take the floor away from her. The leader should take the initiative in these cases to ensure that male members of the group do not intimidate the female members. Below is a hypothetical conversation which suggests how this can be done:

Mary: "The third clause in this contract does not allow for the best means for tax depreciation. You see . . ."

John: "Another thing, the delivery dates should be checked on by the production division."

Leader: "Just a second, John. I think we need to hear exactly what Mary had in mind when she said we could do better tax-wise. We can then go back to you. Mary, could you give us some details?"

9.2 Types of Meetings

Face-to-face meetings can be divided into several types. A meeting is defined as a session in which most or all persons communicate with every other member. Meetings are characterized by full participation. Gatherings where full participation is not expected are defined as assemblies. The Japanese believe that participation must be as complete as possible when decisions must be made. When no decisions need to be developed, then total participation is not a prerequisite. However, even sessions organized to share information may demand discussion. Giving information is not the same as understanding the message. A manager may call an assembly so that she can deliver a message. Later, she can chair a number of smaller meetings to see if the workers really understand or approve of what was said earlier.

Gatherings convened solely to inform members of an already-made decision are called assemblies. These are sessions characterized by a one-way communication pattern and are seldom found in Japanese businesses. Assemblies are dominated by one or more persons while the majority of the participants listens. One measure of whether or not a meeting is an assembly is the extent to which those present take part in the discussion. If the leader talks more than the others, then the meeting is in danger of becoming an assembly. The persons present are better described as an audience since their participation is limited to listening.

Assemblies may involve as few as two persons where only one delivers information while the other listens, or they may involve millions receiving the same message through television. The number of the participants is less important than how much communication is exchanged by all parties. A true meeting involves full participation among those present.

Unfortunately, most of us would rather chair an assembly than take part in a meeting in the true sense of the word. In an assembly the audience listens (hopefully) politely and at least sits quietly. The leader has the illusion that he is in total control and that everyone is absorbing what he is saying. The reader is invited to remember how much he or she benefited from high school assemblies to evaluate the usefulness of this type of meeting. Ego building though such assemblies may be to the leaders, their usefulness is otherwise nil. What is communicated in an assembly can nearly always be better expressed on paper.

Written down, a message can be better understood and assimilated. People listen less than they talk and few hear the complete oral message. Leaders should keep assemblies as few and as short as possible since they accomplish so little. Using the high school model again, an assembly becomes memorable only when all present cheer or otherwise take part during the assembly. Even a spitball thrown on the stage during a dull assembly awakens interest. At least a spitball is a sign of participation and breaks the monotomy.

Japanese Meetings

The Japanese manner of holding meetings can be best understood through two concepts, *Nemawashi* and *Matomari*. *Nemawashi* ("going around the roots") is a gardening term and is translated as the necessity of digging around the root system of a tree being transplanted. The gardner makes certain that he does not kill the tree by digging into the root system. In the same way decisions must be made in such a way that members' morale does not decrease and harmonious relations are not disturbed. The process of making a decision must contribute to the workers' morale as well as solving a problem.

To the Japanese executive, a meeting achieves more than a decision or the exchange of information. A meeting allows the chairperson to evaluate the emotional temperatures of those involved. Voting or making the final decision is delayed until the feelings of all of those present are expressed. A meeting is held to "go around the roots" by making sure the interests of those involved and their feelings have been considered.

Americans believe that the process of making a decision and hammering out managerial consensus necessitates conflict and person-to-person confrontation. Meetings involve yelling, expressions of anger, and displays of aggression. Doing so gives a participant the image that he is forceful as well as a fighter. Americans see the possible achievement of an agreement as a challenge to overcome someone. Someone imposes his will on someone else. It is at this time that personality conflicts explode into open conflict. Meetings in America can quickly become arenas where opponents polarize and refuse to compromise or agree. Meetings have little to do with problem solutions as such and more with conflicting parties scoring points against each other and letting off steam.

It is also assumed that participants can be friends again after a meeting and that there will be no long-lasting hard feelings. This, of course, is a naive belief. Hurt feelings and hostility are seldomed defined as part of the game and forgotten. Only a saint forgives someone who has just yelled at and demeaned him, and few of us are saints. Instead most of us in this situation would maintain an outward facade of friendliness while hoping for revenge someday. These conflicts can divide an office into feuding cliques. Like the Hatfields and the McCoys, managerial cliques continue their feuds long after the reasons to do so have been forgotten.

The Japanese do not allow conflict to become so public, and the process of *nemawashi* is one of the techniques used to ensure co-worker harmony. Within a managerial context, *nemawashi* involves achieving agreement for a proposed project *before* members meet together. A formal meeting occurs after agreement has been achieved, not before. The initiator or sponsor of a particular project will informally and behind-the-scenes present his ideas and meet any objections as they emerge.

Nemawashi prevents conflicts from becoming public. Going behind the scenes mutes any disagreement which exists and encourages full discussion and participation in informal settings. These private meetings give conflicting parties opportunities to settle their differences privately. Lasting disagreements among group members are frowned upon in Japan. Corporate members who disagree can use the *nemawashi* procedure to develop mutually satisfactory compromises before the conflict becomes so public that no one is willing retreat. Once made public, conflicts spread to other areas. Few conflicts can be limited only to one or a few matters.

If total acceptance cannot be obtained, then the sponsor either continues to alter his proposal or else dismisses it. Proposals which cause dissension are rejected in favor of those that maintain harmony. The intensive consultation demanded by the *nemawashi* process keeps conflicts from ever developing. *Nemawashi* does not allow a sponsor of a project to become too aggressive in pushing for acceptance. Eventually, this sponsor will realize that further compromise is impossible and that a few persons will never be convinced to accept a given proposal. When all arguments are rejected, then the idea is given up.

On the other hand, it is easier to cede a point or two in private. Concessions under the *nemawashi* process will be made in private rather than in public. Public concessions are likely to be seen as signs of weaknesses, and no one wants to lose face in front of everyone. As important, private consultations make any discussions personal ones. When that happens, giving in or accepting a compromise places a debt on the other person. He will have to compromise in the future to exchange one debt with another.

The Japanese keep careful accounts of their debts. A person who has accepted a favor will be expected to do something in return. Whoever cedes a point today can expect a similar compromise from the other person someday. Discussing and negotiating disagreements in private means personal favors can be exchanged. *Nemawashi* binds co-workers in a net of mutual debts and in an on-going exchange of favors. The process reinforces harmony.

When all principals reach an agreement, a meeting can be formally called, and the already-made decision is officially proposed and accepted. Disagreements have already been ironed out, and the final session is more a reinforcement of the group's harmony *(wa)* than a potential "head-busting" occasion.

There are times when prior consulting is impossible, such as when a project is not yet completely developed and detailed. Yet there may be a need to disuss a matter before the participants are ready to make a public stand. In these instances, the technique of *matomari* is used. *Matomari* is used when decision-makers are faced with a complex problem but there has not been a chance for prior informal consultation behind-the-scenes.

Matomari works in this way. A meeting is called and the chief executive presents a problem and its solution. A corporation president proposes that the company enter the American market. He wants to see if a general consensus can be reached before detailed plans are made on the feasibility of his idea.

Each person states his own reaction to the proposal at hand in turn. He does not offer a final decision but rather only a vague reaction. He then sits back to listen to what the others say. *Matomari* allows each executive to state part of his position or feeling and to listen. As person after person offers off-the-cuff opinions, the listeners will shift their positions in reaction to the others.

Gradually everyone's positions will become more and more definite as each participant takes a more and more definite stand. Those who take strong exception to a proposal will say so in a less and less ambiguous manner or else change their position. Eventually a consensus will develop as participants exchange views and begins to compromise.

If a number of participants are strongly against a project, then the proposal will be dropped or tabled and the meeting adjourned. The sponsor may then try to convince his opponents informally through the *nemawashi* method. If no one feels strongly against the topic and most have indicated their tentative support, then more detailed preparation can be made. A go-ahead signal has been given.

9.3 How to Conduct a Meeting

In meetings where full participation is wanted, the person with the highest amount of formal authority should talk less than any other person present. Listening more than talking forces the others to participate. The leader should contribute only when facts are needed, when the discussion wanders from the matter at hand, or when there is a long lull in the conversation. The leader should be a moderator.

The purposes and benefits of meetings will not be achieved if the group's leader is the most active participant. There is a simple rule guiding how leaders should act in a meeting: the more the leader talks, the less worthwhile the meeting. A corollary to this rule is that a leader should talk less than the others. In the Japanese fashion, the best leader is the silent leader. He sits and listens. When the leader dominates, the subordinates do not voice their criticisms. By dominating a discussion, the leader does not give others a chance to contribute any useful suggestions before it is too late. All they can do is listen and agree to whatever the senior official is presenting. The over-active leader fools himself into thinking agreement and consensus have been achieved when they have not.

This is especially true when a chief executive or division chief has carefully prepared for a meeting but has not allowed others to do the same. He may want to present a pet project as completely as possible and he maintains secrecy to surprise his audience.

This practice is good drama but bad management. It's human nature to want to keep a project as secret as possible, partly because doing so forestalls criticism. No one can criticize what he doesn't know. Keeping a future presentation secret also gives a person more time to prepare. It's a temptation to keep a future presentation secret until it has been polished an reworked. A completed presentation gives the impression that the proposal is the result of effortless efficiency. It's like working a crossword puzzle with a pen instead of with a pencil with an eraser. Both give the impression of efficiency and self-confidence. By keeping the early stages of a proposal secret, no one knows the false starts and dead ends earlier encountered.

By contrast, the Japanese expect and encourage managers to discuss fully any proposals in their early stages. One reason for this willingness to share preliminary information is that it is easier to get and receive criticisms when a plan is half-formed than when it is completed. Less work has been expended and the originator is less ego-involved in an incomplete proposal than when it is ready for full inspection. Few of us welcome criticism after a plan is completed. We listen to others better when a proposal is in the formative stage. At that time, the planner tells himself that any flaws would have been dealt with by him eventually. He is not as defensive to critics as he would be later.

On the other hand, presenting proposal informally before it is complete "asks" others for advice. They are encouraged to see the proposal with a critical eye. The person who wants to encourage as much contribution as possible should make it a habit of presenting preliminary proposals with the beginning statement that, "This is not finished and I'd like to get your reactions. If you have any suggestions, I'd appreciate you giving them to me. It needs lots of changes." It may be hard to be humble and ask for input, but only then will others contribute effectively.

Others can more easily suggest changes in a proposal when it is incomplete than when it is fully formed. It's easier to add a room to a house when it is in the blueprint stage than when it has already been built. Early consultation makes second thoughts less costly and ensures that small errors do not develop into formidable flaws.

The manager who refuses to share knowledge with subordinates during the early stages of a project does not become aware of a plan's problems until it is too late. Lack of preparation forces subordinates to remain quiet when faced with a completed proposal. If convinced that their superior has more material than they, they have to also assume he knows more. They have no choice but to keep quiet and keep any doubts they have to themselves.

Team members may feel so competent that they resent outside supervision, even if this supervision takes the form of reports. They may want to keep their activities secret until a task has been completed. To these persons, keeping secrets is a sign of independence and a source of pride. The manager faced with such a situation should insist on periodic progress reports. Then he is in a better position to judge progress and to prevent problems from developing unnoticed (Brown, 1979:3). Periodically scheduled meetings encourage workers and manager to review progress of work being done. In this situation, meetings need to be held to keep non-members, such as the superior or supervisor, informed. The participants must be encouraged to dominate the discussion while the leader keeps quiet. His responsibility is to keep the others talking. His role is to collect information and not to dispense it.

Since people are usually unwilling to discuss unfinished projects, leaders in this situation should communicate only positive reinforcement and emotional support. They should offer positive messages to encourage the presenters and give them courage to continue. The leader who nods his head and says, "that sounds good; it's promising", is being effective. Criticism should be impersonal and gentle rather than personal and insulting. The leader is presiding over meetings because he and other want to be kept informed. Criticizing preliminary, unfinished proposals makes the participants insecure and nervous. Their reaction is to say less next time. At the minimum, they will try to say whatever they think the critics want to hear. Under such conditions, the leader will be later surprised when he finds that others have little enthusiasm for a project he thinks has already been discussed and accepted.

Group participants aim more of their talk to the leader than to non-leaders. There is the tendency to want to impress the leader more than the other persons present. When a leader talks too much, the other members ignore each other and focus all of their attention on the leader. Talking then becomes a succession of dialogues where one person talks to the leader; then the second person talks to the leader, and so on. If there is no free discussion among all members present the meeting will degenerate into a sequence of leader-follower talks. The comments of the subordinates become less and less critical and more and more supportive. A leader in such a situation gets his ego puffed up, but little constructive work will get done.

The way to avoid this mutual admiration is for the leader to encourage members to talk to each other instead of only to the leader. Members with equal prestige are more likely to criticize each other than a superior. The leader learns much more when the others talk to each other. They are more familiar with the issue being discussed and they know each others' strengths and weaknesses. By listening when the subordinates talk to each other, the leader can discover points of conflicts and areas of tension as well as pick up factual information.

When the leader does less talking than anyone else, the others are less likely to know his stand on a proposal and will be less able to decide how to agree for the sake of agreeing. They are freer to innovate and support a position because of its intrinsic qualities rather because they think the leader approves. The Japanese saying "management sits; it does not do" is a worthwhile guide for American managers.

A Japanese session leader might be considered by Americans to be super-fluous since he seems to do so little during a meeting. But this is incorrect. Doyle and Straus (1976) prefer the term "facilitator" rather than "leader" and it is in that sense that the term leader is used in this book and by the Japanese. It is important to understand that we are concerned here with meetings which are called because input by the participants are needed. There are obviously times when workers are gathered to inform them of facts or a new policy. In these instances, the leader gives his message, answers questions if anyone is brave enough to admit to not understanding a point, and then leaves with the impression that he has performed correctly. Even in this very authoritarian context where communication is essentially one-way, there is the high likeli-hood that many persons have not completely understood what has been presented. But few in the audience will dare ask questions. It's not an efficient use of everyone's time.

When the leader says less than the others he forces the members of a group to become active participants. Silence is painful and embarrassing, and those present will feel obligated to end this gap, especially if prodded by the leader. Americans begin to feel very uncomfortable after thirty or so seconds of silence. When the group is small and the leader can easily look everyone directly in the eye, such silence will seldom last more than a minute, usually much less. If no one speaks, the leader can ask someone to contribute and start the conversation. But that is usually unnecessary. The effective "silent" leader begins the meeting by making a general comment, such as, "Now tell me what you've got."

The Japanese are aware that Americans feel uncomfortable when no one speaks. A negotiating strategy the Japanese use is to stare at an American and say nothing. This often causes panic after a few moments and unnerves American negotiators. To the Japanese, a silent pause is understood to mean the person is thinking. Breaks in the conversation are acceptable, especially when more talk might cause tension.

By doing little talking except to encourage others to contribute, the leader is establishing a climate making full participation easier. His silence makes clear the rules guiding the meeting. He is indicating that the others are expected to talk and contribute. It is also clear that when a leader says little the participants do not know how he feels about a project or specific solution. Instead of reinforcing his own conclusions the participants become freer to contribute more original and personal ideas.[1]

---

[1] Conformity because of group loyalty or fear of being different is an American as well as a Japanese phenomenon. See Janis (1972).

Silence is a useful tool for another reason. Silence is embarrassing and painful. No one likes to be stared at by a superior while he's waiting for him to say something. One such experience is usually enough. The next time this person attends a meeting with the same people he will be prepared to say something and to contribute. This is especially so when the silent participant realizes that those who speak are not criticized or punished by the leader when they contribute. Even those who hate to talk in public will steel themselves to contribute when keeping silent is embarrasing and talking is rewarded. Good leaders know listening and offering emotional support encourage effective participation.

It is extremely difficult for Americans to remain silent and to listen more than they talk. American managers feel that they must take charge of any situation involving subordinates. By dominating a meeting the American manager shows that he is competent and doing the work expected of a manager. This is foreign to the Japanese manager. We have seen that a Japanese will patiently encourage the full participation of others until they have reached a consensus.

Pascale and Athos (1981b) suggest that the "silent manager" must discipline himself and let others make decisions. This passive managerial philosophy forces others to solve their own problems as well as to contribute. This is an especially useful policy to follow when problems develop from personality conflicts. Instead of calling the conflicting workers and deciding for one party over another, the silent leader encourages the opponents to talk to each other and to arrive at a mutually satisfactory solution.

Personal conflicts are placed in their proper perspective when they are made public and presented to a superior. The superior faced with two employees whose quarrels are endangering morale and production does well to bring these two together and listen to their complaints. He listens to each in turn and says little except to indicate he is listening. He can then tell them to solve their differences now or face the (unspecified) consequences. By saying little else he forces them to solve their problems themselves. Legitimate grievances have to be met, of course. But most personal conflicts have emotional and irrational causes and are not susceptible to logic. Saying nothing forces the conflicting parties to work through their complaints.

San Diego's Kyota Ceramic, the American subsidiary of Kyocera of Japan, owns a house where employees can meet after hours to eat, drink, and talk about their business problems. Superiors bring together at this meeting place individuals who are at loggerheads. Thus production and sales personnel can be brought together to discuss their mutual problems in an informal atmosphere. It is here that salesmen can mention that certain customers need faster delivery than others. Or production engineers can point out that special delivery schedules cause certain production problems. Discussions over food and drinks are friendlier than when they take place in a more formal setting such as a conference room. More American companies should set aside an area where employees can meet informally in a friendly setting to settle their conflicts themselves. A "silent leader" in these circumstances encourages compromise and cooperation.

The "silent leader" also indicates by his silence that he depends on subordinates. This encourages them to participate in the decision-making process. Japanese executives encourage others to make decisions. Ideally, this practice will be copied by others down the line. Managerial styles tend to be copied by subordinates. Encouraging others to make more and more decisions becomes a model for others. Over time, a "silent manager" will find that subordinates – and their subordinates in turn – will increasingly use initiative after they are encouraged to participate in meetings. Doing so will force them to make more and more decisions. This frees the senior executive to makes decisions that can be better made at a higher level. It is more productive to solve problems at the lowest possible organizational level. The process begins when superiors rely on their subordinates and become "silent leaders".

When faced with a problem, the typical Japanese executive indicates that a problem exists and that it must be solved by those most affected by it. At the same time, he also says that he does not expect to interfere in the problem's solutions. Those involved are told that they must find a solution which is mutually satisfactory or all parties will be blamed for threatening the company's *wa*. The more active American executive is tempted to get involved in solving any problem which comes across his desk. He would also probably alientate one or all parties, lower morale, and make enemies all at the same time.

Many conflicts in an organization arise because of personality factors. Someone wants to enlarge his department's responsibilities or wants to increase his power to the detriment of another person. Or two persons honestly support different solutions/policies for the same problem. Such conflicts are best handled at their sources. A manager's best policy is to do as little as possible except point out that a solution must be found as soon as possible. As an added motivation, there should also be the understanding that everyone will suffer if the superior intervenes because no one can agree.

Richard Tanner Pascale and Anthony G. Athos (1981a) strongly recommend that American executives develop a more passive managerial style to force subordinates to become more independent. One strategy they recommend is one of "indirection". When decisiveness is not necessary, be vague. Indecisiveness is a virtue when choices are vague or when the standards for making a decision are inadequate.

This passiveness forces other group members to contribute their ideas. They cannot agree with a leader if he doesn't show a preference. Being vague allows participants to contribute without fear of contradicting the leader. Japanese executives use non-commitment frequently to encourage others to use their initative. In addition, vagueness allows an executive to keep his options open. A Japanese manager doesn't want to make a stand until a proposal has been carefully studied by everyone else. He can always reject or accept a proposal later without embarassment after the experts have had their say.

9.4 Everyone a Participant

Studies of worker productivity indicate that tasks are always performed slowly at first until the work becomes more familiar. Workers, whether managers or not, need time to learn their duties and get into the rhythms of their work. In the same way, workers also need time to learn how to work together. It takes a while for individuals to become a team. Managers must be patient when members of a new group learn to interact together. This first stage is an especially delicate period. Leaders tend to be impatient during this time. It's easier, though wrong, to force persons to act together, distribute tasks, and generally organize activities. It's also more efficient to begin by telling subordinates exactly what needs to be done and how to do it.

But this is a short-sighted practice. Japanese executives spend considerable time and patience training future leaders. They offer their subordinates more freedom to act on their own even when they could solve many problems on their own rather than waiting for their subordinates to flounder and eventually find correct solutions. Japanese policy is very strict on this point: subordinates should make as many decisions as possible. Even if they are not as effective as senior executives at first, they will become so eventually. Americans working in Japanese subsidiaries are often very uncomfortable with this policy. American managers normally report to their Japanese superiors to present problems and suggest possible solutions. The expectation is that the Japanese superiors would decide on a solution and issue appropriate directions (Tsurumi, 1976:229). These Americans, following their own experiences, expect their Japanese leaders to take charge, issue orders, and "act" like leaders.

The Japanese executives would point out that if the Americans could identify the problem, then it was up to them to identify the solution. Upper level managers are available for crises which can't be solved at lower levels, but middle management is essentially on its own. The Japanese, on their own part, believe that their American subordinates are too willing to ask for help when they are expected to solve problems themselves.

This passiviness on the part of the Japanese is associated with a tolerance for mistakes. Japanese managers are more lenient when subordinates make mistakes since any experience is a learning one in the long run. The Japanese do not say, "One mistake and you're fired!" This is more of an American stance. Rather, Japanese leaders are more likely to say; "Take your time and do your best! Everyone makes mistakes and it take time to learn to cooperate."

American leaders should learn to be more patient. Most mistakes are not important ones, and potentially costly failures can be stopped before too much damage is done. Leaders must take a long-range view of their responsibilities. One of these responsibilities is to train the next leaders of the organization. Such training takes place only when workers are given increasingly more and more responsibility and freedom.

Teamwork is achieved only when the leader forces his subordinates to work together and gives them the time to learn teamwork.' This can be done by allowing workers to use their own initiative. The leader "sits" and is "invisible", and encourages all other members to interact with each other and not just with himself. Participants get used to working together as active equals. A team spirit will emerge and make all members of the team more productive. They will help, encourage, and motivate each other instead of spending their time agreeing with the leader. When he does less the leader achieves more by getting more from his fellow workers. This is a major advantage of Japanese managerial practices: the leader works to encourage others to be more motivated and to take the initiative. He is part of a team instead of the dominant tyrant of a work group. Meanwhile, this leader has a number of persons who perform responsible, important work. He can devote himself to tasks that only he can do.

There will be times when members at a meeting will stop talking. This will first happen when all or most members have contributed their first thoughts or when a few participants have dominated the discussion and have said what they wanted to present. The leader's duty at this time is to ask those who have not contributed to do so. All work groups contain members who will participate less in open discussion. They may be shy, unprepared, or feel that their prestige in the group is too low to allow them to participate. It is easier for these persons to allow others to dominate a meeting. The leader must encourage their participation.

Some workers may have been bullied by others into a dominant-submission relationship. These will end up being supportive of their own informal leaders and contribute little except to inflate the bullies' egos. Such teams should be broken up as quickly as possible. It is necessary that team members interact on an equal basis. Members will have different skills and talent to offer the group.

That's a plus. Any team benefits when the members' talent are varied. Hopefully, one skill will complement another. Even when participants are specialized, together they offer a range of skills. This can only happen when participants are equals. Allowing a few to dominate others is counterproductive. If the leader should not dominate, no one else certainly should. Everyone must be encourage to contribute equally.

The leader must not allow some members to remain silent and he must force them to contribute even if this means asking outright for their opinion. Full participation is necessary because only then can the leader receive the widest range of input. Allowing some members to remain silent only encourages those who are more aggressive to dominate more and more the meeting. Only their views are presented and most persons present will wish they had never come.

There are several dangers in allowing the more aggressive members to dominate. Listening to only a few members reduces the likelihood that all points-of-view are heard. The more a few dominate, the less others will feel free to contribute. It is important that all members feel that all must take part during a discussion.

As important, allowing a few to dominate a debate or presentation gives them too much power. There is always the danger that these tyrants can become power brokers and empire builders, since they control a number of other persons. Leadership is partly a matter of habit on the part of leaders and followers, and those who dominate during a previous meeting will also expect to take over during the next one. People slip into certain roles, and being the leader in the past prepares us to act in the same way in the future.[2] Similarly, some participants will adopt the follower roles. They will allow others to take the initiative and look to them for leadership. These people fall into the habit of saying little that is constructive. The leader must make certain that no one person or persons is allowed to adopt the leadership role. If that happens, a few subordinates increasingly dominate, and the chance to develop a consensus decision structure is lost.

To ensure equality of participations, the group leader must force all members to contribute once or more during each meeting. A member may be too shy or unprepared the first few times he attends. But he will begin to contribute when he realizes that he is expected to contribute *every* time there is a meeting. This person will soon become prepared as he finds he cannot hide behind the more active members.

---

[2] This role-taking in a group is a common phenomenon. Two other commonly found roles in addition to leader and follower are the clown and the nay-sayer. The clown makes jokes and asides at his own expense and others, and contributes litte except dubious humor. The nay-sayer is in the habit of criticizing everything and of making only negative comments.

Meetings will be awkward at first because many members will be psychologically unable to contribute. They have adopted the role of the follower and may
not be able to do much at first except agree with those who talk the most. But
if the leader indicates that all members must accept a more active role, they
will increasingly participate. Waiting for people to learn to contribute is hard
for a leader, but he must be patient.

There is one technique that can be used to encourage full participation as well
as to develop an atmosphere of informality and involvement. This technique
involves asking at the beginning of a meeting that each participant relate a
success story to the other members. This allows each member to brag a little
and as well as to participate. Success-telling starts the meetings on a positive
note and delays for a while any complaints the members want to express. If
asking for success stories is too awkward or embarrassing for some members,
the leader can always ask for a progress report from each participant. Asking
what everyone is doing forces participation as well as informs the group on
everyone's activities.

The leader needs to listen eventually to all complaints, but it is difficult to
change the atmosphere of a meeting after a negative mood has developed.
Members may be eager to voice their complaints and problems first since these
must be met and solved. It is natural to want to discuss what is most
bothersome. Unfortunately, many complaints cannot be solved immediately
or in public. Many complainers merely want to express their feelings and don't
really expect solutions. Leaders do better to encourage subordinates to come
to them privately to discuss their complaints and needs.

Pessimism may get out of hand if all members become eager to present their
own problems. Complaints feed on one another and once begun, people
compete to see who can complain the most and the loudest. This activity is
unproductive because the voicing of complaints may be done not to receive
help but merely to receive sympathy. A complainer may not really be listening
to the contents of the answers; he is too involved in his own feelings. No real
information is exchanged and the participants become more and more upset.
Soon there is no room for good news or constructive, cooperative behavior.

This can be avoided by beginning a meeting on a positive tone. The leader asks
each participant to relate to the others a success story of one type or another.
And the speaker gets immediate praise for the good job done. All of us enjoy
the opportunity to receive a little praise for our successes; the Japanese are no
exception. Some of the talk during an after-hour office party at some bar will
always consist of an exchange of congratulations for past work.

Success-telling, aside from its emotional benefits, is also educational. Members essentially tell each other how certain situations were faced and how
certain problems were solved. The listeners get hints on how they themselves

can handle a difficult customer or how to solve a production problem. Since most of us feel that we are as good or better than our co-workers, hearing of their successes gives us the confident feeling that we can do as well or better.

Then too, success-telling gives the impression that, as the stories show, any problem can be solved. Divisions and departments, as well as work groups, develop over time their own mythologies. It does no harm for a supervisor to encourage positive image building in his section. Once the personnel are convinced they are part of a successful team they will convince themselves they too are superior.

Full and directed discussions use the diverse abilities of all of the members, and a good leader will staff a group with people who have different abilities and different ways of arriving at solutions. Individuals differ from each other in how they work and visualize problems. Some enjoy detailed analysis while others prefer a more general orientation. These two types complement each other. The encouragement of full participation utilizes the different talents of those present. In this case individuals can be more productive working together bei stimulating one another than by working alone. When working together, the individual weaknesses and biases may be balanced by the others' strengths (Maier and Hayes, 1962). Unilateral action on the part of a leader destroys any advantages that differing point of views offer a group.

Conflicting points of view may be threatening to some. The leader must make sure that the discussion remains on a friendly, cooperative level. When he talks the leader should be encouraging and supporting rather than presenting his views or his criticisms. If a disagreement does arise which seems to be unsolvable, he should, as the Japanese do, adjourn the meeting and calm ruffled feelings before another session is called.

9.5 Exploratory and Leap-Frog Meetings

A meeting which has as its purpose the search for new solutions is defined as exploratory. Exploratory meetings are distinguished by the fact that the solution or end result of the meeting is unknown. Meetings may be convened after a decision has been made and their purposes are to distribute tasks, established ground rules (time schedules, etc.), or to hold progress reports. But exploratory meetings are meetings whose solutions are as yet unknown.

These meetings demand collective creativity and a high amount of mutual support. These have been called barnstorming and buzz sessions. Exploratory meetings demand leaders who say very little and who guide the discussions rather than dictate their directions. In such a meeting the leader encourages and never criticizes. To criticize will inhibit the one who was criticized and the others who now fear being criticized in turn.

When the leader speaks, any difference between what he says and what others have presented threatens the latter. If the leader wishes to receive new ideas (or criticisms) he must be willing to keep his thoughts to himself, to listen, and to never criticize. In a harmoniously-run group, ideas will come so swiftly that weak presentations will more likely be ignored than criticized. Being ignored is punishment enough, but its much less painful.

The executive who has responsibility over a large number of subordinates from different organizational levels can hold leap-frog meetings (Foy, 1980). Leap-frog meetings involve personnel from different organizational levels. These meetings help reduce the disadvantages of increasing organizational complexity and social distance caused by increasing size. The Japanese executives continuously hold leap-frog meetings. This may be as simple as walking through the shop floor and talking to the workers or visiting a division to have tea with the members. The senior official asks a few questions and listens for any subtle hints of low morale and friction.

Leap-frog meetings show workers that senior officials are in fact personally interested in their problems. They also make large companies into temporarily smaller and more personal ones. For a leap-frog meeting to work the senior official must listen and not make policy statements and excuses. He must also be willing to react to whatever is said when it's appropriate.

Leap-frog meetings can take many forms. The only limitations are a manager's imagination. Peter A. Magowan, of Safeway Stores, Inc., was given the task when he became Safeway's Chief Executive Officer of revitalizing the company. To do this, Magowan wanted to not only motivate his employees, but also wanted to place into practice as many new, innovative ideas as possible.

One procedure adopted by Magowan was to conduct a series of leap-frog meetings. Magowan meets with store employees around the country to listen to their suggestions. This forces Magowan to be away from his office about one week in three. His rationale is that Safeway's employees at the retail level deal with customers on a daily basis and are themselves continuously immersed in work. They should be able to spot local problems and changing tastes before those in the central office can.

Magowan also attends award banquets and makes himself as visible as possible to his 160,000-plus employees. As an added bonus, Magowan's absences from his office forces others to make more decisions and take on added responsibility. When he does return to his Oakland, California office, he is not immunated by petty problems better handled at a lower level. Like successful Japanese senior executives, Magowan devotes considerable amounts of time listening to his employees and being a "silent leader". He listens, and he does immerse himself in administrative details better handled by others. Being "silent" does not mean being idle and unavailable. It means not doing what others can do.

Nothing flatters a group of workers more than receiving a second visit from a superior who returns to answer their grievances and complaints. Or at the very least, a short note could be sent stating that a complaint or suggestion will be handled in a certain way. If nothing needs to be done, a thank you expressing gratitude is always appreciated. Unlike Japanese workers, American workers seldom receive pats on the back and positive reinforcement.

The last requirement for a successful leap-frog meeting is that the intermediate manager – the foreman or departmental director – must not present. This may seem unnecessary to mention but many supervisors will want to be present, if for no other reasons than to intimidate their subordinates and to ensure that their own superiors hear nothing negative. The visitor can always talk to a foreman privately later to hear his side of the story.

9.6 The Freeloaders

Those who refuse to participate creatively during a meeting offer two general dangers for which the leader must be alert. These seemingly non-participants – which I designate as freeloaders – will nevertheless contribute something to the meeting, however minimal. One such "contribution" is to complain after a meeting has been adjourned. It's easy to complain when nothing else has been contributed. These free-loaders don't feel loyal to a solution because they haven't been involved in its development. Freeloaders who feel forced to say something will either join the majority and begin a bandwagon movement, or else they will ask for a delay before a decision can be reached. Either strategy makes the freeloader feel comfortable because each ploy is essentially a camouflage for non-participation.

Freeloaders join a bandwagon because being part of a majority is always safe. They end up on the winning side; if the project ends in a failure this nontalker can place the blame on others. Why the freeloader has adopted this strategy is clear enough. He says little until he senses that either a consensus has been reached or that one proposal or another is supported by the majority. These strategies are characteristic of the well-recognized yes-man.

This tendency for some members of a team to contribute little except agreement or delay tactics is obviously a very real danger in the Japanese corporation. The search for complete consensus encourages some members to contribute little to the group until a majority develops. Few participants will want to propose potentially creative suggestions if there is any chance that these ideas will disturb the group's harmony (wa) or if the majority might reject some propositions. The American manager is better able to limit the number of free-loaders if he chooses, since our culture encourages individuality more than

Japan's. But this individuality must be carefully nurtured or it will collapse under the weight of the silent freeloaders.

Freeloaders, if they cannot join a bandwagon, will not commit themselves to any position. This is done by trying to delay the group's making a decision. The usual ploy for these non-talkers if pushed for their participation is to suggest that a decision can't be made yet and that more facts are needed. Since few decisions can ever be made based on all the facts, it is always easy to ask for more information. Freeloaders have little if anything to contribute, and they can protect their inaction by proposing that any further discussion be postponed until later.

Every reader has attended a meeting during which some members sit silently and noncommitedly for a period of time, when suddenly one suggests that a delay is needed before a decision can be made. Then another joins in to also say more information is needed. Suddenly a bandwagon begins to roll for a postponement of decision making. The leader has lost control of the meeting and any momentum achieved is on the verge of slipping away. The freeloaders have won another victory for noncommitment.

The leader can forestall this delay by stating clearly at the beginning of the meeting that a decision must be made. He can remind the participants when suggestions for delays and more information are made that a decision has to be achieved and then continue to probe for more constructive participation.

If a delay is feasible and the leader thinks that more information is needed so that a collective decision can be made, then the meeting can be adjourned. There are unfortunate consequences if demands for a delay is accepted, however. Meetings which do not complete their tasks give the participants the feeling that little, if anything, has been accomplished. Now the members believe that they have attended another meeting which turned out to be nonproductive. This make them hesitant to expect much more in the future.

It is much better not to call for a meeting unless the organizer feels confident that a decision can be made; the alternative is to announce at the start that a decision may not be reached and that the purpose of the meeting is exploratory. If that is the case, the leader should summarize the ideas and suggestions presented during the session. This will end the meeting on a more positive note. This is not the best way to start a meeting, since saying that a decision might not be made during the session begins the meeting on a negative note. The members might not try as hard if they accept the idea that the session will not be productive. It is better to have a series of mini-meetings and allocate tasks. Hold a formal meeting only when you think a decision is possible.

If a delay is unavoidable, a useful strategy is to first ask those wishing a delay the specific reasons for the postponement of a decision. The leader openly writes down each reason and asks if there are any other comments. Then he appoints one or more subcommittees or individuals to gather the information listed. This shows the participants that the leader is listening to them and takes their requests seriously.

If the leader appoints as researchers those who asked for more information in the first place, he thereby places the responsibility for any more delay on those who are responsible for the delay. Freeloaders soon become aware that their delaying tactics give them more work. They will soon realize that asking for delays is an expensive way of avoiding responsibility. Freeloaders become more cautious about interrupting without their making any positive contributions if they have to pay for their actions.

On the other hand, freeloaders may merely be shy and not used to public speaking, and their requests for delays may be valid. Giving them the responsibility of providing missing information offers the leader the chance of evaluating their talents. These special assignments gives these non-talkers the opportunity to get valuable experience as they become more knowledgable about the problems discussed. It may be that someone who gives the impression of being a freeloader is in reality a non-talker who is unused to speaking up in public. This type of participant may have adopted a passive role because it's more comfortable to say nothing. Group leaders are forced to encourage this person to develop more self-confidence.

Another strategy which encourages potential freeloaders to contribute to the group is for the leader so assign each of them a specific duty before the meeting. This keeps the non-talkers from hiding under a cloak of anonymity and forces them to recognize that the leader values specific preparations and expects the same of them. The non-talkers will also be forced to prepare themselves for a meeting if they know they will be expected to contribute. Forced participation not only ensures a wider range of argument, but also forces traditional "yes-men" to develop a more forceful and, hopefully, a more independent style. The leader must make sure that no one is allowed to stay silent, even if this means at first longer meetings and less decisive discussions. After a time, all members will become more prepared and self-assured.

9.7 How Many Members?

How large should a meeting be? The correct answer depends on the purpose of the meeting. Size of membership balances two conflicting tendencies. Smaller size results in greater efficiency and more intense relationships among members. If you want to achieve a goal as quickly as possible and want to turn individuals into a team, then your committee should be as small as is practical. In this instance, a team or committee with a task to complete should have between five and twelve members. Informal seating is possible when less than fifteen persons meet together, everyone can participate, and "free-riders" find it difficult not to participate. Unfortunately, a larger group contains more freeloaders, and a core of members will do most of the work anyway. From this point-of-view, groups where the members need to meet often and arrive at joint decisions should have less than fifteen members.

On the other hand, a group should be larger when implementation of a decision needs the cooperation of a large number of persons. Decisions made by a small group may not be accepted by those excluded from attending the deliberations. The Japanese solve this dilemma by using persons as organizational "links". Each member of a small group is expected to report to other groups to see if their members support consensus. This is a time-consuming process but the alternative is to get everyone together even this means fifty or more persons.

Larger groups do not encourage more contribution; the free-rider problem becomes more acute when twenty or more persons meet together. Further, large groups encourage participants to become audiences. For a high level of contribution, reduce the number of persons who will work together.

The use of links is time-consuming. A meeting is held and a consensus reached. But this consensus is not final, since the links must report to other groups and hold their meetings. Then the original members meet again to report. Any changes must then be discussed by the sub-groups and back again.

Japanese leaders force themselves to be patient as deliberations go back and forth from central group through the links to the sub-group and back. Experience has taught them that while agreement takes a long time, not achieving complete agreement before implementation is even more wasteful in the long-run.

There is one great advantage to holding a large number of time-consuming, low-membership meetings to forge a common decision. Simply put, the more time it takes to make a decision, the more time participants have to change their minds. First decisions are often incorrect and based on individualistic criteria. It takes time to achieve a consensus by adjusting to others' opinions. Decision-making meetings should be learning experiences as well as sessions. Extensive discussions provide this opportunity as members present, defend, and change positions.

William T. Carnes points out in his book *Effective Meetings for Busy People* (1980), that no one can correctly predict the future. Every decision will have to be changed, if only because experience shows how a decision can be improved. The longer it takes to make a decision, the better it should be. When full consensus has been finally reached, there should be fewer weaknesses in the decision. While many decisions must be made quickly, speedy decision-making is not efficient. Groups are likely to make mistakes when circumstances demand snap decisions. Leaders can ask for quick decisions, but this will not ensure arriving at better decisions.

Carnes (1980) presents a law for groups: *A decision never really becomes final.* If a decision works, the chances of further change become less with time, but participants should be ready to change a decision at any time. Again, this is made easier when done a group setting. The Japanese see this as an opportunity for improvement: schedules become shorter, expansion goes faster, quality improves. Arriving at a decision in Japan demand extensive consultation, many meetings, and much compromise. This consultation continues after a project has begun. Members of a group expect to be kept current on a project's progress. When this is done, it is easier for them to discover emerging weaknesses and make appropriate changes.

Individuals, when they make individual decisions, are more likely to become attached to them. It's hard for someone to admit that a previous decision might not be completely correct. On the other hand, group decisions have already achieved previous compromise, and no one member "owns" a proposal. It's easier for a group which has arrived at a joint decision to continue the pattern of compromise and cooperation and change that decision whenever it becomes necessary.

This makes flexibility a way of life. If compromise takes place before a decision is made official, it's also easy to change it afterwards. This allows the Japanese to adjust to changing conditions very quickly. Change occurs faster and with less social friction in Japanese corporations than in American companies.

Flexibility is the result of compromise and extensive consultation. This demands full participation by those responsible for making a decision and carrying it out. This is achieved when groups are small. Smaller groups may take more time to arrive at a decision, but they are more efficient in the long run.

9.8 The Benefits of Full Participation

One of the advantages of full participation during meetings is that it leads to fuller participation in other settings. Generally, those who keep quiet during a meeting will be listeners in more informal discussions. Or, as is often the case, those defined as quiet in one situation will not be listened to elsewhere. Even when these persons try contribute, they will not be accepted by others as possible contributors. Some become defined as followers and non-contributors (or freeloaders) just as others are defined as leaders or clowns. Non-contributors adopt a submissive role, and they will are not taken seriously when they actually have something to contribute.

Another bonus when full participation is achieved is that co-workers discuss the agenda with one another before a specific meeting is held. Few of us want to be part of the minority, and often a person will not participate in a discussion until he discovers which side the majority will adopt. Then he will make meaningless sounds of agreement and support. We can call this person the "silent conformist". He contributes little to a discussion until he feels it is safe to support one side or another. If you allow the silent conformist to keep silent, he will do so until he senses how a consensus will develop. He contributes little until he can become part of a landslide of agreement. There is a way to shortcut a silent conformisty.

Force this person to contribute *before* a decision is reached. He will either have to say something which is noncommittal or else will be forced to be more helpful. A good leader at this point pushers such a person to state a position. After a few meetings, the silent conformist will begin to exhibit more initiative, if only to keep from being stared at when asked to contribute. This takes time. I have already stated the obvious; it takes time to develop an efficient, self-governing group whose members eventually take charge on their own initiative.

Rensis Likert (1961) found that people who have participated in a decision are more likely to accept its final form than those who have not been consulted. Prior consulting makes participants into co-sponsors. This enhances the chances that a decision, once made, will be carried out in the expected manner. The Japanese term "co-destiny" fits well here. The participants share a common destiny and sense of responsibility because they have participated fully during the early stage of the decision-making process. The challenge to superiors is to make certain all members of a group participate in a manner so that they feel responsible for the final decision. This can be achieved by being as silent as possible. Let the others discuss a problem and make a final decision. How else will they learn? Executives – and leaders of all types – should learn that they must not become indispensible.

The Japanese use group participation as a strategy for cooperation, and the same result can be accomplished by Americans. A Japanese worker expects cooperation from another team member by emphasizing that they both share a common tie. Since group interests are more important than individual interests, group membership forces members to become aware of their similar interests. Full participation emphasizes that participants have common identity and responsibilities. Complete and equal participation makes consensus more probable than does open conflict.

Participants are forced to make concessions when they work together. This is due to the fact that each participant brings a unique view to the discussion. Every member, potentially, can make some unique contribution. Participation forces all members of a work group to listen to – and hopefully learn from – all other members. Full participation encourages a more tolerant attitude toward others as participants learn that others too have contributions to make.

This results in a positive and productive give-and-take situation as the members take into account the concerns and contributions of others. Full participation ensures that everyone has at least the option to contribute to the solution of a problem, even if some have to surrender parts of their pet ideas. As a result, the end product emerging from full participation has the imprint of all present. The solution becomes a group solution. Since everyone can recognize his own contribution, however small, each participant feels as if each has done worthwhile work.

Full participation also makes each member into a leader. After all, contributing at least part of the solution to a team's problems allows a member to feel as if he is partly in charge, since his own participation has made a positive contribution. It is well known that leaders tend to be more self-confident than non-leaders. (Gibb, 1969). Leaders also have higher feelings of work satisfaction and are better adjusted psychologically (Mann, 1959), because their contributions as leaders give them self-confidence and satisfaction. Success makes a person more assured. That is why Cattell and Stice (1954) found that group leaders were less anxious and nervous than average members. Success and being able to contribute to a group are visible signs that a person has talents worthy of the respect of others.

Full participation is more than a learning experience when members listen to each other instead of only themeselves. Participation also allows participants to contribute; when they do they will become more self-assured and more self-confident that they are, in fact, worthy of respect. Participation causes a person to feel as if he is a leader among leaders instead of an ignored follower. The Japanese are adept in this process. They encourage full participation so that all members of a group have to contribute to a final decision. When that happens, morale goes up and everyone supports a final decision. The Japanese work long hours, and they take a long time (to Americans) to arrive at a final decision. But the effort and time are well worth the result.

People do not have an inborn leadership personality. Leadership is a trait which is developed through trial and error. Work situations can be structured so that leaders emerge as members are encouraged to take part in group discussions and decision-making. Japanese corporations encourage workers to feel as if each has input into the decision-making process. This in turn results in the feeling that he now has the responsibility to take the initative in his work. By encouraging full participation, the Japanese encourage all members of a group to be co-leaders. If a Japanese team gives off the impression that no one stands out enough to be pointed out as the leader and one in charge, it is not because all members are followers. Instead, no one stands out because all are expected to perform the duties of a leader.

Then too, as Arnold S. Tannenbaum has pointed out, participation is ego-enhancing. Participation makes the person feel more important and worthy of respect. After all, being allowed to perform more important work signifies that one is worthy of doing so. (Tannenbaum, 1966:98). Numerous studies (Tannenbaum, et al. 1974) have shown that workers at the higher levels of organization have much higher work satisfaction than those holding lower-level positions. Full participation in the decision-making process decreases the negative effects of hierarchy. Allowing lower-level workers to make work-related decisions and accept more responsibility increase their self-images. They are sharing the work done by superiors.

Participation reduces the frustrations associated with holding a low-level position. For the Japanese, full participation and consensus decision-making make it easier to wait for promotion. While a Japanese lower-level manager may be forced to wait for promotion until seniority makes promotion automatic, he is consoled by the fact that he can enjoy performing the duties of an office long before he formally holds that office. Later, he will have to learn that, he too, must cede decisions to subordinates. By then, the new-superior has learned that his responsibility is not to make decisions. His task is to ensure *wa* and encourage future executives to make decisions.

Full participation also increases morale because it makes work more interesting. Asking for contributions means asking someone to become a generalist. Few problems are solved in a vacuum. Those who accept responsibility will find themselves forced to develop new skills. That is why Japanese executives encourage frequent job rotation and constant skill-upgrading. Arnold S. Tannenbaum (1966:98) feels that workers who have been challenged to stretch their faculties in one area will perform better in another. At the very least, they have been forced to think about what they are doing. Full participation also offers variety. This refreshes workers and they can return to their former duties with a renewed interest.

Worker Recognition

Encouraging full participation results in other benefits which reduce supervisory problems. All workers need to be recognized. But many organizations prevent individual recognition by not encouraging the publicity of accomplishments. Lack of visibility may not be a conscious policy, but often a worker finds that few persons are aware of his performance. This inhibits the development of pride in one's work.

Many projects and duties are so specialized that no one outside of a few co-workers realize their complexity or can understand what in fact was done. Also, supervisors can smother their subordinates' recognition by being too domineering. The supervisor who says; "Just please me and don't worry about anyone else; I'll protect you from them", is in danger of making his subordinates into unsung heroes (Roseman, 1981). Unsung heroes develop negative self-concepts and dependency upon the one who knows their worth.

Pleasing only one person, even if a direct superior, does not offer enough recognition. We all need a larger audience to applause us. Ignored workers don't have the opportunity to develop any self-respect. The worker who doesn't receive messages of worth will gradually decide that what he is doing is not worthwhile. Work is seldom evaluated apart from the praise the actor receives or does not receive. Work often has little intrinsic value unless others also value the work. People who receive no or little outside recognition eventually lose pride in their work and will attempt to do less and less. Unsung work gradually grinds to a halt. We have all known workers who are isolated and whose work is unappreciated. These persons will be eventually do only enough to get by.

There is nothing sadder than a man who feels no one appreciates his work. He will be the one who comes home and when his wife asks what happened at the office will answer, "nothing". He could explain he wrote four memos, met with the vice-president for thirty minutes to discuss hiring policies, and met with his own superior where he was told to finish up the next year's division's budget by next week. These actions mean little to outsiders and will also gradually mean nothing to him.

But the same man could, after a long day, tell his wife that he had been told by the president that he expects next year's budget will be a gem like last year's, and that while at the watercooler someone mentioned that one of his memos made a lot of sense. The content of these activities may mean little, but receiving recognition makes them extremely worthwhile. One of the reasons bureaucracies are so often characterized by low morale and low productivitiy is that work often disappears into the system and no one receives any positive feedback. Giving and receiving praise is a necessary part of all meetings. Session leaders should congratulate at least one person during the beginning of a meeting. Such an action sets a positive and cooperative tone to the rest of the meeting and builds up the self-confidence of those praised.

9.9 Practical Suggestions

It is important that the leader remember that, although he is in charge, the reason for calling for a problem-solving meeting is to get advice from the participants. He should not be a star who dominates the actions and thoughts of the participants. Participative management succeeds only when the leader honestly and continuously seeks the contribution of the participants. Below are examples of how the leader should behave if the goal of a meeting is full participation and involvement:

* The leader should not involve himself in a dialogue with a specific person. This can either embarrass a participant or encourage a two-way conversation which may destroy spontaneous interaction.

* The leader should write down all solutions without evaluation. There should be a personal notepad or a blackboard. This action tells the other participants the leader will entertain all ideas and that he has no personal preconceptions he wants the group to accept. The notes can be later used as record of the proceedings if necessary.

* Never probe. Asking questions for more information gives the participants the feeling that the leader disapproves or approves a certain point. Let the other members ask each other for clarification. Probes from the leader make a contributor defensive. Remember the best leader is the silent leader.

* Be alert for when group members are ready for the close of the meeting to happen. If conversation drags and there are pauses after someone talks, it is best to summarize the points already discussed and adjourn.

* The leader is responsible for the solutions made by the group. If persons are asked to make decisions then the leader must accept both the decisions and the responsibility. Don't call for a meeting if you have already reached a suitable solution to a problem.

* The leader's contribution should be more emotional than factual. Give members encouragement and praise. Emotional support is more effective than criticism. Let members openly evaluate and criticize each other.

* Don't be impatient. Groups develop their own rhythms and pace. Some groups take more time to begin to be effective than others.

* Set a positive tone as quickly as possible. Begin a meeting by praising its past accomplishments and by indicating high expectations for future behavior.

* Keep meetings short. For most issues, meetings should last between sixty and ninety minutes, or less. It's better to hold two short meeting than one long one. Meetings become increasingly inefficient after an hour or so.

Chapter 10
How to Conduct Business with the Japanese

10.1 Japanese Business Etiquette

Having discussed how the Japanese work together we can now turn our attention to how Americans can work with the Japanese. Many Americans assume that while most Japanese are different from Americans, executives and managers from each country can easily deal with one another. The reasoning is that while the Japanese and American cultures are different in many ways, there is one universal (i.e. American) way of doing business. Nothing is further from the truth. Japanese executives differ from their American counterparts as much as Japanese and American factory floor workers differ from each other.

The Japanese business person is part of the Japanese culture. Americans who expect to do "business as usual" when dealing with the Japanese will be sadly disappointed. It's necessary to remember that each country has different cultural patterns of conducting business. In English-speaking countries, Americans find bewildering differences in how business is done in the United States and in Great Britain, Australia, or even Canada. There are even greater differences between the United States and Japan, though any difficulty deriving from these cultural differences can be overcome with preparation.

I will assume that an American is in Japan to negotiate a contract with a large Japanese corporation. The problem is knowing how to behave properly. Acting otherwise insults your Japanese host, causes misunderstandings, and ensures complete failure to complete a deal. Even when both the American and Japanese parties want to negotiate successfully, cultural misunderstandings result in communication breakdowns.

The Business Card

Japanese society is both hierarchical and group-centered. As a result, Japanese executives do not like to interact with strangers whom they cannot place in a prestige level relative to them. Everyone must be categorized and classified by group membership and prestige level before comfortable interaction begins. This is especially important when a Japanese is meeting another Japanese for the first time. The Japanese language contains different forms depending on whether one is speaking to someone with a superior or inferior status. The same problem exists when a Japanese meets a foreigner for the first time. He wants to know how much prestige and respect the other person can command.

Non-Japanese should make certain a Japanese knows who the foreigner works for, how important the company is, etc.

The Japanese feel uncomfortable with strangers until each knows the other's status level and social identity. When Japanese businessmen first meet, their first act is to exchange business cards. This allows identification according to rank and prestige. Now they know how much respect should be given and who should begin and direct the conversation. The pecking order has been established.

Americans travelling in Japan on business, or even when expecting to deal extensively with Japanese in the United States, should have an ample supply of business cards. In fact, a business card should be included in early correspondences.

Japanese executives themselves keep business cards on file and use them for reference. Cards are easy to read and refer to. An American's business card should be printed in English on one side and Japanese on the other. Each side should give name, title, employer, address, and telephone number. Your title should be as specific as possible. A general term such as "engineer" or "accountant" is not enough. The Japanese need to know your exact position so that you can be defined precisely in terms of organizational authority and responsibility.

Working for a large Japanese corporation is a matter of great prestige, and Japanese strangers want to locate each other in terms of work identities before they can begin to feel relaxed with one another. That is why Japanese corporate employees with pretensions toward respectability will not only be proud of their official titles (often inflated), but will also want to exchange business cards. For one thing, employees of the larger and higher prestige companies automatically receive respect from others. By the same token, Americans from larger, well-known companies should stress their affiliations. Doing so gives them easier access and more attention than would be otherwise. Be prepared to exchange cards often. Present the side with the Japanese script right-side-up. Presenting a card upside down is discourteous.

Business cards are kept in view during meetings. A Japanese talking to foreigners for the first time places their cards on the table or desk in front of him for reference. Foreign names are hard to remember and pronounce correctly, especially when there has been introductions to a large number of persons. Business cards are used as memory joggers. A Japanese feels embarrassed when he confuses people or uses their names incorrectly. Business cards help avoid this problem.

Travel as a Group

Remember that the Japanese are group-oriented. It is better to go to Japan with other fellow executives and co-workers. Bring a number of assistants instead of going alone. The word "individual" in Japanese has the connotation of being selfish, so a person working alone is automatically suspect. Having a large entourage gives the impression that you're taking the project being discussed seriously. The more important the project, the larger will be the number of Japanese who will want to meet you.

The Japanese negotiate in groups. The chances that you will deal alone with a higher official are very small. If you go alone you will be outnumbered. Having others with you means that the Japanese don't have to focus on you all of the time. Talking to only one person who is a near-stranger makes the Japanese nervous. Being out-numbered, you will tire more quickly and make mistakes.

The Japanese may not take you seriously if you're alone. They make decisions through group consensus, and they will assume you do the same. Not all Japanese, especially those who are older, completely understand the American way of doing business.

When negotiating over a period of time, you will notice that your opposite members come and go. The people you're dealing with will change constantly. The reason for this is that every member in a Japanese corporation must be fully informed on matters that deal with his expertise and responsibility. Some specialists will attend a meeting and then leave when the topics they're interested in have been discussed. Also, some officials attend for symbolic reasons. They may want to indicate their interest or support by attending part of one session or another. These will leave after a while and they mean no disrespect when doing so. Some Japanese will fall asleep ("listening with one's eyes shut") during a presentation. This should be ignored since their attendance is what is needed, not their understanding. These persons will rely on experts and specialists to make recommendations on technical matters. A rotation of contacts does not mean disinterest or that "passing the buck" is taking place.

The reverse is truer. More participants means greater interest. Be calm when a newly-arrived participant asks very technical questions which have been discussed earlier. He will have carefully discussed the matter with other Japanese co-workers and he's not the only one who needs added information. They will understand if you don't have instant answers to everything and you can easily ask for more time to prepare yourself. Just make an appointment to discuss the matter at a specific time. If something is brought up which is not on the agenda, say you need to present more data to answer fully and suggest discussing this point the next day or so.

There will be times when the Japanese signal to each other and even whisper among themselves. They mean no disrespect. They are merely checking with each other, deciding what to ask next, and finding out what progress has been made. Continue talking to whoever asked the last question.

Preliminary technical details during Japanese negotiations are handled at lower levels than in the United States. Decisions in a Japanese corporation are formalized only when all persons involved agree. Encourage your assistants meet with your host's aides. Senior executives are generalists in training and will agree to a contract only when their more specialized assistants recommend doing so. This will take time. Expect delays until all of the Japanese agree with one another. The American practices of head-to-head confrontation and "let-others-fill-in-the-details-later" will not work in Japan.

Don't forget that corporate promotion is automatic and based on seniority during most of a person's career. Japanese corporations also follow a policy of frequent rotation from department to department for middle managers. A division head may not be well versed in the technical details of his department, and he depends on his younger experts to help him make a final decision. A leader will invite experts to attend negotiation meetings, and the negotiators will change from day to day. You may have to repeat the same points several times to different persons. Don't assume this is a sign of inefficiency; it's instead a feature of the way the Japanese do business. The more persons you can convince, the more likely a proposal will be accepted.

Unfortunately, some persons may attend a few meetings out of curiosity or to gain experience. Don't worry when people come and go. Even temporary visitors will have an impact on the final decision. The Japanese are also meeting with one another to discuss your proposals. They are spending more time on your affairs than you are.

You are expected to show deference and respect to senior officials. But lower-level employees must also be taken very seriously. Answer all questions and requests for specific data no matter who makes the request. The person asking the questions may be only a lower-level specialist, but his decision will be respected, and he may have been invited because of his expertise. Also, some questions may be too embarrassing for a senior official to ask. He may be afraid that a question might make him look ignorant or worse. It's normal in this situation for a Japanese to have an assistant to ask such questions.

Executives in Japan are expected to listen more than they talk. A leader who defers to a junior member is nevertheless involved though he may not give that impression. He is not expected to dominate the sessions. You should also let your assistants answer questions and ask for clarifications. This shows the Japanese you trust your own colleagues and that you are also a good team member.

Having others with you gives you another bonus. Some of the Japanese may not feel comfortable in dealing directly with you. They may feel that some questions are too delicate or else they are too embarrassed to tell you something directly. In these instances, information can be passed on to you indirectly through other members of your party. A lower level member of the Japanese negotiating team can pass on negative information to a lower level American negotiator more easily than could higher levels members.

Use an Interpreter/Translator

Use a local interpreter/translator whenever possible. The local person will be familiar with the local scene and can help with local matters, such as recommending a restaurant or bar for further meetings, or other facilities. You should also bring your own interpreter (local or otherwise) along to all social functions, if any, to make discussions easier. When entertaining, your interpreter can help you make the evening relaxed as well as useful.

Your Japanese counterpart will also have his own interpreter who will as a courtesy translate for you as well as for his/her own employers. But asking someone else's translator to work constantly is a very dangerous idea. First of all, translating is very difficult work. Having your own translator means the opposite interpreter can rest now and then. Few translators can work efficiently for several hours without a rest.

As important, your own translator supports your interests. You can assume he is more interested in your affairs than the translator from the other side of the table.[1] He will work harder to help you. It is wise to discuss what went on during a meeting with your own translator as soon as convenient. Japanese is a high-context language, meaning that a word can have several meanings based on the context of the sentence, how it is said, and the gestures of the speaker. Many Japanese words with different meanings also sound the same.

A translator may not want to say to you in front of everyone that a previous speaker is probably lying or is showing disinterest. The Japanese acknowledge that there can be a big difference between what is being said and what is really meant. A de-briefing session with your own interpreter will be more likely to discover these fine points without embarrassing those involved. Japanese negotiators may expect your translator to tell you later the true meaning of what is being said. Your translator should be thought of as a co-partner as much as possible. If he has enough information, he will be atuned to the subtleties of the negotiations.

---

[1] In the same way, it's dangerous and ultimately self-defeating to ask an opponent's lawyer for advice. Many Japanese interpreters are female, and Japanese executives are used to interpreters of either sex. Choose an interpreter on the basis of skill rather than gender.

Be patient with your interpreter. He or she may take notes, ask a question or two to clear up an obscure point, and stop to look up a word in a pocket dictionary. These are all standard procedures. Your interpreter will probably make up his own glossary of technical terms likely to be used. This is not a sign of incompetence. He is merely trying to prepare a list of words not commonly used which might be necessary. No translator can be expected to know every word in the English and Japanese languages.

There is sometimes little relationship between the number of words said in Japanese and in English. Don't ask your interpreter if he's made an error when he translates a Japanese paragraph into two or three English words. Your Japanese counterpart may have included several polite phrases and references to his being unschooled, humble, etc., which do not need to be translated. Doubting your translator in front of everyone makes him lose face as well as causes him to become nervous. The de-briefing sessions will answer any questions you may have.

One warning about Japanese interpreters. Free-lance interpreters are generally taught foreign languages as part of a Liberal Arts curriculum; as a result, they may not be familiar with technical terms or concepts. Talk with your interpreter before the negotiating sessions begin so he can prepare a special vocabulary. It is best to give an interpreter copies of speeches, if any, and contracts and specifications before a meeting. Have an assistant go over with your interpreter all material and relevant matters before they are presented. This might mean sending an assistant to Japan a few days before your arrival to confer with your local interpreter.

A prepared and rehearsed interpreter is well worth the extra time and cost. Few interpreters are as nimble as the one who when forced to translate a joke completely meaningless in the second language, saved the day by saying, "the honorable guest has just told a joke which is untranslatable into Japanese. When I nod my head, please laugh loudly."

If you hire an interpreter, hire him for a long period in order to obtain at least conditional loyalty. If you go back to Japan, make certain you hire the same interpreter. The loyalty of your Japanese employees, even if temporary, is a necessity for anyone hoping to do business in Japan.

The American Translator's Association (109 Croton Ave., Ossining, N. Y. 10562) publishes a directory of licensed translators and interpreters who have passed examinations in their languages. In addition, the annual publication *The Literary Marketplace* contains a list of translators/interpreters. Persons expecting to use such services should plan ahead. While a rough translation can usually be gotten fairly quickly, translations of technical terms take more time. Then too, a translator may have to covert American measures into the metric system. Many English terms may not have simple Japanese equivalents, especially slang and technical terms. Translation is as much an art as a science, and long, complex documents may demand more than one translating session. As with anything when dealing with the Japanese, expect to spend more time than what is "normal" in the United States.

Get an Introduction

Japanese old hands insist that initial business contacts should be made through third parties (see, for example the useful brochure "Doing Business in Japan" by the Japan External Trade Organization (1982)). This is not always necessary, and even some foreigners in Japan have begun potentially profitable ventures without using a third party. But these are in the minority.

It may be hard as well as time-consuming for a Japanese to respond to a stranger's letter. The letter must first be translated and then sent to the correct office or individual. Most letters, especially from lesser-known foreign companies, will not contain enough information that can be acted upon by all concerned. Few corporate employees will respond to a foreign letter on only his own responsibility.

The strategy most likely to achieve a successful connection is to use third parties to provide introductions rather making a "cold" contact. Someone who personally knows both parties is best. He can give needed information, begin the trust process, and provide a bridge between two strangers.

The problem is that a Japanese executive will not want to give a direct "no" to someone. An American beginning negotiations may not realize his Japanese counterparts have no interest in what he has to offer but are too polite to say so. Plausible reasons for delay after delay are offered until the American finally gets suspicious that he has been rejected.

It is easier for a Japanese to give a direct denial through a third party when necessary. A third party, if respected by both sides, forces the Japanese to respond to overtures more positively. He doesn't want to offend the mediator and he owes him at least a hearing. The mediator *(chukaisha)* is a common fixture in Japanese affairs, much like a marriage broker, and is widely used.

The *chukaisha* may be a professional middle-man interested in bringing two parties together. He may even make a profitable living as a professional contact. This person offers a valuable service in a society where correct behavior and face-to-face interaction are so important. Banks, trading companies, and lawyers often serve as third parties.

There are many mediators in Japan. They are able to speed up a shipment through customs and help a foreigner thread his way through the maze of government bureaucracy with some speed and effectiveness.

A warning. If a Japanese performs a favor for you, he will expect something in return. Be liberal when someone who has helped you asks you to do something. This is normal and completely expected.

The Japanese External Trade Organization (JETRO) has published a comprehensive guide (The Bank of Tokyo, Ltd., 1983) which describes the laws and other regulations dealing with foreigners doing business in Japan. This work lists all laws related to setting up enterprises in Japan, as well as all necessary documents, tax regulations, employment standards, international regulations, etc.

At the end of the English language section, this handbook also lists all government administrative units concerned with international trade. There are also sections listing Japanese law and accounting firms with international experience, research institutes (these are very influencial in Japan), chambers of commerce, and other associations and centers useful to foreigners in Japan. This handbook provides lists of potential mediators and local contacts for Americans.

The U.S. embassy in Japan is also prepared to help Americans. U.S. embassy personnel can often provide introductions as well as vital information on local laws and national conditions. The address is:

Commercial Attache
Embassy of the United States of America
Tameike Tokyo Bldg.
Tokyo, Japan

Be Formal During Business Hours

Business persons from the United States tend to be among the most informal in the world. We may think of ourselves as "all business" and "hardheaded", but foreigners view us as often childish, and certainly as too friendly during inopportune times. This may be part of our charm, but our friendliness also irritates foreigners. Act formally with strangers when you first meet. All business relations except with colleagues are more formal than in the United States. From this preference for formality comes a number of rules listed below that Americans should be wise to follow. An axiom that is useful is never to say anything you don't mean and never promise anything that can't be delivered. Americans, foreigners find, are prone to toss vague invitations ("come and see us sometimes") and to assume instant friedships with near-strangers. Japanese retain a core of privacy which acquaintances are not allowed to penetrate. People have to earn being friends and achieve an informal relationship. It's best to wait and let the other person make the first overtures of friendship.

One problem is that an American visiting Japan for business purposes is a stranger who will soon leave. Few people want to invest emotional capital and time on someone who will soon leave the country, whether it will be months or years.

Use Last Names and Titles

Always use a person's last name and title, if any, when being first introduced. Corporate, professional, and honorific titles are sources of pride to the Japanese. If someone is introduced to you as "doctor" or if a title is prominent on a business card, use the title and surname. Someone with a Ph. D. would expect to be called "Doctor Tanaka." It does no harm to be more polite than usual.

By the same token, do not call someone by his first name, even if you've seen this person before or often. Japanese adults call each other "Mr." or "Mrs." though they have known each other for years. Doing otherwise shows a lack of respect. It's best to let the Japanese gently tell you when first names can be used, probably during a party. If such a level of intimacy is reached, nevertheless remain formal in public and during negotiating sessions unless specifically told to be more informal.

While using the surnames and titles of your Japanese opposites, introduce yourself and your American partners in a formal manner. The Japanese find it disconcerting when an American takes off his coat, rolls up his sleeves, and suggests that everyone call him "Tex", his partner "Billy Bob", and his chief engineer "Sam". Such familiarities in Japan are reserved for school chums and some family members. They are out of place in a negotiating session.

For your part, introduce yourself formally. When introducing a number of Americans, mention the last name and official position of each one. Make sure you pay special attention to the oldest members of the Japanese party. Since age and position are highly correlated in Japan, don't slight senior parties even when they seem to be relatively inactive. Older Japanese should not be ignored during a negotiating session even when they are relatively silent. Talk to the senior members of the Japanese team even when you're answering a question asked by someone else. They should be included in the conversation through eye contact at regular intervals. General questions should be aimed at these senior officials. They will indicate who should answer you, and this will give the assistants the permission to talk.

Sell Yourself and Your Company

While your posture and behavior should be formal during business meetings, especially the early negotiating sessions, the Japanese do not expect the personal element to be completely left out. Instead, he prepared to spend the first series of meetings selling yourself and your company. The Japanese want to first know that you and your company are reliable and worthy of a long-term relationship. Make sure the Japanese negotiators know something about your own background. This includes the universities attended, family situation, hobbies, and professional and practical experience.

If you attended a high-prestige university, then by all means mention your alma mater as quickly as possible. Japanese executives rank each other according to the prestige of the universities attended and do the same with Americans if they can. If your university is not well-known, describe where it is located and its better points. The Japanese are curious about anything American and they want to know as much as possible about you.

The same applies to describing your company. Your proposals will be given more serious attention if you can describe your company as a stable, dependable, trustworthy, and long-lasting institution. Don't stretch the truth, since the Japanese have independent sources of information. They will already have gathered a fat dossier on your company (including biographies of senior executives) before beginning serious negotiations. Their bank will have researched your company's financial standing and recent history. It is accepted to be from a small and growing company. The sin is lying or exaggerating your company's record.

As you describe your company, don't emphasize how profitable it is or how much money the Japanese can make if negotiations are successful. Money and profits shouldn't be mentioned until the final stages of negotiations. Let the Japanese take the initiative when its time to begin discussions of a financial nature. When that stage is reached, the Japanese have decided that a business relation with you is both possible and advantageous, and they are willing to begin serious negotiations. Instead of bragging about how profitable an agreement would be, describe how good your company is. If possible, try to mention how dedicated your company is to public service and community improvements. When introducing yourself, include a thumbnail sketch of your company's charitable contributions, if any. While doing so, stress your company's ability to deliver superlative service and its policy of loyalty to suppliers and customers.

The customer is king in Japan. Buyers expect to be treated with respect. If you wish to sell to the Japanese, try to project an image of being humble and eager to provide excellent service to customers. Stress that your company wants to establish harmonious relationships. The monetary aspects can be brought up in the later sessions. The first order of business is to gain the trust of the Japanese. This is not the time to discuss how ruthlessly you deal with competitors or how unhappy the Japanese will be if they don't deal with you. Such posturing is seen as threatening and arrogant.

A strategy which can be used to begin the process of gaining the trust of the Japanese is to provide them with a dossier of your company and its leaders. Such a folder should include community awards won by the company and executives, as well as any recognition showing that the company is service oriented. This folder should also contain bank and other references, as well as descriptions (and pictures) of your company's products.

It's bad form to appear selfish and concerned only with profits. Ideally, companies in Japan exist to enrich the nation, customers, and employers before stockholders and executives. Boasting about your company's profits is counterproductive. Such financial data will be collected independently by your Japanese hosts. If they expect to enter into a long-term relationship with your company, your Japanese negotiators will investigate your company thoroughly. It is best to stress what your products or organization can do for customers and the Japanese company. Stress service rather than profits.

Dress Conservatively

The Japanese act and speak formally, and they also dress conservatively. The basic corporate uniform in Japan is a dark (preferably black) suit, tie, and white shirt. Even corporate janitors and clerks wear coats and ties if working indoors. Otherwise everyone, including the plant managers and foremen, wear the company's jacket or windblazer. The latter is more common in factories. Dark suits are acceptable in part because, to the Japanese, black denotes joy. Assuming that the color black is a gloomy one reflects an American value and not Japanese. Americans should also dress conservatively while in Japan. Loud colors or outrageous styles suggest to the Japanese that the wearer is untrustworthy or else he would conform to more traditional styles. Respect for age is a Japanese, and Japanese elders dress conservatively; they set the tone for corporate fashions.

If you live in California and work for a recently-established company, you probably are used to wearing informal clothing styles. If so, you may not have any formal business suits that would be approved by Japanese businessmen. One solution is to visit Hong Kong a few days before you begin negotiations in Japan. Between sight-seeing trips in Hong Kong, visit a tailor recommended by your hotel and order several suits. After a few days and a few fittings, you'll have an acceptable wardrobe. Avoid pure-silk shirts. They tend not to keep their looks if the seams are not sewn with the correct material. A stay in Hong Kong is always enjoyable, though hotel rooms are expensive, but a few day's visit in Hong Kong eases the transition due to jet lag.

Formal Body Language

An irritating habit the Japanese find in Americans is that Americans act relaxed at inappropriate moments. Americans believe that behaving in a relaxed manner indicates friendliness and trust. Such behavior goes along with the belief that all participants are equal to one another and that formality is a needless ritual. Seating by rank is a major consideration among business associates. If visiting a Japanese office, the hosts have already carefully planned a seating arrangement and American guests will be told where to sit. The Japanese are more formal than Americans with strangers, especially at the office.

Sit correctly or formally. Never slouch or lean back. This can be interpreted by the Japanese as discourtesy or disinterest. Leaning back and looking at the ceiling may be seen in America as if a person is in deep thought; the Japanese interpret the position as indicating boredom. If you are visiting Japanese business associates, let them be the hosts and direct the ceremonies. Never act as if you are in control or at your own office. A guest should be passive and served by the hosts. The Japanese and the British both dislike Americans who act too aggresively. Let the hosts suggest what to do next. Taking the first step and asking for a drink, for example, suggests your host is not doing his duty.

Similarly, the Japanese feel uncomfortable when Americans sit on the corner of their desks. The Japanese don't know how to react to this. Do they remain standing? Or are they expected to sit on another's desk? The same dismay as felt when an American visits a Japanese office and sits on his host's desk. This type of informality is insulting to the Japanese.

Don't Get Mad

The Japanese prefer to hide their emotions, especially anger, frustration, disappointment, and arrogance. They might – and often do – experience these emotional states, but it's bad etiquette to express them. This is reflected in the proverb, "the hawk hides his talons." In essence, emotions that might disrupt relationships are best kept from being expressed.

For an American, shouting, yelling, pounding on the table, and displaying anger are counter-productive. The often-used American negotiating tactics of intimidation are counter-productive in Japan. For example, an commonly-used American negotiating tactic is to establish a time limit and threaten to stop negotiations when the limit has been reached. This tactic is doomed to failure unless the Japanese are desparate to sign a contract. Even then, the memory of having been rushed into an agreement will keep them from wanting to continue the relationship beyond necessary limits.

A time limit should not be established unless absolutely necessary. The Japanese can act quickly when there is a sense of urgency or crisis. At other times, a "take-it-or-leave-it-right-now" will be rejected by Japanese corporate executives. Being pushed in this way is seen as insulting and as a sign of weakness. The Japanese do give in, and they cede points, but they do so in a face-saving manner. They will give in when necesssary, but only in a face-saving way which may take some time.

Showing anger and acting in a threatening manner is a bad tactic for another reason. The Japanese want to establish long-term relationships. They will resist signing an agreement with someone they don't like or can't get along with. In Japan, acting angry is defined as either a loss of control or as a sign of immaturity. It's best for American to use logic and fact rather than emotion to reach an agreement with the Japanese.

Americans can show emotion. Businessmen can exhibit happiness and disappointment. These are permissible emotions in a business setting. Friendship can also be exhibited. Giving a gift which shows personal interest and effort is done often. An American who shows an interest in a special activity will often find that his Japanese hosts will try to satisfy that interest. An interest in history will provide a Japanese with the opportunity to offer a special tour of a temple or other attraction. Americans can do the same. A Japanese executive who plays golf (most do) would appreciate a special gift with a golfing theme.

Howard F. Van Zandt (1970), who spent over twenty-five years in Japan, offers the illustration of a Japanese friend who gave him a bowl of bamboo which he had himself carefully transplanted and nurtured. Americans who show the more positive emotions of friendship and interest will find their Japanese hosts more cooperative.

On the other hand, the Japanese try very hard to read the emotional states of foreigners. It's probably futile to try to hide or mask completely a feeling. Someone who dislikes the Japanese and Japanese culture will not be able to hide the fact. The Japanese were forced to mask their feelings and cooperate with often-arrogant, intollerant Americans during the post-war occupation and the "years of the hungry cage." Now, however, the Japanese can afford to reject foreign relations with those they don't like.

10.2 Negotiating with the Japanese

Prepare to take two to three, some say six, times longer to arrive at an agreement than you're used to in the States. The wish to hurry through an agreement is one of the most common complaints foreigners have against Americans. Except when dealing with Germans, British, or the Swiss, signing a contract with any foreign group takes a longer time than is customary in the United States.

Negotiations nearly always take more time in Japan. I have already mentioned that the Japanese language is a high-density language. A message in Japanese can imply a number of meanings. By contrast, English is a low-context language, and it is relatively easy for a speaker using English to state clearly and factually what he wants to communicate. The Japanese language also conveys emotional moods and feelings better than facts. Boye De Mente (1981:105) finds that the Japanese understand only about 85 percent of what is being said when talking together (others suggest lower percentages). Many words have multiple meanings, and the emphasis on being polite means that what is heard is not always what the speaker really wants to say or is vocalizing. To avoid misunderstandings, the Japanese repeat main points of what they want to convey.

Asking a question may give the impression that the speaker has not been clear enough. To ask a question indicates criticism of the speaker who failed to communicate adequately. Asking a question might also suggest that the questioner has not been listening or is too stupid to understand what has been said. All in all, keeping quiet may be the wisest policy for a Japanese. More talk will clear everything up eventually. That is why the Japanese are willing to take a long time negotiating with each other and foreigners. Americans should be prepared to repeat every point in an agreement a number of times in different ways. Even then, the chances are that some parts of an eventual agreement will be misunderstood by one party or another.

Boye De Mente, who has lived in Japan for a large number of years, illustrates how Americans and Japanese can misunderstand each other even when the same words are used. In his book *The Japanese Way of Doing Business* (1981:115), De Mente uses the term "sincerity" *(Makoto)* as an example of language confusion. To Americans, being sincere means being honest, trustworthy and open; to place all of one's cards on the table, as it were. To the Japanese, being *Makoto* means to insure harmony and good will among all parties; *wa,* in short (De Mente, 1981:113–5). *Makoto* can mean at times not openly disagreeing or delaying telling an associate a contract contains impossible clauses and conditions. Being "sincere" to the Japanese often means being emotionally supportive. For Americans, being sincere means being factually true. The same attitude is seen differently by the Japanese and Americans.

Never force the Japanese to reject a proposal in public. It is very difficult to reopen negotiation once a project or clause has been publicly rejected. Don't insist on a formal response if the Japanese negotiators seem unwilling to do so. Demanding a response to a "take it or leave it" ultimatum will result in a negative response (Kobayashi, 1984). Keeping quiet at this point leaves room for future compromise. There is always the chance that the Japanese will agree to a previously-rejected part of an agreement in order to gain another point. If a part of an agreement seems to be "forgotten" or ignored by the Japanese negotiators, say nothing and go on to the next section. You can always go back to a neglected condition and find out in more informal settings why a resistance to its acceptance exists.

Wait for bad news to be offered in a private setting. It's easier then to change positions through further negotiations. You can always re-offer a proposal later even if it means camouflaging it so that its previous rejection can be ignored.

Americans doing business in Japan should never forget that a third party is always present when Japanese and non-Japanese negotiate. This third party is the Japanese government. More specifically, all business with foreigners involve the Ministry of International Trade and Industry (MITI) to one extent or another. MITI helps plan the future economy, and this ministry expects importer-exporters to accept its "guidance" and "suggestions". Companies planning large-scale expansion projects must receive the approval of MITI (Adams, 1970).

Many negotiations are slowed down because a Japanese negotiator wants to make certain that MITI or other ministries approve of the venture. This takes time. If MITI has to be consulted, like any other Japanese office, it does not make decisions quickly. During the negotiations, the American negotiator might ask the Japanese whether they should talk to MITI officials, or whether the project being discussed already enjoys their approval.

The influence of the MITI, Economic Planning Agency, the Ministry of Finance and other ministries can cause bewilderment. Take the example of a government official who visits a Japanese negotiating to build a plant in America as part of a joint venture. The official might say, "I suggest you change this provision and eliminate this clause." Nothing is written, and no document passes hands, but the "advice" has to be accepted. Otherwise the government might punish the offending company when export licenses are needed, when foreign credits are exchanged, etc. There are many ways the government can punish a company which ignores its "advice."

The Japanese partner will try to keep the American negotiators informed, but it may be hard for him to say explicitly that a contract deletion is demanded by part of the Japanese government (Kobayashi, 1970). The American should listen carefully to the reasons, if any, given for a contractual change. Don't accuse your counterpart of arbitrarily making new demands. He may be just as unhappy as you are. After all, he's caught in the middle and he's negotiating with two parties, you and his government.

Japanese also have to consider their suppliers and "child companies". The negotiating Japanese partner dares not ignore the effects a contract would have on suppliers. The American negotiator might have to talk to sub-contractors and get their approval. An executive, for example, may feel obligated to help a "child company" because of past favors and old debts. It may be necessary to include third parties into the negotiations because your Japanese counterparts wants to help an old friend or a "child company".

Once a mutually satisfactory agreement has been reached, the Americans need to review the contract periodically (Tsurumi, 1984:326). The Japanese believe that business relations should change as conditions change as well as be long-term. They see nothing unusual in wanting to change parts of contract when conditions warrant a change. Japanese-American joint venture agreements must be seen as flexible. Re-negotiations on a regular, six month basis, are profitable for both sides. The whole agreement need not be re-hashed at every meeting. But difficulties and problems can be brought up at this time.

Yoshi Tsurumi (1984:319) recommends annual informal "study sessions" for Japanese and American partners and business associates. These show concern for the other party, increase familiarity, and make future action more possible. These informal sessions can easily cover future as well as current projects. They prepare the Japanese for future expansion and increased ventures. In the long run, such sessions save time and increase the probability of future successes. Future actions go faster once a stable relationship has been developed with Japanese business partners. Future contacts and business expansions will take less time. Americans consistently conducting business with the Japanese are able to deal with a limited number of Japanese counterparts. Lower-level managers are responsible for day-to-day decisions, and they make many decisions without passing requests from one person to another.

Accept Delays

The need for preliminary extensive discussions among the Japanese results in necessary time lags between negotiating sessions. If a new point is raised by the Americans, the Japanese negotiators will have to consult extensively with their co-employers. Each agreement is reached through the achieving of a consensus, and each new step takes time.

The Japanese negotiators do not want to ignore you while they discuss your proposals. They will therefore ask to be able to escort you around Tokyo to see the sights. That these tours take place during the work day should not dismay you. Rejecting such tours and insisting that you're in Japan solely "to do business" is a mistake. Common Japanese courtesy demands that the foreigner foreigner is suitably entertained and shown Japan. The Japanese are proud of their culture and country. They take pleasure in showing off the sights and their accomplishments. These tours allow time between negotiating sessions. It takes time to achieve a consensus and agreements are seldom reached quickly. The Japanese negotiators will suggest that you rest for a few days because they realize they need some time before the next meeting.

Finally, a tour of local temples or of a subsidiary's plant allows for informal discussions to take place. The Japanese are highly work-oriented and dislike wasting time. When they suggest a negotiating break to allow the Americans to visit the sights, the reason for this delay is most likely to be business-related. It may that there is a chance that a point is in danger of disrupting the negotations. The Japanese negotiators may want to hint at their disagreement in pleasant surroundings, such as a temple garden.

If you sense that an impasse has been reached, you can propose that the next session be delayed a day or so. The Japanese will quickly agree if they in fact want a delay. You can always say you have already made reservations for the next day if they volunteer to escort you around. You can also plead that you need to prepare a report to your own superiors. These responses allow you to gracefully reject having your Japanese hosts asign you someone to guide you around. Remember, though, that these tours can be a substitute for formal negotiating sessions. They should not be always rejected.

10.3 After an Agreement

If time is available, American guests ought to celebrate in some fashion when an agreement with the Japanese has been reached. These celebrations show that the Americans are glad that an agreement has been mutually agreed to and that the relationship is now a personal one. Gestures appreciated by the Japanese would be a supper/banquet hosted by the Americans and special gifts to commemorate the occasion. If the Americans are selling to the Japanese, they should host a ceremony to commemorate and celebrate reaching an agreement. This act "thanks" the buyers for becoming customers and as a result members of the corporate family. It the Americans are the host, they should remember that close relationships and formality continue after the Japanese agree to a business deal.

An act which indicates the importance the American partners place on an agreement is hiring a photographer to take pictures of the event (Graham and Sano, 1984:97). The photographs can be enlarged and sent later. The Americans should sign the copies to make them more personal.

Gifts should be offerred at this time, ideally those with some symbolic content. A company from the state of Georgia might present Japanese senior officials with Georgian granite or marble paperweights with the company's logo on it. The Americans would mention that the stones were quarried in Georgia and stand for durability and strength. Like the President of the United States, the American senior executives can distribute the pens (with the official logo) which were used to sign the contracts to everyone present.

John L. Graham and Yoshino Sano (1984) warn against the American tendency to act relaxed and informally once a formal agreement is reached. Many contracts in the United States are sent in their final forms through the mail to be signed. In Japan, however, signing ceremonies are important formal affairs and should not be omitted.

The Uses of Silence and Body Language

The Japanese talk less than Americans when they communicate. This is partly because the Japanese favour intuitive communication. The listener should "understand" much more than what is being verbally expressed ("The eyes say as much as the mouth"). Then too, leaders in Japan maintain dignity by keeping silent and saying as little as possible (Masao, 1976). Japanese executives prefer to speak in short sentences or not at all; subordinates are expected to understand nods, grunts, hand movements and the meaning in a stance.

The Japanese also use quiet pauses to think. Americans see periods of silences as negative messages and as withdrawls. A pause may merely mean the Japanese speaker wants to be very sure what he will say next. He's also studying you and the others in the room. An American should not try to fill up these pauses. If he's finished what he wants to say and he sees no visible reaction or response, he should wait. A response will come eventually.

When to Talk Japanese

The Japanese language is a very difficult one for Americans. The pronunciation is fairly straightforward and easier to learn than Thai or Manadarin Chinese, since they both extensively use tone to convey meaning. The same sound will mean different things according to whether your voice rises or falls as you say the same word. This problem does not exist in Japanese. But the grammar and the forms of the Japanese language are complex. Learning the proper protocols takes years to conquer properly. Like the French, the Japanese take their language very seriously; it's considered to be an important part of their cultural heritage and must be used correctly.

There is no chance for someone going to Japan for business or tourist reasons to learn an adequate Japanese vocabulary and grammar. However, you can learn a few phrases, especially the polite ones (such as thank you, good morning, please, and good evening), fairly easily. Your Japanese hosts will be flattered if you make the effort to learn a few words of Japanese. But these language attempts must take place during informal occasions.

It is important not to use your guidebook vocabulary during formal business negotiations. Practice your Japanese during informal periods, preferably in the evening during meals and bar hops. During business sessions, use English and your interpreter. Mediocre knowledge of Japanese might mislead the Japanese into thinking you can understand them fluently. Finding out you can't after a few bursts of Japanese embarrasses your hosts. Very limited knowledge of Japanese forces the Japanese to listen to "babytalk" for a while before business can begin. Why torture your hosts unnecessarily? You can give each other language lessons during more informal meetings.

Tipping

Tipping in Japan is almost always unnecessary. Hotels and restaurants include a service charge. The exceptions are the smallest family restaurants and Japanese-style inns *(ryokan)*. Japanese inns give complete responsibility for room service to one person. She will serve meals as well as take care of the room. She should be given a tip – in an envelope – at the beginning of your stay. Other persons can be given special rewards for extra-ordinary service, but this is usually unnecessary. For someone who has given service for a length of time, such as a guide, a "goodby" gift is more appropriate than money.

Gift Giving

The Japanese frequently exchange gifts. Gifts are signs of gratitude and friendliness. More importantly, gifts are ritual exchanges used to cement relationships. The manager of a new store will visit every retail establishment in the neighborhood and offer a small gift to each owner as a symbol that they are not direct competitors and that the new owners want the become part of the neighborhood. Wedding guests are given gifts by the host as a gesture of thanks for attending the lavish ceremony.

Gifts are usually given when paying a social call, and business associates commonly exchange gifts. A frequent visitor to Japan should learn when to offer gifts to suppliers and buyers as well as business partners. At the minimum, cards should be sent at Christmas and during other special occasions. The Japanese may not celebrate Christmas, but they appreciate the gesture.

The Japanese exchange gifts on many occasions, and two times of the year set aside for special gift-giving: July and December. These seasons *(ochugen* and *oseibo,* respectively) are times when corporate employees receive their semi-annual bonuses. Everyone gives gifts during these two times to repay former favors and as a way of recognizing that social ties exist with friends, relatives and business associates. This exchange is so prevasive that twenty-six percent of annual sales in Japan's department stores are accounted for during July and December (Popham, 1983).

Americans should be prepared to give gifts to their Japanese colleagues. Large department stores in Japan offer advice on which gifts are appropriate and all employ English-speaking personnel to help the foreigner. There are several rules to follow, however, for gift giving.

The first rule is *don't give too much.* Gifts become obligations in Japan, and a well-meaning gift may impose a hardship on the recipient, since one gift demands another of about the same value. When giving a gift for the first time, make it a simple, inexpensive one. It will express your friendliness better than an expensive one which becomes a burdensome debt to repay. For business associates, articles with a value of roughly $ 10–20 are adequate unless you first receive something of greater value.

The second rule is *don't give a bulky gift.* Space in Japanese houses is at a premium. Gifts that clutter and take up too much space (and remind the recipient of an obligation) are not welcomed. A popular gift in Japan is a melon. Its stem has been cut specially to form a graceful arc, it comes handsomely wrapped, and is appropriately expensive.

The Japanese themselve exchange gifts that can be consumed: boxes of teas, instant coffee, even detergent and soap. The most traditional gifts are edible seaweed, dried mushrooms, dried fish, vegetable oil, spices, and condiments for the summer picnics. Winter gifts are often seaweed, vegetable oil, condiments, and dairy products. Canned goods, whiskey, and noodles are always popular (Popham, 1983).

For the foreigner who expects to offer a gift, a stop in the duty-free store of the airport before leaving the United States can be profitable. Imported alcohol is expensive in Japan and always appreciated. The wise traveller buys his alcohol quota before landing in Japan. Fountain pens are also liked in Japan and elsewhere in the Far East.

The last rule is *offer a personal gift.* Give something which has a personal touch as well as utility. Remember that the Japanese admire special objects as gifts. Give something that reflects a special interest of the recipient or the donor. An engineer might appreciate a special drafting instrument. A professor would enjoy an English language book. If you work or live near a university, keep in mind collegiate mementos, especially if your Japanese hosts have ties with an American university. A T-shirt or sportshirt with a school emblem is a correct gift.

Like the Europeans, Japanese adults as well as children enjoy candy. Americans define sweets as a child's prerogative although they're adult foods in other countries. That's why fancy candies can be found in Europe and Japan rather than in the United States. I have sat in a French salon after a six course meal and been offered a choice of chocolates. The scene of a number of well-dressed French persons eating bon bons and sipping after-dinner drinks is a foreign one to Americans.

There is no shame in American adults offering sweets to Japanese. The candy in question ought to be fancy, imported (European) ones, or else those that represent America's uniqueness. American sweets such as maple candy are appropriate. Japanese weather is often humid; make certain the candy is well wrapped, preferably in individual bite-sized portions.

Fine craftsmanship is also appreciated in Japan. Desk sets, engraved nameplates, and small carvings make fine gifts. Gifts typically American – native art and curios – can be offered. A stuffed jack rabbit sporting small deer horns (a Texas Jackalope) would not be appreciated. Be serious in what you give, since humor does not always successfully carry over from one culture to another. The first gifts should be small and easily consumed. A translator/interpreter and Japanese colleagues are good guides to use for advice on gifts and who should be the recipients. Asking a Japanese friend what you should give to another is flattering and would be taken seriously. Remember that asking such a favor from a Japanese entails a debt. Your Japanese friend would expect a favor in return.

The Fear of Saying No

The greatest problem experienced by Americans when dealing with the Japanese stems from the difficulty the latter have in presenting a negative message, or even saying "no" openly. Even the Japanese sometimes have a hard time determining that someone means "no" when he says the opposite in order to avoid embarrassment.

The reason for this is that the Japanese dislike disappointing someone; they don't want to openly insult a possible partner. Harmony is given such a high value in Japan that a negative reply is often given a positive twist. A Japanese dares not to be too assertive, since such behavior will be defined by others as too aggressive or individualistic. A negative answer, when given, will be balanced by a more positive statement which seems to hold some hope. If a negative statement is made, the foreigner should listen carefully and pay attention for what follows. The positive part may be mere camouflage and verbal noise and is not expected to be believed.

Americans often misunderstand a statement that has both negative and positive parts. We tend to be optimistic and assume that the positive phrase offers a chance for success. The Japanese, by contrast, tend to interpret a mixed statement in more negative terms. Masaaki Imai (1981:5) states that the Japanese have a long list (he says endless) of negative phrases hidden in encouraging, more positive blankets:

I think it's a wonderful idea, but...
We are interested in your proposition, but we need to consider this clause.

There are countless of other possibilities. The point is that the Japanese don't wish to embarrass themselves or others by a direct denial.

That is one reason why roughly half of all marriages in Japan today are arranged by go-betweens and professional matchmakers. A matchmaker will introduce two persons and allow them to be together for a short while. If either wishes to discontinue the relationship, than the matchmaker can diplomatically inform the other person later.

Such fear of embarrassment is reflected in the Japanese terms *"Tatemae"* and *"honne"*. *"Tatemae"* is being polite and saying what your listener wants to hear. It is agreement in order to avoid a confrontation, as when a worker agrees with a superior. *"Honne"* is honest talk; what the speaker really feels and wants to say if he dared.

Even a straight "yes" or "maybe" is hard to interpret. The Japanese word for "yes" is *"hai"*, and it is used often in conversation. At times a *"hai!"* merely means "I'm listening", or "I'm here", as when talking on the telephone. Mothers will say *"hai"* frequently to their children while paying attention elsewhere. A *"hai"* may not, and usually does not, mean that a Japanese agrees with you; nor does he mean that he is committed to what is being said. This response means "I see your point", or "I understand", or, "I hear you". There is no agreement implied. It is more an instrument of etiquette than an empirical statement.

Sharing Information

Americans hoping to conduct business with the Japanese should be prepared to deliver extensive presentations. These presentations must be extremely detailed. They should involve charts, diagrams, samples, models and extensive documentation, such as blueprints and photographs.

There are a number of reasons of all of this necessary detail. First, Japanese education is detailed and concrete. Lessons plod from one specific point to the next, making learning easier. Complicated topics are broken down into smaller, easier-to-learn sub-units. Adult Japanese continue to prefer material that is presented in detailed fashion.

Secondly, many Japanese have to be consulted before a decision can be reached. They will have questions of their own to ask their colleagues. A lack of information embarrasses the Japanese negotiators and forces them to ask the Americans for further clarifications. It's better to present as much information as possible the first time. Not having basic data at one's fingertips causes the American presenters to appear as if they didn't care enough to be throughly prepared. They lose face if they act confused or ignorant. There may be times when the Japanese do not want to ask questions which might indicate their ignorance and thus embarrass them. An American might assume that a point is so elemental that everyone understands what is involved. In this case, the Japanese negotiator would avoid asking for further clarification. It is better to present too much than too little.

Finally, the Japanese will ask very detailed questions in order to make certain that they understand other points clearly. It's dangerous to assume that unsaid points are understood by all participants in a cross-cultural setting. What is assumed by one party may not be so by the other. Those who have experience negotiating with foreigners are extra-cautious. They have learned to their disadvantage that nothing should be taken for granted.

Since Japanese negotiators will discuss your proposal with many other persons, some of whom are experts in certain specialities, Americans should consider giving the Japanese copies of all materials presented during negotiations, including models and other visual aids. If the Japanese negotiators are enthusiastic about your proposal, they become your cheering section. They should be given as much support as possible to present your case their own way. On the other hand, if your negotiating counterparts are luke-warm toward your proposal, complete data might convince third parties that your proposal has value.

Howard Van Zandt (1970) points out that the written word is highly respected by the Japanese. A person whose data support what is being said is more likely to be believed. The Japanese verbal language contains many homonyms, and many terms when spoken have more than one meaning. Visual displays and documentation allow the Japanese a more dependable understanding of what Americans have said. Giving the Japanese copies of all presentations and documentation encourages the Japanese to trust what you have said.

On the other hand, American negotiators should be willing to ask for whatever information they need. If the Americans have been open and trustful with whatever information was asked for, it is appropriate for them to point out that a fair exchange of data necessitates more cooperation from the Japanese. If the Japanese seem to be asking for more information than is necessary, point out that such information is seldom given and that before you do so, you need to know why such data are needed. The Japanese are not above asking for more information than is relevant just to find out more about American state-of-the art technology. Some requests for information are due more to curiosity than to the needs of the negotiation.

10.4 Visiting Japan

I have consistently used the masculine form when discussing Japanese business. This is because virtually all Japanese decision-makers are male. The few Japanese managers who are female form a very small minority. Females are simply not allowed into managerial ranks. There will be female clerks, secretaries, and interpeters, but very few managers and executives. Today's corporate world is a man's world and very few women have managerial responsibility. Almost all of the corporate personnel you'll deal with will be male unless a woman has developed her own company.

Moreover, Japanese wives are absent from most business activities, even those that are purely social. Pedestrians in Tokyo around nine or ten o'clock in the evening will all be either male corporate employees or the women who serve them: hostesses, bar girls, etc. Wives will be at home at this time. They are very nearly completely divorced from their husband's world of business. Don't expect to be invited to a Japanese home. The Japanese don't ordinarily entertain at home, especially when foreigners are involved. The hostess would want to offer the most ornate meal possible. This is both expensive and time-consuming and most Japanese apartments are too small for extensive entertaining. It's easier to entertain outside the home, and this involves primarily males.

Then too, a Japanese wife may not speak English or she may speak it badly and is embarrassed to do so. This puts a strain on possible home visits. The Japanese entertain only long-standing close friends and relatives at home. Even co-workers would not expect to be invited to a colleague's home; nor would neighbors. Americans are invited occasionally into Japanese homes, and these occasions should be considered as marks of favor and not as usual practice.

By all means take your wife or husband on a business trip to Japan. But your spouse would not be expected to be a guest at most business functions. It would cause strain and embarrassment to suggest off-handly that your host's wife and yours might go shopping together. The Japanese business world is separate from family. Only those Japanese who have lived in the United States for a extended period would not be shaken if an American brought his wife to social affairs, unless she were specifically invited.

Japanese business men, especially those who are younger, are able to deal with and negotiate with females as long as they are foreigners. American businesswomen need not be excluded from dealing with the Japanese. They should act and dress sedately, and be circumspect when attending social events. But the Japanese can deal with foreign women on a business level. Foreigners do many strange things, and the Japanese are adept in meeting such challenges. Women who come to Japan on business are defined as foreign business persons rather than females. No American executive should feel hesitant in sending a woman to Japan to negotiate or conduct business.

Jet Lag and Arrival in Japan

Jet lag is a problem for Americans who travel to Japan. At first you feel alert in the early morning and feel sleepy in the afternoon. Since preliminary negotiations have the purpose of getting acquainted and establishing a personal relationship, your hosts will probably entertain you royally. There will be restaurant dining, evening parties, and opportunities for extended drinking, if only to respond and to offer toasts. All of this will further aggravate the fatigue due to jet lag.

Try to land in Japan in the late afternoon or early evening. After flying for over twelve hours, arriving at your hotel in the evening forces you to adjust to local sleep patterns, and you'll be tired anyway. Most business travelers into Japan land at Narita airport, outside of Tokyo. Tokyo is the business as well as government center of Japan and all corporations have offices in the city. Tokyo is usually the first destination of an American visitor.

It will take about two hours to go from your plane to your Tokyo hotel. The usual procedure is to disembark from your plane, pick up your luggage, and pass through customs. These are easy to do and the efficiency of the personnel makes this stage pass quickly and painlessly, unless your luggage has been lost. The airport has English-speaking employees present to help you if there are any difficulties at this stage.

Once through customs, you will have to make several choices in how you will proceed to your hotel. The following are the most common and economic paths. I will assume no one is there to meet you.

Currency exchange facilities are available beyond the customs and passport checking areas. Exchange some dollars for Yen currency at this point. The next step is to decide whether to take an airport express bus or an airport limousine bus into Tokyo proper. English signs are clear and informative. There are also an adequate number of English-speaking officials to help.

Express buses go directly into Tokyo and the major hotels, and take roughly a little less than two hours to do so. These buses leave the airport at long intervals and are not always conveniently available. Airport limousines operate more frequently. Their routes go from the airport to the Tokyo Terminal (pronounced Tee-Cat by the Japanese), and the journey takes roughly eighty minutes. TCAT is in a more central location than the airport vis a vis Tokyo. Once there, taxis are available to drive you to your hotel, taking probably about thirty minutes or so.

If someone offers to meet you at the airport, you might suggest meeting at TCAT. This will save your host time, perhaps several hours, since most Japanese will have to commute to central Tokyo and then to TCAT. A more considerate reply is to ask your hosts not to meet you either at the airport or at TCAT. You can always plead fatigue and jet lag, which will be true. Also, you will probably be too tired to deal adequately with strangers at this time. Meeting business associates after you arrive at your hotel and have taken the time to be rested save everyone a lot of inconvenience.

Some destinations from TCAT are reached more quickly by taking a toll highway. Your taxi driver will ask you if you wish to pay the toll, which is extra. He may know only the English word, 'Toll". The toll charge is a bargain.

Many taxi drivers don't speak or understand English. It's wisest to have on hand the address of your hotel. Show the driver the hotel's card or confirmation letter and the ride begins. Welcome to Tokyo.[2]

The Businessman's Hotel

The typical hotel used by first-time foreigners will be a world-class hotel. The personnel there are used to foreigners and many speak English. These hotels also offer a complete line of services useful to foreign businessmen: international telephone connections, meeting facilities, money exchange facilities, translators, etc. If you wish to telephone a Japanese contact, the hotel staff can telephone for you and ask in Japanese for the person you want.

These hotels offer extensive shopping facilities in their basements. Their arcades offer a very wide selection of services (tourist facilities, transportation, business services, secretarial facilities, barber shops) catering to foreigners, as well as restaurants, clothing stores, newspaper and book kiosks, and souvenir shops. While expensive, they are not exorbitant and they are convenient. Most busy foreigners can do all of their shopping within their hotel's basements. If

---

[2] There are a number of guides for Tokyo and Japan in general easily available in English in Japan and the United States. An excellent introduction to Japan and Japanese culture can be found in *Japan A Country* (1983) published by the U.S. Government Printing Office.

there is time, visit one of Japan's large department stores. They offer everything one might want and more, as well as English-speaking clerks.

Finally, no foreigner needs to starve while in Japan. Your hotel will house a number of restaurants, typically each specializing in a different national cuisine: Continental (usually French), Japanese, Chinese, Korean, and those offering Kobe beef. Japanese and English menus are displayed outside each restaurant so a prospective client can see if a restaurant offers the correct fare. These restaurants are expensive.

The more adventurous can easily wander around the hotel for a few blocks and discover the local cuisine at a lower price. Except in certain slum areas, Japanese cities are as safe or safer than cities in Europe and much safer than those in the United States. One of my favorite meals in Japan was in a ten-table restaurant three blocks from a world-class hotel. My wife and I wandered around a Tokyo suburb taking photographs until we discovered this small restaurant and that we were hungry. We were the only Americans there and no one spoke English. Eventually the son, daughter, father, and mother came to stare at us from the doorway of the kitchen. In spite of the attention we got, the noodle soup was delicious and the meal pleasant. As we left, all of the members of the family came out of the kitchen to wish us well. The Japanese are curious about Americans, and foreigners in general are stared at. This is not done from discourtesy but from interest.

Should you wish to economize and experiment, be adventurous and stroll outside your hotel. The nearest railway station will have a large basement-arcade with shops and restaurants. You can find gifts as well as restaurants there. Or walk around on your own. There are always small restaurants around.

Finding a restaurant is easy. Tokyo has thousands of restaurants. Some are exclusive, or nearly so, and will not accept strangers or foreigners. Your hotel staff and tourist bulletins can give information as to reservations and other details.

When strolling, you will find that while signs are illegible, each restaurant has visible to pedestrians one or more display cases containing numbered plastic models of the main dishes and their prices. This is for the convenience of visitors from the provinces as well as from foreign countries. These models allowed chefs to show off their skills in producing new dishes and were a means of advertising the dishes offered.

Walk by a number of restaurants until you see a dish you favor. Once inside, take the waiter outside and point to the dish or combinations you wish, and ask for your beverage. You can order even at the smallest ten-table restaurant without your knowing Japanese or the staff being able to speak English.

Be careful of your choice, since some models may lack fine details. What looked like chicken pieces on a skewer to the author was actually squid. While good, chicken would have been more welcomed. Try broiled eel if given the chance, especially at one of the many booths found outside most temples and tourist attractions.

Tokyo also contains an uncountable number of small coffee shops. Japanese businessmen like to leave their offices and drink coffee where it is quiet and private. These are good, quiet places when privacy or rest is needed. Don't hesitate to suggest going to a coffee shop for a more comfortable, informal setting. The Japanese do it all of the time. These are also places where a tourist can sit down, find a toilet, and rest awhile for the price of a cup of coffee.

References

Abegglen, James C. (1958): *The Japanese Factory*. Glencoe, Ill. Free Press.

Adams, Thomas (1969): "Though Western Eyes". Pp. 13–225 in Thomas Morton Adams and N. Kobayashi (eds.): *The World of Japanese Business*. Tokyo: Kodansha Intl. Ltd.

Alston, Jon P. (1982): "Awarding Bonuses the Japanese Way". *Business Horizons* 25 (September-October): 46–50.

Amsden, Davida M. and Robert T. Amsden, eds. (1976): *QC Circles: Applications, Tools, and Theory*. Milwaukee, Wisconsin: American Society for Quality Control.

Axelrod, Robert (1984): *The Evolution of Cooperation*. New York: Basic Books, Inc.

Ballon, Robert (1980): "Management Style". Pp. 115–30 in Paul Norbury and Geoffrey Bownas (eds.): *Business in Japan A Guide to Japanese Practice and Procedure* (Revised Edition). Boulder, Colorado: Westview Press.

Bank of Tokyo, Ltd. (1983): *Setting Up Enterprises in Japan*. Tokyo: Japan External Trade Organization.

Barmash, Isadore (1976): *For the Good of the Company*. New York: Grosset and Dunlap, Publishers.

Barra, Ralph (1983): *Putting Quality Circles to Work*. New York: McGraw-Hill Book Company.

Becker, Franklin (1981): *Workspace. Creating Environments in Organizations*. New York: Praeger.

Bedford, Leslie (1981): "Japan's Educational System". Pp. 236–44 in Bradley M. Richardson and Taizo Ueda (eds.): *Business and Society in Japan*. New York: Praeger.

Bennett, Amanda (1984): "China's Legal System Irks Westerners". *Wall Street Journal* (April, 5): 5.

Bill, Richard (1982): "Robots. No Blue Collars for Japanese Factory". *The Eagle* (March 13): A1.

Blau, Peter M. (1955): *Dynamics of Bureaucracy*. Chicago: University of Chicago Press.

Boas, Marx and Steve Chain (1976): *Big Mac. The Unauthorized Story of McDonald's*. New York: E. P. Dutton and Company, Inc.

Bolling, Richard and John Bowles (1982): *America's Competitive Edge. How to Get Our Country Moving Again*. New York: McGraw-Hill Book Co.

Braverman, Harry (1974): *Labor and Monopoly Capital. The Degradation of Work in the Twentieth Century*. New York: Monthly Review Press.

Broadbridge, Seymour A. (1966): *Industrial Dualism in Japan*. London: F. Cass.

Brooks, Malcolm J. and Archie Kaplan (1972): "The Office Environment: Space, Planning, and Affective Behavior." *Human Factors* 14 (October): 373–92.

Brown, Ronald (1979): *The Practical Manager's Guide to Excellence in Management*. New York: American Management Association.

Brzezinski, Zbigniew (1972): *The Fragile Blossom: Crisis and Change in Japan*. New York: Harper and Row.

Burck, Charles G. (1981): "How GM Stays Ahead". *Fortune* 103 (March 9): 48–56.

Burck, Charles G. (1982): "Can Detroit Catch Up". *Fortune* 105 (February 8): 34–39.

Bureau of Labor Statistics (1983): "A BLS Reader on Productivity." Bulletin 2171 (June). U.S. Department of Labor.

Bureau of Labor Statistics (1983): "Productivity and the Economy: A Chartbook." Bulletin 2172 (June). U.S. Department of Labor.

Buss, Dale D. (1982): "Japanese-Owned Auto Plants in the U.S. Present a Tough Challenge for the UAW." *Wall Street Journal* (March 23): 22.

Bylinsky, Gene (1981): "The Japanese Score on a US Fumble." *Fortune* 103 (June 1): 68–72.

Carnes, William T. (1980): *Effective Meetings for Busy People.* New York: McGraw-Hill Book Co.

Cattell, Raymond B. and Glenn F. Stice (1954): "Four Formulae for Selecting Leaders on the Basis of Personality." *Human Relations* 7 (November): 493–507.

Chapman, William (1981): "Japan: The Land of Few Lawyers." *Halt* 2 (Spring): 12.

Chira, Susan (1984): "New Spirit at an Auto Plant." *The New York Times* (August 24): 29 ff.

Christopher, Robert C. (1983): *The Japanese Mind: The Goliath Explained.* New York: Simon and Schuster.

Clark, Rodney (1979): *The Japanese Company.* New Haven: Yale University Press.

Clark, Russell D. (1971): "Group-Induced Shift Toward Risk: A Critical Appraisal." *Psychological Bulletin* 76 (October): 251–270.

Clayton, Karen (1983): "Contracts-Seeing Double." *PHP* 14 (October): 20–31.

Clayton, Stephen (1984): "More Lawyers than Meets the Eye." *PHP* 15 (November): 7–17.

Coch, Lester and John R. P. French (1948): "Overcoming Resistance to Change." *Human Relations* 1 (4): 512–532.

Cole, David E. (1981): "Analysis of U.S. and Japanese Automotive Technology." In: Robert E. Cole (1981b).

Cole, Robert E. (1971): *Japanese Blue Collar.* Berkeley, California: University of California Press.

Cole, Robert E. (1979): *Work, Mobility and Participation.* Berkeley, California: University of California Press.

Cole, Robert E. (1980): "Will QC Circles Work in the U.S.?" *Quality Progress* 13 (July): 30–33.

Cole, Robert E. (1981a): "Quality Control Practices in the Auto Industry." In Robert E. Cole (1981b).

Cole, Robert E. (1981b): *The Japanese Automobile Industry: Model and Challenge for the Future?* Ann Arbor, Michigan: The University of Michigan Center for Japanese Center for Japanese Studies.

Crosby, Philip B. (1980): *Quality is Free. The Art of Making Quality Certain.* Chicago: Mentor.

Crosby, Philip B. (1984): *Quality Without Tears. The Art of Hassle-Free Management.* New York: McGraw-Hill Company.

Davidson, William H. (1984): *The Amazing Race. Winning the Technorivalry with Japan.* New York: John Wiley and Sons.

Davis, Stanley A. (1982): *Managing and Organizing Multinational Corporations.* New York: Pergamon Press.

De Mente, Boye (1981): *The Japanese Way of Doing Business. The Psychology of Management in Japan.* Englewood Cliffs, New Jersey: Prentice-Hall, Inc.

De Vos, George A. (1965): "Achievement Orientation, Social Self-Identity, and Japanese Economic Growth." *Asian Survey* 5 (December): 575–589.

De Vos, George A. (1973): *Socialization for Success: Cultural Psychology of the Japanese.* Berkeley, California: The University of California Press.

Deacon, Richard (1983): *Kempei. A History of the Japanese Secret Service.* New York: Beaufort Books, Inc.

Dean, Andrea O. (1977): "Evaluation of an Open Office Landscape: AIA Headquarters." *American Institute of Architects Journal* 66 (July): 32–38.

Di Giorgio, Brent S. (1981): "Management and Labor Cooperate in Increased Productivity." *Supervision* 42 (January): 5–7.

Doi, L. Takeo (1974): "Amae: A Key Concept for Understanding Japanese Personality Structure." Pp. 145–154 in T. S. Lebra and W. P. Lebra (1974): *Japanese Culture and Behavior. Selected Readings.* Honolulu: The University Press of Hawaii.

Donnelly Mirrors, Inc. (1983): *DMI Handbook. You and Your Company.* Holland, Michigan: Donnelly Mirrors, Inc.

Doyle, Michael and David Straus (1976): *How to Make Meetings Work.* New York: Playboy Paperbacks.

Drucker, Peter F. (1971): "What we can Learn from Japanese Management." *Harvard Business Review* 49 (March–April): 110-122.

Drucker, Peter F. (1983): "Thomas Watson's Principles of Modern Management." *Esquire* 101 (December): 193ff.

Engel, Herbert M. (1983): *How to Delegate. A Guide to Getting Things Done.* Houston: Gulf Publishing Company.

Fields, George (1983): *From Bonsai to Levi's. When West Meets East: An Insider's Surprising Account of How the Japanese Live.* New York: Macmillan Publishing Company.

Fisher, John E. (1977): 'Playing Favorites in Large Organizations." *Business Horizons* 20 (June): 68–74.

Fishwick, Marshall (1983): *Ronald Revisited. The World of Ronald McDonald.* Bowling Green, Ohio: Bowling Green University Popular Press.

Foy, Nancy (1980): *The Yin and Yang of Organizations.* New York: William Morrow and Company.

Fruin, W. Mark (1983): *Kikkoman.* Cambridge, Mass.: Harvard University Press.

Furstenberg, F. (1974): *Why the Japanese Have Been So Successful.* New York: Hippocrene Press.

Gibb, C. A. (1969): "Leadership". Pp. 877–920 in G. Lindzey and E. Aronson (eds.): *The Handbook of Social Psychology.* Volume Two. Reading, Mass.: Addison-Wesley.

Gibney, Frank (1982): *Miracle By Design. The Real Reasons Behind Japan's Economic Success.* New York: Time Books.

Gibson, W. David (1981): "Why Lunch is Free at Texasgulf." *The Wall Street Journal* (September 20): 9ff.

Golden, Arthur (1982): "Group Think in Japan Inc." *The New York Times Magazine* (December 5): 133ff.

Gooding, Judson (1970): "Blue-Collar Blues on the Assembly Line." *Fortune* 82 (July): 70ff.

Gordon, Thomas (1977): *Leader Effectiveness Training.* New York: P. H. Wyden Books.

Gould, Rowland (1970): *The Matsushita Phenomenon*. Tokyo: The Diamond Publishing Co., Ltd.

Gould, William B. (1984): *Japan's Reshaping of American Labor Law*. Cambridge, Mass.: The MIT Press.

Gouldner, Alvin M. (1954): *Patterns of Industrial Bureaucracy*. New York: The Free Press.

Graham, John L. (1981): "A Hidden Cause of America's Trade Deficit with Japan." *The Columbia World Journal of Business* 16 (Fall): 5–13.

Graham, John L. and Yoshihiro Sano (1984): *Smart Bargaining. Doing Business with the Japanese*. Cambridge, Mass.: Ballinger Publishing Company.

Gryna, Frank M. Jr. (1981): *Quality Circles. A Team Approach to Problem Solving*. New York: AMACOM.

Hall, Robert W. (1983): *Zero Inventories*. Homewood, Illinois: Dow Jones-Irvin.

Hanami, Tadashi (1979): *Labor Relations in Japan Today*. New York: Kodansha International, Ltd.

Harragan, Betty Lehan (1977): *Games Your Mother Never Taught You. Corporate Gamesmanship for Women*. New York: Warner Books.

Harragan, Betty Lehan (1983): *Knowing the Score. Play-by-Play Directions for Women in the Job*. New York: St. Martin's Press.

Hayes, Robert A. (1981): "Why Japanese Factories Work." *Harvard Business Review* 59 (July–August): 56–66.

Heider, Fritz (1958): *The Psychology of Interpersonal Relations*. New York: John Wiley and Sons.

Homans, George C. (1974): *Social Behavior in its Elementary Forms*. New York: Harcourt Brace Jovanovich.

Hsu, Francis L. K. (1974): *Iemoto: The Heart of Japan*. Cambridge, Mass.: Schenkman Publishing Co.

Hunt, Morton (1982): "How the Mind Works." *The New York Time Magazine* (January 24): 30 ff.

Husen, Torstein (1967): *International Study of Achievement in Mathematics: A Comparison of Twelve Countries* (Volume 2). New York: John Wiley and Sons.

Imai, Masaaki (1975): *Never Take Yes for an Answer. An Inside Look at Japanese Business for Foreign Businessmen*. Tokyo: The Simul Press, Inc.

Imai, Masaaki (1981): *16 Ways to Avoid Saying No*. Tokyo: The Das Nippon Printing Co., Ltd.

Ishii, Takemochi (1983): "Introducing Robots Smoothly." *Look Japan* 29 (June 10): 25 ff.

Janis, Irving (1972): *Victims of Groupthink*. Boston, Mass.: Houghton Mifflin Company.

Japan External Trade Organization (1982): "Doing Business With Japan." JETRO Marketing Series 8. Tokyo: JETRO.

Johnson, Charmers (1982): *MITI and the Japanese Miracle*. Stanford, California: Stanford University Press.

Juran, J. M. (1978): "Japanese and Western Quality: A Contrast in Methods and Results." *Management Review* 67 (1): 27–45.

Juran, J. M. (1981): "Product Quality-A Prescription for the West. Part 2." *Management Review* 70 (July): 57–61.

Kahn, Herman (1971): *The Emerging Japanese Superstate*. Englewood Cliffs, New Jersey: Prentice-Hall.

Kamata, Satoshi (1982): *Japan in the Passing Lane. An Insider's Account of Life in a Japanese Auto Factory*. New York: Pantheon Books.

Kanter, Rosabeth Moss (1977): *Men and Women of the Corporation*. New York: Basic Books.

Kasarda, John D. (1974): "The Structural Implications of Social System Size." *American Sociological Review* 39 (February): 19–28.

Keidel, Arthur (1981): "Income Distribution in Contemporary Japan." Pp. 125–134 in Bradley M. Richardson and Taizo Ueda: *Business and Society in Japan*. New York: Praeger Publishers.

Kidder, Tracy (1981): *The Soul of a New Machine*. Boston, Mass.: Little, Brown and Company.

Kim, Ken I. and Harold I. Lunde (1982): "Quality Circles: Why they Work in Japan and How We Can Make Them Work in the United States." In: Lee and Schwendiman (1982).

King, Sarah Sanderson and Michael J. King (1983): "Hamburger University." In: Fishwick (1983).

Knoz, S. (1979): "Quality Circles: Japanese Success Story." *Industrial Engineering* 11 (1): 24–27.

Kobayashi, Kaoru (1984): "How to Win a Negotiation-Japanese Style." *Japanese Economic Journal* (July): 24.

Kobayashi, N. (1970): "All-around Company Training: Key to Success." *Journal of Japanese Trade and Industry* 2 (September–October).

Kojima, Akira (1983): "Gap in Use of Robots is Widening Between Japan and Western Nations." *Japanese Economic Journal* 21 (May): 18.

Kotkin, Joel and Yoriko Kishimoto (1984): "Rising Sons." *INC* 6 (April): 146–156.

Kroc, Ray with Robert Anderson (1977): *Grinding it Out. The Making of McDonald's*. Chicago: Henry Regnery Company.

Kuzniar, Paul (1982): "Eastmen Kodak: A Model Japanese Company." *Business and Public Affairs* 9 (1): 3–4.

Lee, John M. (1974): "Songs of Companies Resound in Japan." Pp. 479 in Edwin O. Reischauer (1974): *Japan*. New York: Arnor Press.

Lee, Sang M. and Gary Schwendiman (1982): *Management by Japanese Systems*. New York: Praeger Publishers.

Levening, Robert, Milton Moskowitz, and Michael Kats (1984): *The 100 Best Companies to Work for in America*. Reading, Mass.: Addison-Wesley Publishing Company.

Lewin, Kurt and Ronald Lippitt (1938): "An Experimental Approach to the Study of Autocracy and Democracy: A Preliminary Note." *Sociometry* 1 (January–April): 292–300.

Likert, Rensis (1961): *New Patterns of Management*. New York: McGraw-Hill Company.

Maier, Norman R. F. and John J. Hayes (1962): *Creative Management*. New York: John Wiley and Sons, Inc.

Main, Jeremy (1981): "How to Battle Your Own Bureaucracy." *Fortune* 103 (June 29): 54–58.

Mans, Jack (1981): "Campbell Soup Co. – 1981 Processor of the Year. Part Two." *Processed Prepared Foods* 150 (October): 42–46.

Marth, Del (1984): "Why Safeway Stopped Playing Safe." *Nation's Business* 72 (August): 40–43.

Masao, Kunihiro (1976): "The Japanese Language and Intercultural Communication."
Pp. 51–73 in Japan Center for International Exchange, *The Silent Power. Japan's Identity and World Role*. Tokyo: The Simul Press.

Masatsugu, Mitsuyuki (1982): *The Modern Samurai Society. Duty, and Dependence in Contemporary Japan*. New York: AMACOM.

McClelland, David C. (1967): *The Achieving Society*. New York: The Free Press.

McGregor, Douglas (1960): *The Human Side of Enterprise*. New York: McGraw-Hill Company, Inc.

McMillan, Charles J. (1984): *The Japanese Industrial System*. Berlin–New York: Walter de Gruyter.

Melman, Seymour (1983): *Profits Without Production*. New York: Alfred A. Knopf.

Miller, L. Keith and Robert L. Hamblin (1963): "Interdependence, Differential Rewarding, and Productivity." *American Sociological Review* 28 (October): 768–778.

Mitsui and Co., Ltd. (1977): *The 100 Year History of Mitsui and Co., Ltd*. Tokyo: Mitsui and Co., Ltd.

Mohr, William L. and Harriet Mohr (1983): *Quality Circles. Changing Images of People at Work*. Reading, Mass.: Addison-Wesley Publishing Company.

Monden, Yasuhiro (1981): "What Makes the Toyoto Production System Really Tick?" *Industrial Engineering* 13 (January): 36–46.

Monroe, Wilbur F. and Eisuke Sakakibara (1977): The Japanese *Industrial Society. Its Organizational, Cultural, and Economic Underpinnings*. Austin, Texas: Bureau of Business Research, The University of Texas at Austin.

Morton, Thomas F. and N. Kobayashi (1970): *The World of Japanese Business*. Tokyo: Kudansha International, Ltd.

Negandhi, Anant R. and B. Rajaram Baliga (1979): *Quest for Survival and Growth. A Comparative Study of American, European, and Japanese Multinationals*. New York: Praeger.

Negandhi, Anant R. and B. Rajaram Baliga (1981): *Tables are Turning. Multinational Companies in the United States*. Cambridge, Mass.: Oelgeschlager, Gunn, and Hain, Publishers, Inc.

Norbeck, Edward (1976): *Changing Japan*. Second Edition. New York: Holt, Rinehart, and Winston.

Oh, Sadaharu and David Falkner (1984): *Sadaharu Oh. A Zen Way of Baseball*. New York: Times Books.

Ohmae, Kenichi (1982): *The Mind of the Strategist. The Art of Japanese Business*. New York: McGraw-Hill Book Company.

Ouchi, William C. (1981): *Theory Z. How American Business Can Meet the Japanese Challenge*. Reading, Mass.: Addison-Wesley Publishing Company.

Ozawa, Terutomo (1980): "Japanese World of Work: An Interpretitive Survey." *MSU Business Topics* 28 (1): 45–56.

Pascale, Richard Tanner (1983): "Zen and the Art of Management." Pp. 510–523 in Eliza B. C. Collins (eds.), *Executive Success: Making it in Management*. New York: John Wiley and Sons.

Pascale, Richard Tanner and Anthony G. Athos (1981a): *The Art of Japanese Management. Applications for American Executives*. New York: Simon and Schuster.

Pascale, Richard Tanner and Anthony G. Athos (1981b): "Deciding When Not to Make Decisions." *The Wall Street Journal* January 4: 26.

Patchen, Martin (1970): *Participation, Achievement, and Involvement on the Job*. Englewood Cliffs, New Jersey: Prentice-Hall.

Peters, Thomas and Robert H. Waterman Jr. (1982): *In Search of Excellence: Lessons from America's Best-Run Companies.* New York: Harper and Row.

Popham, Peter (1983): "Say it with Salad Oil." *PHP* 14 (June): 33–38.

Puick, Vladimir, Monica L. Wolford, and John Mai-Marquez (1984): "Comparisons of Management Mobility in the U.S. and Japanese Automobile Industries." Working paper No. 378 Division of Research, Graduate School of Business Administration, the University of Michigan (April).

Rapport, Anatol and Albert M. Chammah (1965): *Prisoner's Dilemma.* Ann Arbor, Michigan: The University of Michigan Press.

Renwick, George W. (1980): "If Australians are Arrogant, Are Americans Boring?" *The Bridge* 5: 2 ff.

Richardson, Bradley M. and Taizo Ueda (1981): *Business and Society in Japan. Fundamentals for Businessmen.* New York: Praeger Publishers.

Richmond, Frederick W. and Michael Kahan (1983): *How to Beat the Japanese at their Own Game.* Englewood Cliffs, New Jersey. Prentice-Hall, Inc.

Roberts, Jon G. (1973): *Mitsui: Three Centuries of Japanese Business.* New York: Weatherhill.

Robson, Mike (1982): *Quality Circles. A Practical Guide.* Adershot, Hants, England: Gower Publishing, Limited.

Rodgers, William (1969): *Think: A Biography of the Watsons and IBM.* New York: The New American Library, Inc.

Rohlen, Thomas P. (1974): *For Harmony and Strength. Japanese White Collar Organizations in Anthropological Perspectives.* Berkeley, California: University of California Press.

Rohlen, Thomas P. (1975): "The Company Work Group." In: Ezra F. Vogel (1975).

Rohlen, Thomas P. (1983): *Japan's High Schools.* Berkeley, California: University of California Press.

Rosen, Barbara (1983): "The Rejected: Refusal of Partnership after Years with Firm can Crush an Attorney." *The Wall Street Journal* (January 3): 1, 24.

Ross, Irwin (1982): "The New UAW Contract. A 'Fortune' Proposal", *Fortune* 105 (February 8): 40–45.

Ross, Joel E. and William C. Ross (1982): *Japanese Quality Circles and Productivity.* Reston, Virginia: Reston Publishing Company, Inc.

Sadamoto, Kuni (1982): *Breaking the Barriers. True Accounts of Oversees Companies in Japan.* Tokyo: Survey Japan.

Sakita, Tetsuo (1982): *Honda Motors. The Men, The Management, The Machines.* Tokyo: Kodansha International, Ltd.

Sakurabayashi, Makoto and Robert J. Ballon (1963): "Labor Management Relations in Modern Japan." Pp. 245–266 in Joseph Roggendorf (1963): *Studies in Japanese Culture. Tradition and Experiment.* Tokyo: Sophia University.

Sanders, Sol (1975): *Honda. The Man and His Machines.* Boston, Mass.: Little, Brown and Company.

Sasaki, Naoto (1982): *Management and Industrial Structure in Japan.* New York: Pergamon Press.

Saso, Mary and Stuart Kirby (1982): *Japanese Industrial Competition to 1990.* Cambridge, Mass.: Abt Books.

Schnapp, John B. (1982): "Soichiro Honda: Japan's Inventive Iconoclast." *The Wall Street Journal* (February 1): 20.

Schonberger, Richard J. (1982): *Japanese Manufacturing Techniques*. New York: The Free Press.

Schreiber, Mark (1983): "The Club, The Team, The Company." *PHP* 14 (December): 18–26.

Shepherd, Shirley (1980): "Improve Productivity with Task Teams." *Training/HRD* 17 (April): 74 ff.

Shiina, Takao (1984): "Bridging the Communication Gap: How IBM Succeeded in Japan." *Journal of Japanese Trade and Industry* 3 (February): 44–47.

Shimada, Haruo (1983): "Japan's Misunderstood Labor-Management Relations." *Look Japan* 29 (June 10): 4–5.

Simison, Robert (1982): "Chrysler is Halting its Assembly Lines Several Times Daily." *The Wall Street Journal* (February 11): 19.

Slater, Philip E. (1958): "Contrasting Correlates of Group Size." *Sociometry* 21 (June): 129–139.

Steinberg, Rafael (1975): *Man and the Organization*. New York: Time-Life Books.

Steiner, Ivan D. (1972): *Group Processes and Productivity*. New York: Academic Press.

Stevens, Mark (1981): *The Big Eight*. New York: Macmillan Publishing Co., Inc.

Swartz, Gary (1983): "The Honorable Art of Saving." *Rotary in Japan* 19 (Winter): 14–17.

Taira, Koji (1970): *Economic Development and the Labor Market in Japan*. New York: Columbia University Press.

Takezawa, Shin-Ichi and Arthur Whitehill (1983): *Work Ways: Japan and America*. Tokyo: The Japan Institute of Labor.

Tanaka, Hideo (1976): *The Japanese Legal System*. Tokyo: The University of Tokyo Press.

Tannenbaum, Arnold S. (1966): *Social Psychology of the Work Organization*. Belmont, California: Wadsworth Publishing Company.

Tannenbaum, Arnold S., Bogdan Kavcic, Menachem Rosner, Mino Vianello, and George Wieser (1974): *Hierarchy in Organizations*. San Francisco. Jossey-Bass, Publishers.

Taylor, Frederick Winslow (1911) *Scientific Management*. New York: Harper and Brothers Publishers.

Trevor, Malcolm (1983): *Japan's Reluctant Multinationals. Japanese Management at Home and Abroad*. London: Frances Pinter, Publishers.

Tsubota, Junjiro (1984): "Lawsuits and Legal Consciousness." *PHP* 15 (November): 26–30.

Tsuda, Masumi (1977) "Study of Japanese Management Development Practices." *Hitotsubashi Journal of Arts and Sciences* 18 (September): 1–19.

Tsurumi, Yoshi (1976): *The Japanese are Coming. A Multinational Interaction of Firms and Politics*. Cambridge, Mass.: Ballinger Publishing Company.

Tsurumi, Yoshi (1984): *Multinational Management Business Strategy and Government Policy. Second Edition*. Cambridge, Mass.: Ballinger Publishing Company.

U.S. Government Printing Office (1983): *Japan. A Country Study*. Washington, D. C.

Upham, Frank K. (1981a): "Law in Japan." In: Richardson and Ueda (1981).

Upham, Frank K. (1981b): "Litigation in Japan." In: Richardson and Ueda (1981).

Van Zandt, Howard F. (1970): "How to Negotiate in Japan." *Harvard Business Review* 48 (November–December): 45–56.

Vander Zanden, James W. (1981): *Social Psychology*. New York: Random House.

Vogel, Ezra F. (1975): *Modern Japanese Organization and Decision-Making*. Berkeley, California: University of California Press.

Vogel, Ezra F. (1979): *Japan as Number One*. Cambridge, Mass.: Harvard University Press.

Waters, Craig R. (1984): "Why Everybody's Talking about 'Just-in-Time'". *INC* 6 (March): 77–90.

Watzlawick, Paul, Janet Bevin and Donald Jackson (1967): *Pragmatics of Human Communication*. New York: Horton.

Wheelwright, Steven C. (1981): "Japan-Where Operations are Really Strategic." *Harvard Business Review* 59 (July–August): 67–74.

Whiting, Robert (1977): *The Chryanthemum and the Bat. Baseball Samurai Style*. New York: Dodd, Mead and Company.

Whiting, Robert (1983): "The Japanese National Sport." *Look Japan* (June 10): 6–7.

Whiting, Robert (1984): "Hired Bats." *PHP* 15 (March): 52–60.

Williams, Marcille Gray (1977): *The New Executive Woman. A Guide to Business Success*. New York: The New American Library.

Woronoff, Jon (1981): *Japan's Wasted Workers*. Tokyo: Lotus Press, Ltd.

Woronoff, Jon (1982a): *Japan. The Coming Social Crisis*. Tokyo: The Lotus Press, Ltd.

Woronoff, Jon (1982b): *Inside Japan, Inc*. Tokyo: Lotus Press, Ltd.

Wrapp, H. Edward (1984): "Good Managers Don't Make Policy Decisions." *Harvard Business Review* 62 (July–August): 8–21.

Wright, J. Patrick (1980): *On a Clear Day you can See General Motors*. New York: Avon Books.

Young, Frank (1983): "Bottoms Up to the Old Year." *PHP* 14 (December): 54–58.

Author Index

Subject Index

de Gruyter Studies in Organization

An international series by internationally known
authors presenting current research in organization.

The Japanese Industrial System
By *Charles J. McMillan*
2nd revised edition
1985. 15,5 x 23 cm. XII, 356 pages. Cloth DM 88,–
ISBN 3 11 010410 5

Political Management
Redefining the Public Sphere
By *Hall Thomas Wilson*
1984. 15,5 x 23 cm. X, 316 pages. Cloth DM 98,–
ISBN 3 11 009902 0

Limits to Bureaucratic Growth
By *Marshall W. Meyer* in Association with *William Stevenson*
and *Stephen Webster*
1985. 15,5 x 23 cm. X, 228 pages. Cloth DM 88,–
ISBN 3 11 009865 2

Guidance, Control and Evaluation in the Public Sector
Edited by *F. X. Kaufmann, G. Majone, V. Ostrom*
1985. 17 x 24 cm. XIV, 830 pages. Cloth DM 198,–
ISBN 3 11 009707 9

International Business in the Middle East
Edited by *Erdener Kaynak*
1986. 15,5 x 23 cm. XVI, 278 pages. Cloth DM 114,–
ISBN 3 11 010321 4

The American Samurai
Blending American and Japanese Managerial Practice
By *Jon P. Alston*
1986. 15,5 x 23 cm. XII, 368 pages. Cloth. DM 105,–
ISBN 3 11 010619 1

Prices are subject to change without notice

WALTER DE GRUYTER · BERLIN · NEW YORK

ORGANIZATION STUDIES

An international multidisciplinary journal devoted to the study of organizations, organizing and the organized in, and between societies.

Editor-in-Chief: David J. Hickson, University of Bradford

Co-Editor: Alfred Kieser, Mannheim

Managing Editor: Susan van der Werff

Editorial Board: F. Agersnap, Copenhagen; K. Azumi, Newark; G. Benguigui, Paris; S. Clegg, Queensland; P. Coetsier, Gent; F. Ferraresi, Turin; J. Hage, Maryland; B. Hedberg, Stockholm; F. Hegner, Berlin; B. Hinings, Alberta; G. Hofstede, Arnhem; J. de Kervasdoué, Paris; C. Lammers, Leiden; B. Mannheim, Haifa; R. Mayntz, Cologne; G. Morgan, Toronto; I. Nonaka, Tokyo; J. Olson, Bergen; J. Padioleau, Florence; J. Pennings, Pennsylvania; G. Salaman, Milton Keynes; B. Stymne, Stockholm; A. Teulings, Amsterdam; H. Thierry, Amsterdam; J.-C. Thoenig, Fontainebleau.

Organization Studies is a supranational journal, based neither on any one nation nor on collaboration between any particular nations. Its aim is to present diverse theoretical and empirical research from all nations, spanning a broad view of organizations and organizing. Its current Editorial Board is drawn from thirteen nations, and its contributors are worldwide.

O. S. is published in English because that language is the most widely read in this field of research. But manuscripts in other languages can be reviewed in those languages prior to translation. O. S. reviews books published in languages other than English to bring them before its international readership, and News and Notes cover conferences and research in many countries.

O. S. has published papers by authors from sociology, political science, management and public administration, psychology and economics. Some among the range of titles are listed overleaf. O. S. is not only about the study of "the organization", though that is central. It is also about the processes of organizing people, whether in business, public services, or public administration and government; and it is about the response of "the organized". It is not only about the contemporary scene, especially differences around the world, but also about the historical developments which have led to that scene.

Subscription rates 1986

Per volume of four issues. Libraries and institutions **DM 118,–** / approx. US $43.70. Individuals (except FRG and Switzerland) **DM 59,–** / approx. US $21.85 (DM-prices are definitive, $-prices are approximate and subject to fluctuations in the exchange rate).

Published in collaboration with the European Group for Organizational Studies (EGOS) and the Maison des Sciences de l'Homme, Paris by

WALTER DE GRUYTER · BERLIN · NEW YORK

Verlag Walter de Gruyter & Co., Genthiner Straße 13, D-1000 Berlin 30, Tel.: (0 30) 2 60 05-0
Walter de Gruyter, Inc., 200 Saw Mill River Road, Hawthorne, N. Y. 10532, Tel.: (914) 747-0110